DATE			

The Works of William James

This volume edited by

Fredson Bowers, Textual Editor
Ignas K. Skrupskelis, Associate Editor

Introduction by
H. S. Thayer

William James in 1910

portrait by Ellen Emmet; courtesy Harvard University Portrait Collection

The Meaning of Truth

William James

HARVARD UNIVERSITY PRESS
Cambridge, Massachusetts
and London, England
1975

CENTER FOR EDITIONS OF
AMERICAN AUTHORS

AN APPROVED TEXT

MODERN LANGUAGE
ASSOCIATION OF AMERICA

®

Library of Congress Cataloging in Publication Data
James, William, 1842–1910.
The meaning of truth.
(The works of William James)
1. Truth. 2. Pragmatism. I. Title.
B832.J4   1975   144′.3   75–30758
ISBN 0–674–55861–8

Foreword

The Meaning of Truth is the second volume to be published in
THE WORKS OF WILLIAM JAMES. As James made clear in his Preface, he felt it important to provide a sequel to *Pragmatism* which
would expand and make clear the pragmatic theory of truth that
had stirred so much excitement and controversy. In it he collected
"all the work of my pen that bears directly on the truth-question."
Six of the essays were written directly in response to criticisms of
Pragmatism by Bertrand Russell and others. At the same time
James, by attacking the rationalistic transcendental tradition in
philosophy, sought with these essays to clear the ground for the
doctrine he called radical empiricism, which will form the subject
of the volume *Essays in Radical Empiricism*.

In editing *The Meaning of Truth* the pattern that was established for *Pragmatism* has been followed. An Introduction deals
with the biographical and historical information relevant to the
text and provides an analysis of its philosophical content and significance. We have been fortunate in having Professor H. S. Thayer
of the City University of New York undertake this task, as he did
for *Pragmatism*. In each case he has provided an essay which constitutes original scholarly work of a high order.

The text has been established by Fredson Bowers, Emeritus Lin-
den Kent Professor of English at the University of Virginia, the
Textual Editor of the WORKS as a whole. Professor Bowers has also

provided a history of the text and the authority of its source documents, together with a textual apparatus which will enable scholars to reconstruct the documents used in the editing. The objective of the textual editing has been to establish a text which comes as close as possible to James's final intentions, while the apparatus and appendixes together provide the documentation for tracing the development of James's thought through the various stages of its creation and expression. The Associate Editor, Professor Ignas K. Skrupskelis of the University of South Carolina, is responsible for the section of reference Notes to the text and for the Index, and in addition he contributed to the documentation of the publishing history.

The editors had the benefit of general policy guidance and many specific suggestions from the Advisory Board of scholars listed in the front matter of this volume, and Professor Thayer received valuable critical suggestions from the Board that were of assistance to him in writing the Introduction. The Board was appointed by the American Council of Learned Societies, under whose sponsorship the WORKS are being edited and published.

The Key to Pagination of Editions at the end of this volume correlates the pages of the present text with those of the original Longmans, Green edition and its subsequent reprintings.

An undertaking such as the present volume requires cooperation from many quarters. The editors wish to express thanks to the following individuals and institutions for their generous help in providing indispensable services, resources, and specialized knowledge.

We are grateful to Mr. Alexander James and to Dr. William Bond of the Houghton Library for permission to utilize and reproduce both printed and manuscript texts in the James Collection at Harvard University, and to Miss Carolyn Jakeman and her staff in the Houghton Library Reading Room for their assistance.

The National Endowment for the Humanities made this volume possible by providing the funds for the editorial work, and Dr. Ronald Berman, Chairman of the Endowment, and Dr. Simone Reagor, Director of the Division of Research Grants, and her colleagues Dr. Geraldine Otremba and Mr. David Wallace have steadily supported the WORKS as the project has developed.

The University of South Carolina has provided the Associate Editor with research assistance, working space, and other facilities.

The Andrew W. Mellon Foundation made a generous and critically important grant in support of the publication of the first four volumes of the WORKS.

Others to whom the editors are grateful for help with this volume are:

Mr. Robert W. Allison, Assistant Curator of MSS. and Archives, Special Collections, of the Joseph Regenstein Library, University of Chicago, was of assistance with the typescript of "W. James's Statement" (p. 218) and gave permission to reproduce a transcript of the typescript and to reproduce one of its pages in facsimile.

The Educators and Librarians Collection, Manuscript Division, Department of Special Collections, Stanford University Libraries, gave permission to record the revisions James made in the carbon typescript of the text of the University of Chicago's ribbon copy of the "Statement" (pp. 214–215). Miss Michele Leiser, Manuscripts Processor at Stanford, was helpful in answering the Textual Editor's questions.

Mr. Kenneth Blackwell, Archivist, made available from the Bertrand Russell Archives, Mills Memorial Library, McMaster University, Hamilton, Ontario, Canada, for publication in this volume, the annotated offprint of Russell's "Transatlantic 'Truth'" in *The Albany Review* (January 1908) and William James's letters to Russell.

Professor Lawrence Wilson Beals of Williams College helped to find James material in the papers of James Bissett Pratt, of which he is custodian, and the Williams College Library gave permission to print James's letters to Pratt.

Mr. Kenneth Lohf, Director of Special Collections, Manuscript Division, at the Columbia University Library, kindly made available the files of F. J. E. Woodbridge, editor of the *Journal of Philosophy, Psychology, and Scientific Methods* and gave permission for appropriate letters to be quoted.

Professor A. Delaunay of the Institut Pasteur, Paris, is to be thanked for his assistance in locating the book *La Vie de Emile Duclaux* (p. 176n.) needed to verify James's quotation and to prepare the comment in the Notes.

The Director of the Interlibrary Loan Division, the University of South Carolina Library, was most helpful in arranging for a number of borrowings to assist Professor Skrupskelis in identifying quotations.

Mrs. Ignas Skrupskelis machined the necessary copies of different editions on the Hinman Collator.

Mrs. Ann Louise McLaughlin, Senior Editor, Harvard University Press, saw the volume through all the necessary stages from copy to print.

Mrs. Jo Ann Boydston examined the text for the seal of the Center for Editions of American Authors.

Mrs. Anne Quigley, Chief Research Assistant to Mr. Bowers, and her assistants, Mrs. Sayre Ellen Dykes, Mrs. Deborah Winn, and Mrs. Mary Mikalson, worked tirelessly and patiently on the many detailed tasks that had to be performed on schedule and with the great precision required by the standards set by the Center for Editions of American Authors. They have a large share of the credit for earning the CEAA seal which this volume carries.

Frederick H. Burkhardt

Contents

Introduction

by

H. S. Thayer

The Meaning of Truth was published in 1909, one year before William James died. The book was intended, the subtitle informs us, as a sequel to *Pragmatism* (1907). But it differs from the earlier work in several fundamental ways. James makes clear in the Preface that this volume is a continuation and clarification of just one theme: the "pivotal part" of *Pragmatism*, namely, its account of truth. The subject matter to be treated is consequently narrower in scope and a less ambitious endeavor than the earlier volume of lectures, whose deceptive simplicity and popular style caused many readers to underestimate the value and depth of often novel analyses and suggestive insights into philosophic issues of science, epistemology, metaphysics, and religion.

In *Pragmatism** James attempted to present a new and comprehensive philosophy, developing it in "broad strokes, and avoiding minute controversy." He conceived it nonetheless as a major effort. It was, he remarked in a letter, "The most important thing I've written yet, and bound, I am sure, to stir up a lot of attention."[1] The lectures that formed the book were delivered to large

---

*All references to *Pragmatism* are to the volume in the series of THE WORKS OF WILLIAM JAMES (Cambridge, Mass.: Harvard University Press, 1975). References to *The Meaning of Truth*, designated in these pages as '*MT*', are to the present volume. All other references to James's works are to first printings except that in footnote 17 to *Essays in Radical Empiricism* in WORKS (1976).

[1]*The Letters of William James* (Boston: Atlantic Monthly Press, 1920), II, 276.

audiences, and much of the sparkle of sagacious humor is there to entertain as well as instruct. *The Meaning of Truth*, on the other hand, consists almost entirely of articles James had published in various journals. Although his style is characteristically vigorous, colloquial, and unpretentious, he is addressing not the public but professional philosophers. *Pragmatism* expresses a sense of urgency and mission in its deliverance of doctrines. *The Meaning of Truth* exhibits confidence in a movement that has established itself, positions won or requiring only further explanation in order to be accepted. Much of the discussion is polemical, and there are signs of James's impatience with some of his critics who continued to misunderstand the ideas in question or failed to take them seriously. Here he was prepared to enter into some of that minute controversy that he had avoided earlier.

The Meaning of Truth, then, is the most complete statement of his theory of truth James has left. This is a highly original and by no means simple theory. It well deserves study as a cardinal doctrine in James's philosophic outlook and an important contribution to our understanding of the meaning and value of the concept of truth.

Pragmatism was a popular and successful book. During James's lifetime it rapidly went through many printings, and served to focus the controversy over truth that had been occupying the journals since 1904. Just before it appeared, James had published his chapter on truth (Lecture VI of *Pragmatism*) in *The Journal of Philosophy, Psychology, and Scientific Methods*.[2] He wrote to F. C. S. Schiller about this: "I find that my own chapter on Truth printed in the J. of P. already, convinces no one as yet, not even my most *gleichgesinnten* cronies. It will have to be worked in by much future labor . . . I think that the theory of truth is the key to all the rest of our positions" (*Letters*, II, 271). It must be acknowledged—and *The Meaning of Truth* bears it out—that the idea of truth is the key to James's position.

By the time *Pragmatism* was published James had begun to tire of the proliferation of critical discussions concerning pragmatic

[2]"Pragmatism's Conception of Truth," *The Journal of Philosophy, Psychology, and Scientific Methods*, 4 (1907), 141–155.

truth. In that year of 1907 he dutifully published seven articles explaining and defending his views; in these the topic of truth predominated. The following year he published four more pieces in the same vein. In the four years between 1904, when the controversy started, and 1908, James wrote and published twenty articles and one book (*Pragmatism*) expounding and defending his tenets.[3] It is not surprising, particularly for one who did not thrive on critical disputes, that by 1908 he was ready to leave further defense of pragmatic truth to Dewey and Schiller and turn his attention to other matters.

Some of the 1907 articles were reprinted in *The Meaning of Truth*. James intended this work as a final statement of his doctrine of truth. Explaining why he has set forth his views once more and reprinted his share of "so much verbal wrangling," he offers two interesting reasons. First, he says he is convinced that an understanding and "definitive settlement" of the pragmatic account of truth "will mark a turning-point in the history of epistemology, and consequently in that of general philosophy" (*MT*, p. 4). Second, he states his belief that the pragmatic theory of truth "is a step of first-rate importance in making radical empiricism prevail" (*MT*, p. 6). Radical empiricism was the epistemological and metaphysical theory of experience that James had worked on concurrently with pragmatism. These were cognate philosophic interests; each developed early in James's intellectual history and matured slowly. In 1904, while occupied with pragmatism, he also published two major essays on radical empiricism.[4] *Essays in Radical Empiricism* appeared in 1912, two years after his death; ten of its twelve chapters are reprintings of articles published in 1904–05.

The exact relation between his pragmatism and radical empiricism seems never to have been entirely distinct in James's mind. He several times asserted the logical separation and independence

---

[3]The reader may verify this by consulting Ralph Barton Perry's *Annotated Bibliography of the Writings of William James* (New York: Longmans, Green, 1920), revised with additions in John J. McDermott, ed., *The Writings of William James* (New York: Random House, 1967), pp. 812–858.

[4]"Does 'Consciousness' Exist?" *The Journal of Philosophy, Psychology, and Scientific Methods*, 1 (1904), 477–491. "A World of Pure Experience," *ibid.*, 1 (1904), 533–543, 561–570.

of these doctrines, saying that one could be accepted without the other. On the other hand, he also conceived some intimate connection between the doctrines of pragmatic truth and radical empiricism.

These and other matters might have become clearer had James lived to write one or more of the technical works, the "system," or the *Weltanschauung* he often longed to complete. In the last ten years of his life he frequently announced his intention to write a "serious, systematic, and syllogistic"[5] book, "a general system of metaphysics," or a "general treatise on philosophy," or a "system of tychistic and pluralistic philosophy of pure experience," a "magnum opus." But distractions of fame and of popular lecturing and writing, and periods of ill health and depression intervened to prevent him from accomplishing his hoped-for "immortal work."[6] With his unfinished *Some Problems of Philosophy* James left a memorandum in which he wrote: "Say it is fragmentary and unrevised . . . Say that I hoped by it to round out my system, which now is too much like an arch built only on one side."[7]

Philosophic Background of the Controversy

In order to understand James's theory of truth and the motivating argument of the present book, it is necessary to consider the specific critical and philosophical setting in which these ideas were formed and stated. The critical discussion over truth occurred in and as a part of a more general tension and clash of philosophies. James's pragmatism and notion of truth, his radical empiricism and pluralism were to a considerable extent developed in criticism of and as alternatives to absolute idealism, the dominant philosophic school in England and America at the turn of the century.

In a famous passage in *Pragmatism* James describes the history

---

[5]Ralph Barton Perry, *The Thought and Character of William James* (Boston: Little, Brown, 1936), II, 338.

[6]For these severally announced intentions see *Letters*, II, 179, 203, 127, and 203 respectively. For the reference to the "immortal work" see Perry, *Thought and Character of William James*, II, 468. Another expressed hope of writing a book "more original and ground-breaking than anything I have yet put forth(!)" is in a letter of Oct. 6, 1907, to his brother Henry; *Letters*, II, 299.

[7]*Some Problems of Philosophy* (New York and London: Longmans, Green, 1911), pp. vii–viii.

of philosophy as consisting "of a certain clash of human temperaments," namely, the "tender-minded" and "tough-minded" (*Pragmatism*, p. 13). The former is Rationalistic (going by principles),
Intellectualistic, Idealistic, Religious, Free-willist, Monistic, Dog-
matical. The tough-minded is Empiricist (going by facts), Sensation-
alistic, Materialistic, Irreligious, Fatalistic, Pluralistic, Skeptical.
In James's day the most skillful and influential spokesman for
a form of tender-minded idealism was F. H. Bradley. The tough-
minded school of empiricists was led by T. H. Huxley, W. K. Clifford, and K. Pearson. The intellectual roots of British idealism
were nurtured primarily in Kantian and Hegelian German idealism. German idealism had its initial transmission through Cole-
ridge, Whewell, Hamilton, Ferrier, and J. H. Stirling, all critical of
the older empiricism of Locke, Berkeley, and Hume. The most
powerful critical proponent of this school was T. H. Green. His attack on the atomistic sensationalism and the associational psychology of Locke and Hume was devastating and considered by many to
apply with equal effect to more recent empirical thinkers such as
Mill, Bain, and Spencer. Green's critical focus was on the inability
of sensationalism to account for relations, and thus, ultimately, its
failure to explain how knowledge was possible at all (*see MT*, p.
79). The relating activity is essential over otherwise discrete sensations and ideas in order that we become aware of unified objects, of
the world, or of ourselves. Since that unifying activity is not given
in sense experience, Green argued for the presence of an ordering,
intellectual consciousness, a living spirit in the world and acting
through individual thinkers. Thus, as James remarked, we have
"a monism of a devout kind."[8]

Led by Green and John and Edward Caird, and thereafter by
Bradley, A. E. Taylor, Bosanquet, Joachim, McTaggart in Britain,
and James's Harvard colleague Josiah Royce, idealism established
itself as the prevailing system of Anglo-American thought. The
philosophic preoccupations here were not only epistemological and
metaphysical; there were also social and moral considerations.
Thus, Green and the Cairds were critics of the utilitarianism of

---

[8]*A Pluralistic Universe* (New York and London: Longmans, Green, 1909), p. 7.

Mill and H. Sidgwick. Against individualistic utilitarianism, idealism advanced theories of the social, collectivistic, or unified nature of political and ethical life; the good and the moral law were embodied in social relationships, in the state, or in a higher spiritual community.

An important impetus to tough-minded philosophy came in the latter part of the nineteenth century after the publication of Darwin's *Origin of Species* (1859). The impact of and interest in Darwin's work was enormous. Darwin and Spencer were forces to be reckoned with. Idealists on the whole took one of two positions; some, like Bradley, tended to eschew or discount this form of empirical science, to remain philosophically unconcerned and aloof from what was, finally, a phenomenon of an unintelligible realm of appearance anyway. Others, like the young John Dewey (or Peirce and Royce), attempted to adopt the theory of evolution as evidence for and integral to a more comprehensive evolutionary idealism.

James regarded pragmatism as a way of mediating between the tender- and the tough-minded philosophies. The idea, as he put it to his audience early in the first lecture of *Pragmatism,* is to derive something of significant value between "an empirical philosophy that is not religious enough, and a religious philosophy that is not empirical enough for your purpose" (p. 15). And in the last words of the final lecture he says: "Between the two extremes of crude naturalism on the one hand and transcendental absolutism on the other, you may find that . . . the pragmatistic or melioristic type of theism is exactly what you require" (p. 144).

James's characterization of the two kinds of temperament whose mutual antagonism marks the history of philosophy might, of course, be questioned. But this is of no moment to us since we are interested rather in how James conceived the problems and what he took to be the direction of philosophy in his own time. His description is revealing of what he understood to be the difficulties, the excesses and shortcomings in the intellectual traditions he had inherited and in which he was situated. By proposing pragmatism as a mediator he did not intend a synthesis of tender and tough outlooks. He was searching for a genuine alternative, a way of critically assimilating some while rejecting other parts of the philosophic legacy. In 1906 he found most persons to be of "a decidedly empiricist proclivity" but desiring, in addition to facts and science, moral and religious values (*Pragmatism*, p. 14). To clarify and resolve these human wants a method of critical analysis and procedure was needed; and James thought he had found this in the theory of pragmatic meaning and truth.

It is of curious interest that William James himself cannot be placed in his own classification of philosophic temperaments. He was a man of extraordinary complexity, of deep internal emotional divisions and conflicting intellectual tendencies. Outwardly (at times) an "adorable genius," as Whitehead said, but inwardly (at times) driven to despair of any worth or hope of accomplishment, James could charm the world but could also entertain possibilities of madness or suicide. We can say, however, that, with important exceptions made for free-will, religious belief, and optimism, he generally inclined to the tough-minded outlook. And with religious idealism the dominant academic philosophy at the time, and because some of James's early work received most criticism from that quarter, the burden of his critical writing was directed against monistic idealism.

We are thus brought back to Bradley, for in opposition to the skillful and effective expression of philosophic idealism James advanced his pluralism, radical empiricism, and pragmatism. According to Bradley, reality is a single whole or unity in, but forever distinct from appearance. Reality "must be single, because plurality, taken as real, contradicts itself." And he adds that since any plurality implies relations, "through its relations, it unwillingly asserts always a superior unity."[9] Indeed all relations and predications lead to contradiction and so are unreal. In all judgments, Bradley argues, there is a difference between subject and predicate, "a difference which, while it persists, shows a failure in thought, but which, if removed, would wholly destroy the special essence of thinking" (*AR*, p. 361). The "main nature" of thinking is that

[9]F. H. Bradley, *Appearance and Reality* (London: Swan Sonnenschein; New York: Macmillan, 1893), p. 519. Further references in the Introduction are to this edition, designated '*AR*'.

"Thought essentially consists in the separation of the 'what' from the 'that.' It may be said to accept this dissolution as its effective principle" (*AR*, p. 360; for a critical notice by James, *MT*, p. 43): Predication and relations cannot represent reality, and they have meaning only in the world of appearance. Bradley is led accordingly to hold that all categorical judgments are to some extent false: "The subject and the predicate, in the end, cannot either *be* the other. If however we stop short of this goal, our judgment has failed to reach truth; while if we attained it, the terms and their relations would have ceased" (*AR*, p. 361). There is always "something else" supporting the predication, a reality which goes beyond the predicate. This something cannot be stated and lies outside of judgment or any progressive series of judgments. Ultimately this "something else" is the wholly real, coherent, self-identical Absolute, "a single and all-inclusive experience, which embraces every partial diversity in concord" (*AR*, p. 147), the object of self-transcendence.

Bradley is classified as a Hegelian, and he constantly cites Hegel as the source of his doctrines; but the critical dialectical structure of his thought is very much like that of Parmenides. One main motif in this dialectic is that, although thought is imperfect and incapable of adequately representing the Absolute, the Absolute Reality is nonetheless the criterion of truth and falsehood, the better and worse, beauty and ugliness (*AR*, p. 552). This is the aim of thought; yet to attain it, thought would have to transcend its inherent 'that'-'what' subject-predicate distinction, and this, says Bradley, is the suicide of thinking (*AR*, p. 168). But since truth is the whole, as Hegel also taught, finiteness of thoughts and judgments is a condition of unreality and thus error (*AR*, p. 541). Each finite thing and each partial truth thus "contradicts" itself in pointing to its opposite, to something more as adding to and completing itself; and in so doing each thing passes beyond itself into its opposite and in turn makes for a wider unity. Since, however, even absolute truth and complete truth must consist of a subject, which would be the whole, and a predicate, Bradley concludes:

Even absolute truth in the end seems thus to turn out erroneous—

And it must be admitted that, in the end, no possible truth is quite true.

It is a partial and inadequate translation of that which it professes to give bodily. And this internal discrepancy belongs irremoveably to truth's proper character (*AR*, p. 544).

All of this must be admitted "in the end," a phrase which, along with "finally" and "in itself" is ubiquitous in the writings of monistic idealists. Here "in the end" means: if you have reasoned carefully the idealistic conclusion will be inevitable. In the end, what can be known is severely limited. And truth, for Bradley, is defined, vaguely, as an ideal of satisfaction, our wanting a coherent whole. "Truth is an ideal expression of the Universe at once coherent and comprehensive": this sentence appeared in a valuable summary account of Bradley's outlook.[10] But for James, such a definition of truth really says very little. In any case, historically it was not only the pragmatists whose doctrine of truth courted unclarity.[11]

Thought and discourse proceed by means of distinctions and relations. For Bradley, however, reality is a differentiated yet seamless whole. Thus, the world of our intellectual efforts, and the world of final satisfaction and truth are severed realms. We can appreciate how difficult it was on this view to understand James's account of truth as the "workings" of ideas in particular cases; of his saying "Our account of truth is an account of truths in the plural, of processes of leading, realized *in rebus*, and having only this quality in common, that they *pay*" (*Pragmatism*, p. 104); of his conception of reality as "plastic," incomplete and in the making, awaiting part of its complexion from the future (*Pragmatism*, p.

[10]"Coherence and Contradiction," *Mind*, n.s. 18 (1909), 492. The article is reprinted in *Essays on Truth and Reality* (Oxford: The Clarendon Press, 1914), pp. 219-244. For James's reaction see "Bradley or Bergson?" *Collected Essays and Reviews* (New York and London: Longmans, Green, 1920), pp. 491-499.

[11]So, for example, this discussion of 'truth' in *Essays on Truth and Reality*, pp. 343-344: "Reality for me . . . is one individual Experience. It is a higher unity above our immediate experience. . . . But, though transcending these modes of experience, it includes them all fully. Such a whole is Reality, and, as against this whole, truth is merely ideal. It is indeed never a mere idea, for certainly there are no mere ideas. It is Reality appearing and expressing itself in that one-sided way which we call ideal. Hence truth is identical with Reality in the sense that, in order to perfect itself, it would have to become Reality. On the other side truth, while it is truth, differs from Reality, and, if it ceased to be different, would cease to be true. But how in detail all this is possible, cannot be understood."

123; he cites this as the important difference between pragmatism and rationalism); and of the possibility of different kinds of particular satisfaction (*Pragmatism*, p. 35). In this use of the concepts of 'truth,' 'reality,' and 'satisfaction,' James appeared to the rationalist mind to be speaking an alien and strange language and inviting intellectual anarchy. Moreover, his refusal to be pedantic and his vividness of expression led more solemn fellow philosophers to wonder whether he was theorizing in earnest or having fun at their expense. James's alliance with F. C. S. Schiller deepened this suspicion in Oxford, where Schiller was regarded as something of an upstart and philosophic prankster in his irreverent attacks on Bradley and absolutism.

Even James's close friend Royce found the new language and doctrines difficult to comprehend fully. For Royce, a fundamental obstacle to developing a theory of truth was explaining the nature of error—a standing problem for monistic idealism. He constructed an ingenious and abstruse argument contending that to err, a judgment would have to disagree with its intended object. But a judging mind would not err about its own immediate ideas: either it knows its own ideas, and its judgments about them cannot err, or it does not know them in which case judgment would be meaningless. To know, however, that a judgment about an external object does or does not agree with that object—and especially to know that a thought is incomplete or inadequately represents its object—would require a more inclusive judgment, one that incorporates both the idea of the object and the object itself. This Royce calls the more "inclusive thought," a thought that includes particular thoughts and their intended objects. Since a judgment about an object cannot of itself "insure agreement with it," what is needed is the containing thought. Error, accordingly, "is an incomplete thought, that to a higher thought, which includes it and its intended object, is known as having failed in the purpose that it more or less clearly had, and that is fully realized in this higher thought." Without this "higher inclusive thought," Royce concludes, "an assertion has no external object, and is no error."[12] In order to realize

[12]*The Religious Aspect of Philosophy* (Boston: Houghton Mifflin, 1885), p. 425. On the "infinite unity of conscious thought to which is present all possible truth," see p. 424; other passages quoted are from pp. 428–432.

and understand truth, we then require an "infinite unity of conscious thought" enveloping all finite thought. This is the "all-including Thought," or "the infinite content of the all-including mind" within which all finite minds, their ideas, and all objects represented by thought are contained. Royce elaborated on this notion of universal consciousness as an "infinite unity" in which was found all possible truth. It was the Absolute experience which related to all individual experiences as an organic whole to its fragmentary parts.

James did not wish to accept this theory of an omnipresent, overruling and, as he viewed it, fatalistic Absolute. But the argument impressed him. He expounded it to Renouvier and in his review of Royce's *The Religious Aspect of Philosophy*.[13] For many years he sought to discover some decisive logical weakness in the argument to justify his initial moral objections. In 1887 he remarked (*Letters*, I, 265): "I have vainly tried to escape from it. I still suspect it of inconclusiveness, but I frankly confess that I am *unable* to overthrow it." Finally, about 1893 he began to see, as he says in a note added to "The Function of Cognition," (*MT*, p. 23) that "any definitely experienceable workings would serve as intermediaries quite as well as the absolute mind's intentions would." The entire recondite apparatus of absolute mind was unnecessary. Knowing, objective reference, and truth and error could be explained perfectly well by an analysis of the activity of finite minds and ideas related to objects within experience, the relations being that of pointing, or leading cognition, through intermediate experience, to the reality or object. With some justice James later remarked about this paper and its argument that it is "the fons et origo of all *my* pragmatism";[14] and he reprinted it as the opening chapter of *The Meaning of Truth*.

The criticism of idealism deepened when it occurred to James that not only could knowledge and truth be explained without

[13]*Atlantic Monthly*, 55 (1885), 840–843; reprinted in *Collected Essays and Reviews*, pp. 276–284. For his letter to Renouvier see Perry, *Thought and Character of William James*, II, 702–705. In a letter to Bradley of July 9, 1895, he comments on Royce's argument, J. C. Kenna, "Ten Unpublished Letters from William James, 1842–1910, to Francis Herbert Bradley," *Mind*, n.s. 35 (1966), 312–313.

[14]From a letter to C. A. Strong, Sept. 17, 1907; James papers in Houghton Library, Harvard (bMS Am. 1092).

having to invoke the Absolute, and without having to depart from or transcend experience, but that the difficult notion of the absolute mind failed to explain any particular feature or event. In *Pragmatism* (p. 17) he offers the methodological pragmatic observation that the notion of "absolute mind" has no determinate empirical consequences: "You can deduce no single actual particular from the notion of it. It is compatible with any state of things whatever being true here below."

James's eventual resolution and reasoned rejection of Royce's doctrine is a central development in the historical formation of his pragmatism and theory of truth. Royce's argument for absolute mind provided the initial challenge to and testing of James's pragmatic conception of thought and action; these theories were further clarified and advanced in the exchanges with Bradley and the idealist school and his criticisms generally of intellectualism.

Bradley was something of an eccentric, and his metaphysical philosophy was far from being dogmatic or orthodox; it is carefully reasoned, often highly original, and deeply skeptical. But other monistic idealists, including Royce, very easily developed the more respectable theological implications of the Whole and the Absolute. Monistic idealism thus provided for religious affiliations and could be viewed as a bulwark against scientific materialism and agnosticism. It was a philosophy which, perhaps because individual selves and "mere" partial and particular experience count for so little in comparison to the all-inclusive Absolute, appealed to genteel sentiments.[15] It proved that the world was good and that present evils are necessary in serving a higher good, and was, therefore, favorably cultivated in the more exclusive academies of higher learning in America and expounded by professors whose training had usually been in theology (see *Pragmatism*, p. 16).

To James, the entire system of monistic idealism appeared labored, highly professional but somewhat insincere in motive and thin in consequences. Indeed, he found it suffocating. He mis-

---

[15]In later writings Royce was to make of his idealism a thoroughly social theory. The very suggestive theory of meaning as a social activity within a community of interpretation (which was close to ideas of Peirce) seems to have had little interest for James.

trusted its respectability—for reality is anything but refined or respectable—its "disdain for the particular, the personal, and the unwholesome,"[16] its discomfort with variety, "its infallible impeccable all-pervasiveness,"[17] and its "block universe." He had a democratic abhorrence for the notion of evil as unreal, or as necessary to the realization of good. On more technical grounds James argued that by making truth a property or possession of reality, or the Absolute, idealists had rendered the concept of 'truth' unknowable and useless. Truth conceived as "an ideal expression of the universe," in Bradley's words, is of little aid in explaining just what conditions define a belief or a statement to be true, and how truths can occur or be known. Against the arguments that had been advanced by Green,[18] concerning the dumbness of sensations and how relations are therefore instituted by thought, or against Bradley's view of relations as unreal, James set forth a central thesis of radical empiricism: "relations between things . . . are just as much matters of direct particular experience, neither more so nor less so, than the things themselves." This, he adds (*MT*, p. 7), makes relations both real and experienced; the parts of experience are held together by relations that are parts of experience. There is no need to appeal to an absolute, or "higher unifying agency" to account for order in experience or a unified world. And this position also affords a genuine and knowable place for pluralities and individuals. Instead of a mysterious Infinite Mind, whose containment and coordinating of a knower and object known defines 'truth' (i.e., Royce's theory), the pragmatic theory, says James, can give a definite account of the truth-relation and in experiential terms.

Finally, although it may be held that the idealists had overindulged the role of mind and thought in their theory of reality, the tough-minded empiricist and agnostic philosophers, such as Spencer, Huxley, Clifford, and Pearson had taken the other extreme to view the world as complete and describable independently of knowing organisms. Against this "naturalism" James

---

[16]*A Pluralistic Universe* (1909), p. 309.

[17]*Essays in Radical Empiricism*, WORKS, p. 142.

[18]For James on Green's argument see *Principles of Psychology* (New York: Henry Holt, 1890), II, 9–13.

stressed the importance of the knower and the presence of human feelings, purposes, and intervening actions to any complete description of the world. "*The* world is surely the *total* world, including our mental reaction. The world *minus* that is an abstraction, useful for certain purposes, but always envelopable. Pure naturalism is surely envelopable in wider teleological or appreciative determinations."[19]

In addition to advancing the doctrines of pluralism, radical empiricism, and pragmatism, James argued that growth and novelty are ultimate traits of reality. Although it was in the last years of his lifetime that he hoped to set forth in detail the metaphysical significance of these ideas, they recur throughout his philosophical thought and writings. A year before his death he commented: "I think the center of my whole *Anschauung*, since years ago I read Renouvier, has been the belief that something is doing in the universe, and that *novelty* is real."[20] This mention of Renouvier is significant; it is a reflection at the end of a life upon its philosophical beginning. For it was in 1869–70, while suffering a severe psychological crisis, that James found in Renouvier's theory of free will a resolution of his despair and the restoration of health (see *Letters*, I, 147). In *Some Problems of Philosophy* James acknowledged this debt in his intended statement of dedication, saying of Renouvier: "he was one of the greatest of philosophic characters, and but for the decisive impression made on me in the seventies by his masterly advocacy of pluralism, I might never have got free from the monistic superstition under which I had grown up" (p. 165).

In order to develop the metaphysical implications of the notions of growth and novelty James had to reckon with the criticisms of the reality and intelligibility of possibility and change advanced by monistic idealists. He had also to work out an alternative to the reductive analysis of change by materialistic empiricists and to defend the idea of novelty against scientific determinists. On this issue James regarded the idealists and the scientific empiricists as alike in taking an Intellectualist or Abstractionist position; in

---

[19]Perry, *Thought and Character of William James*, II, 476.
[20]From a letter to James Ward, June 27, 1909; see Perry, II, 656.

each case change, growth, novelty, and genuine variety are either denied outright or given "sterile" and schematic representations untrue to the thick, deep, moving character of reality.

These critical reflections led James also to believe that logico-mathematical analyses of time, motion, and infinity were inadequate for expressing the fully continuous character of conscious experience and of reality. Although he had no objection to the construction and analysis of formal and mathematical systems, he mistrusted the philosophical claims often made for these disciplines as providing complete and final explanations of reality or revealing the ultimate metaphysical categories of the world. Peirce, among others, accused him of refusing to acknowledge the value of exact thinking. It must be said that what James was refusing to accept was not exact thought for its own sake or as an ideal but rather the view that exact systems mirror a corresponding exactness in reality or that such systems yield the final truth concerning the nature of things. In any event, in accord with his opposition to this form of Intellectualism, James enthusiastically greeted the work of Bergson. And while he had anticipated some of those ideas in his own earlier philosophizing, he addressed Bergson as a "magician" whose work constituted a turning-point of thought. He wrote him: "I feel that at bottom we are fighting the same fight. . . . The position we are rescuing is 'Tychism' and a really growing world" (*Letters*, II, 292). He felt that Bergson had killed Intellectualism. But for the less enthusiastic response of Peirce and Dewey, James might have been tempted further to pursue the more mystical and irrational tendencies in Bergson's outlook. As to this later development of his thought, however, no more need be said here. It remains in what follows to examine more carefully James's theory of truth.

THE MEANING OF TRUTH

I pass now from the more historical concerns that affected the growth and formation of James's theory of truth, to that theory itself. It was an unusually controversial theory, and the present volume reinforces this impression. The controversy stemmed from fundamental differences of entire philosophical positions and orientation to an extent not fully realized by any of the parties to it; but the conspicuous point of conflict was in the concept of truth.

On this matter James is open to criticism for devoting so much attention to the polemical aspects of the discussion of truth that he was deterred from setting forth a careful and rounded statement of his theory. The fifteen chapters of *The Meaning of Truth* contain treatments, and divers essays on the notion of truth. Because it is central to an understanding of James's philosophy and influence, it is worth attempting to exhibit the essential interconnections of these sundry treatments and separate analyses and arguments, in the hope of providing a unified formulation of James's theory. This attempt requires a reconstruction and piecing together of the leading ideas and intentions in his several expositions into a schematic and coherent whole. We can then consider briefly some of the standing critical difficulties that have been addressed to and associated with the theory.

At the outset it is important to be clear upon one point that should have received some attention by James and his critics, for much misunderstanding and irrelevant argumentation would have been avoided. I refer to the fact that when James argues for his conception of truth it should not be thought that he is arguing against or rejecting all other theories of truth. The reason this caused misunderstanding is that it is natural to assume that when a philosopher sets forth his theory on some subject he is denying other theories on that subject and, implicitly at least, treating them as erroneous. So it was assumed that in offering his theory of pragmatic truth James meant to deny and exclude any other version of truth from what he took to be the right view of the meaning of that concept. But this was not the case. On the contrary, James was attempting a remolding rather than a renunciation of older ideas. He was concerned with clarifying, deepening, and extending the application of the more familiarly received conception, and with accounting for the function of the concept of truth in contexts which remained ignored or inexplicable by traditional theories. Thus, occasionally he will claim that his doctrine includes, absorbs, and supports others; that "Pragmatic truth contains the whole of intellectualist truth and a hundred other things in addition" (*MT*, p. 111).

The generally accepted "dictionary" definition of 'truth' in James's day was: the agreement of ideas with reality (falsehood being the disagreement of an idea with reality). He acknowledges this definition (for example, *Pragmatism*, p. 96, and *MT*, p. 117). For Bradley, since truth is Reality, agreement would be conceived as the harmony and unity of Reality with (or in) itself. For Royce the agreement lies between fragmentary judgments and the whole of Absolute Truth, within an Absolute Mind. But James first asks, what specifically is *meant* by 'agreement'? And he finds the idealists and intellectualists producing no very clear answer. It is not that what they say is wrong, he contends, but that their use of 'agreement' is uninformative. Accordingly, he develops the pragmatic meaning of the concept. He took a similar critical view of the notion of truth as correspondence. He does not reject the thesis that truth is the correspondence of ideas or statements with reality, but again he finds the formulation vague (*MT*, pp. 44–45, 105). In each case we need and do not have an explanation of what the complete conditions are that constitute an 'agreement' or 'correspondence.' Overstating it somewhat, James concludes that these definitions of 'truth' tell us no more than that what is true *is* true (*MT*, p. 128).

In order to understand James's theory of truth we must recognize, then, not one exclusive theory, but two stages and two fundamental ways through which claims and ascriptions of truth proceed. There is first what we may for convenience call *cognitive truth* (drawing on the discussion of "cognitio," *MT*, p. 50, although by "cognitive truth" here we do not mean a "copy" theory of thoughts and things). This is the conception of truth that James accepts but judges of little philosophical value. This is dictionary truth in its simplest abstract form, namely, as the agreement (or correspondence) between beliefs and statements and what these may be said to be about. 'Truth' characterizes the circumstances that pertain when what is believed or stated to be the case *is* the case. Such circumstances might pertain, for example, between the belief or statement that it is raining, and the occurrence of raining. This is a doctrine of truth according to which what is believed or stated "agrees" or "corresponds" with the subject matter it "describes" or is "about." This is not to be confused with a more recent theory in which to say "true" is to express *agreement* with a statement made in an appropriately related context.[21] For our present purposes it is not necessary to attempt a more accurate definition of 'cognitive truth' (and to do so is not an easy task). There is secondly *pragmatic truth*, the doctrine James advocated and the subject of his book.

There are important conditions holding in common for cognitive truth and pragmatic truth as well as important differences. However, if the distinction is sound, and is, as I believe, in accord with James's own views, it has the merit of reducing and clearing up a mass of confused opinions and misapprehensions that grew between James and his critics.

Keeping now to this distinction, we can say that an idea (judgment, statement), to be true or false, must at least be cognitively true or false—it will or will not "agree" or "correspond" with reality. James does not deny this, as some critics mistakenly charged, nor is he rightly accused of rejecting the law of excluded middle, or the existence of a reality external to thought and belief (in *MT* see p. 8, and the Third and Fourth misunderstandings of pragmatism in Ch. VII). On the other hand, an idea could be cognitively true and yet *pragmatically* neither true nor false. The appearance of paradox here is easily dispelled when we consider that the class of cognitive truths (and falsehoods) is wider than that of pragmatic truth; some cognitive truths have no pragmatic significance or "cash value," but they are no less true (cognitively) for that. Thus, cognitive truth is a necessary but not sufficient condition of pragmatic truth.

Among the cognitive truths whose pragmatic truth or falsehood might in this way be indeterminate (or whose truth value, like cash value, might even fluctuate, as will be explained later), are those James characterizes as our accumulated "stock of *extra* truths,

---

[21]For this analysis developed by P. F. Strawson and its assimilation to Dewey's theory of truth see Gertrude Ezorsky, "Truth in Context," *The Journal of Philosophy*, 60 (1963), 113–135. For a survey of James and Dewey on truth and their theories discussed in the light of other contemporary views see Ezorsky's article, "Pragmatic Theory of Truth," in Paul Edwards, ed., *The Encyclopedia of Philosophy*, 6 (New York: Macmillan & Free Press; London: Collier-Macmillan, 1967), 427–430.

of ideas . . . true of merely possible situations" (*Pragmatism*, p. 98). When an extra truth is needed to meet some emergency in conduct or solve some problem, "it passes from cold-storage to do work in the world." But in so passing into the world it becomes more than cognitive truth; for with its needed function and practical use it has issued in pragmatic truth. If we incorporate this distinction in a paraphrase of one of James's well known pronouncements we can say of such occasions of an activated truth: it is useful because it is true (cognitively) or it is true (pragmatically) because it is useful. This accords with his further comment that: "True is the name for whatever idea starts the verification-process, useful is the name for its completed function in experience." For these reasons, considering James's primary interest in that smaller class of truths that come out of cold-storage and acquire distinctively pragmatic value, his doctrine might be more accurately described as a theory of pragmatic truth rather than a pragmatic theory of truth.

The foregoing distinction meets one of the most frequent and serious charges of irrationalism and subjectivity directed against James's theory. As a consequence of his account of truth, he was accused of maintaining that a belief or statement could be true for some persons and false for others (hence the claim that he had abandoned the law of excluded middle). This is largely a misunderstanding. What James did in effect hold was: a cognitively true statement might be neither true nor false pragmatically for some persons (that is, roughly, not pragmatically significant), while pragmatically true for others (that is, pragmatically significant). Moreover, on his theory the "same" statement, or linguistic form, might differ in pragmatic truth and meaning in different contexts, because the pragmatic meaning and truth of beliefs and statements are alike determined to some extent by factors in the occasion and particular circumstances in which they are entertained or asserted.

It can be seen that pragmatic truth requires further additional conditions for its realization than is the case for cognitive truth. If we ask what these further conditions may be we are led to the main ideas of James's theory.

Introduction

In *Pragmatism* James says:

> the question 'what is *the* truth?' is no real question (being irrelative to all conditions) and . . . the whole notion of *the* truth is an abstraction from the fact of truths in the plural, a mere useful summarizing phrase like *the* Latin Language or *the* Law (pp. 115–116).

He is not claiming, it is to be noticed, that an abstract definition of *the* truth is impossible or wrong.[22] The dictionary definition has its summarizing uses, and in this he may be understood to be referring to what we have been calling *cognitive* truth. But such truth, he says, is "irrelative to all conditions." The determination of pragmatic truth, however, requires a specification of certain kinds of conditions. James often remarked that the conditions in question are not those of merely believing what is pleasant or believing that the consequences of an idea will be useful or wishing whatever one wants to be true. One basic condition of the theory and definition of pragmatic truth is found in the concept of *working*. A true idea is one that works. The notion of the working of a belief or statement is explained, in turn, as entailing a certain kind of satisfaction, one in which there is a resolution of initially uncertain or discordant circumstances or an adaptation to an environment or the location of some needed or intended object (a practical or theoretical object-ive). The concept of 'working' supplies the pragmatic meaning of the doctrine of truth as "agreement." Pragmatism, James says, in *Meaning of Truth*:

> defines 'agreeing' to mean certain ways of 'working,' be they actual or

---

[22]As will be argued below, the notion of *cognitive truth* as a necessary but not sufficient condition of pragmatic truth is important. It resolves a multitude of objections raised against James's theory. It is unfortunate that James did not make this point clearer, but he was absorbed in developing the distinctively *pragmatic* aspect of truth in the "working" and "satisfactory" functions. Still, that he did recognize what I have here called "cognitive truth" can be seen, in addition to the passages cited in the text, in *MT* when, (e.g., p. 118) he refers to just such true statements and beliefs as "inertly and statically true only by courtesy: they practically pass for true; but you *cannot define what you mean* by calling them true without referring to their functional possibilities." In *Pragmatism*, he says: "Truth with a big T, and in the singular, claims abstractly to be recognized, of course" (p. 111). And he speaks of rationalist definitions of truth as trivial, but adds: "They are absolutely true, of course, but absolutely insignificant until you handle them pragmatically" (p. 109). This truth, with the big T, is what we are here pointing to as cognitive truth.

potential. Thus, for my statement "the desk exists" to be true of a desk recognized as real by you, it must be able to lead me to shake your desk, to explain myself by words that suggest that desk to your mind.... Reference then to something determinate, and some sort of adaptation to it worthy of the name of agreement, are thus constituent elements in the definition of any statement of mine as 'true' (pp. 117–118).

Again quoting *Pragmatism* in his Preface, James says:

To 'agree' in the widest sense with a reality, *can only mean to be guided either straight up to it or into its surroundings* .... Any idea that helps us to *deal*, whether practically or intellectually, with either the reality or its belongings, that doesn't entangle our progress in frustrations, that *fits*, in fact, and adapts our life to the reality's whole setting, will agree sufficiently to meet the requirement. It will hold true of that reality (p. 102).

The concept of 'working' is essential in the explanation of pragmatic truth. If we recall James's interpretation of the purposive nature of thought and the instrumental character of concepts, we can appreciate even more clearly the argument here concerning the working and adaptational function of true ideas.

Let us consider James's theory more closely. The theory, as I shall try to show, formulates three fundamental conditions that must be fulfilled if a belief (or statement, or judgment) is to be pragmatically true. A survey of these three conditions will then enable us to construct a general definition of William James's doctrine of truth.

(1) The first condition is that of cognitive truth. To be true, the objective reference of a belief or statement must be the case. James says "The truth of the idea is one relation of it to the reality." He often mentions the role of "objective reference" and comments: "My mind was so filled with the notion of objective reference that I never dreamed that my hearers would let go of it" (*MT*, p. 128). Falsehood then would be an erroneously intended or purported objective reference; affirming something to be the case when in fact it is not. This is the main feature of what James regards as the *realism* of pragmatic truth (*see MT*, Ch. IX and pp. 104 ff.). The pragmatist "posits ... a reality and a mind with ideas. What, now, he asks, can make those ideas true of that reality?" (*MT*, p. 104)

The complete answer remains to be developed below, but one part of it is before us: to be true, the idea must agree or correspond with reality.

(2) The second condition of pragmatic truth has to do with the idea of the assimilating of new forms of experience into the existing system of our beliefs or, as James puts it, the marrying of old opinions with new facts.

In criticizing the idealists' identification of truth with reality, James argues that the order of sensible experience and facts is neither true nor false. Changes and additions to the content of this order "simply *come* and *are*. Truth is *what we say about them*" (*Pragmatism*, p. 36). And among the important things we say is how certain occurrences of experience are signs of other experiences, how "One bit of it can warn us to get ready for another bit, can 'intend' or be 'significant of' that remoter object. The object's advent is the significance's verification" (*ibid.*, p. 99). This organization of beliefs about facts and relations among the items of experience is one part of our system of truth and knowledge. The other part consists of what James calls "relations among purely mental ideas" (*ibid.*, p. 100). He refers to such "absolute, or unconditional" beliefs as that "1 and 1 make 2" or that "white differs less from gray than it does from black." These definitional truths or "principles" are necessary for organizing systems of logical and mathematical ideas and relations and ordering the sensible facts of experience. They provide possible ways in which to arrange and interpret the facts of experience so as to reliably anticipate future experience. "This marriage of fact and theory is endlessly fertile." Of these two orders, James continues,

Between the coercions of the sensible order and those of the ideal order, our mind is thus wedged tightly. Our ideas must agree with realities, be such realities concrete or abstract, be they facts or be they principles, under penalty of endless inconsistency and frustration (*ibid.*, p. 101).

Thus, we find ourselves endowed with a stock of beliefs, our system of knowledge, acquired partly through experience and partly as an inheritance from our ancestors and our culture. It may happen, James points out, that certain experiences may strain some of our old beliefs: we may be contradicted by somebody or may contradict ourselves, or we may discover facts that are incompatible with a belief. "The result is an inward trouble" from which we seek to escape. Some modification of our beliefs or a reinterpretation of the facts, or both, is demanded. The critical process of and readjustment in the mass of one's opinions continues,

until at last some new idea comes up which he can graft upon the ancient stock with a minimum of disturbance of the latter, some idea that mediates between the stock and the new experience and runs them into one another most felicitously and expediently.

This new idea is then adopted as the true one. It preserves the older stock of truths with a minimum of modification . . . New truth is always a go-between, a smoother-over of transitions (*Pragmatism*, p. 35).

This is how new truth "marries old opinion to new fact," James adds, and different ideas and theories accomplish this integrative function with varying degrees of success from different points of view, so that to some degree "everything here is plastic."

James emphasizes the controlling importance of the old truths. We seek to preserve them and we depend on them even when making revisions among them. Conservatism is the strategy. If an experience so novel as to threaten most of our fundamental beliefs occurred, we would incline, if possible, to ignore it or classify it as illusory. As to the skeptical possibility that all our beliefs are mistaken or illusory, we might retort that it is only within the accepted stock of our beliefs—or some part of it—that we are given criteria for distinguishing the real from the illusory; it makes little sense to question the veracity of the system as a whole. James does, however, remark that some of our most firmly established old beliefs could be subject to revision with the advent of new experience. He alludes to the transformation, at the time of his writing in 1907, "of logical and mathematical ideas, a transformation which seems even to be invading physics" (*Pragmatism*, p. 37).

Since alternative theories and organization of beliefs for interpreting experience are available, there is no one absolute "right" way of viewing reality, no one true theory. Reality is what it is known *as*, James is fond of saying (and on which see the note to

33.11, p. 171 below). And what an object is known *as* depends on a certain prior focusing of interests and needs that guide conceptualization, and partly upon similarly conditioned terminations in sense experience (thus *MT*, p. 76).

Since we live in a common world, we learn to conceptualize in common, or because we conceptualize in common, we posit a common world. In either case, James argues, we eschew solipsism and we share in and use alike the stock of old truths. Our confidence in this system of beliefs is increased through "face to face" verification of beliefs with experience, or by more elaborate and extended indirect verifications. But although we share a common system of knowledge, we are each to some extent differently situated in it and the uses we make of it. These individuating differences of perspective and interest, of needs and purposes, allow for James some variations among persons as to how the world is viewed, relativism in decisions about how it is to be "carved" and categorized, and what things are known *as*.

The third condition of pragmatic truth is the most novel and controversial part of James's theory.

(3) For an idea to be true of reality, it "must point to or lead towards *that* reality and no other, and . . . the pointings and leadings must yield satisfaction as their result" (*MT*, p. 104). Here, I believe, we find the most distinctive characteristic of William James's theory of truth. Pragmatic truth is not a property of ideas or statements but of the circumstances and events in which an idea or statement contributes to an action with a beneficial and satisfactory outcome. The mere occurrence of a feeling of satisfaction does not suffice for truth; it is indispensable for (pragmatic) truth but insufficient "unless reality be also incidentally led to" (*MT*, p. 106). James does not argue that satisfaction *is* truth or alone determines truth. Beliefs about events and objects supposed real but which do not exist would be false "in spite of all their satisfactoriness" (*MT*, pp. 8, 106). He recognizes the "notorious" fact that "the temporarily satisfactory is often false" (*MT*, p. 54). And he protests against associating this idea of satisfaction with his "Will to Believe" argument (*MT*, pp. 86–87).

In "The Function of Cognition" (Ch. I of *MT*) James argued

that the test of the truth and meaning of ideas was their termination in "definite percepts," that is, the sensations to which they lead or which can be derived from them. In later parts of *The Meaning of Truth* a less subjective and philosophically more realistic position is taken; the truth of beliefs will be how they terminate in reality: "there can be no truth if there is nothing to be true about. . . . This is why as a pragmatist I have so carefully posited 'reality' *ab initio*, and why, throughout my whole discussion, I remain an epistemological realist" (*MT*, p. 106).

The process of *working* or *leading* is thus described by James as a continuous order of psychological and physical events linking the entertainment of an idea "as a *terminus a quo* in someone's mind and some particular reality as a *terminus ad quem*" (*MT*, pp. 129–130). The idea has an instrumental function; it is "an instrument for enabling us the better to *have to do* with the object and to act about it" (*MT*, p. 80). Successive ideas can then be regarded as increasingly more true of an object when subjected to the corrective process of critical inquiry and testing. In this case the pragmatic meaning of "Absolute truth" would be "an ideal limit to the series of successive termini . . . the ideal notion of an ultimate completely satisfactory terminus" (*MT*, pp. 88–89) or "an ideal opinion in which all men might agree" (*MT*, pp. 142, 143; also p. 76, and *Pragmatism*, pp. 106–107). It is the entire process of events mediating between an idea and its object and issuing in satisfactory terminations of sensation and action that determine truth. "Such mediating events *make* the idea 'true' " (*MT*, p. 109). These are or make possible the "functional workings" of ideas or statements (*MT*, p. 122). Concerning this notion of 'workings' two observations are necessary.

(a) James occasionally ascribes to ideas, beliefs, and statements certain inhering tendencies or properties which, under appropriate conditions, are causative factors in the mediating process through which verification and truth occur. So far as I know, he never completely developed this notion; but it has a role in his analyses of thinking, and the concept of 'tendencies' is prominent in the famous discussion of the "stream of thought" in *The Principles of Psychology* (I, ch. IX). He can be seen to ascribe dispositional properties to ideas (beliefs and statements, the latter construed as occasions of stating something) when he argues: "The trueness of an idea must mean *something definite in it that determines its tendency to work.*" He goes on to maintain that just as a man's mortality—which is the possibility of his death—is to be understood as "something in man that accounts for his tendency towards death," so there "is something of this sort in the idea" that accounts for its tendency to "work." There is also "something" in "bread that accounts for its tendency to nourish." In one of his clearest statements he then describes the complexity of causal and dispositional conditions that constitute the 'working' of an idea:

What that something is in the case of truth psychology tells us: the idea has associates peculiar to itself, motor as well as ideational; it tends by its place and nature to call these into being, one after another; and the appearance of them in succession is what we mean by the 'workings' of the idea. According to what they are, does the trueness or falseness which the idea harbored come to light. These tendencies have still earlier conditions which, in a general way, biology, psychology and biography can trace. This whole chain of natural causal conditions produces a resultant state of things in which new relations, not simply causal, can now be found, or into which they can now be introduced—the relations namely which we epistemologists study, relations of adaptation, of substitutability, of instrumentality, of reference and of truth (*MT*, p. 96).

(b) The other observation concerning the 'working' of ideas and statements is the importance James attaches to the presence of an interest or need. The causal working tendencies just discussed are relative to specific interests and needs; the working that issues in pragmatic truth, issues accordingly in satisfactions. Truth, James says, is an "adaptive relation," and he asks: "What meaning, indeed, can an idea's truth have save its power of adapting us either mentally or physically to a reality?" (*MT*, p. 130). This recognition of human purposes guiding our thinking led him to regard truth as one species of good: "The true is the name of whatever proves itself to be good in the way of belief, and good, too, for definite, assignable reasons" (*Pragmatism*, p. 42). And it is this aspect of the 'working' of thought that James referred to as its "expediency," saying "'*The true'* ... *is only the expedient in the way of our thinking* ... expedient in the long run and on the whole" (*MT*, p. 4, or *Pragmatism*, p. 106). It should be evident, then, that the satisfaction of "some vital human need" (*MT*, p. 5) is one further necessary condition of pragmatic truth (although not of cognitive truth).

These last tenets prompted the most controversy and misunderstanding in critical discussions of James's theory. But before turning to these difficulties, we may sum up this part of our discussion: for an idea (belief, judgment, statement) to be pragmatically true three conditions are to be fulfilled. The idea must:

*1. Be cognitively true.

*2. Be compatible with the older body of truths.

*3. Work. It must provide some satisfaction of a need or purpose (recalling the two aspects of 'working' just discussed). In short, "thoughts are true which guide us to *beneficial interaction* with sensible particulars" (*MT*, p. 51).

In this schematic form we are given a general definition of James's conception of 'truth.'

We can even cast this general definition in the distinctively pragmatic form that Peirce recommended for explicating the meaning of abstract concepts. Put very roughly, his counsel was: to determine the meaning of terms like 'force,' or 'hard,' one should formulate a description of the use of the term in contexts of experiment and testing; how the term is applied and the consequences of that application will yield a description of its meaning.[23] Thus, as an

---

[23]Charles Sanders Peirce, *Collected Papers* (Cambridge, Mass.: Harvard University Press, 1931–1958), V, 248–271, where Peirce applies the analysis to the concepts of 'hardness,' 'weight,' 'force,' and 'reality.' See I, 337, where Peirce says: "Take any general term whatever. I say of a stone that it is *hard*. That means that so long as the stone remains hard, every essay to scratch it by the moderate pressure of a knife will surely fail. To call the stone *hard* is to predict that no matter how often you try the experiment, it will fail every time." See also V, 273: "if one can define accurately all the conceivable experimental phenomena which the affirmation or denial of a concept could imply, one will have therein a complete definition of the concept." This theory is discussed in H. S. Thayer, *Meaning and Action* (New York: Bobbs-Merrill, 1968), pp. 86–101. The application of Peirce's method of analysis of meaning to James's doctrine of truth was suggested to me by Morton White; see *The Age of Analysis* (New York: New American Library, Mentor Books, 1955), pp. 157–158; but my development of the idea here takes a different line from his.

example, Peirce says we mean by 'hard'—or that something x is hard—if you perform the experimental operation, O, of scratch-testing on x, it would result as a consequence that x will not be scratched. The explication proceeds by specifying a certain experimental situation, E (the presence of x and conditions for scratch-testing), an operation, O (scratch-testing), and general result, R (would not be scratched by many substances in repeated cases of testing). So, to say "x is hard" means: if E, and O, then R (x would not be scratched). Now we can fit our definition of James's concept of truth into this explicative scheme as follows. We want to consider the meaning of "P is true" where 'P' is a belief or statement which, as a necessary first step, we take to be cognitively true (so fulfilling condition *1). We take P as part of a situation E, which includes personal needs and interests to be satisfied, as discussed (in 3.(b)) above. "P is true" then means: If E, and O (that is, acting on P, the "leading" of P) then R (that is, P would fulfill conditions *2 and *3). Briefly, the truth of P on James's theory comes to mean: if P fulfills *1, and is acted upon, P would fulfill *2 and *3. In this way P would become pragmatically true and verified in the manner and under the conditions that particularly interested James.

To avoid misunderstanding, it should be added that the above sequence of three conditions in which I have represented James's theory of truth is not proposed as a temporal order—or order of discovery—according to which truth will occur first in a cognitive sense and thence, in successive stages, fulfill conditions *2 and *3. The three conditions are to be construed solely as logical conditions and hence as components of the *definition* of pragmatic truth, not as phases of the process of *verification*.

It remains finally to consider some of the major difficulties directed to James's theory. We need not reopen all of the original controversy—much of which is now of limited historical curiosity —but some of the criticisms, notably those advanced by Moore, Russell, Pratt, and Lovejoy, are of interest and relevance. The most important of these can be briefly sketched and commented on in the light of the above definition. Let us, for convenience, use the expression 'Belief-assertion' so as to capture the objective of truth ascriptions for James. He mentions ideas, beliefs, judgments, and statements as alike capable of truth or falsehood; but—especially in his express doubts about construing propositions as abstract capsules containing truth or falsehood as properties (*MT*, p. 151)—it is clear that he is interested in contexts in which acts of believing and asserting occur as constituents and are the occasions of pragmatic truth or falsehood.[24]

Of the various objections to James's theory, three have generally been regarded as the most serious.

First: James maintains a Belief-assertion is true if it works or is expedient. But, it will be objected, a false Belief-assertion under certain circumstances can be expedient. It may be useful for us to have someone believe a lie. It might be useful to believe other persons exist even if they did not (Russell's argument, *MT*, p. 149). The Belief-assertion "God exists" may be useful, or work, for some persons, even if God does not exist (*MT*, Preface, p. 6, and notice James's reference to this "slander," p. 147). Finally, some true Belief-assertion might not be expedient. As to this kind of objection we are now in a position to see how it turns on a confusing of senses of 'truth' (senses *1, *2, and *3). The critical force of the instances adduced against James here derives from the supposition that he meant to equate 'truth' and 'working' or 'useful.' But he did not argue that 'true' = 'useful' (thus *MT*, pp. 148–150). The useful is a sign (not infallibly so) of truth; but as we have seen, for a Belief-assertion to be pragmatically true, conditions other than *3 are required. Lastly, while a (cognitively) false Belief-assertion might be useful or expedient in some particular case, in "the long run" a false Belief-assertion will conflict with our old stock of truths (that is, *2) and so will eventually prove not to "work." Hence, although every pragmatically true Belief-assertion is useful, not every useful Belief-assertion is pragmatically true.

Second: James errs in failing to recognize the difference between

---

[24]In these pages I have followed James's language in assigning truth or falsity severally to ideas, beliefs, judgments, and statements. As to statements, I think it is clear that James was construing these as events of utterance (or inscription) in linguistic occasions, as true or false. These would be token instances of types of linguistic forms and expressions. The use here of 'Belief-assertion' is intended to represent these several kinds of token instance of truth or falsehood for James.

the truth of a Belief-assertion and the useful effects of believing that Belief-assertion, for he equates 'x is true' with 'it is useful to believe x' (see *MT*, p. 149). But this is a misrepresentation. James says: "The social proposition 'other men exist' and the pragmatist proposition 'it is expedient to believe that other men exist' come from different universes of discourse. . . . The first expresses the object of a belief, the second tells of one condition of the belief's power to maintain itself" (*MT*, p. 150). Misunderstanding on this point has led to some ridicule of pragmatism: A company of philosophers staying the night at an Inn are informed by the host that the establishment is on fire. Concerned to determine the truth of this report, all but one of the philosophers look about the rooms; the one, the pragmatist, asks himself instead what will be expedient for him to believe. If he is a pessimist, and heavily insured, he will conclude the announcement is false and go to bed; but if he reflects on the value of life he will decide the host is telling the truth and will join his colleagues in rushing outside. The parable depends on ignoring the role of conditions *1 and *2 in establishing pragmatic truth; it also overlooks such pronouncements as: "Truth . . . is manifestly incompatible with waywardness on our part. Woe to him whose beliefs play fast and loose with the order which realities follow in his experience: they will lead him nowhere or else make false connexions" (*Pragmatism*, p. 99).

Third: James confuses *truth* and *verification*. This has been a persistent criticism (see his discussion, *MT*, p. 108, of the sixth misunderstanding of pragmatism, his reply to Pratt, pp. 94 ff., and the note to 93.1, p. 181 below). Clearly, the verification of some Belief-assertion, or corroborating our belief in it, is distinct from the truth of that Belief-assertion. In order to be verifiable at all—or be subject to verification—a Belief-assertion would have to be either true or false; the truth value is logically prior to and distinct from the verification. So too, an unverified Belief-assertion remains either true or false, verification neither creating nor being truth. Furthermore, knowing what we mean by a belief being true, and knowing whether the belief *is* true are distinct (for we can know what the truth of "the earth is flat" would mean, although in fact the statement is false). All of this is to say that cognitive truth and verification cannot be equated. James, however, was interested in verification as a process under conditions *2 and *3, rather than *1 (which latter he may have taken for granted). It is the workings of a Belief-assertion as constituting its pragmatic truth that he also called verification, thus seeming to treat truth and verification as synonymous. He says that an idea "is *made* true by events. Its verity *is* . . . a process: the process namely of its verifying itself, its veri-*fication*. Its validity is the process of its valid-*ation*" (*MT*, pp. 3–4). But the process he speaks of here, in which verity is verification, is the fulfilling of conditions *2 and *3. The process, as we might rephrase it, *makes* out of otherwise mere cognitive truth (of *1), pragmatic truth; and verities (of *1) become veri-*fications* (of *2 and *3). Still, cognitive truth and verification remain distinctly different in meaning.

It would be more judicious to decide that James was vague rather than glaringly mistaken about verification. And he would have helped to advance understanding and reduce futile controversy if he had clearly developed and distinguished his doctrine of pragmatic verification from more generally accepted notions of testing and confirmation.

In conclusion, it might be asked why, considering its importance, James was not more explicit in acknowledging the notion of cognitive truth which can be found alternately suggested, employed, and alluded to in his writings. One reason, we have seen, is that the general idea of "absolute" truth, made so much of by many of his contemporaries, held little interest for James. It was truths in the plural and the particular verification procedures and their specific contributions to the control and clarification of experience that he regarded as of primary philosophic importance. He does, however, recognize "absolute" truth as a regulative ideal; it means "what no farther experience will ever alter" (*Pragmatism*, p. 106). This serves as an ideal of "potential better truth," a stimulus to continued investigation. Accordingly, although certain past systems of thought, such as Ptolemaic astronomy or Euclidean space "were expedient for centuries," we now consider them as "only relatively true, or true within those borders of exexperience." But James concludes, " 'Absolutely' they are false"

(*Pragmatism,* p. 107). The absolute condition here is our cognitive truth. And of this absolute sense of truth functioning as a regulative ideal he says: "the proposition 'There *is* absolute truth' is the only absolute truth of which we can be sure" (*MT,* p. 143). On the other hand, he was wary of the danger of hypostatizing concepts as the names of essences. Now the concept of "absolute truth" can readily be made to eventuate in a theory of *the* Truth as an integral part of absolute Reality. James had witnessed philosophers in his day thus affirming a "non-utilitarian, haughty, refined, remote, exalted" conception of "objective truth" as an "absolute correspondence of our thoughts with an equally absolute reality" (*Pragmatism,* p. 38). In short, he saw the idea of absolute truth leading all too easily to monistic idealism. He was to focus on this form of hypostatization calling it "vicious abstractionism" (*MT,* Ch. XII, and p. 135), namely, when what is selectively referred to by a concept is taken as the only real feature in an otherwise "originally rich phenomenon," and all other features are denied and expunged. In wanting to keep clear of such abstractionism James was uneasy about the notion of a single "absolute" definition of truth. The one dictionary definition, he feared, if made too much of, could encourage discounting the importance of truths in the plural and verification processes on the grounds that these are "nothing but" instances of the one absolute truth and thus, merely the partial aspects of one ideal reality.

On this I think we must observe that, though his critical reservations concerning abstractionism are on the whole cogent, James underestimated the value of general definitions and the legitimate use of very general and abstract concepts in philosophy. In the present instance, because of his interest in the role of particular truths and verifications of belief, he was occasionally misled into supposing that knowledge of the "absolute" meaning of 'truth' would entail possession of absolute knowledge. He thus confused the quite distinct ideas of one fixed "absolute" meaning of 'truth' and the probabilistic character of knowledge. He thought that to understand the meaning of truth in some absolute sense might constitute a denial of the relative, mutable, and fallible nature of the confirmation of hypotheses and beliefs. Apparently he failed to see that an absolute definition of 'truth' is not incompatible with the idea that knowledge never attains absolute certainty or that confirmation of belief is of degrees and, in the light of new knowledge, is subject to change and even disconfirmation.[25] On these points James was frequently inconsistent and mistaken. But these same points form part of the reason why the notion of cognitive truth, while present in James's theorizing, receives little emphasis.

CONCLUSION

The object of the above interpretation and reformulation of James's argument has been both to clarify and suggest some of the very real philosophical merits of his theory of truth. In bringing this discussion to a close I do not wish to leave the impression that I think no serious difficulties remain to be encountered in his writings on truth. There are merits, but there are also shortcomings; and some of each have been formative in diverse ways in the critical and speculative currents of later philosophic thought.

The Meaning of Truth did not create the stir that *Pragmatism* had two years before. The prevailing sense was that James had not succeeded in dealing directly with the criticisms that his earlier work had prompted; that doctrines had been restated rather than questions answered. F. C. S. Schiller, not surprisingly, wrote a glowing piece for *Mind* (Bradley having declined to write a review). The brief notice in *The Journal of Philosophy, Psychology, and Scientific Methods* simply characterized the book as a challenge to non-pragmatists to meet this more formidable statement of the pragmatic theory of truth.[26] In a critical review in the *Philosophical Review*, George T. Ladd (see note to 10.12, p. 168 below) found a "constant shifting of the two questions" concerning what truth *is*, and *how* truth is arrived at—a criticism frequently made of James.

[25]This critical problem in James is discussed by Israel Scheffler, *Four Pragmatists* (New York: Humanities Press, 1974), pp. 112–116.

[26]F. C. S. Schiller's review is in *Mind*, n.s. 19 (1910), 258–263. John E. Russell's review, *The Journal of Philosophy, Psychology, and Scientific Methods*, 7 (1910), 22–24. A favorable précis by E. Baron appeared in *Revue de Philosophie*, 16 (1910), 426–428. A mildly sympathetic and substantial review appeared in the *Revue Philosophique*, 70 (1910), 643–649. But the reviewer, Lionel Dauriac, prefaces his discussion with the observation that, although James is engaged in making a serious case for his philosophy, pragmatism is not taken seriously in Europe.

Generally, he was regarded as having perpetuated the older controversial issues rather than resolving them in his new book. Further attention to these questions was diverted by the publication of *A Pluralistic Universe* (1909) in which James carried his pragmatic convictions and criticism of monistic idealism into the camp of the opposition by presenting these lectures in Oxford. The lectures and the idea of radical empiricism and pluralism advanced in them aroused considerable interest. With James's untimely death in 1910 the moot notion of truth in the particular manner and terms in which he had dealt with it began to lose some of its urgency; new developments in philosophy coming from Moore and Russell in England and the changing course of American pragmatism under Dewey, among other forces, effected a reconsideration and alteration of the forms in which the nature of the problem of truth was identified and discussed. And for a time James's influence and relevance was felt to lie rather in his contributions to psychology and his philosophical analysis of consciousness and of the idea of pure experience.

I hope, however, that contrary to the familiar imputation that James had indulged in hasty and indefensible pronouncements on truth, the preceding has made it evident that this theory was an unusually ambitious undertaking. For what he was attempting was to show how complex interrelated, psychological, moral, epistemological and metaphysical considerations converge in the idea of *truth*, if the philosophic implications and significance of that idea are to be clarified, and if its function as a ruling condition of successful conduct in a malleable and changing world is to be understood. The concept of truth, for James, was accordingly envisaged and developed as integral to a more inclusive philosophic system and as an essential linking of two principle parts: a critical (rather than descriptive) theory of behavior and a metaphysics of experience. The vision was never entirely fixed and the system never fully articulated.

I suggest that this was the dominant motivation of the theme of *The Meaning of Truth*, namely, the quest for a coherent and comprehensive philosophic expression of the varied forms and ends of human action and experience, and of how it is possible for thought to be a source of alteration, novelty, and value in the world of which it is also an objective condition and part. This aim, however, was almost destined to be conceived imperfectly by a man of James's mercurial intellectual temperament and deep distrust of system-building and certainty and finality in philosophy.

This is not how James has usually been interpreted. His theory of truth is usually explained as resulting from an interest in justifying religious and metaphysical convictions. The contention then being that if a religious belief "works," it is true. This is an elliptical way of characterizing James's view of truth. No doubt the great importance of his father's Swedenborgian religious investigations and the early influence of his father's friend Emerson had a deep emotional effect on his thinking. And this was reinforced by encountering Renouvier's writings in a later period of crisis, which contributed to James's lifelong appreciation of the subtle psychological value and 'working' functions of religious belief. Furthermore, as a psychologist, James took an almost clinical interest in the pathology of belief, and how, under specific circumstances, differing kinds of beliefs could lead to beneficial adaptations to the world. Thus, he attempted to show how religious and metaphysical beliefs as well as ordinary moral and esthetic aspirations could be pragmatically meaningful and, in special cases, self-fulfilling and perhaps true. But there is another way of viewing this pragmatic defense of moral and emotional interests and of taking the conduct they inspire seriously. It may appear on one side as an apologia for religious yearnings; it can even have been partly that. But the sword cuts two ways. By arguing that religious and metaphysical assertions can be pragmatically meaningful claims to truth, James was also showing these to be serious hypotheses rather than closed dogmas. He was thus encouraging the extended application of critical inquiry, of pragmatic analysis and justification to the spheres of religion and metaphysics. So viewed, James's pragmatism was not a retreat from reason or defense of unreason; it was an enlarging of the subject matter of reason where dogma had hitherto often prevailed.

The ultimate value of thought, for William James, is its power of directing and transforming sensory experience, its terminations in specific forms of illumination and action. How and in what measure is ordinary experience clarified and made serviceable to human needs and to our individual and socially shared wants and satisfactions? Such is James's pragmatic critique of the uses of intelligence. The critique is central to his conception of philosophy. Philosophy is not an isolated, esoteric, and autonomous discipline. Its full significance emerges with wider terminations in the traffic of human affairs and individual conduct. Truth is essential here both as a controlling end and a clarification of procedures for successful and creative action. For James truth is not constitutive of a realm of being or of essence, but a regulative ideal for the effective organization of human energies in conscientious interaction with environing reality and prospective goods.*

*This introduction was written while I was a member of The Institute for Advanced Study, Princeton, for the academic year 1974–75. Partial support for this work as part of a more extensive study was provided by the National Endowment for the Humanities under Grant F74-588.

The Meaning of Truth

A Sequel to 'Pragmatism'

Preface

The pivotal part of my book named *Pragmatism* is its account of the relation called 'truth' which may obtain between an idea (opinion, belief, statement, or what not) and its object. "Truth," I there say, "is a property of certain of our ideas. It means their 'agreement,' as falsity means their disagreement, with 'reality.' Pragmatists and intellectualists both accept this definition as a matter of course. . . .

"Where our ideas [do] not copy definitely their object, what does agreement with that object mean? . . . Pragmatism asks its usual question. 'Grant an idea or belief to be true,' it says, 'what concrete difference will its being true make in anyone's actual life? What experiences [may] be different from those which would obtain if the belief were false? How will the truth be realized? What, in short, is the truth's cash-value in experiential terms?' The moment pragmatism asks this question, it sees the answer: *True ideas are those that we can assimilate, validate, corroborate and verify. False ideas are those that we cannot.* That is the practical difference it makes to us to have true ideas; that, therefore, is the meaning of truth, for it is all that truth is known-as.

"The truth of an idea is not a stagnant property inherent in it. Truth *happens* to an idea. It *becomes* true, is *made* true by events.

3

Its verity *is* in fact an event, a process: the process namely of its verifying itself, its veri-*fication*. Its validity is the process of its valid-*ation*.[1]

"To 'agree' in the widest sense with a reality *can only mean to be guided either straight up to it or into its surroundings, or to be put into such working touch with it as to handle either it or something connected with it better than if we disagreed*. Better either intellectually or practically! ... Any idea that helps us to *deal*, whether practically or intellectually, with either the reality or its belongings, that doesn't entangle our progress in frustrations, that *fits*, in fact, and adapts our life to the reality's whole setting, will agree sufficiently to meet the requirement. It will hold true of that reality.

" '*The true*,' to put it very briefly, *is only the expedient in the way of our thinking, just as 'the right' is only the expedient in the way of our behaving*. Expedient in almost any fashion; and expedient in the long run and on the whole, of course; for what meets expediently all the experience in sight won't necessarily meet all farther experiences equally satisfactorily. Experience, as we know, has ways of *boiling over*, and making us correct our present formulas."

This account of truth, following upon the similar ones given by Messrs. Dewey and Schiller, has occasioned the liveliest discussion. Few critics have defended it, most of them have scouted it. It seems evident that the subject is a hard one to understand, under its apparent simplicity; and evident also, I think, that the definitive settlement of it will mark a turning-point in the history of epistemology, and consequently in that of general philosophy. In order to make my own thought more accessible to those who hereafter may have to study the question, I have collected in the volume that follows all the work of my pen that bears directly on the truth-question. My first statement was in 1884, in the article that begins the present volume. The other papers follow in the order

---

[1] But "verifi*ability*," I add, "is as good as verification. For one truth-process completed there are a million in our lives that function in [the] state of nascency. They turn us *towards* direct verification; lead us into the *surroundings* of the objects they envisage; and then, if everything runs on harmoniously, we are so sure that verification is possible that we omit it, and are usually justified by all that happens."

4

of their publication. Two or three appear now for the first time.

One of the accusations which I oftenest have had to meet is that of making the truth of our religious beliefs consist in their 'feeling good' to us, and in nothing else. I regret to have given some excuse for this charge, by the unguarded language in which, in the book *Pragmatism,* I spoke of the truth of the belief of certain philosophers in the absolute. Explaining why I do not believe in the absolute myself (p. 78 [*ed.,* WORKS, p. 43]), yet finding that it may secure 'moral holidays' to those who need them, and is true in so far forth (if to gain moral holidays be a good),[2] I offered this as a conciliatory olive-branch to my enemies. But they, as is only too common with such offerings, trampled the gift under foot and turned and rent the giver. I had counted too much on their good will—oh for the rarity of christian charity under the sun! Oh for the rarity of ordinary secular intelligence also! I had supposed it to be matter of common observation that, of two competing views of the universe which in all other respects are equal, but of which the first denies some vital human need while the second satisfies it, the second will be favored by sane men for the simple reason that it makes the world seem more rational. To choose the first view under such circumstances would be an ascetic act, an act of philosophic self-denial of which no normal human being would be guilty. Using the pragmatic test of the meaning of concepts, I had shown the concept of the absolute to *mean* nothing but the holiday giver, the banisher of cosmic fear. One's objective deliverance, when one says 'the absolute exists,' amounted, on my showing, just to this, that 'some justification of a feeling of security in presence of the universe' exists, and that systematically to refuse to cultivate a feeling of security would be to do violence to a tendency in one's emotional life which might well be respected as prophetic.

Apparently my absolutist critics fail to see the workings of their own minds in any such picture, so all that I can do is to apologize, and take my offering back. The absolute is true in *no* way then, and least of all, by the verdict of the critics, in the way which I assigned!

My treatment of 'God,' 'freedom,' and 'design' was similar.

---

[2] *Op. cit.,* p. 75 [WORKS, pp. 41–42].

Reducing, by the pragmatic test, the meaning of each of these concepts to its positive experienceable operation, I showed them all to mean the same thing, viz., the presence of 'promise' in the world. 'God or no God?' means 'promise or no promise?' It seems to me that the alternative is objective enough, being a question as to whether the cosmos has one character or another, even tho our own provisional answer be made on subjective grounds. Nevertheless christian and non-christian critics alike accuse me of summoning people to say 'God exists,' *even when he doesn't exist*, because forsooth in my philosophy the 'truth' of the saying doesn't really mean that he exists in any shape whatever, but only that to say so feels good.

Most of the pragmatist and anti-pragmatist warfare is over what the word 'truth' shall be held to signify, and not over any of the facts embodied in truth-situations; for both pragmatists and anti-pragmatists believe in existent objects, just as they believe in our ideas of them. The difference is that when the pragmatists speak of truth, they mean exclusively something about the ideas, namely their workableness; whereas when anti-pragmatists speak of truth they seem most often to mean something about the objects. Since the pragmatist, if he agrees that an idea is 'really' true, also agrees to whatever it says about its object; and since most anti-pragmatists have already come round to agreeing that, if the object exists, the idea that it does so is workable; there would seem so little left to fight about that I might well be asked why instead of reprinting my share in so much verbal wrangling, I do not show my sense of 'values' by burning it all up.

I understand the question and I will give my answer. I am interested in another doctrine in philosophy to which I give the name of radical empiricism, and it seems to me that the establishment of the pragmatist theory of truth is a step of first-rate importance in making radical empiricism prevail. Radical empiricism consists first of a postulate, next of a statement of fact, and finally of a generalized conclusion.

The postulate is that the only things that shall be debatable among philosophers shall be things definable in terms drawn from experience. [Things of an unexperienceable nature may exist ad libitum, but they form no part of the material for philosophic debate.]

The statement of fact is that the relations between things, conjunctive as well as disjunctive, are just as much matters of direct particular experience, neither more so nor less so, than the things themselves.

The generalized conclusion is that therefore the parts of experience hold together from next to next by relations that are themselves parts of experience. The directly apprehended universe needs, in short, no extraneous trans-empirical connective support, but possesses in its own right a concatenated or continuous structure.

The great obstacle to radical empiricism in the contemporary mind is the rooted rationalist belief that experience as immediately given is all disjunction and no conjunction, and that to make one world out of this separateness, a higher unifying agency must be there. In the prevalent idealism this agency is represented as the absolute all-witness which 'relates' things together by throwing 'categories' over them like a net. The most peculiar and unique, perhaps, of all these categories is supposed to be the truth-relation, which connects parts of reality in pairs, making of one of them a knower, and of the other a thing known, yet which is itself contentless experientially, neither describable, explicable, nor reduceable to lower terms, and denotable only by uttering the name 'truth.'

The pragmatist view, on the contrary, of the truth-relation is that it has a definite content, and that everything in it is experienceable. Its whole nature can be told in positive terms. The 'workableness' which ideas must have, in order to be true, means particular workings, physical or intellectual, actual or possible, which they may set up from next to next inside of concrete experience. Were this pragmatic contention admitted, one great point in the victory of radical empiricism would also be scored, for the relation between an object and the idea that truly knows it, is held by rationalists to be nothing of this describable sort, but to stand outside of all possible temporal experience; and on the relation, so interpreted, rationalism is wonted to make its last most obdurate rally.

7

Now the anti-pragmatist contentions which I try to meet in this volume can be so easily used by rationalists as weapons of resistance, not only to pragmatism but to radical empiricism also (for if the truth-relation were transcendent, others might be so too), that I feel strongly the strategical importance of having them definitely met and got out of the way. What our critics most persistently keep saying is that tho workings go with truth, yet they do not constitute it. It is numerically additional to them, prior to them, explanatory *of* them, and in no wise to be explained *by* them, we are incessantly told. The first point for our enemies to establish, therefore, is that *something* numerically additional and prior to the workings is involved in the truth of an idea. Since the *object* is additional, and usually prior, most rationalists plead *it*, and boldly accuse us of denying it. This leaves on the bystanders the impression—since we cannot reasonably deny the existence of the object—that our account of truth breaks down, and that our critics have driven us from the field. Altho in various places in this volume I try to refute the slanderous charge that we deny real existence, I will say here again, for the sake of emphasis, that the existence of the object, whenever the idea asserts it 'truly,' is the only reason, in innumerable cases, why the idea does work successfully, if it work at all; and that it seems an abuse of language, to say the least, to transfer the word 'truth' from the idea to the object's existence, when the falsehood of ideas that won't work is explained by that existence as well as the truth of those that will.

I find this abuse prevailing among my most accomplished adversaries. But once establish the proper verbal custom, let the word 'truth' represent a property of the idea, cease to make it something mysteriously connected with the object known, and the path opens fair and wide, as I believe, to the discussion of radical empiricism on its merits. The truth of an idea will then mean only its workings, or that in it which by ordinary psychological laws sets up those workings; it will mean neither the idea's object, nor anything 'saltatory' inside the idea, that terms drawn from experience cannot describe.

One word more, ere I end this preface. A distinction is sometimes made between Dewey, Schiller and myself, as if I, in supposing the object's existence, made a concession to popular prejudice which they, as more radical pragmatists, refuse to make. As I myself understand these authors, we all three absolutely agree in admitting the transcendency of the object (provided it be an experienceable object) to the subject, in the truth-relation. Dewey in particular has insisted almost ad nauseam that the whole meaning of our cognitive states and processes lies in the way they intervene in the control and revaluation of independent existences or facts. His account of knowledge is not only absurd, but meaningless, unless independent existences be there of which our ideas take account, and for the transformation of which they work. But because he and Schiller refuse to discuss objects and relations 'transcendent' in the sense of being *altogether trans-experiential,* their critics pounce on sentences in their writings to that effect to show that they deny the existence *within the realm of experience* of objects external to the ideas that declare their presence there.[3] It seems incredible that educated and apparently sincere critics should so fail to catch their adversary's point of view.

What misleads so many of them is possibly also the fact that the universes of discourse of Schiller, Dewey, and myself are panoramas of different extent, and that what the one postulates explicitly the other provisionally leaves only in a state of implication, while the reader thereupon considers it to be denied. Schiller's universe is the smallest, being essentially a psychological one. He starts with but one sort of thing, truth-claims, but is led ultimately to the independent objective facts which they assert, inasmuch as the most successfully validated of all claims is that such facts are there. My universe is more essentially epistemological. I start with two things,

---

[3] It gives me pleasure to welcome Professor Carveth Read into the pragmatistic church, so far as his epistemology goes. See his vigorous book, *The Metaphysics of Nature,* 2d Edition, Appendix A. (London, Black, 1908.) The work *What is Reality?* by Francis Howe Johnson (Boston, 1891), of which I make the acquaintance only while correcting these proofs, contains some striking anticipations of the later pragmatist view. *The Psychology of Thinking,* by Irving E. Miller (New York, Macmillan Co., 1909), which has just appeared, is one of the most convincing pragmatist documents yet published, tho it does not use the word 'pragmatism' at all. While I am making references, I cannot refrain from inserting one to the extraordinarily acute article by H. V. Knox, in the *Quarterly Review* for April, 1909.

the objective facts and the claims, and indicate which claims, the facts being there, will work successfully as the latter's substitutes and which will not. I call the former claims true. Dewey's panorama, if I understand this colleague, is the widest of the three, but I refrain from giving my own account of its complexity. Suffice it that he holds as firmly as I do to objects independent of our judgments. If I am wrong in saying this, he must correct me. I decline in this matter to be corrected at second hand.

I have not pretended in the following pages to consider all the critics of my account of truth, such as Messrs. Taylor, Lovejoy, Gardiner, Bakewell, Creighton, Hibben, Parodi, Salter, Carus, Lalande, Mentré, McTaggart, G. E. Moore, Ladd and others, especially not Professor Schinz, who has published under the title of *Anti-pragmatisme* an amusing sociological romance. Some of these critics seem to me to labor under an inability almost pathetic, to understand the thesis which they seek to refute. I imagine that most of their difficulties have been answered by anticipation elsewhere in this volume, and I am sure that my readers will thank me for not adding more repetition to the fearful amount that is already there.

95 IRVING ST., CAMBRIDGE (MASS.),
    August, 1909.

Contents

I

The Function of Cognition[1]

The following inquiry is (to use a distinction familiar to readers of Mr. Shadworth Hodgson) not an inquiry into the 'how it comes,' but into the 'what it is' of cognition. What we call acts of cognition are evidently realized through what we call brains and their events, whether there be 'souls' dynamically connected with the brains or not. But with neither brains nor souls has this essay any business to transact. In it we shall simply assume that cognition *is* produced, somehow, and limit ourselves to asking what elements it contains, what factors it implies.

Cognition is a function of consciousness. The first factor it implies is therefore a state of consciousness wherein the cognition shall take place. Having elsewhere used the word 'feeling' to designate generically all states of consciousness considered subjectively, or without respect to their possible function, I shall then say that, whatever elements an act of cognition may imply besides, it at least implies the existence of a *feeling*. [If the reader share the current antipathy to the word 'feeling,' he may substitute for it, wherever I use it, the word 'idea,' taken in the old broad Lockian sense, or he

---

[1] Read before the Aristotelian Society, December 1, 1884, and first published in *Mind*, vol. x (1885).—This, and the following articles have received a very slight verbal revision, consisting mostly in the omission of redundancy.

may use the clumsy phrase 'state of consciousness,' or finally he may say 'thought' instead.]

Now it is to be observed that the common consent of mankind has agreed that some feelings are cognitive and some are simple facts having a subjective, or, what one might almost call a physical, existence, but no such self-transcendent function as would be implied in their being pieces of knowledge. Our task is again limited here. We are not to ask, "How is self-transcendence possible?" We are only to ask, "How comes it that common sense has assigned a number of cases in which it is assumed not only to be possible but actual? And what are the marks used by common sense to distinguish those cases from the rest?" In short, our inquiry is a chapter in descriptive psychology—hardly anything more.

Condillac embarked on a quest similar to this by his famous hypothesis of a statue to which various feelings were successively imparted. Its first feeling was supposed to be one of fragrance. But to avoid all possible complication with the question of genesis, let us not attribute even to a statue the possession of our imaginary feeling. Let us rather suppose it attached to no matter, nor localized at any point in space, but left swinging *in vacuo*, as it were, by the direct creative *fiat* of a god. And let us also, to escape entanglement with difficulties about the physical or psychical nature of its 'object,' not call it a feeling of fragrance or of any other determinate sort, but limit ourselves to assuming that it is a feeling of q. What is true of it under this abstract name will be no less true of it in any more particular shape (such as fragrance, pain, hardness) which the reader may suppose.

Now, if this feeling of q be the only creation of the god, it will of course form the entire universe. And if, to escape the cavils of that large class of persons who believe that *semper idem sentire ac non sentire* are the same,[2] we allow the feeling to be of as short a duration as they like, that universe will only need to last an in-

---

[2] 'The Relativity of Knowledge,' held in this sense, is, it may be observed in passing, one of the oddest of philosophic superstitions. Whatever facts may be cited in its favor are due to the properties of nerve-tissue, which may be exhausted by too prolonged an excitement. Patients with neuralgias that last unremittingly for days can, however, assure us that the limits of this nerve-law are pretty widely drawn. But if we physically could get a feeling that should last eternally unchanged, what atom

finitesimal part of a second. The feeling in question will thus be reduced to its fighting weight, and all that befals it in the way of a cognitive function must be held to befal in the brief instant of its quickly snuffed-out life—a life, it will also be noticed, that has no other moment of consciousness either preceding or following it.

Well now, can our little feeling, thus left alone in the universe—for the god and we psychological critics may be supposed left out of the account—can the feeling, I say, be said to have any sort of a cognitive function? For it to *know*, there must be something to be known. What is there, on the present supposition? One may reply, "the feeling's content q." But does it not seem more proper to call this the feeling's *quality* than its content? Does not the word 'content' suggest that the feeling has already dirempted itself as an act from its content as an object? And would it be quite safe to assume so promptly that the quality q of a feeling is one and the same thing with a feeling of the quality q? The quality q, so far, is an entirely subjective fact which the feeling carries so to speak endogenously, or in its pocket. If anyone pleases to dignify so simple a fact as this by the name of knowledge, of course nothing can prevent him. But let us keep closer to the path of common usage, and reserve the name knowledge for the cognition of 'realities,' meaning by realities things that exist independently of the feeling through which their cognition occurs. If the content of the feeling occur nowhere in the universe outside of the feeling itself, and perish with the feeling, common usage refuses to call it a reality, and brands it as a subjective feature of the feeling's constitution, or at the most as the feeling's *dream*.

For the feeling to be cognitive in the specific sense, then, it must be self-transcendent; and we must prevail upon the god to *create a reality outside of it* to correspond to its intrinsic quality q. Thus only can it be redeemed from the condition of being a solipsism. If now the new-created reality *resemble* the feeling's quality q, I say that the feeling may be held by us *to be cognizant of that reality*.

---

of logical or psychological argument is there to prove that it would not be felt as long as it lasted, and felt for just what it is, all that time? The reason for the opposite prejudice seems to be our reluctance to think that so *stupid* a thing as such a feeling would necessarily be, should be allowed to fill eternity with its presence. An interminable acquaintance, leading to no knowledge-*about*—such would be its condition.

This first instalment of my thesis is sure to be attacked. But one word before defending it. 'Reality' has become our warrant for calling a feeling cognitive; but what becomes our warrant for calling anything reality? The only reply is—the faith of the present critic or inquirer. At every moment of his life he finds himself subject to a belief in *some* realities, even tho his realities of this year should prove to be his illusions of the next. Whenever he finds that the feeling he is studying contemplates what he himself regards as a reality, he must of course admit the feeling itself to be truly cognitive. We are ourselves the critics here; and we shall find our burden much lightened by being allowed to take reality in this relative and provisional way. Every science must make some assumptions. *Erkenntnisstheoretiker* are but fallible mortals. When they study the function of cognition, they do it by means of the same function in themselves. And knowing that the fountain cannot go higher than its source, we should promptly confess that our results in this field are affected by our own liability to err. *The most we can claim is, that what we say about cognition may be counted as true as what we say about anything else.* If our hearers agree with us about what are to be held 'realities,' they will perhaps also agree to the reality of our doctrine of the way in which they are known. We cannot ask for more.

Our terminology shall follow the spirit of these remarks. We will deny the function of knowledge to any feeling whose quality or content we do not ourselves believe to exist outside of that feeling as well as in it. We may call such a feeling a dream if we like; we shall have to see later whether we can call it a fiction or an error.

To revert now to our thesis. Some persons will immediately cry out, "How *can* a reality resemble a feeling?" Here we find how wise we were to name the quality of the feeling by an algebraic letter q. We flank the whole difficulty of resemblance between an inner state and an outward reality, by leaving it free to anyone to postulate as the reality whatever sort of thing he thinks *can* resemble a feeling—if not an outward thing, then another feeling like the first one—the mere feeling q in the critic's mind for example. Evading thus this objection, we turn to another which is sure to be urged.

It will come from those philosophers to whom 'thought,' in the sense of a knowledge of relations, is the all in all of mental life; and who hold a merely feeling consciousness to be no better—one would sometimes say from their utterances, a good deal worse—than no consciousness at all. Such phrases as these, for example, are common to-day in the mouths of those who claim to walk in the footprints of Kant and Hegel rather than in the ancestral English paths: "A perception detached from all others, left out of the 'heap which we call a mind,' being out of all relation, has no qualities—is simply nothing. We can no more 'consider' it than we can see vacancy." "It is simply in itself—fleeting, momentary, unnameable (because, while we name it, it has become another), and for the same reason unknowable, the very negation of knowability." "Exclude from what we have considered real all qualities constituted by relation, we find that none are left."

Altho such citations as these from the writings of Professor Green might be multiplied almost indefinitely, they would hardly repay the pains of collection, so egregiously false is the doctrine they teach. Our little supposed feeling, whatever it may be, from the cognitive point of view, whether a bit of knowledge or a dream, is certainly no psychical zero. It is a most positively and definitely qualified inner fact, with a complexion all its own. Of course there are many mental facts which it is *not*. It knows q, if q be a reality, with a very minimum of knowledge. It neither dates nor locates it. It neither classes nor names it. And it neither knows itself as a feeling, nor contrasts itself with other feelings, nor estimates its own duration or intensity. It is, in short, if there is no more of it than this, a most dumb and helpless and useless kind of thing.

But if we must describe it by so many negations, and if it can say nothing *about* itself or *about* anything else, by what right do we deny that it is a psychical zero? And may not the 'relationists' be right after all?

In the innocent looking word 'about' lies the solution of this riddle; and a simple enough solution it is when frankly looked at. A quotation from a too seldom quoted book, the *Exploratio Philosophica* of John Grote (London, 1865), p. 60, will form the best introduction to it.

"Our knowledge," writes Grote, "may be contemplated in either of two ways, or, to use other words, we may speak in a double manner of the 'object' of knowledge. That is, we may either use language thus: we *know* a thing, a man, etc.; or we may use it thus: we know such and such things *about* the thing, the man, etc. Language in general, following its true logical instinct, distinguishes between these two applications of the notion of knowledge, the one being γνῶναι, noscere, kennen, connaître, the other being εἰδέναι, scire, wissen, savoir. In the origin, the former may be considered more what I have called phenomenal—it is the notion of knowledge as *acquaintance* or familiarity with what is known: which notion is perhaps more akin to the phenomenal bodily communication, and is less purely intellectual than the other: it is the kind of knowledge which we have of a thing by the presentation to the senses or the representation of it in picture or type, a 'vorstellung'. The other, which is what we express in judgments or propositions, what is embodied in 'begriffe' or concepts without any necessary imaginative representation, is in its origin the more *intellectual* notion of knowledge. There is no reason however why we should not express our knowledge, whatever its kind, in either manner, provided only we do not confusedly express it, in the same proposition or piece of reasoning, in both."

Now obviously if our supposed feeling of q is (if knowledge at all) only knowledge of the mere acquaintance-type, it is milking a he-goat, as the ancients would have said, to try to extract from it any deliverance *about* anything under the sun, even about itself. And it is as unjust, after our failure, to turn upon it and call it a psychical nothing, as it would be, after our fruitless attack upon the billy-goat, to proclaim the non-lactiferous character of the whole goat-tribe. But the entire industry of the hegelian school in trying to shove simple sensation out of the pale of philosophic recognition is founded on this false issue. It is always the 'speechlessness' of sensation, its inability to make any 'statement,'[3] that is held to make the very notion of it meaningless, and to justify the student of knowledge in scouting it out of existence. 'Significance,' in the sense

[3] See, for example, Green's Introduction to Hume's *Treatise of Human Nature*, p. 36.

18

of standing as the sign of other mental states, is taken to be the sole function of what mental states we have; and from the perception that our little primitive sensation has as yet no significance in this literal sense, it is an easy step to call it first meaningless, next senseless, then vacuous, and finally to brand it as absurd and inadmissible. But in this universal liquidation, this everlasting slip, slip, slip, of direct acquaintance into knowledge-*about*, until at last nothing is left about which the knowledge can be supposed to obtain, does not all 'significance' depart from the situation? And when our knowledge about things has reached its never so complicated perfection, must there not needs abide alongside of it and inextricably mixed in with it some acquaintance with *what* things all this knowledge is about?

Now, our supposed little feeling gives a *what*; and if other feelings should succeed which remember the first, its *what* may stand as subject or predicate of some piece of knowledge-about, of some judgment, perceiving relations between it and other *whats* which the other feelings may know. The hitherto dumb *q* will then receive a name and be no longer speechless. But every name, as students of logic know, has its 'denotation'; and the denotation always means some reality or content, relationless *ab extra* or with its internal relations unanalyzed, like the *q* which our primitive sensation is supposed to know. No relation-expressing proposition is possible except on the basis of a preliminary acquaintance with such 'facts,' with such contents, as this. Let the *q* be fragrance, let it be toothache, or let it be a more complex kind of feeling, like that of the full-moon swimming in her blue abyss, it must first come in that simple shape, and be held fast in that first intention, before any knowledge *about* it can be attained. The knowledge *about* it is *it* with a context added. Undo *it*, and what is added cannot be *context*.[4]

4 If A enters and B exclaims, "Didn't you see my brother on the stairs?" we all hold that A may answer, "I saw him, but didn't know he was your brother"; ignorance of brotherhood not abolishing power to see. But those who, on account of the unrelatedness of the first facts with which we become acquainted, deny them to be 'known' to us, ought in consistency to maintain that if A did not perceive the relationship of the man on the stairs to B, it was impossible he should have noticed him at all.

Let us say no more then about this objection, but enlarge our thesis, thus: If there be in the universe a *q* other than the *q* in the feeling, the latter may have acquaintance with an entity ejective to itself; an acquaintance moreover, which, as mere acquaintance, it would be hard to imagine susceptible either of improvement or increase, being in its way complete; and which would oblige us (so long as we refuse not to call acquaintance knowledge) to say not only that the feeling is cognitive, but that all qualities of feeling, *so long as there is anything outside of them which they resemble,* are feelings *of* qualities of existence, and perceptions of outward fact.

The point of this vindication of the cognitive function of the first feeling lies, it will be noticed, in the discovery that *q* does exist elsewhere than in it. In case this discovery were not made, we could not be sure the feeling was cognitive; and in case there were nothing outside to be discovered, we should have to call the feeling a dream. But the feeling itself cannot make the discovery. Its own *q* is the only *q* it grasps; and its own nature is not a particle altered by having the self-transcendent function of cognition either added to it or taken away. The function is accidental; synthetic, not analytic; and falls outside and not inside its being.[5]

A feeling feels as a gun shoots. If there be nothing to be felt or hit, they discharge themselves *ins blaue hinein.* If, however, something starts up opposite them, they no longer simply shoot or feel, they hit and know.

But with this arises a worse objection than any yet made. We the

---

[5] It seems odd to call so important a function accidental, but I do not see how we can mend the matter. Just as, if we start with the reality and ask how it may come to be known, we can only reply by invoking a feeling which shall *reconstruct* it in its own more private fashion; so, if we start with the feeling and ask how it may come to know, we can only reply by invoking a reality which shall *reconstruct* it in its own more public fashion. In either case, however, the datum we start with remains just what it was. One may easily get lost in verbal mysteries about the difference between quality of feeling and feeling of quality, between receiving and reconstructing the knowledge of a reality. But at the end we must confess that the notion of real cognition involves an unmediated dualism of the knower and the known. See Bowne's *Metaphysics,* New York, 1882, pp. 403–412, and various passages in Lotze, *e.g., Logic,* § 308. ['Unmediated' is a bad word to have used.—1909.]

critics look on and see a real q and a feeling of q; and because the two resemble each other, we say the one knows the other. But what right have we to say this until we know that the feeling of q means to stand for or represent just that *same* other q? Suppose, instead of one q, a number of real q's in the field. If the gun shoots and hits, we can easily see which one of them it hits. But how can we distinguish which one the feeling knows? It knows the one it stands for. But which one *does* it stand for? It declares no intention in this respect. It merely resembles; it resembles all indifferently; and resembling, *per se,* is not necessarily representing or standing-for at all. Eggs resemble each other, but do not on that account represent, stand for, or know each other. And if you say this is because neither of them is a *feeling,* then imagine the world to consist of nothing but toothaches, which *are* feelings, feelings resembling each other exactly—would they know each other the better for all that?

The case of q being a bare quality like that of toothache-pain is quite different from that of its being a concrete individual thing. There is practically no test for deciding whether the feeling of a bare quality means to represent it or not. It can *do* nothing to the quality beyond resembling it, simply because an abstract quality is a thing to which nothing can be done. Being without context or environment or *principium individuationis,* a quiddity with no hæcceity, a platonic idea, even duplicate editions of such a quality (were they possible), would be indiscernible, and no sign could be given, no result altered, whether the feeling meant to stand for this edition or for that, or whether it simply resembled the quality without meaning to stand for it at all.

If now we grant a genuine pluralism of editions to the quality q, by assigning to each a *context* which shall distinguish it from its mates, we may proceed to explain which edition of it the feeling knows, by extending our principle of resemblance to the context too, and saying the feeling knows the particular q whose context it most exactly duplicates. But here again the theoretic doubt recurs: duplication and coincidence, are they knowledge? The gun shows which q it points to and hits, by *breaking* it. Until the feeling can show us which q it points to and knows, by some equally flagrant token, why are we not free to deny that it either points to or knows any one of the *real q*'s at all, and to affirm that the word 'resemblance' exhaustively describes its relation to the reality?

Well, as a matter of fact, every actual feeling *does* show us, quite as flagrantly as the gun, which *q* it points to; and practically in concrete cases the matter is decided by an element we have hitherto left out. Let us pass from abstractions to possible instances, and ask our obliging *deus ex machina* to frame for us a richer world. Let him send me, for example, a dream of the death of a certain man, and let him simultaneously cause the man to die. How would our practical instinct spontaneously decide whether this were a case of cognition of the reality, or only a sort of marvellous coincidence of a resembling reality with my dream? Just such puzzling cases as this are what the 'society for psychical research' is busily collecting and trying to interpret in the most reasonable way.

If my dream were the only one of the kind I ever had in my life, if the context of the death in the dream differed in many particulars from the real death's context, and if my dream led me to no action about the death, unquestionably we should all call it a strange coincidence, and naught besides. But if the death in the dream had a long context, agreeing point for point with every feature that attended the real death; if I were constantly having such dreams, all equally perfect, and if on awaking I had a habit of *acting* immediately as if they were true and so getting 'the start' of my more tardily instructed neighbors—we should in all probability have to admit that I had some mysterious kind of clairvoyant power, that my dreams in an inscrutable way meant just those realities they figured, and that the word 'coincidence' failed to touch the root of the matter. And whatever doubts anyone preserved would completely vanish, if it should appear that from the midst of my dream I had the power of *interfering* with the course of the reality, and making the events in it turn this way or that, according as I dreamed they should. Then at least it would be certain that my waking critics and my dreaming self were dealing with the *same*.

And thus do men invariably decide such a question. *The falling of the dream's practical consequences* into the real world, and the *extent* of the resemblance between the two worlds are the criteria they instinctively use.[6] All feeling is for the sake of action, all feeling results in action—to-day no argument is needed to prove these truths. But by a most singular disposition of nature which we may conceive to have been different, *my feelings act upon the realities within my critic's world.* Unless, then, my critic can prove that my feeling does not 'point to' those realities which it acts upon, how can he continue to doubt that he and I are alike cognizant of one and the same real world? If the action is performed in one world, that must be the world the feeling intends; if in another world, *that* is the world the feeling has in mind. If your feeling bear no fruits in my world, I call it utterly detached from my world; I call it a solipsism, and call its world a dream-world. If your toothache do not prompt you to *act* as if I had a toothache, nor even as if I had a separate existence; if you neither say to me, "I know now how you must suffer!" nor tell me of a remedy, I deny that your feeling, however it may resemble mine, is really cognizant of mine. It gives no *sign* of being cognizant, and such a sign is absolutely necessary to my admission that it is.

Before I can think you to mean my world, you must affect my world; before I can think you to mean much of it, you must affect

---

[6] The thoroughgoing objector might, it is true, still return to the charge, and, granting a dream which should completely mirror the real universe, and all the actions dreamed in which should be instantly matched by duplicate actions in this universe, still insist that this is nothing more than harmony, and that it is as far as ever from being made clear whether the dream-world refers to that other world, all of whose details it so closely copies. This objection leads deep into metaphysics. I do not impugn its importance, and justice obliges me to say that but for the teachings of my colleague, Dr. Josiah Royce, I should neither have grasped its full force nor made my own practical and psychological point of view as clear to myself as it is. On this occasion I prefer to stick steadfastly to that point of view; but I hope that Dr. Royce's more fundamental criticism of the function of cognition may ere long see the light. [I referred in this note to Royce's *Religious aspect of philosophy*, then about to be published. This powerful book maintained that the notion of *referring* involved that of an inclusive mind that shall own both the real *q* and the mental *q*, and use the latter expressly as a representative symbol of the former. At the time I could not refute this transcendentalist opinion. Later, largely through the influence of Professor D. S. Miller (see his essay 'The meaning of truth and error,' in the *Philosophical Review* for 1893, vol. 2, p. 403) I came to see that any definitely experienceable workings would serve as intermediaries quite as well as the absolute mind's intentions would.]

much of it; and before I can be sure you mean it *as I do,* you must affect it *just as I should* if I were in your place. Then I, your critic, will gladly believe that we are thinking, not only of the same reality, but that we are thinking it *alike,* and thinking of much of its extent.

Without the practical effects of our neighbor's feelings on our own world, we should never suspect the existence of our neighbor's feelings at all, and of course should never find ourselves playing the critic as we do in this article. The constitution of nature is very peculiar. In the world of each of us are certain objects called human bodies, which move about and act on all the other objects there, and the occasions of their action are in the main what the occasions of our action would be, were they our bodies. They use words and gestures, which, if we used them, would have thoughts behind them—no mere thoughts *überhaupt,* however, but strictly determinate thoughts. I think you have the notion of fire in general, because I see you act towards this fire in my room just as I act towards it—poke it and present your person towards it, and so forth. But that binds me to believe that if you feel 'fire' at all, *this* is the fire you feel. As a matter of fact, whenever we constitute ourselves into psychological critics, it is not by dint of discovering which reality a feeling 'resembles' that we find out which reality it means. We become first aware of which one it means, and then we suppose that to be the one it resembles. We see each other looking at the same objects, pointing to them and turning them over in various ways, and thereupon we hope and trust that all of our several feelings resemble the reality and each other. But this is a thing of which we are never theoretically sure. Still, it would practically be a case of *grübelsucht,* if a ruffian were assaulting and drubbing my body, to spend much time in subtle speculation either as to whether his vision of my body resembled mine, or as to whether the body he really *meant* to insult were not some body in his mind's eye, altogether other from my own. The practical point of view brushes such metaphysical cobwebs away. If what he have in mind be not *my* body, why call we it a body at all? His mind is inferred by me as a term, to whose existence we trace the things that happen. The inference is quite void if the term, once inferred, be separated from its connexion with the body that made me infer it, and connected with another that is not mine at all. No matter for the metaphysical puzzle of how our two minds, the ruffian's and mine, *can* mean the same body. Men who see each other's bodies sharing the same space, treading the same earth, splashing the same water, making the same air resonant, and pursuing the same game and eating out of the same dish, will never practically believe in a pluralism of solipsistic worlds.

Where, however, the actions of one mind seem to take no effect in the world of the other, the case is different. This is what happens in poetry and fiction. Everyone knows *Ivanhoe*, for example; but so long as we stick to the story pure and simple without regard to the facts of its production, few would hesitate to admit that there are as many different Ivanhoes as there are different minds cognizant of the story.[7] The fact that all these Ivanhoes *resemble* each other does not prove the contrary. But if an alteration invented by one man in his version were to reverberate immediately through all the other versions, and produce changes therein, we should then easily agree that all these thinkers were thinking the *same* Ivanhoe, and that, fiction or no fiction, it formed a little world common to them all.

[7] That is, there is no *real* 'Ivanhoe,' not even the one in Sir Walter Scott's mind as he was writing the story. That one is only the *first* one of the Ivanhoe-solipsisms. It is quite true we can make it the real Ivanhoe if we like, and then say that the other Ivanhoes know it or do not know it, according as they refer to and resemble it or no. This is done by bringing in Sir Walter Scott himself as the author of the real Ivanhoe, and so making a complex object of both. This object, however, is not a story pure and simple. It has dynamic relations with the world common to the experience of all the readers. Sir Walter Scott's Ivanhoe got itself printed in volumes which we all can handle, and to any one of which we can refer to see which of our versions be the true one, *i. e.*, the original one of Scott himself. We can see the manuscript; in short we can get back to the Ivanhoe in Scott's mind by many an avenue and channel of this real world of our experience—a thing we can by no means do with either the Ivanhoe or the Rebecca, either the Templar or the Isaac of York, of the story taken simply as such, and detached from the conditions of its production. Everywhere, then, we have the same test: can we pass continuously from two objects in two minds to a third object which seems to be in *both* minds, because each mind feels every modification imprinted on it by the other? If so, the first two objects named are derivatives, to say the least, from the same third object, and may be held, if they resemble each other, to refer to one and the same reality.

Having reached this point, we may take up our thesis and improve it again. Still calling the reality by the name of q and letting the critic's feeling vouch for it, we can say that any other feeling will be held cognizant of q, provided it both resemble q, and refer to q, as shown by its either modifying q directly, or modifying some other reality, p or r, which the critic knows to be continuous with q. Or more shortly, thus: *The feeling of q knows whatever reality it resembles, and either directly or indirectly operates on.* If it resemble without operating, it is a dream; if it operate without resembling, it is an error.[8]

It is to be feared that the reader may consider this formula rather insignificant and obvious, and hardly worth the labor of so many pages, especially when he considers that the only cases to

---

[8] Among such errors are those cases in which our feeling operates on a reality which it does partially resemble, and yet does not intend: as for instance, when I take up your umbrella, meaning to take my own. I cannot be said here either to know your umbrella, or my own, which latter my feeling more completely resembles. I am mistaking them both, misrepresenting their context, etc.

We have spoken in the text as if the critic were necessarily one mind, and the feeling criticized another. But the criticized feeling and its critic may be earlier and later feelings of the same mind, and here it might seem that we could dispense with the notion of operating, to prove that critic and criticized are referring to and meaning to represent the *same*. We think we see our past feelings directly, and know what they refer to without appeal. At the worst, we can always fix the intention of our present feeling and *make* it refer to the same reality to which any one of our past feelings may have referred. So we need no 'operating' here, to make sure that the feeling and its critic mean the same real q. Well, all the better if this is so! We have covered the more complex and difficult case in our text, and we may let this easier one go. The main thing at present is to stick to practical psychology, and ignore metaphysical difficulties.

One more remark. Our formula contains, it will be observed, nothing to correspond to the great principle of cognition laid down by Professor Ferrier in his *Institutes of Metaphysic* and apparently adopted by all the followers of Fichte, the principle, namely, that for knowledge to be constituted there must be knowledge of the knowing mind along with whatever else is known: not q, as we have supposed, but q *plus myself*, must be the least I can know. It is certain that the common sense of mankind never dreams of using any such principle when it tries to discriminate between conscious states that are knowledge and conscious states that are not. So that Ferrier's principle, if it have any relevancy at all, must have relevancy to the metaphysical possibility of consciousness at large, and not to the practically recognized constitution of cognitive consciousness. We may therefore pass it by without further notice here.

which it applies are *percepts,* and that the whole field of symbolic or conceptual thinking seems to elude its grasp. Where the reality is either a material thing or act, or a state of the critic's consciousness, I may both mirror it in my mind and operate upon it—in the latter case indirectly, of course—as soon as I perceive it. But there are many cognitions, universally allowed to be such, which neither mirror nor operate on their realities.

In the whole field of symbolic thought we are universally held both to intend, to speak of, and to reach conclusions about—to know, in short—particular realities, without having in our subjective consciousness any mind-stuff that resembles them even in a remote degree. We are instructed about them by language which awakens no consciousness beyond its sound; and we know *which* realities they are by the faintest and most fragmentary glimpse of some remote context they may have and by no direct imagination of themselves. As minds may differ here, let me speak in the first person. I am sure that my own current thinking has *words* for its almost exclusive subjective material, words which are made intelligible by being referred to some reality that lies beyond the horizon of direct consciousness, and of which I am only aware as of a terminal *more* existing in a certain direction, to which the words might lead but do not lead yet. The *subject,* or *topic,* of the words is usually something towards which I mentally seem to pitch them in a backward way, almost as I might jerk my thumb over my shoulder to point at something, without looking round, if I were only entirely sure that it was there. The *upshot,* or *conclusion,* of the words is something towards which I seem to incline my head forwards, as if giving assent to its existence, tho all my mind's eye catches sight of may be some tatter of an image connected with it, which tatter, however, if only endued with the feeling of familiarity and reality, makes me feel that the whole to which it belongs is rational and real, and fit to be let pass.

Here then is cognitive consciousness on a large scale, and yet what it knows, it hardly resembles in the least degree. The formula last laid down for our thesis must therefore be made more complete. We may now express it thus: *A percept knows whatever reality it directly or indirectly operates on and resembles; a con-*

ceptual feeling, or thought, knows[9] *a reality, whenever it actually or potentially terminates in a percept that operates on or resembles that reality, or is otherwise connected with it or with its context.* The latter percept may be either sensation or sensorial idea; and when I say the thought must *terminate* in such a percept, I mean that it must ultimately be capable of leading up thereto—by the way of practical experience, if the terminal feeling be a sensation; by the way of logical or habitual suggestion, if it be only an image in the mind.

Let an illustration make this plainer. I open the first book I take up, and read the first sentence that meets my eye: "Newton saw the handiwork of God in the heavens as plainly as Paley in the animal kingdom." I immediately look back and try to analyze the subjective state in which I rapidly apprehended this sentence as I read it. In the first place there was an obvious feeling that the sentence was intelligible and rational and related to the world of realities. There was also a sense of agreement or harmony between 'Newton,' 'Paley,' and 'God.' There was no apparent image connected with the words 'heavens,' or 'handiwork,' or 'God'; they were words merely. With 'animal kingdom' I think there was the faintest consciousness (it may possibly have been an image of the steps) of the Museum of Zoology in the town of Cambridge where I write. With 'Paley' there was an equally faint consciousness of a small dark leather book; and with 'Newton' a pretty distinct vision of the right-hand lower corner of a curling periwig. This is all the mind-stuff I can discover in my first consciousness of the meaning of this sentence, and I am afraid that even not all of this would have been present had I come upon the sentence in a genuine reading of the book, and not picked it out for an experiment. And yet my consciousness was truly cognitive. The sentence is 'about' realities which my psychological critic—for we must not forget him—acknowledges to be such, even as he acknowledges my distinct feeling that they *are* realities, and my acquiescence in the general rightness of what I read of them, to be true knowledge on my part.

---

[9] Is an incomplete 'thought about' that reality, that reality is its 'topic,' etc.

Now what justifies my critic in being as lenient as this? This singularly inadequate consciousness of mine, made up of symbols that neither resemble nor affect the realities they stand for—how can he be sure it is cognizant of the very realities he has himself in mind?

He is sure because in countless like cases he has seen such inadequate and symbolic thoughts, by developing themselves, terminate in percepts that practically modified and presumably resembled his own. By 'developing' themselves is meant obeying their tendencies, following up the suggestions nascently present in them, working in the direction in which they seem to point, clearing up the penumbra, making distinct the halo, unravelling the fringe, which is part of their composition, and in the midst of which their more substantive kernel of subjective content seems consciously to lie. Thus I may develope my thought in the Paley direction by procuring the brown leather volume and bringing the passages about the animal kingdom before the critic's eyes. I may satisfy him that the words mean for me just what they mean for him, by showing him *in concreto* the very animals and their arrangements, of which the pages treat. I may get Newton's works and portraits; or if I follow the line of suggestion of the wig, I may smother my critic in seventeenth-century matters pertaining to Newton's environment, to show that the word 'Newton' has the same *locus* and relations in both our minds. Finally I may, by act and word, persuade him that what I mean by God and the heavens and the analogy of the handiworks, is just what he means also.

My demonstration in the last resort is to his *senses*. My thought makes me act on his senses much as he might himself act on them, were he pursuing the consequences of a perception of his own. Practically then *my* thought terminates in *his* realities. He willingly supposes it, therefore, to be *of* them, and inwardly to *resemble* what his own thought would be, were it of the same symbolic sort as mine. And the pivot and fulcrum and support of his mental persuasion, is the sensible operation which my thought leads me, or may lead, to effect—the bringing of Paley's book, of Newton's portrait, etc., before his very eyes.

In the last analysis, then, we believe that we all know and think about and talk about the same world, because *we believe our PER-CEPTS are possessed by us in common.* And we believe this because the percepts of each one of us seem to be changed in consequence of changes in the percepts of someone else. What I am for you is in the first instance a percept of your own. Unexpectedly, how-ever, I open and show you a book, uttering certain sounds the while. These acts are also your percepts, but they so resemble acts of yours with feelings prompting them, that you cannot doubt I have the feelings too, or that the book is one book felt in both our worlds. That it is felt in the same way, that my feelings of it re-semble yours, is something of which we never can be sure, but which we assume as the simplest hypothesis that meets the case. As a matter of fact, we never *are* sure of it, and, as *erkenntniss-theoretiker*, we can only say that of feelings that should *not* re-semble each other, both could not know the same thing at the same time in the same way.[10] If each holds to its own percept as the reality, it is bound to say of the other percept, that, tho it may *intend* that reality, and prove this by working change upon it, yet, if it do not resemble it, it is all false and wrong.[11]

If this be so of percepts, how much more so of higher modes of thought! Even in the sphere of sensation individuals are probably different enough. Comparative study of the simplest conceptual elements seems to show a wider divergence still. And when it comes to general theories and emotional attitudes towards life, it is indeed time to say with Thackeray, "My friend, two different universes walk about under your hat and under mine."

What can save us at all and prevent us from flying asunder into a chaos of mutually repellent solipsisms? Through what can our several minds commune? Through nothing but the mu-tual resemblance of those of our perceptual feelings which have this power of modifying one another, *which are mere dumb*

---

[10]Tho both might terminate in the same thing and be incomplete thoughts 'about' it.

[11]The difference between Idealism and Realism is immaterial here. What is said in the text is consistent with either theory. A law by which my percept shall change yours directly is no more mysterious than a law by which it shall first change a phys-ical reality, and then the reality change yours. In either case you and I seem knit into a continuous world, and not to form a pair of solipsisms.

knowledges-of-acquaintance, and which must also resemble their realities or not know them aright at all. In such pieces of knowledge-of-acquaintance all our knowledge-about must end, and carry a sense of this possible termination as part of its content. These percepts, these *termini,* these sensible things, these mere matters-of-acquaintance, are the only realities we ever directly know, and the whole history of our thought is the history of our substitution of one of them for another, and the reduction of the substitute to the status of a conceptual sign. Contemned tho they be by some thinkers, these sensations are the mother-earth, the anchorage, the stable rock, the first and last limits, the *terminus a quo* and the *terminus ad quem* of the mind. To find such sensational *termini* should be our aim with all our higher thought. They end discussion; they destroy the false conceit of knowledge; and without them we are all at sea with each other's meaning. If two men act alike on a percept, they believe themselves to feel alike about it; if not, they may suspect they know it in differing ways. We can never be sure we understand each other till we are able to bring the matter to this test.[12] This is why metaphysical discussions are so much like fighting with the air; they have no practical issue of a sensational kind. 'Scientific' theories, on the other hand, always terminate in definite percepts. You can deduce a possible sensation from your theory and, taking me into your laboratory, prove that your theory is true of my world by giving me the sensation then and there. Beautiful is the flight of conceptual reason through the upper air of truth. No wonder philosophers are dazzled by it still, and no wonder they look with some disdain at the low earth of feeling from which the goddess launched herself aloft. But woe to her if she return not home to its acquaintance; *Nirgends haften dann die unsicheren Sohlen*—every crazy wind will take her, and, like a fire-balloon at night, she will go out among the stars.

---

[12] "There is no distinction of meaning so fine as to consist in anything but a possible difference of practice. . . . It appears, then, that the rule for attaining the [highest] grade of clearness of apprehension is as follows: Consider what effects, which might conceivably have practical bearings, we conceive the object of our conception to have. Then, our conception of these effects is the whole of our conception of the object." Charles S. Peirce: 'How to make our Ideas clear,' in *Popular Science Monthly,* New York, January, 1878, p. 293.

Note.—The reader will easily see how much of the account of the truth-function developed later in *Pragmatism* was already explicit in this earlier article, and how much came to be defined later. In this earlier article we find distinctly asserted:

1. The reality, external to the true idea;

2. The critic, reader, or epistemologist, with his own belief, as warrant for this reality's existence;

3. The experienceable environment, as the vehicle or medium connecting knower with known, and yielding the cognitive *relation*;

4. The notion of *pointing*, through this medium, to the reality, as one condition of our being said to know it;

5. That of *resembling* it, and eventually *affecting* it, as determining the pointing to *it* and not to something else.

6. The elimination of the 'epistemological gulf,' so that the whole truth-relation falls inside of the continuities of concrete experience, and is constituted of particular processes, varying with every object and subject, and susceptible of being described in detail.

The defects in this earlier account are:

1. The possibly undue prominence given to resembling, which altho a fundamental function in knowing truly, is so often dispensed with;

2. The undue emphasis laid upon operating on the object itself, which in many cases is indeed decisive of that being what we refer to, but which is often lacking, or replaced by operations on other things related to the object.

3. The imperfect development of the generalized notion of the *workability* of the feeling or idea as equivalent to that *satisfactory adaptation* to the particular reality, which constitutes the truth of the idea. It is this more generalized notion, as covering all such specifications as pointing, fitting, operating or resembling, that distinguishes the developed view of Dewey, Schiller, and myself.

4. The treatment, on page 39 [*ed.*, 31.4–12], of percepts as the only realm of reality. I now treat concepts as a co-ordinate realm.

The next paper represents a somewhat broader grasp of the topic on the writer's part.

II

The Tigers in India[1]

There are two ways of knowing things, knowing them immediately or intuitively, and knowing them conceptually or representatively. Altho such things as the white paper before our eyes can
be known intuitively, most of the things we know, the tigers now
in India, for example, or the scholastic system of philosophy, are
known only representatively or symbolically.

Suppose, to fix our ideas, that we take first a case of conceptual
knowledge; and let it be our knowledge of the tigers in India, as
we sit here. Exactly what do we *mean* by saying that we here know
the tigers? What is the precise fact that the cognition so confidently
claimed is *known-as*, to use Shadworth Hodgson's inelegant but
valuable form of words?

Most men would answer that what we mean by knowing the
tigers is having them, however absent in body, become in some
way present to our thought; or that our knowledge of them is
known as presence of our thought to them. A great mystery is
usually made of this peculiar presence in absence; and the scholastic philosophy, which is only common sense grown pedantic,
would explain it as a peculiar kind of existence, called *intentional*

[1] Extracts from a presidential address before the American Psychological Association, published in the *Psychological Review*, vol. ii, p. 105 (1895).

33

inexistence, of the tigers in our mind. At the very least, people would say that what we mean by knowing the tigers is mentally *pointing* towards them as we sit here.

But now what do we mean by *pointing,* in such a case as this? What is the pointing known-as, here?

To this question I shall have to give a very prosaic answer— one that traverses the prepossessions not only of common sense and scholasticism, but also those of nearly all the epistemological writers whom I have ever read. The answer, made brief, is this: The pointing of our thought to the tigers is known simply and solely as a procession of mental associates and motor consequences that follow on the thought, and that would lead harmoniously, if followed out, into some ideal or real context, or even into the immediate presence, of the tigers. It is known as our rejection of a jaguar, if that beast were shown us as a tiger; as our assent to a genuine tiger if so shown. It is known as our ability to utter all sorts of propositions which don't contradict other propositions that are true of the real tigers. It is even known, if we take the tigers very seriously, as actions of ours which may terminate in directly intuited tigers, as they would if we took a voyage to India for the purpose of tiger-hunting and brought back a lot of skins of the striped rascals which we had laid low. In all this there is no self-transcendency in our mental images *taken by themselves.* They are one phenomenal fact; the tigers are another; and their pointing to the tigers is a perfectly commonplace intra-experiential relation, *if you once grant a connecting world to be there.* In short, the ideas and the tigers are in themselves as loose and separate, to use Hume's language, as any two things can be; and pointing means here an operation as external and adventitious as any that nature yields.[2]

I hope you may agree with me now that in representative knowledge there is no special inner mystery, but only an outer chain of

---

[2] A stone in one field may 'fit,' we say, a hole in another field. But the relation of 'fitting,' so long as no one carries the stone to the hole and drops it in, is only one name for the fact that such an act *may* happen. Similarly with the knowing of the tigers here and now. It is only an anticipatory name for a further associative and terminative process that *may* occur.

physical or mental intermediaries connecting thought and thing. *To know an object is here to lead to it through a context which the world supplies.* All this was most instructively set forth by our colleague D. S. Miller at our meeting in New York last Christmas, and for re-confirming my sometime wavering opinion, I owe him this acknowledgment.[3]

Let us next pass on to the case of immediate or intuitive acquaintance with an object, and let the object be the white paper before our eyes. The thought-stuff and the thing-stuff are here indistinguishably the same in nature, as we saw a moment since, and there is no context of intermediaries or associates to stand between and separate the thought and thing. There is no 'presence in absence' here, and no 'pointing,' but rather an allround embracing of the paper by the thought; and it is clear that the knowing cannot now be explained exactly as it was when the tigers were its object. Dotted all through our experience are states of immediate acquaintance just like this. Somewhere our belief always does rest on ultimate data like the whiteness, smoothness, or squareness of this paper. Whether such qualities be truly ultimate aspects of being, or only provisional suppositions of ours, held-to till we get better informed, is quite immaterial for our present inquiry. So long as it is believed in, we see our object face to face. What now do we mean by 'knowing' such a sort of object as this? For this is also the way in which we should know the tiger if our conceptual idea of him were to terminate by having led us to his lair?

This address must not become too long, so I must give my answer in the fewest words. And let me first say this: So far as the white paper or other ultimate datum of our experience may be considered to enter also into someone else's experience, and we, in knowing it, are held to know it there as well as here; so far, again, as it may be considered to be a mere mask for hidden molecules that other now impossible experiences of our own might some day lay bare to view; so far it is a case of tigers in India again, for, the things known being absent experiences, the knowing can

[3] See Dr. Miller's articles on Truth and Error, and on Content and Function, in the *Philosophical Review*, July, 1893, and Nov., 1895.

only consist in passing smoothly towards them through the intermediary context that the world supplies. But if our own private vision of the paper be considered in abstraction from every other event, as if it constituted by itself the universe (and it might perfectly well do so, for aught we can understand to the contrary), then the paper seen and the seeing of it are only two names for one indivisible fact which, properly named, is *the datum, the phenomenon, or the experience.* The paper is in the mind and the mind is around the paper, because paper and mind are only two names that are given later to the one experience, when, taken in a larger world of which it forms a part, its connexions are traced in different directions.[4] *To know immediately, then, or intuitively, is for mental content and object to be identical.* This is a very different definition from that which we gave of representative knowledge; but neither definition involves those mysterious notions of self-transcendency and presence in absence which are such essential parts of the ideas of knowledge, both of philosophers and of common men.[5]

---

[4] What is meant by this is that 'the experience' can be referred to either of two great associative systems, that of the experiencer's mental history, or that of the experienced facts of the world. Of both of these systems it forms part, and may be regarded, indeed, as one of their points of intersection. One might let a vertical line stand for the mental history; but the same object, O, appears also in the mental history of different persons, represented by the other vertical lines. It thus ceases to

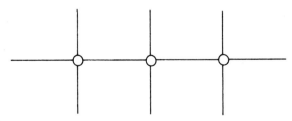

be the private property of one experience, and becomes, so to speak, a shared or public thing. We can track its outer history in this way, and represent it by the horizontal line. [It is also known representatively at other points of the vertical lines, or intuitively there again, so that the line of its outer history would have to be looped and wandering, but I make it straight for simplicity's sake.] In any case, however, it is the same *stuff* that figures in all the sets of lines.

[5][The reader will observe that the text is written from the point of view of naif realism or common sense, and avoids raising the idealistic controversy.]

III

Humanism and Truth[1]

Receiving from the Editor of *Mind* an advance proof of Mr. Bradley's article on 'Truth and Practice,' I understand this as a hint to me to join in the controversy over 'Pragmatism' which seems to have seriously begun. As my name has been coupled with the movement, I deem it wise to take the hint, the more so as in some quarters greater credit has been given me than I deserve, and probably undeserved discredit in other quarters falls also to my lot.

First, as to the word 'pragmatism.' I myself have only used the term to indicate a method of carrying on abstract discussion. The serious meaning of a concept, says Mr. Peirce, lies in the concrete difference to someone which its being true will make. Strive to bring all debated conceptions to that 'pragmatic' test, and you will escape vain wrangling: if it can make no practical difference which of two statements be true, then they are really one statement in two verbal forms; if it can make no practical difference whether a given statement be true or false, then the statement has no real meaning. In neither case is there anything fit to quarrel about: we may save our breath, and pass to more important things.

[1] Reprinted, with slight verbal revision, from *Mind*, vol. xiii, N. S., p. 457 (October, 1904). A couple of interpolations from another article in *Mind*, 'Humanism and truth once more,' in vol. xiv, have been made.

All that the pragmatic method implies, then, is that truths should *have* practical[2] consequences. In England the word has been used more broadly still, to cover the notion that the truth of any statement *consists* in the consequences, and particularly in their being good consequences. Here we get beyond affairs of method altogether; and since my pragmatism and this wider pragmatism are so different, and both are important enough to have different names, I think that Mr. Schiller's proposal to call the wider pragmatism by the name of 'humanism' is excellent and ought to be adopted. The narrower pragmatism may still be spoken of as the 'pragmatic method.'

I have read in the past six months many hostile reviews of Schiller's and Dewey's publications; but with the exception of Mr. Bradley's elaborate indictment, they are out of reach where I write, and I have largely forgotten them. I think that a free discussion of the subject on my part would in any case be more useful than a polemic attempt at rebutting these criticisms in detail. Mr. Bradley in particular can be taken care of by Mr. Schiller. He repeatedly confesses himself unable to comprehend Schiller's views, he evidently has not sought to do so sympathetically, and I deeply regret to say that his laborious article throws, for my mind, absolutely no useful light upon the subject. It seems to me on the whole an *ignoratio elenchi*, and I feel free to disregard it altogether.

The subject is unquestionably difficult. Messrs. Dewey's and Schiller's thought is eminently an induction, a generalization working itself free from all sorts of entangling particulars. If true, it involves much restatement of traditional notions. This is a kind of intellectual product that never attains a classic form of expression when first promulgated. The critic ought therefore not to be too sharp and logic-chopping in his dealings with it, but should weigh it as a whole, and especially weigh it against its possible alternatives. One should also try to apply it first to one instance, and then to another to see how it will work. It seems to me that it is emphatically not a case for instant execution, by conviction of in-

---

[2] ['Practical' in the sense of *particular*, of course, not in the sense that the consequences may not be *mental* as well as physical.]

trinsic absurdity or of self-contradiction, or by caricature of what it would look like if reduced to skeleton shape. Humanism is in fact much more like one of those secular changes that come upon public opinion overnight, as it were, borne upon tides 'too deep for sound or foam,' that survive all the crudities and extravagances of their advocates, that you can pin to no one absolutely essential statement, nor kill by any one decisive stab.

Such have been the changes from aristocracy to democracy, from classic to romantic taste, from theistic to pantheistic feeling, from static to evolutionary ways of understanding life—changes of which we all have been spectators. Scholasticism still opposes to such changes the method of confutation by single decisive reasons, showing that the new view involves self-contradiction, or traverses some fundamental principle. This is like stopping a river by planting a stick in the middle of its bed. Round your obstacle flows the water and 'gets there all the same.' In reading some of our opponents, I am not a little reminded of those catholic writers who refute darwinism by telling us that higher species cannot come from lower because *minus nequit gignere plus,* or that the notion of transformation is absurd, for it implies that species tend to their own destruction, and that would violate the principle that every reality tends to persevere in its own shape. The point of view is too myopic, too tight and close to take in the inductive argument. Wide generalizations in science always meet with these summary refutations in their early days; but they outlive them, and the refutations then sound oddly antiquated and scholastic. I cannot help suspecting that the humanistic theory is going through this kind of would-be refutation at present.

The one condition of understanding humanism is to become inductive-minded oneself, to drop rigorous definitions, and follow lines of least resistance 'on the whole.' "In other words," an opponent might say, "resolve your intellect into a kind of slush." "Even so," I make reply—"if you will consent to use no politer word." For humanism, conceiving the more 'true' as the more 'satisfactory' (Dewey's term), has sincerely to renounce rectilinear arguments and ancient ideals of rigor and finality. It is in just this temper of renunciation, so different from that of pyrrhonistic scepticism, that the spirit of humanism essentially consists. Satisfactoriness has to be measured by a multitude of standards, of which some, for aught we know, may fail in any given case; and what is more satisfactory than any alternative in sight, may to the end be a sum of *pluses* and *minuses*, concerning which we can only trust that by ulterior corrections and improvements a maximum of the one and a minimum of the other may some day be approached. It means a real change of heart, a break with absolutistic hopes, when one takes up this inductive view of the conditions of belief.

As I understand the pragmatist way of seeing things, it owes its being to the break-down which the last fifty years have brought about in the older notions of scientific truth. "God geometrizes," it used to be said; and it was believed that Euclid's elements literally reproduced his geometrizing. There is an eternal and unchangeable 'reason'; and its voice was supposed to reverberate in *Barbara* and *Celarent*. So also of the 'laws of nature,' physical and chemical, so of natural history classifications—all were supposed to be exact and exclusive duplicates of pre-human archetypes buried in the structure of things, to which the spark of divinity hidden in our intellect enables us to penetrate. The anatomy of the world is logical, and its logic is that of a university professor, it was thought. Up to about 1850 almost everyone believed that sciences expressed truths that were exact copies of a definite code of non-human realities. But the enormously rapid multiplication of theories in these latter days has well-nigh upset the notion of any one of them being a more literally objective kind of thing than another. There are so many geometries, so many logics, so many physical and chemical hypotheses, so many classifications, each one of them good for so much and yet not good for everything, that the notion that even the truest formula may be a human device and not a literal transcript has dawned upon us. We hear scientific laws now treated as so much 'conceptual shorthand,' true so far as they are useful but no farther. Our mind has become tolerant of symbol instead of reproduction, of approximation instead of exactness, of plasticity instead of rigor. 'Energetics,' measuring the bare face of sensible phenomena so as to describe in a single formula all their changes of 'level,' is the last word of this scientific humanism, which indeed leaves queries enough outstanding as to the reason for so curious a congruence between the world and the mind, but which at any rate makes our whole notion of scientific truth more flexible and genial than it used to be.

It is to be doubted whether any theorizer to-day, either in mathematics, logic, physics or biology, conceives himself to be literally re-editing processes of nature or thoughts of God. The main forms of our thinking, the separation of subjects from predicates, the negative, hypothetic and disjunctive judgments, are purely human habits. The ether, as Lord Salisbury said, is only a noun for the verb to undulate; and many of our theological ideas are admitted, even by those who call them 'true,' to be humanistic in like degree.

I fancy that these changes in the current notions of truth are what originally gave the impulse to Messrs. Dewey's and Schiller's views. The suspicion is in the air nowadays that the superiority of one of our formulas to another may not consist so much in its literal 'objectivity,' as in subjective qualities like its usefulness, its 'elegance' or its congruity with our residual beliefs. Yielding to these suspicions, and generalizing, we fall into something like the humanistic state of mind. Truth we conceive to mean everywhere, not duplication, but addition; not the constructing of inner copies of already complete realities, but rather the collaborating with realities so as to bring about a clearer result. Obviously this state of mind is at first full of vagueness and ambiguity. 'Collaborating' is a vague term; it must at any rate cover conceptions and logical arrangements. 'Clearer' is vaguer still. Truth must bring clear thoughts, as well as clear the way to action. 'Reality' is the vaguest term of all. The only way to test such a program at all is to apply it to the various types of truth, in the hope of reaching an account that shall be more precise. Any hypothesis that forces such a review upon one has one great merit, even if in the end it prove invalid: it gets us better acquainted with the total subject. To give the theory plenty of 'rope' and see if it hangs itself eventually is better tactics than to choke it off at the outset by abstract accusations of self-contradiction. I think therefore that a decided effort at sympathetic mental play with humanism is the provisional attitude to be recommended to the reader.

When I find myself playing sympathetically with humanism, something like what follows is what I end by conceiving it to mean.

Experience is a process that continually gives us new material to digest. We handle this intellectually by the mass of beliefs of which we find ourselves already possessed, assimilating, rejecting, or rearranging in different degrees. Some of the apperceiving ideas are recent acquisitions of our own, but most of them are common-sense traditions of the race. There is probably not a common-sense tradition, of all those which we now live by, that was not in the first instance a genuine discovery, an inductive generalization like those more recent ones of the atom, of inertia, of energy, of reflex action, or of fitness to survive. The notions of one Time and of one Space as single continuous receptacles; the distinction between thoughts and things, matter and mind; between permanent subjects and changing attributes; the conception of classes with sub-classes within them; the separation of fortuitous from regularly caused connexions; surely all these were once definite conquests made at historic dates by our ancestors in their attempts to get the chaos of their crude individual experiences into a more shareable and manageable shape. They proved of such sovereign use as *denkmittel* that they are now a part of the very structure of our mind. We cannot play fast and loose with them. No experience can upset them. On the contrary, they apperceive every experience and assign it to its place.

To what effect? That we may the better foresee the course of our experiences, communicate with one another, and steer our lives by rule. Also that we may have a cleaner, clearer, more inclusive mental view.

The greatest common-sense achievement, after the discovery of one Time and one Space, is probably the concept of permanently existing things. When a rattle first drops out of the hand of a baby, he does not look to see where it has gone. Non-perception he accepts as annihilation until he finds a better belief. That our perceptions mean *beings*, rattles that are there whether we hold them in our hands or not, becomes an interpretation so luminous of what happens to us that, once employed, it never gets forgotten. It applies with equal felicity to things and persons, to the objective and to the ejective realm. However a Berkeley, a Mill, or a Cornelius may criticize it, it *works*; and in practical life we never think of 'going back' upon it, or reading our incoming experiences in any other terms. We may, indeed, speculatively imagine a state of 'pure' experience before the hypothesis of permanent objects behind its flux had been framed; and we can play with the idea that some primeval genius might have struck into a different hypothesis. But we cannot positively imagine to-day what the different hypothesis could have been, for the category of trans-perceptual reality is now one of the foundations of our life. Our thoughts must still employ it if they are to possess reasonableness and truth.

This notion of a *first* in the shape of a most chaotic pure experience which sets us questions, of a *second* in the way of fundamental categories, long ago wrought into the structure of our consciousness and practically irreversible, which define the general frame within which answers must fall, and of a *third* which gives the detail of the answers in the shapes most congruous with all our present needs, is, as I take it, the essence of the humanistic conception. It represents experience in its pristine purity to be now so enveloped in predicates historically worked out that we can think of it as little more than an *Other*, of a *That*, which the mind, in Mr. Bradley's phrase, 'encounters,' and to whose stimulating presence we respond by ways of thinking which we call 'true' in proportion as they facilitate our mental or physical activities and bring us outer power and inner peace. But whether the Other, the universal *That*, has itself any definite inner structure, or whether, if it have any, the structure resembles any of our predicated *whats*, this is a question which humanism leaves untouched. For us, at any rate, it insists, reality is an accumulation of our own intellectual inventions, and the struggle for 'truth' in our progressive dealings with it is always a struggle to work in new nouns and adjectives while altering as little as possible the old.

It is hard to see why either Mr. Bradley's own logic or his metaphysics should oblige him to quarrel with this conception. He might consistently adopt it *verbatim et literatim*, if he would, and simply throw his peculiar absolute round it, following in this the good example of Professor Royce. Bergson in France, and his disciples, Wilbois the physicist and Leroy, are thoroughgoing humanists in the sense defined. Professor Milhaud also appears to be one; and the great Poincaré misses it by only the breadth of a hair. In Germany the name of Simmel offers itself as that of a humanist of the most radical sort. Mach and his school, and Hertz and Ostwald must be classed as humanists. The view is in the atmosphere and must be patiently discussed.

The best way to discuss it would be to see what the alternative might be. What is it indeed? Its critics make no explicit statement, Professor Royce being the only one so far who has formulated anything definite. The first service of humanism to philosophy accordingly seems to be that it will probably oblige those who dislike it to search their own hearts and heads. It will force analysis to the front and make it the order of the day. At present the lazy tradition that truth is *adæquatio intellectûs et rei* seems all there is to contradict it with. Mr. Bradley's only suggestion is that true thought "must correspond to a determinate being which it cannot be said to make," and obviously that sheds no new light. What is the meaning of the word to 'correspond'? Where is the 'being'? What sort of things are 'determinations,' and what is meant in this particular case by 'not to make'?

Humanism proceeds immediately to refine upon the looseness of these epithets. We correspond in *some* way with anything with which we enter into any relations at all. If it be a thing, we may produce an exact copy of it, or we may simply feel it as an existent in a certain place. If it be a demand, we may obey it without knowing anything more about it than its push. If it be a proposition, we may agree by not contradicting it, by letting it pass. If it be a relation between things, we may act on the first thing so as to bring ourselves out where the second will be. If it be something inaccessible, we may substitute a hypothetical object for it, which, having the same consequences, will cipher out for us real results. In a general way we may simply *add our thought to it*; and if it *suffers the addition*, and the whole situation harmoniously prolongs and enriches itself, the thought will pass for true.

As for the whereabouts of the beings thus corresponded to, altho they may be outside of the present thought as well as in it, humanism sees no ground for saying they are outside of finite experience itself. Pragmatically, their reality means that we submit to them, take account of them, whether we like to or not, but this we must perpetually do with experiences other than our own. The whole system of what the present experience must correspond to 'adequately' may be continuous with the present experience itself. Reality, so taken as experience other than the present, might be either the legacy of past experience or the content of experience to come. Its determinations for *us* are in any case the adjectives which our acts of judging fit to it, and those are essentially humanistic things.

To say that our thought does not 'make' this reality means pragmatically that if our own particular thought were annihilated the reality would still be there in some shape, tho possibly it might be a shape that would lack something that our thought supplies. That reality is 'independent' means that there is something in every experience that escapes our arbitrary control. If it be a sensible experience it coerces our attention; if a sequence, we cannot invert it; if we compare two terms we can come to only one result. There is a push, an urgency, within our very experience, against which we are on the whole powerless, and which drives us in a direction that is the destiny of our belief. That this drift of experience itself is in the last resort due to something independent of all possible experience may or may not be true. There may or may not be an extra-experiential 'ding an sich' that keeps the ball rolling, or an 'absolute' that lies eternally behind all the successive determinations which human thought has made. But within our experience *itself* at any rate, humanism says, some determinations show themselves as being independent of others; some questions, if we ever ask them, can only be answered in one way; some beings, if we ever suppose them, must be supposed to have

45

existed previously to the supposing; some relations, if they exist ever, must exist as long as their terms exist.

Truth thus means, according to humanism, the relation of less fixed parts of experience (predicates) to other relatively more fixed parts (subjects); and we are not required to seek it in a relation of experience as such to anything beyond itself. We can stay at home, for our behavior as experients is hemmed in on every side. The forces both of advance and of resistance are exerted by our own objects, and the notion of truth as something opposed to waywardness or license inevitably grows up solipsistically inside of every human life.

So obvious is all this that a common charge against the humanistic authors 'makes me tired.' "How can a deweyite discriminate sincerity from bluff?" was a question asked at a philosophic meeting where I reported on Dewey's *Studies*. "How can the mere[3] pragmatist feel any duty to think truly?" is the objection urged by Professor Royce. Mr. Bradley in turn says that if a humanist understands his own doctrine, he "must hold . . . any idea however mad to be the truth if any one will have it so." And Professor Taylor describes pragmatism as believing anything one pleases and calling it truth.

Such a shallow sense of the conditions under which men's thinking actually goes on seems to me most surprising. These critics appear to suppose that, if left to itself, the rudderless raft of our experience must be ready to drift anywhere or nowhere. Even tho there were compasses on board, they seem to say, there would be no pole for them to point to. There must be absolute sailing-directions, they insist, decreed from outside, and an independent chart of the voyage added to the 'mere' voyage itself, if we are ever to make a port. But is it not obvious that even tho there be such absolute sailing-directions in the shape of pre-human standards of truth that we *ought* to follow, the only guarantee that we shall in fact follow them must lie in our human equipment. The 'ought'

[3] I know of no 'mere' pragmatist, if *mereness* here means, as it seems to, the denial of all concreteness to the pragmatist's thought.

would be a *brutum fulmen* unless there were a felt grain inside of our experience that conspired. As a matter of fact the devoutest believers in absolute standards must admit that men fail to obey them. Waywardness is here, in spite of the eternal prohibitions, and the existence of any amount of reality *ante rem* is no warrant against unlimited error *in rebus* being incurred. The only *real* guarantee we have against licentious thinking is the circumpressure of experience itself, which gets us sick of concrete errors, whether there be a trans-empirical reality or not. How does the partisan of absolute reality know what this orders him to think? He cannot get direct sight of the absolute; and he has no means of guessing what it wants of him except by following the humanistic clues. The only truth that he himself will ever practically *accept* will be that to which his finite experiences lead him of themselves. The state of mind which shudders at the idea of a lot of experiences left to themselves, and that augurs protection from the sheer name of an absolute, as if, however inoperative, that might still stand for a sort of ghostly security, is like the mood of those good people who, whenever they hear of a social tendency that is damnable, begin to redden and to puff, and say "Parliament or Congress ought to make a law against it," as if an impotent decree would give relief.

All the *sanctions* of a law of truth lie in the very texture of experience. Absolute or no absolute, the concrete truth *for us* will always be that way of thinking in which our various experiences most profitably combine.

And yet, the opponent obstinately urges, your humanist will always have a greater liberty to play fast and loose with truth than will your believer in an independent realm of reality that makes the standard rigid. If by this latter believer he means a man who pretends to know the standard and who fulminates it, the humanist will doubtless prove more flexible; but no more flexible than the absolutist himself if the latter follows (as fortunately our present-day absolutists do follow) empirical methods of inquiry in concrete affairs. To consider hypotheses is surely always better than to dogmatize *ins blaue hinein.*

Nevertheless this probable flexibility of temper in him has been used to convict the humanist of sin. Believing as he does, that truth lies *in rebus*, and is at every moment our own line of most propitious reaction, he stands forever debarred, as I have heard a learned colleague say, from trying to convert opponents, for does not their view, being *their* most propitious momentary reaction, already fill the bill? Only the believer in the *ante-rem* brand of truth can on this theory seek to make converts without self-stultification. But can there be self-stultification in urging any account whatever of truth? Can the definition ever contradict the deed? "Truth is what I feel like saying"—suppose that to be the definition. "Well, I feel like saying that, and I want you to feel like saying it, and shall continue to say it until I get you to agree." Where is there any contradiction? Whatever truth may be said to be, that is the kind of truth which the saying can be held to carry. The *temper* which a saying may comport is an extra-logical matter. It may indeed be hotter in some individual absolutist than in a humanist, but it need not be so in another. And the humanist, for his part, is perfectly consistent in compassing sea and land to make one proselyte, if his nature be enthusiastic enough.

"But how *can* you be enthusiastic over any view of things which you know to have been partly made by yourself, and which is liable to alter during the next minute? How is any heroic devotion to the ideal of truth possible under such paltry conditions?"

This is just another of those objections by which the anti-humanists show their own comparatively slack hold on the realities of the situation. If they would only follow the pragmatic method and ask: "What is truth *known-as*? What does its existence stand for in the way of concrete goods?"—they would see that the name of it is the *inbegriff* of almost everything that is valuable in our lives. The true is the opposite of whatever is instable, of whatever is practically disappointing, of whatever is useless, of whatever is lying and unreliable, of whatever is unverifiable and unsupported, of whatever is inconsistent and contradictory, of whatever is artificial and eccentric, of whatever is unreal in the sense of being of no practical account. Here are pragmatic reasons with a vengeance why we should turn to truth—truth saves us from a world of that complexion. What wonder that its very name awakens loyal feeling! In particular what wonder that all little provisional fool's paradises of belief should appear contemptible in comparison with its bare pursuit! When absolutists reject humanism because they feel it to be untrue, that means that the whole habit of their mental needs is wedded already to a different view of reality, in comparison with which the humanistic world seems but the whim of a few irresponsible youths. Their own subjective apperceiving mass is what speaks here in the name of the eternal natures and bids them reject our humanism—as they apprehend it. Just so with us humanists, when we condemn all noble, clean-cut, fixed, eternal, rational, temple-like systems of philosophy. These contradict the *dramatic temperament* of nature, as our dealings with nature and our habits of thinking have so far brought us to conceive it. They seem oddly personal and artificial, even when not bureaucratic and professional in an absurd degree. We turn from them to the great unpent and unstayed wilderness of truth as we feel it to be constituted, with as good a conscience as rationalists are moved by when they turn from our wilderness into their neater and cleaner intellectual abodes.[4]

This is surely enough to show that the humanist does not ignore the character of objectivity and independence in truth. Let me

---

[4] [I cannot forbear quoting as an illustration of the contrast between humanist and rationalist tempers of mind, in a sphere remote from philosophy, these remarks on the Dreyfus 'affaire,' written by one who assuredly had never heard of humanism or pragmatism. "Autant que la Révolution, l'Affaire est désormais une de nos 'origines'. Si elle n'a pas fait ouvrir le gouffre, . . . c'est elle du moins qui a rendu patent et visible le long travail souterrain qui, silencieusement, avait préparé la séparation entre nos deux camps d'aujourd'hui, pour écarter enfin, d'un coup soudain, *la France des traditionalistes, (poseurs de principes, chercheurs d'unité, constructeurs de systèmes a priori) et la France éprise du fait positif et de libre examen;*—la France révolutionnaire et romantique si l'on veut, celle qui met très haut l'individu, qui ne veut pas qu'un juste périsse fût-ce pour sauver la nation, et qui cherche la vérité dans toutes ses parties aussi bien que dans une vue d'ensemble. . . . Duclaux ne pouvait pas concevoir qu'on préférât quelque chose à la vérité. Mais il voyait bien autour de lui de fort honnêtes gens qui, mettant en balance la vie d'un homme et la raison d'Etat, lui avouaient de quel poids léger ils jugeaient une simple existence individuelle, pour innocente qu'elle fût. *C'étaient des classiques, des gens à qui l'ensemble seul importe.*" *La Vie de Emile Duclaux*, par Mme. Em. D., Laval, 1906, pp. 243, 247–248.]

turn next to what his opponents mean when they say that to be true, our thoughts must 'correspond.'

The vulgar notion of correspondence here is that the thoughts must *copy* the reality—cognitio fit per *assimiliationem* cogniti et cognoscentis; and philosophy, without having ever fairly sat down to the question, seems to have instinctively accepted this idea: propositions are held true if they copy the eternal thought; terms are held true if they copy extra-mental realities. Implicitly, I think that the copy-theory has animated most of the criticisms that have been made on humanism.

A priori, however, it is not self-evident that the sole business of our mind with realities should be to copy them. Let my reader suppose himself to constitute for a time all the reality there is in the universe, and then to receive the announcement that another being is to be created who shall know him truly. How will he represent the knowing in advance? What will he hope it to be? I doubt extremely whether it could ever occur to him to fancy it as a mere copying. Of what use to him would an imperfect second edition of himself in the new comer's interior be? It would seem pure waste of a propitious opportunity. The demand would more probably be for something absolutely new. The reader would conceive the knowing humanistically, "the new comer," he would say, "must *take account of my presence by reacting on it in such a way that good would accrue to us both*. If copying be requisite to that end, let there be copying; otherwise not." The essence in any case would not be the copying, but the enrichment of the previous world.

I read the other day, in a book of Professor Eucken's, a phrase, *"Die erhöhung des vorgefundenen daseins,"* which seems to be pertinent here. Why may not thought's mission be to increase and elevate, rather than simply to imitate and reduplicate, existence? No one who has read Lotze can fail to remember his striking comment on the ordinary view of the secondary qualities of matter, which brands them as 'illusory' because they copy nothing in the thing. The notion of a world complete in itself, to which thought comes as a passive mirror, adding nothing to fact, Lotze says is irrational. Rather is thought itself a most momentous part of fact, and the whole mission of the pre-existing and insufficient world of matter may simply be to provoke thought to produce its far more precious supplement.

'Knowing,' in short, may, for aught we can see beforehand to the contrary, be *only one way of getting into fruitful relations with reality,* whether copying be one of the relations or not.

It is easy to see from what special type of knowing the copy-theory arose. In our dealings with natural phenomena the great point is to be able to foretell. Foretelling, according to such a writer as Spencer, is the whole meaning of intelligence. When Spencer's 'law of intelligence' says that inner and outer relations must 'correspond,' it means that the distribution of terms in our inner time-scheme and space-scheme must be an exact copy of the distribution in real time and space of the real terms. In strict theory the mental terms themselves need not answer to the real terms in the sense of severally copying them, symbolic mental terms being enough, if only the real dates and places be copied. But in our ordinary life the mental terms are images and the real ones are sensations, and the images so often copy the sensations, that we easily take copying of terms as well as of relations to be the natural significance of knowing. Meanwhile much, even of this common descriptive truth, is couched in verbal symbols. If our symbols *fit* the world, in the sense of determining our expectations rightly, they may even be the better for not copying its terms.

It seems obvious that the pragmatic account of all this routine of phenomenal knowledge is accurate. Truth here is a relation, not of our ideas to non-human realities, but of conceptual parts of our experience to sensational parts. Those thoughts are true which guide us to *beneficial interaction* with sensible particulars as they occur, whether they copy these in advance or not.

From the frequency of copying in the knowledge of phenomenal fact, copying has been supposed to be the essence of truth in matters rational also. Geometry and logic, it has been supposed, must copy archetypal thoughts in the Creator. But in these abstract spheres there is no need of assuming archetypes. The mind is free to carve so many figures out of space, to make so many numerical collections, to frame so many classes and series, and it can analyze and compare so endlessly, that the very superabundance of the resulting ideas makes us doubt the 'objective' pre-existence of their models. It would be plainly wrong to suppose a God whose thought consecrated rectangular but not polar co-ordinates, or Jevons's notation but not Boole's. Yet if, on the other hand, we assume God to have thought in advance of every *possible* flight of human fancy in these directions, his mind becomes too much like a hindoo idol with three heads, eight arms and six breasts, too much made up of superfœtation and redundancy for us to wish to copy it, and the whole notion of copying tends to evaporate from these sciences. Their objects can be better interpreted as being created step by step by men, as fast as they successively conceive them.

If now it be asked how, if triangles, squares, square roots, genera, and the like, are but improvised human 'artefacts,' their properties and relations can be so promptly known to be 'eternal,' the humanistic answer is easy. If triangles and genera are of our own production we can keep them invariant. We can make them 'timeless' by expressly decreeing that on *the things we mean* time shall exert no altering effect, that they are intentionally and it may be fictitiously abstracted from every corrupting real associate and condition. But relations between invariant objects will themselves be invariant. Such relations cannot be happenings, for by hypothesis nothing shall happen to the objects. I have tried to show in the last chapter of my *Principles of Psychology*[5] that they can only be relations of comparison. No one so far seems to have noticed my suggestion, and I am too ignorant of the development of mathematics to feel very confident of my own view. But if it were correct it would solve the difficulty perfectly. Relations of comparison are matters of direct inspection. As soon as mental objects are mentally compared, they are perceived to be either like or unlike. But once the same, always the same, once different, always different, under these timeless conditions. Which is as much as to say that truths concerning these man-made objects are necessary and eternal. We can change our conclusions only by changing our data first.

The whole fabric of the *a priori* sciences can thus be treated as a man-made product. As Locke long ago pointed out, these sciences have no immediate connexion with fact. Only *if* a fact can be humanized by being identified with any of these ideal objects, is

[5] Vol. ii, pp. 641 ff.

what was true of the objects now true also of the facts. The truth itself meanwhile was originally a copy of nothing; it was only a relation directly perceived to obtain between two artificial mental things.[6]

We may now glance at some special types of knowing, so as to see better whether the humanistic account fits. On the mathematical and logical types we need not enlarge further, nor need we return at much length to the case of our descriptive knowledge of the course of nature. So far as this involves anticipation, tho that *may* mean copying, it need, as we saw, mean little more than 'getting ready' in advance. But with many distant and future objects, our practical relations are to the last degree potential and remote. In no sense can we now get ready for the arrest of the earth's revolution by the tidal brake, for instance; and with the past, tho we suppose ourselves to know it truly, we have no practical relations at all. It is obvious that, altho interests strictly practical have been the original starting-point of our search for true phenomenal descriptions, yet an intrinsic interest in the bare describing function has grown up. We wish accounts that shall be true, whether they bring collateral profit or not. The primitive function has developed its demand for mere exercise. This theoretic curiosity seems to be the characteristically human *differentia,* and humanism recognizes its enormous scope. A true idea now means not only one that prepares us for an actual perception. It means also one that might prepare us for a merely possible perception, or one that, if spoken, would suggest possible perceptions to others, or suggest actual perceptions which the speaker cannot share. The *ensemble* of perceptions thus thought of as either actual or possible form a system which it is obviously advantageous to us to get into a stable and consistent shape; and here it is that the common-sense notion of permanent beings finds triumphant use. Beings acting outside of the thinker explain, not only his actual perceptions, past and future, but his possible perceptions and those of everyone else. Accordingly they gratify our theoretic need in a supremely beautiful way. We pass from our immediate actual through them into the foreign and the potential, and back again into the future actual,

[6] [Mental things which are realities of course within the mental world.]

accounting for innumerable particulars by a single cause. As in those circular panoramas, where a real foreground of dirt, grass, bushes, rocks and a broken-down cannon is enveloped by a canvas picture of sky and earth and of a raging battle, continuing the foreground so cunningly that the spectator can detect no joint; so these conceptual objects, added to our present perceptual reality, fuse with it into the whole universe of our belief. In spite of all berkeleyan criticism, we do not doubt that they are really there. Tho our discovery of any one of them may only date from now, we unhesitatingly say that it not only *is*, but *was* there, if, by so saying, the past appears connected more consistently with what we feel the present to be. This is historic truth. Moses wrote the Pentateuch, we think, because if he didn't, all our religious habits will have to be undone. Julius Cæsar was real, or we can never listen to history again. Trilobites were once alive, or all our thought about the strata is at sea. Radium, discovered only yesterday, must always have existed, or its analogy with other natural elements, which are permanent, fails. In all this, it is but one portion of our beliefs reacting on another so as to yield the most satisfactory total state of mind. That state of mind, we say, sees truth, and the content of its deliverances we believe.

Of course, if you take the satisfactoriness concretely, as something felt by you now, and if, by truth, you mean truth taken abstractly and verified in the long run, you cannot make them equate, for it is notorious that the temporarily satisfactory is often false. Yet at each and every concrete moment, truth for each man is what that man 'troweth' at that moment with the maximum of satisfaction to himself; and similarly, abstract truth, truth verified by the long run, and abstract satisfactoriness, long-run satisfactoriness, coincide. If, in short, we compare concrete with concrete and abstract with abstract, the true and the satisfactory do mean the same thing. I suspect that a certain muddling of matters hereabouts is what makes the general philosophic public so impervious to humanism's claims.

The fundamental fact about our experience is that it is a process of change. For the 'trower' at any moment, truth, like the visible area round a man walking in a fog, or like what George Eliot calls "the wall of dark seen by small fishes' eyes that pierce a span in the wide Ocean," is an objective field which the next moment enlarges and of which it is the critic, and which then either suffers alteration or is continued unchanged. The critic sees both the first trower's truth and his own truth, compares them with each other, and verifies or confutes. *His* field of view is the reality independent of that earlier trower's thinking with which that thinking ought to correspond. But the critic is himself only a trower; and if the whole process of experience should terminate at that instant, there would be no otherwise known independent reality with which *his* thought might be compared.

The immediate in experience is always provisionally in this situation. The humanism, for instance, which I see and try so hard to defend, is the completest truth attained from my point of view up to date. But, owing to the fact that all experience is a process, no point of view can ever be *the* last one. Every one is insufficient and off its balance, and responsible to later points of view than itself. You, occupying some of these later points in your own person, and believing in the reality of others, will not agree that my point of view sees truth positive, truth timeless, truth that counts, unless they verify and confirm what it sees.

You generalize this by saying that any opinion, however satisfactory, can count positively and absolutely as true only so far as it agrees with a standard beyond itself; and if you then forget that this standard perpetually grows up endogenously inside the web of the experiences, you may carelessly go on to say that what distributively holds of each experience, holds also collectively of all experience, and that experience as such and in its totality owes whatever truth it may be possessed-of to its correspondence with absolute realities outside of its own being. This evidently is the popular and traditional position. From the fact that finite experiences must draw support from one another, philosophers pass to the notion that experience *überhaupt* must need an absolute support. The denial of such a notion by humanism lies probably at the root of most of the dislike which it incurs.

But is this not the globe, the elephant and the tortoise over again? Must not something end by supporting itself? Humanism is willing to let finite experience be self-supporting. Somewhere being must immediately breast nonentity. Why may not the advancing front of experience, carrying its immanent satisfactions and dissatisfactions, cut against the black inane as the luminous orb of the moon cuts the cærulean abyss? Why should anywhere the world be absolutely fixed and finished? And if reality genuinely grows, why may it not grow in these very determinations which here and now are made?

In point of fact it actually seems to grow by our mental determinations, be these never so 'true.' Take the 'great bear' or 'dipper' constellation in the heavens. We call it by that name, we count the stars and call them seven, we say they were seven before they were counted, and we say that whether anyone had ever noted the fact or not, the dim resemblance to a long-tailed (or long-necked?) animal was always truly there. But what do we mean by this projection into past eternity of recent human ways of thinking? Did an 'absolute' thinker actually do the counting, tell off the stars upon his standing number-tally, and make the bear-comparison, silly as the latter is? Were they explicitly seven, explicitly bear-like, before the human witness came? Surely nothing in the truth of the attributions drives us to think this. They were only implicitly or virtually what we call them, and we human witnesses first explicated them and made them 'real.' A fact virtually pre-exists when every condition of its realization save one is already there. In this case the condition lacking is the act of the counting and comparing mind. But the stars (once the mind considers them) themselves dictate the result. The counting in no wise modifies their previous nature, and, they being what and where they are, the count cannot fall out differently. It could then *always* be made. *Never* could the number seven be questioned, *if the question once were raised.*

We have here a quasi-paradox. Undeniably something comes by the counting that was not there before. And yet that something was *always true.* In one sense you create it, and in another sense you *find* it. You have to treat your count as being true beforehand, the moment you come to treat the matter at all.

Our stellar attributes must always be called true, then; yet none the less are they genuine additions made by our intellect to the world of fact. Not additions of consciousness only, but additions of 'content.' They copy nothing that pre-existed, yet they agree with what pre-existed, fit it, amplify it, relate and connect it with a 'wain,' a number-tally, or what not, and build it out. It seems to me that humanism is the only theory that builds this case out in the good direction, and this case stands for innumerable other kinds of case. In all such cases, odd as it may sound, our judgment may actually be said to retroact and to enrich the past.

Our judgments at any rate change the character of *future* reality by the acts to which they lead. Where these acts are acts expressive of trust—trust, *e.g.*, that a man is honest, that our health is good enough, or that we can make a successful effort—which acts may be a needed antecedent of the trusted things becoming true, Professor Taylor says[7] that our trust is at any rate *untrue when it is made, i.e.*, before the action; and I seem to remember that he disposes of anything like a faith in the general excellence of the universe (making the faithful person's part in it at any rate more excellent) as a 'lie in the soul.' But the pathos of this expression should not blind us to the complication of the facts. I doubt whether Professor Taylor would himself be in favor of practically handling trusters of these kinds as liars. Future and present really mix in such emergencies, and one can always escape lies in them by using hypothetic forms. But Mr. Taylor's attitude suggests such absurd possibilities of practice that it seems to me to illustrate beautifully how self-stultifying the conception of a truth that shall merely register a standing fixture may become. Theoretic truth, truth of passive copying, sought in the sole interests of copying as such, not because copying is *good for something,* but because copying ought *schlechthin* to be, seems, if you look at it coldly, to be an almost preposterous ideal. Why should the universe, existing in itself, also exist in copies? How *can* it be copied in the solidity of its objective fulness? And even if it could, what would the motive be? "Even the hairs of your head are numbered." Doubtless they are, virtually; but why, as an absolute proposition, *ought*

---

[7] In an article criticizing Pragmatism (as he conceives it) in the *McGill University Quarterly* published at Montreal, for May, 1904.

the number to become copied and known? Surely knowing is only one way of interacting with reality and adding to its effect.

The opponent here will ask: "Has not the knowing of truth any substantive value on its own account, apart from the collateral advantages it may bring? And if you allow theoretic satisfactions to exist at all, do they not crowd the collateral satisfactions out of house and home, and must not pragmatism go into bankruptcy, if she admits them at all?" The destructive force of such talk disappears as soon as we use words concretely instead of abstractly, and ask, in our quality of good pragmatists, just what the famous theoretic needs are known-as and in what the intellectual satisfactions consist.

Are they not all mere matters of *consistency*—and emphatically *not* of consistency between an absolute reality and the mind's copies of it, but of actually felt consistency among judgments, objects, and habits of reacting, in the mind's own experienceable world? And are not both our need of such consistency and our pleasure in it conceivable as outcomes of the natural fact that we are beings that do develop mental *habits*—habit itself proving adaptively beneficial in an environment where the same objects, or the same kinds of objects, recur and follow 'law'? If this were so, what would have come first would have been the collateral profits of habit as such, and the theoretic life would have grown up in aid of these. In point of fact, this seems to have been the probable case. At life's origin, any present perception may have been 'true'—if such a word could then be applicable. Later, when reactions became organized, the reactions became 'true' whenever expectation was fulfilled by them. Otherwise they were 'false' or 'mistaken' reactions. But the same class of objects needs the same kind of reaction, so the impulse to react consistently must gradually have been established, and a disappointment felt whenever the results frustrated expectation. Here is a perfectly plausible germ for all our higher consistencies. Nowadays, if an object claims from us a reaction of the kind habitually accorded only to the opposite class of objects, our mental machinery refuses to run smoothly. The situation is intellectually unsatisfactory.

Theoretic truth thus falls *within* the mind, being the accord of some of its processes and objects with other processes and objects—

'accord' consisting here in well-definable relations. So long as the satisfaction of feeling such an accord is denied us, whatever collateral profits may seem to inure from what we believe in are but as dust in the balance—provided always that we are highly organized intellectually, which the majority of us are not. The amount of accord which satisfies most men and women is merely the absence of violent clash between their usual thoughts and statements and the limited sphere of sense-perceptions in which their lives are cast. The theoretic truth that most of us think we 'ought' to attain to is thus the possession of a set of predicates that do not explicitly contradict their subjects. We preserve it as often as not by leaving other predicates and subjects out.

In some men theory is a passion, just as music is in others. The form of inner consistency is pursued far beyond the line at which collateral profits stop. Such men systematize and classify and schematize and make synoptical tables and invent ideal objects for the pure love of unifying. Too often the results, glowing with 'truth' for the inventors, seem pathetically personal and artificial to bystanders. Which is as much as to say that the purely theoretic criterion of truth can leave us in the lurch as easily as any other criterion, and that the absolutists, for all their pretensions, are 'in the same boat' concretely with those whom they attack.

I am well aware that this paper has been rambling in the extreme. But the whole subject is inductive, and sharp logic is hardly yet in order. My great trammel has been the non-existence of any definitely stated alternative on my opponents' part. It may conduce to clearness if I recapitulate, in closing, what I conceive the main points of humanism to be. They are these:

1. An experience, perceptual or conceptual, must conform to reality in order to be true.

2. By 'reality' humanism means nothing more than the other conceptual or perceptual experiences with which a given present experience may find itself in point of fact mixed up.[8]

3. By 'conforming,' humanism means taking account-of in such

___

[8] This is meant merely to exclude reality of an 'unknowable' sort, of which no account in either perceptual or conceptual terms can be given. It includes of course any amount of empirical reality independent of the knower. Pragmatism is thus 'epistemologically' realistic in its account.

a way as to gain any intellectually and practically satisfactory result.

4. To 'take account-of' and to be 'satisfactory' are terms that admit of no definition, so many are the ways in which these requirements can practically be worked out.

5. Vaguely and in general, we take account of a reality by *preserving* it in as unmodified a form as possible. But, to be then satisfactory, it must not contradict other realities outside of it which claim also to be preserved. That we must preserve all the experience we can and minimize contradiction in what we preserve, is about all that can be said in advance.

6. The truth which the conforming experience embodies may be a positive addition to the previous reality, and later judgments may have to conform to *it*. Yet, virtually at least, it may have been true previously. Pragmatically, virtual and actual truth mean the same thing: the possibility of only one answer, *when once the question is raised*.

IV

The Relation between Knower and Known[1]

Throughout the history of philosophy the subject and its object have been treated as absolutely discontinuous entities; and thereupon the presence of the latter to the former, or the 'apprehension' by the former of the latter, has assumed a paradoxical character which all sorts of theories had to be invented to overcome. Representative theories put a mental 'representation,' 'image,' or 'content' into the gap, as a sort of intermediary. Common-sense theories left the gap untouched, declaring our mind able to clear it by a self-transcending leap. Transcendentalist theories left it impossible to traverse by finite knowers, and brought an absolute in to perform the saltatory act. All the while, in the very bosom of the finite experience, every conjunction required to make the relation intelligible is given in full. Either the knower and the known are:

(1) the self-same piece of experience taken twice over in different contexts; or they are

(2) two pieces of *actual* experience belonging to the same subject, with definite tracts of conjunctive transitional experience between them; or

(3) the known is a *possible* experience either of that subject or

[1] Extract from an article entitled 'A World of Pure Experience,' in the *Journal of Philosophy, etc.,* September 29, 1904.

61

another, to which the said conjunctive transitions *would* lead, if sufficiently prolonged.

To discuss all the ways in which one experience may function as the knower of another, would be incompatible with the limits of this essay. I have treated of type 1, the kind of knowledge called perception, in an article in the *Journal of Philosophy*, for September 1, 1904, called 'Does consciousness exist?' This is the type of case in which the mind enjoys direct 'acquaintance' with a present object. In the other types the mind has 'knowledge-about' an object not immediately there. Type 3 can always formally and hypothetically be reduced to type 2, so that a brief description of that type will now put the present reader sufficiently at my point of view, and make him see what the actual meanings of the mysterious cognitive relation may be.

Suppose me to be sitting here in my library at Cambridge, at ten minutes' walk from 'Memorial Hall,' and to be thinking truly of the latter object. My mind may have before it only the name, or it may have a clear image, or it may have a very dim image of the hall, but such an intrinsic difference in the image makes no difference in its cognitive function. Certain *extrinsic* phenomena, special experiences of conjunction, are what impart to the image, be it what it may, its knowing office.

For instance, if you ask me what hall I mean by my image, and I can tell you nothing; or if I fail to point or lead you towards the Harvard Delta; or if, being led by you, I am uncertain whether the Hall I see be what I had in mind or not; you would rightly deny that I had 'meant' that particular hall at all, even tho my mental image might to some degree have resembled it. The resemblance would count in that case as coincidental merely, for all sorts of things of a kind resemble one another in this world without being held for that reason to take cognizance of one another.

On the other hand, if I can lead you to the hall, and tell you of its history and present uses; if in its presence I feel my idea, however imperfect it may have been, to have led hither and to be now *terminated*; if the associates of the image and of the felt hall run parallel, so that each term of the one context corresponds serially, as I walk, with an answering term of the other; why then my soul was prophetic, and my idea must be, and by common consent would be, called cognizant of reality. That percept was what I *meant*, for into it my idea has passed by conjunctive experiences of sameness and fulfilled intention. Nowhere is there jar, but every later moment continues and corroborates an earlier one.

In this continuing and corroborating, taken in no transcendental sense, but denoting definitely felt transitions, *lies all that the knowing of a percept by an idea can possibly contain or signify.* Wherever such transitions are felt, the first experience *knows* the last one. Where they do not, or where even as possibles they cannot, intervene, there can be no pretence of knowing. In this latter case the extremes will be connected, if connected at all, by inferior relations—bare likeness or succession, or by 'withness' alone. Knowledge of sensible realities thus comes to life inside the tissue of experience. It is *made*; and made by relations that unroll themselves in time. Whenever certain intermediaries are given, such that, as they develope towards their terminus, there is experience from point to point of one direction followed, and finally of one process fulfilled, the result is that *their starting-point thereby becomes a knower and their terminus an object meant or known.* That is all that knowing (in the simple case considered) can be known-as, that is the whole of its nature, put into experiential terms. Whenever such is the sequence of our experiences we may freely say that we had the terminal object 'in mind' from the outset, even altho *at* the outset nothing was there in us but a flat piece of substantive experience like any other, with no self-transcendency about it, and no mystery save the mystery of coming into existence and of being gradually followed by other pieces of substantive experience, with conjunctively transitional experiences between. That is what we *mean* here by the object's being 'in mind.' Of any deeper more real way of its being in mind we have no positive conception, and we have no right to discredit our actual experience by talking of such a way at all.

I know that many a reader will rebel at this. "Mere intermediaries," he will say, "even tho they be feelings of continuously growing fulfilment, only *separate* the knower from the known, whereas what we have in knowledge is a kind of immediate touch of the one by the other, an 'apprehension' in the etymological sense of the word, a leaping of the chasm as by lightning, an act by which two terms are smitten into one over the head of their distinctness. All these dead intermediaries of yours are out of each other, and outside of their termini still."

But do not such dialectic difficulties remind us of the dog dropping his bone and snapping at its image in the water? If we knew any more real kind of union *aliunde,* we might be entitled to brand all our empirical unions as a sham. But unions by continuous transition are the only ones we know of, whether in this matter of a knowledge-about that terminates in an acquaintance, whether in personal identity, in logical predication through the copula 'is,' or elsewhere. If anywhere there were more absolute unions, they could only reveal themselves to us by just such conjunctive results. These are what the unions are *worth,* these are all that *we can ever practically mean* by union, by continuity. Is it not time to repeat what Lotze said of substances, that to *act like* one is to *be* one? Should we not say here that to be experienced as continuous is to be really continuous, in a world where experience and reality come to the same thing? In a picture gallery a painted hook will serve to hang a painted chain by, a painted cable will hold a painted ship. In a world where both the terms and their distinctions are affairs of experience, conjunctions that are experienced must be at least as real as anything else. They will be 'absolutely' real conjunctions, if we have no transphenomenal absolute ready, to derealize the whole experienced world by, at a stroke.

So much for the essentials of the cognitive relation where the knowledge is conceptual in type, or forms knowledge 'about' an object. It consists in intermediary experiences (possible, if not actual) of continuously developing progress, and, finally, of fulfilment, when the sensible percept which is the object is reached. The percept here not only *verifies* the concept, proves its function of knowing that percept to be true, but the percept's existence as the terminus of the chain of intermediaries *creates* the function. Whatever terminates that chain was, because it now proves itself to be, what the concept 'had in mind.'

The towering importance for human life of this kind of knowing lies in the fact that an experience that knows another can figure as its *representative*, not in any quasi-miraculous 'epistcmological' sense, but in the definite practical sense of being its *substitute* in various operations, sometimes physical and sometimes mental, which lead us to its associates and results. By experimenting on our ideas of reality, we may save ourselves the trouble of experimenting on the real experiences which they severally mean. The ideas form related systems, corresponding point for point to the systems which the realities form; and by letting an ideal term call up its associates systematically, we may be led to a terminus which the corresponding real term would have led to in case we had operated on the real world. And this brings us to the general question of substitution.

What, exactly, in a system of experiences, does the 'substitution' of one of them for another mean?

According to my view, experience as a whole is a process in time, whereby innumerable particular terms lapse and are superseded by others that follow upon them by transitions which, whether disjunctive or conjunctive in content, are themselves experiences, and must in general be accounted at least as real as the terms which they relate. What the nature of the event called 'superseding' signifies, depends altogether on the kind of transition that obtains. Some experiences simply abolish their predecessors without continuing them in any way. Others are felt to increase or to enlarge their meaning, to carry out their purpose, or to bring us nearer to their goal. They 'represent' them, and may fulfil their function better than they fulfilled it themselves. But to 'fulfil a function' in a world of pure experience can be conceived and defined in only one possible way. In such a world transitions and arrivals (or terminations) are the only events that happen, tho they happen by so many sorts of path. The only function that one experience can perform is to lead into another experience; and the only fulfilment we can speak of is the reaching of a certain experienced end. When one experience leads to (or can lead to) the same end as another, they agree in function. But the whole system of experiences as they are immediately given presents itself as a quasi-chaos through which one can pass out of an initial term in many directions and yet end in the same terminus, moving from next to next by a great many possible paths.

Either one of these paths might be a functional substitute for another, and to follow one rather than another might on occasion be an advantageous thing to do. As a matter of fact, and in a general way, the paths that run through conceptual experiences, that is, through 'thoughts' or 'ideas' that 'know' the things in which they terminate, are highly advantageous paths to follow. Not only do they yield inconceivably rapid transitions; but, owing to the 'universal' character[2] which they frequently possess, and to their capacity for association with one another in great systems, they outstrip the tardy consecutions of the things themselves, and sweep us on towards our ultimate termini in a far more labor-saving way than the following of trains of sensible perception ever could. Wonderful are the new cuts and the short-circuits the thought-paths make. Most thought-paths, it is true, are substitutes for nothing actual; they end outside the real world altogether, in wayward fancies, utopias, fictions or mistakes. But where they do re-enter reality and terminate therein, we substitute them always; and with these substitutes we pass the greater number of our hours.[3]

Whosoever feels his experience to be something substitutional

[2] Of which all that need be said in this essay is that it also can be conceived as functional, and defined in terms of transitions, or of the possibility of such.

[3] This is why I called our experiences, taken all together, a quasi-chaos. There is vastly more discontinuity in the sum total of experiences than we commonly suppose. The objective nucleus of every man's experience, his own body, is, it is true, a continuous percept; and equally continuous as a percept (tho we may be inattentive to it) is the material environment of that body, changing by gradual transition when the body moves. But the distant parts of the physical world are at all times absent from us, and form conceptual objects merely, into the perceptual reality of which our life inserts itself at points discrete and relatively rare. Round their several objective nuclei, partly common and partly discrete, of the real physical world, innumerable thinkers, pursuing their several lines of physically true cogitation, trace paths that intersect one another only at discontinuous perceptual points, and the rest of the time are quite incongruent; and around all the nuclei of shared 'reality' floats the vast cloud of experiences that are wholly subjective, that are non-substitutional, that find not even an eventual ending for themselves in the perceptual world—the mere day-dreams and joys and sufferings and wishes of the individual minds. These exist *with* one another, indeed, and with the objective nuclei, but out of them it is probable that to all eternity no inter-related system of any kind will ever be made.

even while he has it, may be said to have an experience that reaches beyond itself. From inside of its own entity it says 'more,' and postulates reality existing elsewhere. For the transcendentalist, who holds knowing to consist in a *salto mortale* across an 'epistemological chasm,' such an idea presents no difficulty; but it seems at first sight as if it might be inconsistent with an empiricism like our own. Have we not explained that conceptual knowledge is made such wholly by the existence of things that fall outside of the knowing experience itself—by intermediary experiences and by a terminus that fulfils? Can the knowledge be there before these elements that constitute its being have come? And, if knowledge be not there, how can objective reference occur?

The key to this difficulty lies in the distinction between knowing as verified and completed, and the same knowing as in transit and on its way. To recur to the Memorial Hall example lately used, it is only when our idea of the Hall has actually terminated in the percept that we know 'for certain' that from the beginning it was truly cognitive of *that*. Until established by the end of the process, its quality of knowing that, or indeed of knowing anything, could still be doubted; and yet the knowing really was there, as the result now shows. We were *virtual* knowers of the Hall long before we were certified to have been its actual knowers, by the percept's retroactive validating power. Just so we are 'mortal' all the time, by reason of the virtuality of the inevitable event which will make us so when it shall have come.

Now the immensely greater part of all our knowing never gets beyond this virtual stage. It never is completed or nailed down. I speak not merely of our ideas of imperceptibles like ether-waves or dissociated 'ions,' or of 'ejects' like the contents of our neighbors' minds; I speak also of ideas which we might verify if we would take the trouble, but which we hold for true altho unterminated perceptually, because nothing says 'no' to us, and there is no contradicting truth in sight. *To continue thinking unchallenged is, ninety-nine times out of a hundred, our practical substitute for knowing in the completed sense.* As each experience runs by cognitive transition into the next one, and we nowhere feel a collision with what we elsewhere count as truth or fact, we commit ourselves to the current as if the port were sure. We live, as it were, upon the front edge of an advancing wave-crest, and our sense of a determinate direction in falling forward is all we cover of the future of our path. It is as if a differential quotient should be conscious and treat itself as an adequate substitute for a traced-out curve. Our experience, *inter alia*, is of variations of rate and of direction, and lives in these transitions more than in the journey's end. The experiences of tendency are sufficient to act upon—what more could we have *done* at those moments even if the later verification comes complete?

This is what, as a radical empiricist, I say to the charge that the objective reference which is so flagrant a character of our experiences involves a chasm and a mortal leap. A positively conjunctive transition involves neither chasm nor leap. Being the very original of what we mean by continuity, it makes a continuum wherever it appears. Objective reference is an incident of the fact that so much of our experience comes as an insufficient and consists of process and transition. Our fields of experience have no more definite boundaries than have our fields of view. Both are fringed forever by a *more* that continuously developes, and that continuously supersedes them as life proceeds. The relations, generally speaking, are as real here as the terms are, and the only complaint of the transcendentalist's with which I could at all sympathize would be his charge that, by first making knowledge to consist in external relations as I have done, and by then confessing that nine-tenths of the time these are not actually but only virtually there, I have knocked the solid bottom out of the whole business, and palmed off a substitute of knowledge for the genuine thing. Only the admission, such a critic might say, that our ideas are self-transcendent and 'true' already, in advance of the experiences that are to terminate them, can bring solidity back to knowledge in a world like this, in which transitions and terminations are only by exception fulfilled.

This seems to me an excellent place for applying the pragmatic method. What would the self-transcendency affirmed to exist in advance of all experiential mediation or termination, be *known-as*? What would it practically result in for *us*, were it true?

It could only result in our orientation, in the turning of our expectations and practical tendencies into the right path; and the right path here, so long as we and the object are not yet face to face (or can never get face to face, as in the case of ejects), would be the path that led us into the object's nearest neighborhood. Where direct acquaintance is lacking, 'knowledge-about' is the next best thing, and an acquaintance with what actually lies about the object, and is most closely related to it, puts such knowledge within our grasp. Ether-waves and your anger, for example, are things in which my thoughts will never *perceptually* terminate, but my concepts of them lead me to their very brink, to the chromatic fringes and to the hurtful words and deeds which are their really next effects.

Even if our ideas did in themselves possess the postulated self-transcendency, it would still remain true that their putting us into possession of such effects *would be the sole cash-value of the self-transcendency for us.* And this cash-value, it is needless to say, is *verbatim et literatim* what our empiricist account pays in. On pragmatist principles therefore, a dispute over self-transcendency is a pure logomachy. Call our concepts of ejective things self-transcendent or the reverse, it makes no difference, so long as we don't differ about the nature of that exalted virtue's fruits—fruits for us, of course, humanistic fruits.

The transcendentalist believes his ideas to be self-transcendent only because he finds that in fact they do bear fruits. Why need he quarrel with an account of knowledge that insists on naming this effect? Why not treat the working of the idea from next to next as the essence of its self-transcendency? Why insist that knowing is a static relation out of time when it practically seems so much a function of our active life? For a thing to be valid, says Lotze, is the same as to make itself valid. When the whole universe seems only to be making itself valid and to be still incomplete (else why its ceaseless changing?) why, of all things, should knowing be exempt? Why should it not be making itself valid like everything else? That some parts of it may be already valid or verified beyond dispute, the empirical philosopher, of course, like anyone else, may always hope.

V

The Essence of Humanism[1]

Humanism is a ferment that has 'come to stay.' It is not a single hypothesis or theorem, and it dwells on no new facts. It is rather a slow shifting in the philosophic perspective, making things appear as from a new centre of interest or point of sight. Some writers are strongly conscious of the shifting, others half unconscious, even tho their own vision may have undergone much change. The result is no small confusion in debate, the half-conscious humanists often taking part against the radical ones, as if they wished to count upon the other side.[2]

If humanism really be the name for such a shifting of perspective, it is obvious that the whole scene of the philosophic stage will change in some degree if humanism prevails. The emphasis of things, their foreground and background distribution, their sizes

[1] Reprinted from the *Journal of Philosophy, Psychology and Scientific Methods*, vol. ii, No. 5, March 2, 1905.

[2] Professor Baldwin, for example. His address 'Selective Thinking' (*Psychological Review*, January, 1898, reprinted in his volume, 'Development and Evolution') seems to me an unusually well written pragmatic manifesto. Nevertheless in 'The Limits of Pragmatism' (*ibid.*, January, 1904), he (much less clearly) joins in the attack.

and values, will not keep just the same.[3] If such pervasive consequences be involved in humanism, it is clear that no pains which philosophers may take, first in defining it, and then in furthering, checking, or steering its progress, will be thrown away.

It suffers badly at present from incomplete definition. Its most systematic advocates, Schiller and Dewey, have published fragmentary programs only; and its bearing on many vital philosophic problems has not been traced except by adversaries who, scenting heresies in advance, have showered blows on doctrines—subjectivism and scepticism, for example—that no good humanist finds it necessary to entertain. By their still greater reticences, the antihumanists have, in turn, perplexed the humanists. Much of the controversy has involved the word 'truth.' It is always good in debate to know your adversary's point of view authentically. But the critics of humanism never define exactly what the word 'truth' signifies when they use it themselves. The humanists have to guess at their view; and the result has doubtless been much beating of the air. Add to all this, great individual differences in both camps, and it becomes clear that nothing is so urgently needed, at the stage which things have reached at present, as a sharper definition by each side of its central point of view.

Whoever will contribute any touch of sharpness will help us to make sure of what's what and who is who. Anyone can contribute such a definition, and, without it, no one knows exactly where he stands. If I offer my own provisional definition of humanism now and here, others may improve it, some adversary may be led to define his own creed more sharply by the contrast, and a certain quickening of the crystallization of general opinion may result.

---

[3] The ethical changes, it seems to me, are beautifully made evident in Professor Dewey's series of articles, which will never get the attention they deserve till they are printed in a book. I mean: 'The Significance of Emotions,' *Psychological Review*, vol. ii, 13; 'The Reflex Arc Concept in Psychology,' *ibid.*, iii, 357; 'Psychology and Social Practice,' *ibid.*, vii, 105; 'Interpretation of Savage Mind,' *ibid.*, ix, 217; 'Green's Theory of the Moral Motive,' *Philosophical Review*, vol. i, 593; 'Self-realization as the Moral Ideal,' *ibid.*, ii, 652; 'The Psychology of Effort,' *ibid.*, vi, 43; 'The Evolutionary Method as Applied to Morality,' *ibid.*, xi, 107, 353; 'Evolution and Ethics,' *Monist*, vol. viii, 321; to mention only a few.

I

The essential service of humanism, as I conceive the situation, is to have seen that *tho one part of our experience may lean upon another part to make it what it is in any one of several aspects in which it may be considered, experience as a whole is self-containing and leans on nothing.* Since this formula also expresses the main contention of transcendental idealism, it needs abundant explication to make it unambiguous. It seems, at first sight, to confine itself to denying theism and pantheism. But, in fact, it need not deny either; everything would depend on the exegesis; and if the formula ever became canonical, it would certainly develope both right-wing and left-wing interpreters. I myself read humanism theistically and pluralistically. If there be a God, he is no absolute all-experiencer, but simply the experiencer of widest actual conscious span. Read thus, humanism is for me a religion susceptible of reasoned defence, tho I am well aware how many minds there are to whom it can appeal religiously only when it has been monistically translated. Ethically the pluralistic form of it takes for me a stronger hold on reality than any other philosophy I know of—it being essentially a *social* philosophy, a philosophy of '*co*,' in which conjunctions do the work. But my primary reason for advocating it is its matchless intellectual economy. It gets rid, not only of the standing 'problems' that monism engenders ('problem of evil,' 'problem of freedom,' and the like), but of other metaphysical mysteries and paradoxes as well.

It gets rid, for example, of the whole agnostic controversy, by refusing to entertain the hypothesis of trans-empirical reality at all. It gets rid of any need for an absolute of the bradleyan type (avowedly sterile for intellectual purposes) by insisting that the conjunctive relations found within experience are faultlessly real. It gets rid of the need of an absolute of the roycean type (similarly sterile) by its pragmatic treatment of the problem of knowledge. As the views of knowledge, reality and truth imputed to humanism have been those so far most fiercely attacked, it is in regard to these ideas that a sharpening of focus seems most urgently required. I proceed therefore to bring the views which *I* impute to humanism in these respects into focus as briefly as I can.

If the central humanistic thesis, printed above in italics, be accepted, it will follow that, if there be any such thing at all as knowing, the knower and the object known must both be portions of experience. One part of experience must, therefore, either

(1) Know another part of experience—in other words, parts must, as Professor Woodbridge says,[4] represent *one another* instead of representing realities outside of 'consciousness'—this case is that of conceptual knowledge; or else

(2) They must simply exist as so many ultimate *thats* or facts of being, in the first instance; and then, as a secondary complication, and without doubling up its entitative singleness, any one and the same *that* in experience must figure alternately as a thing known and as a knowledge of the thing, by reason of two divergent kinds of context into which, in the general course of experience, it gets woven.[5]

This second case is that of sense-perception. There is a stage of thought that goes beyond common sense, and of it I shall say more presently; but the common-sense stage is a perfectly definite halting-place of thought, primarily for purposes of action; and, so long as we remain on the common-sense stage of thought, object and subject *fuse* in the fact of 'presentation' or sense-perception—the pen and hand which I now *see* writing, for example, *are* the physical realities which those words designate. In this case there is no self-transcendency implied in the knowing. Humanism, here, is only a more comminuted *identitätsphilosophie*.

In case (1), on the contrary, the representative experience *does transcend itself* in knowing the other experience that is its object. No one can talk of the knowledge of the one by the other without seeing them as numerically distinct entities, of which the one lies beyond the other and away from it, along some direction and with some interval, that can be definitely named. But, if the talker be a

---

[4] In *Science*, November 4, 1904, p. 599.

[5] This statement is probably excessively obscure to anyone who has not read my two articles 'Does Consciousness Exist?' and 'A World of Pure Experience' in the *Journal of Philosophy*, vol. i, 1904.

humanist, he must also see this distance-interval concretely and pragmatically, and confess it to consist of other intervening experiences—of possible ones, at all events, if not of actual. To call my present idea of my dog, for example, cognitive of the real dog means that, as the actual tissue of experience is constituted, the idea is capable of leading into a chain of other experiences on my part that go from next to next and terminate at last in vivid sense-perceptions of a jumping, barking, hairy body. Those *are* the real dog, the dog's full presence, for my common sense. If the supposed talker is a profound philosopher, altho they may not *be* the real dog for him, they *mean* the real dog, are practical substitutes for the real dog, as the representation was a practical substitute for them, that real dog being a lot of atoms, say, or of mind-stuff, that lie *where* the sense-perceptions lie in his experience as well as in my own.

III

The philosopher here stands for the stage of thought that goes beyond the stage of common sense; and the difference is simply that he 'interpolates' and 'extrapolates,' where common sense does not. For common sense, two men see the same identical real dog. Philosophy, noting actual differences in their perceptions, points out the duality of these latter, and interpolates something between them as a more real terminus—first, organs, viscera, etc.; next, cells; then, ultimate atoms; lastly, mind-stuff perhaps. The original sense-termini of the two men, instead of coalescing with each other and with the real dog-object, as at first supposed, are thus held by philosophers to be separated by invisible realities with which, at most, they are conterminous.

Abolish, now, one of the percipients, and the interpolation changes into 'extrapolation.' The sense-terminus of the remaining percipient is regarded by the philosopher as not quite reaching reality. He has only carried the procession of experiences, the philosopher thinks, to a definite, because practical, halting-place somewhere on the way towards an absolute truth that lies beyond.

The humanist sees all the time, however, that there is no absolute transcendency even about the more absolute realities thus conjectured or believed in. The viscera and cells are only possible percepts following upon that of the outer body. The atoms again, tho we may never attain to human means of perceiving them, are still defined perceptually. The mind-stuff itself is conceived as a kind of experience; and it is possible to frame the hypothesis (such hypotheses can by no logic be excluded from philosophy) of two knowers of a piece of mind-stuff and the mind-stuff itself becoming 'confluent' at the moment at which our imperfect knowing might pass into knowing of a completed type. Even so do you and I habitually conceive our two perceptions and the real dog as confluent, tho only provisionally, and for the common-sense stage of thought. If my pen be inwardly made of mind-stuff, there is no confluence *now* between that mind-stuff and my visual perception of the pen. But conceivably there might come to be such confluence; for, in the case of my *hand*, the visual sensations and the inward feelings of the hand, its mind-stuff, so to speak, are even now as confluent as any two things can be.

There is, thus, no breach in humanistic epistemology. Whether knowledge be taken as ideally perfected, or only as true enough to pass muster for practice, it is hung on one continuous scheme. Reality, howsoever remote, is always defined as a terminus within the general possibilities of experience; and what knows it is defined as an experience *that 'represents' it, in the sense of being substitutable for it in our thinking* because it leads to the same associates, *or in the sense of 'pointing to it' through a chain of other experiences that either intervene or may intervene.*

Absolute reality here bears the same relation to sensation as sensation bears to conception or imagination. Both are provisional or final termini, sensation being only the terminus at which the practical man habitually stops, while the philosopher projects a 'beyond,' in the shape of more absolute reality. These termini, for the practical and the philosophical stages of thought respectively, are self-supporting. They are not 'true' of anything else, they simply *are*, are *real*. They 'lean on nothing,' as my italicized formula said. Rather does the whole fabric of experience lean on them, just as the whole fabric of the solar system, including many relative positions, leans, for its absolute position in space, on any one of its constituent stars. Here, again, one gets a new *identitätsphilosophie* in pluralistic form.

IV

If I have succeeded in making this at all clear (tho I fear that brevity and abstractness between them may have made me fail), the reader will see that the 'truth' of our mental operations must always be an intra-experiential affair. A conception is reckoned true by common sense when it can be made to lead to a sensation. The sensation, which for common sense is not so much 'true' as 'real,' is held to be *provisionally* true by the philosopher just in so far as it *covers* (abuts at, or occupies the place of) a still more absolutely real experience, in the possibility of which, to some remoter experient, the philosopher finds reason to believe.

Meanwhile what actually *does* count for true to any individual trower, whether he be philosopher or common man, is always a result of his *apperceptions*. If a novel experience, conceptual or sensible, contradict too emphatically our pre-existent system of beliefs, in ninety-nine cases out of a hundred it is treated as false. Only when the older and the newer experiences are congruous enough to mutually apperceive and modify each other, does what we treat as an advance in truth result. In no case, however, need truth consist in a relation between our experiences and something archetypal or trans-experiential. Should we ever reach absolutely terminal experiences, experiences in which we all agreed, which were superseded by no revised continuations, these would not be *true*, they would be *real*, they would simply *be*, and be indeed the angles, corners, and linchpins of all reality, on which the truth of everything else would be stayed. Only such *other* things as led to these by satisfactory conjunctions would be 'true.' Satisfactory connexion of some sort with such termini is all that the word 'truth' means. On the common-sense stage of thought sense-presentations serve as such termini. Our ideas and concepts and scientific theories pass for true only so far as they harmoniously lead back to the world of sense.

I hope that many humanists will endorse this attempt of mine to trace the more essential features of that way of viewing things. I feel almost certain that Messrs. Dewey and Schiller will do so. If the attackers will also take some slight account of it, it may be that discussion will be a little less wide of the mark than it has hitherto been.

VI

A Word More about Truth[1]

My failure in making converts to my conception of truth seems, if I may judge by what I hear in conversation, almost complete. An ordinary philosopher would feel disheartened, and a common choleric sinner would curse God and die, after such a reception. But instead of taking counsel of despair, I make bold to vary my statements, in the faint hope that repeated droppings may wear upon the stone, and that my formulas may seem less obscure if surrounded by something more of a 'mass' whereby to apperceive them.

For fear of compromising other pragmatists, whoe'er they be, I will speak of the conception which I am trying to make intelligible, as my own conception. I first published it in the year 1885, in the first article reprinted in the present book. Essential theses of this article were independently supported in 1893 and 1895 by Professor D. S. Miller[2] and were repeated by me in a presidential address on 'The knowing of things together'[3] in 1895. Professor Strong, in an article in the *Journal of Philosophy, etc.*,[4] entitled 'A naturalistic

---

[1] Reprint from the *Journal of Philosophy*, July 18, 1907.
[2] *Philosophical Review*, vol. ii, p. 408, and *Psychological Review*, vol. ii, p. 533.
[3] The relevant parts of which are printed above, p. 43 [*ed.*, p. 33].
[4] Vol. i, p. 253.

theory of the reference of thought to reality,' called our account 'the James-Miller theory of cognition,' and, as I understood him, gave it his adhesion. Yet, such is the difficulty of writing clearly in these penetralia of philosophy, that each of these revered colleagues informs me privately that the account of truth I now give—which to me is but that earlier statement more completely set forth—is to him inadequate, and seems to leave the gist of real cognition out. If such near friends disagree, what can I hope from remoter ones, and what from unfriendly critics?

Yet I feel so sure that the fault must lie in my lame forms of statement and not in my doctrine, that I am fain to try once more to express myself.

I

Are there not some general distinctions which it may help us to agree about in advance? Professor Strong distinguishes between what he calls 'saltatory' and what he calls 'ambulatory' relations. 'Difference,' for example, is saltatory, jumping as it were immediately from one term to another, but 'distance' in time or space is made out of intervening parts of experience through which we ambulate in succession. Years ago, when T. H. Green's ideas were most influential, I was much troubled by his criticisms of english sensationalism. One of his disciples in particular would always say to me, "Yes! *terms* may indeed be possibly sensational in origin; but *relations*, what are they but pure acts of the intellect coming upon the sensations from above, and of a higher nature?" I well remember the sudden relief it gave me to perceive one day that *space*-relations at any rate were homogeneous with the terms between which they mediated. The terms were spaces, and the relations were other intervening spaces.[5] For the Greenites space-relations had been saltatory, for me they became thenceforward ambulatory.

Now the most general way of contrasting my view of knowledge with the popular view (which is also the view of most epistemologists) is to call my view ambulatory, and the other view saltatory;

[5] See my *Principles of Psychology*, vol. ii, pp. 148–153.

and the most general way of characterizing the two views is by saying that my view describes knowing as it exists concretely, while the other view only describes its results abstractly taken.

I fear that most of my recalcitrant readers fail to recognize that what is ambulatory in the concrete may be taken so abstractly as to appear saltatory. Distance, for example, is made abstract by emptying out whatever is particular in the concrete intervals—it is reduced thus to a sole 'difference,' a difference of 'place,' which is a logical or saltatory distinction, a so-called 'pure relation.'

The same is true of the relation called 'knowing,' which may connect an idea with a reality. My own account of this relation is ambulatory through and through. I say that we know an object by means of an idea, whenever we ambulate towards the object under the impulse which the idea communicates. If we believe in so-called 'sensible' realities, the idea may not only send us towards its object, but may put the latter into our very hand, make it our immediate sensation. But, if, as most reflective people opine, sensible realities are not 'real' realities, but only their appearances, our idea brings us at least so far, puts us in touch with reality's most authentic appearances and substitutes. In any case our idea brings us into the object's neighborhood, practical or ideal, gets us into commerce with it, helps us towards its closer acquaintance, enables us to foresee it, class it, compare it, deduce it—in short, to deal with it as we could not were the idea not in our possession.

The idea is thus, when functionally considered, an instrument for enabling us the better to *have to do* with the object and to act about it. But it and the object are both of them bits of the general sheet and tissue of reality at large; and when we say that the idea leads us towards the object, that only means that it carries us forward through intervening tracts of that reality into the object's closer neighborhood, into the midst of its associates at least, be these its physical neighbors, or be they its logical congeners only. Thus carried into closer quarters, we are in an improved situation as regards acquaintance and conduct; and we say that through the idea we now *know* the object better or more truly.

My thesis is that the knowing here is *made* by the ambulation through the intervening experiences. If the idea led us nowhere, or *from* that object instead of towards it, could we talk at all of its having any cognitive quality? Surely not, for it is only when taken in conjunction with the intermediate experiences that it gets related to *that particular object* rather than to any other part of nature. Those intermediaries determine what particular knowing function it exerts. The terminus they guide us to tells us what object it 'means,' the results they enrich us with 'verify' or 'refute' it. Intervening experiences are thus as indispensable foundations for a concrete relation of cognition as intervening space is for a relation of distance. Cognition, whenever we take it concretely, means determinate 'ambulation,' through intermediaries, from a *terminus a quo* to, or towards, a *terminus ad quem*. As the intermediaries are other than the termini, and connected with them by the usual associative bonds (be these 'external' or be they logical, *i. e.*, classificatory, in character), there would appear to be nothing especially unique about the processes of knowing. They fall wholly within experience; and we need use, in describing them, no other categories than those which we employ in describing other natural processes.

But there exist no processes which we cannot also consider abstractly, eviscerating them down to their essential skeletons or outlines; and when we have treated the processes of knowing thus, we are easily led to regard them as something altogether unparalleled in nature. For we first empty idea, object and intermediaries of all their particularities, in order to retain only a general scheme, and then we consider the latter only in its function of giving a result, and not in its character of being a process. In this treatment the intermediaries shrivel into the form of a mere space of separation, while the idea and object retain only the logical distinctness of being the end-terms that are separated. In other words, the intermediaries which in their concrete particularity form a bridge, evaporate ideally into an empty interval to cross, and then, the relation of the end-terms having become saltatory, the whole hocus-pocus of *erkenntnisstheorie* begins, and goes on unrestrained by further concrete considerations. The idea, in 'meaning' an object separated by an 'epistemological chasm' from itself, now executes what Professor Ladd calls a '*salto mortale*'; in knowing the object's nature, it now 'transcends' its own. The object in turn becomes 'present' where it is really absent, etc.; until a scheme remains upon our hands, the sublime paradoxes of which some of us think that nothing short of an 'absolute' can explain.

The relation between idea and object, thus made abstract and saltatory, is thenceforward opposed, as being more essential and previous, to its own ambulatory self, and the more concrete description is branded as either false or insufficient. The bridge of intermediaries, actual or possible, which in every real case is what carries and defines the knowing, gets treated as an episodic complication which need not even potentially be there. I believe that this vulgar fallacy of opposing abstractions to the concretes from which they are abstracted, is the main reason why my account of knowing is deemed so unsatisfactory, and I will therefore say a word more on that general point.

Any vehicle of conjunction, if *all* its particularities are abstracted from it, will leave us with nothing on our hands but the original disjunction which it bridged over. But to escape treating the resultant self-contradiction as an achievement of dialectical profundity, all we need is to restore some part, no matter how small, of what we have taken away. In the case of the epistemological chasm the first reasonable step is to remember that the chasm was filled with *some* empirical material, whether ideational or sensational, which performed *some* bridging function and saved us from the mortal leap. Restoring thus the indispensable modicum of reality to the matter of our discussion, we find our abstract treatment genuinely useful. We escape entanglement with special cases without at the same time falling into gratuitous paradoxes. We can now describe the general features of cognition, tell what on the whole it *does for us*, in a universal way.

We must remember that this whole inquiry into knowing grows up on a reflective level. In any real moment of knowing, what we are thinking of is our object, not the way in which we ourselves are momentarily knowing it. We at this moment, as it happens, have knowing itself for our object; but I think that the reader will agree that his present knowing of that object is included only abstractly, and by anticipation, in the results he may reach. What he concretely has before his mind, as he reasons, is some supposed objective instance of knowing, as he conceives it to go on in some other person, or recalls it from his own past. As such, he, the critic, sees it to contain both an idea and an object, and processes by which the knower is guided from the one towards the other. He sees that the idea is remote from the object, and that, whether through intermediaries or not, it genuinely *has to do* with it. He sees that it thus works beyond its immediate being, and lays hold of a remote reality; it jumps across, transcends itself. It does all this by extraneous aid, to be sure, but when the aid has come, it *has* done it and the result is secure. Why not talk of results by themselves, then, without considering means? Why not treat the idea as simply grasping or intuiting the reality, of its having the faculty anyhow, of shooting over nature behind the scenes and knowing things immediately and directly? Why need we always lug in the bridging?—it only retards our discourse to do so.

Such abstract talk about cognition's results is surely convenient; and it is surely as legitimate as it is convenient, *so long as we do not forget or positively deny, what it ignores.* We may on occasion say that our idea meant *always* that particular object, that it led us there because it was *of* it intrinsically and essentially. We may insist that its verification follows upon that original cognitive virtue in it—and all the rest—and we shall do no harm so long as we know that these are only short cuts in our thinking. They are positively true accounts of fact *as far as they go,* only they leave vast tracts of fact out of the account, tracts of fact that have to be reinstated to make the accounts literally true of any real case. But if, not merely passively ignoring the intermediaries, you actively deny them[6] to be even potential requisites for the results you are so struck by, your epistemology goes to irremediable smash. You are as far off the track as an historian would be, if, lost in admiration of Napoleon's personal power, he were to ignore his marshals and his armies, and were to accuse you of error in describing his conquests as effected by their means. Of such abstractness and one-sidedness I accuse most of the critics of my own account.

[6]This is the fallacy which I have called 'vicious intellectualism' in my book *A Pluralistic Universe*, Longmans, Green & Co., 1909.

In the second lecture of the book *Pragmatism,* I used the illustration of a squirrel scrambling round a tree-trunk to keep out of sight of a pursuing man: both go round the tree, but does the man go round the squirrel? It all depends, I said, on what you mean by 'going-round.' In one sense of the word the man 'goes round,' in another sense he does not. I settled the dispute by pragmatically distinguishing the senses. But I told how some disputants had called my distinction a shuffling evasion and taken their stand on what they called 'plain honest english going-round.'

In such a simple case few people would object to letting the term in dispute be translated into its concreter equivalents. But in the case of a complex function like our knowing they act differently. I give full concrete particular value for the ideas of knowing in every case I can think of, yet my critics insist that 'plain honest English knowing' is left out of my account. They write as if the minus were on my side and the plus on theirs.

The essence of the matter for me is that altho knowing can be both abstractly and concretely described, and altho the abstract descriptions are often useful enough, yet they are all sucked up and absorbed without residuum into the concreter ones, and contain nothing of any essentially other or higher nature, which the concrete descriptions can be justly accused of leaving behind. Knowing is just a natural process like any other. There is no ambulatory process whatsoever, the results of which we may not describe, if we prefer to, in saltatory terms, or represent in static formulation. Suppose, *e.g.,* that we say a man is 'prudent.' Concretely, that means that he takes out insurance, hedges in betting, looks before he leaps. Do such acts *constitute* the prudence? *are* they the man quâ prudent? Or is the prudence something by itself and independent of them? As a constant habit in him, a permanent tone of character, it is convenient to call him prudent in abstraction from any one of his acts, prudent in general and without specification, and to say the acts follow from the pre-existing prudence. There are peculiarities in his psycho-physical system that make him act prudently; and there are tendencies to association in our thoughts that prompt some of them to make for truth and others for error. But would the man be prudent in the absence of each and all of the acts? Or would the thoughts be true if they had no associative or impulsive tendencies? Surely we have no right to oppose static essences in this way to the moving processes in which they live embedded.

My bedroom is above my library. Does the 'aboveness' here mean aught that is different from the concrete spaces which have to be moved-through in getting from the one to the other? It means, you may say, a pure topographic relation, a sort of architect's plan among the eternal essences. But that is not the full aboveness, it is only an abbreviated substitute that on occasion may lead my mind towards truer, *i.e.*, fuller, dealings with the real aboveness. It is not an aboveness *ante rem*, it is a *post rem* extract from the aboveness *in rebus*. We may indeed talk, for certain conveniences, as if the abstract scheme preceded, we may say "I must go up stairs because of the essential aboveness," just as we may say that the man "does prudent acts because of his ingrained prudence," or that our ideas "lead us truly because of their intrinsic truth." But this should not debar us on other occasions from using completer forms of description. A concrete matter of fact always remains identical under any form of description, as when we say of a line, now that it runs from left to right, and now that it runs from right to left. These are but names of one and the same fact, one more expedient to use at one time, one at another. The *full* facts of cognition, whatever be the way in which we talk about them, even when we talk most abstractly, stand inalterably given in the actualities and possibilities of the experience-continuum.[7] But my critics treat my own more concrete talk as if *it* were the kind that sinned by its inadequacy, and as if the full continuum left something out.

A favorite way of opposing the more abstract to the more concrete account is to accuse those who favor the latter of 'confounding psychology with logic.' Our critics say that when we are asked what truth *means*, we reply by telling only how it is *arrived-at*.

[7] The ultimate object or terminus of a cognitive process may in certain instances lie beyond the direct experience of the particular cognizer, but it, of course, must exist as part of the total universe of experience whose constitution, with cognition in it, the critic is discussing.

But since a meaning is a logical relation, static, independent of time, how can it possibly be identified, they say, with any concrete man's experience, perishing as this does at the instant of its production? This, indeed, sounds profound, but I challenge the profundity. I defy anyone to show any difference between logic and psychology here. The logical relation stands to the psychological relation between idea and object only as saltatory abstractness stands to ambulatory concreteness. Both relations need a psychological vehicle; and the 'logical' one is simply the 'psychological' one disemboweled of its fulness, and reduced to a bare abstractional scheme.

A while ago a prisoner, on being released, tried to assassinate the judge who had sentenced him. He had apparently succeeded in conceiving the judge timelessly, had reduced him to a bare logical meaning, that of being his 'enemy and persecutor,' by stripping off all the concrete conditions (as jury's verdict, official obligation, absence of personal spite, possibly sympathy) that gave its full psychological character to the sentence as a particular man's act in time. Truly the sentence *was* inimical to the culprit; but which idea of it is the truer one, that bare logical definition of it, or its full psychological specification? The anti-pragmatists ought in consistency to stand up for the criminal's view of the case, treat the judge as the latter's logical enemy, and bar out the other conditions as so much inessential psychological stuff.

II

A still further obstacle, I suspect, stands in the way of my account's acceptance. Like Dewey and like Schiller, I have had to say that the truth of an idea is determined by its satisfactoriness. But satisfactoriness is a subjective term, just as idea is; and truth is generally regarded as 'objective.' Readers who admit that satisfactoriness is our only *mark* of truth, the only sign that we possess the precious article, will still say that the objective relation between idea and object which the word 'truth' points to is left out of my account altogether. I fear also that the association of my poor name with the 'will to believe' (which 'will,' it seems to me, ought to play no part in this discussion) works against my credit in some quarters. I fornicate with that unclean thing, my adversaries may think, whereas your genuine truth-lover must discourse in huxleyan heroics, and feel as if truth, to be real truth, ought to bring eventual messages of death to all our satisfactions. Such divergences certainly prove the complexity of the area of our discussion; but to my mind they also are based on misunderstandings, which (tho with but little hope of success) I will try to diminish by a further word of explanation.

First, then, I will ask my objectors to define exactly what *sort* of thing it is they have in mind when they speak of a truth that shall be absolute, complete and objective; and then I will defy them to show me any conceivable standing-room for such a kind of truth outside the terms of my own description. It will fall, as I contend, entirely within the field of my analysis.

To begin with, it must obtain between an idea and a reality that is the idea's object; and, as a predicate, it must apply to the idea and not to the object, for objective realities are not *true*, at least not in the universe of discourse to which we are now confining ourselves, for there they are taken as simply *being*, while the ideas are true *of* them. But we can suppose a series of ideas to be successively more and more true of the same object, and can ask what is the extreme approach to being absolutely true that the last idea might attain to.

The maximal conceivable truth in an idea would seem to be that it should lead to an actual merging of ourselves with the object, to an utter mutual confluence and identification. On the common-sense level of belief this is what is supposed really to take place in sense-perception. My idea of this pen verifies itself through my percept; and my percept is held to *be* the pen for the time being—percepts and physical realities being treated by common sense as identical. But the physiology of the senses has criticized common sense out of court, and the pen 'in itself' is now believed to lie beyond my momentary percept. Yet the notion once suggested, of what a completely consummated acquaintance with a reality might be like, remains over for our speculative purposes. *Total conflux of the mind with the reality* would be the absolute limit of truth, there could be no better or more satisfying knowledge than that.

Such total conflux, it is needless to say, is *already explicitly provided for, as a possibility, in my account of the matter.* If an idea should ever lead us not only *towards,* or *up to,* or *against,* a reality, but so close that we and the reality should *melt together,* it would be made absolutely true, according to me, by that performance.

In point of fact philosophers doubt that this ever occurs. What happens, they think, is only that we get nearer and nearer to realities, we approximate more and more to the all-satisfying limit; and the definition of actually, as distinguished from imaginably, complete and objective truth, can then only be that it belongs to the idea that will lead us as *close up against the object* as in the nature of our experience is possible, literally *next* to it, for instance.

Suppose, now, there were an idea that did this for a certain objective reality. Suppose that no further approach were possible, that nothing lay between, that the next step would carry us right *into* the reality; then that result, being the next thing to conflux, would make the idea true in the maximal degree that might be supposed practically attainable in the world which we inhabit.

Well, I need hardly explain that *that degree of truth is also provided for in my account of the matter.* And if satisfactions are the marks of truth's presence, we may add that any less true substitute for such a true idea would prove less satisfactory. Following its lead, we should probably find out that we did not quite touch the terminus. We should desiderate a closer approach, and not rest till we had found it.

I am, of course, postulating here a standing reality independent of the idea that knows it. I am also postulating that satisfactions grow *pari passu* with our approximation to such reality.[8] If my critics challenge this latter assumption, I retort upon them with the former. Our whole notion of a standing reality grows up in the form of an ideal limit to the series of successive termini to

---

[8] Say, if you prefer to, that *dis*satisfactions decrease *pari passu* with such approximation. The approximation may be of any kind assignable—approximation in time or in space, or approximation in kind, which in common speech means 'copying.'

which our thoughts have led us and still are leading us. Each terminus proves provisional by leaving us unsatisfied. The truer idea is the one that pushes farther; so we are ever beckoned on by the ideal notion of an ultimate completely satisfactory terminus. I, for one, obey and accept that notion. I can conceive no other objective *content* to the notion of ideally perfect truth than that of penetration into such a terminus, nor can I conceive that the notion would ever have grown up, or that true ideas would ever have been sorted out from false or idle ones, save for the greater sum of satisfactions, intellectual or practical, which the truer ones brought with them. Can we imagine a man absolutely satisfied with an idea and with all its relations to his other ideas and to his sensible experiences, who should yet *not* take its content as a true account of reality? The *matter* of the true is thus absolutely identical with the matter of the satisfactory. You may put either word first in your ways of talking; but leave out that whole notion of *satisfactory working* or *leading* (which is the essence of my pragmatistic account) and call truth a static logical relation, independent even of *possible* leadings or satisfactions, and it seems to me you cut all ground from under you.

I fear that I am still very obscure. But I respectfully implore those who reject my doctrine because they can make nothing of my stumbling language, to tell us in their own name—*und zwar* very concretely and articulately!—just how the real, genuine and absolutely 'objective' truth which they believe in so profoundly, *is* constituted and established. They musn't point to the 'reality' itself, for truth is only our subjective relation to realities. What is the nominal essence of this relation, its logical definition, whether or not it be 'objectively' attainable by mortals?

Whatever they may say it is, I have the firmest faith that my account will prove to have allowed for it and included it by anticipation, as one possible case in the total mixture of cases. There is, in short, no *room* for any grade or sort of truth outside of the framework of the pragmatic system, outside of that jungle of empirical workings and leadings, and their nearer or ulterior terminations, of which I seem to have written so unskilfully.

VII

Professor Pratt on Truth

I[1]

Professor J. B. Pratt's paper in the *Journal of Philosophy* for June 6, 1907, is so brilliantly written that its misconception of the pragmatist position seems doubly to call for a reply.

He asserts that, for a pragmatist, truth cannot be a relation between an idea and a reality outside and transcendent of the idea, but must lie "altogether within experience," where it will need "no reference to anything else to justify it"—no reference to the object, apparently. The pragmatist must "reduce everything to psychology," aye, and to the psychology of the immediate moment. He is consequently debarred from saying that an idea that eventually gets psychologically verified *was* already true before the process of verifying was complete; and he is equally debarred from treating an idea as true provisionally so long as he only believes that he *can* verify it whenever he will.

Whether such a pragmatist as this exists, I know not, never having myself met with the beast. We can define terms as we like; and if that be my friend Pratt's definition of a pragmatist, I can only concur with his anti-pragmatism. But, in setting up the weird type, he quotes words from me; so, in order to escape being classed

[1] Reprinted from the *Journal of Philosophy, etc.*, August 15, 1907 (vol. iv, p. 464).

by some reader along with so asinine a being, I will reassert my own view of truth once more.

Truth is essentially a relation between two things, an idea, on the one hand, and a reality outside of the idea, on the other. This relation, like all relations, has its *fundamentum*, namely, the matrix of experiential circumstance, psychological as well as physical, in which the correlated terms are found embedded. In the case of the relation between 'heir' and 'legacy' the *fundamentum* is a world in which there was a testator, and in which there is now a will and an executor; in the case of that between idea and object, it is a world with circumstances of a sort to make a satisfactory verification process, lying around and between the two terms. But just as a man may be called an heir and treated as one before the executor has divided the estate, so an idea may practically be credited with truth before the verification process has been exhaustively carried out—the existence of the mass of verifying circumstance is enough. Where potentiality counts for actuality in so many other cases, one does not see why it may not so count here. We call a man benevolent not only for his kind acts paid in, but for his readiness to perform others; we treat an idea as 'luminous' not only for the light it has shed, but for that we expect it will shed on dark problems. Why should we not equally trust the truth of our ideas? We live on credits everywhere; and we use our ideas far oftener for calling up things connected with their immediate objects, than for calling up those objects themselves. Ninety-nine times out of a hundred the only use we should make of the object itself, if we were led up to it by our idea, would be to pass on to those connected things by its means. So we continually curtail verification-processes, letting our belief that they are possible suffice.

What *constitutes the relation* known as truth, I now say, is just the *existence in the empirical world of this fundamentum of circumstance surrounding object and idea* and ready to be either short-circuited or traversed at full length. So long as it exists, and a satisfactory passage through it between the object and the idea is possible, that idea will both *be* true, and will *have been* true of that object, whether fully developed verification has taken place or not. The nature and place and affinities of the object of course play as vital a part in making the particular passage possible as do the nature and associative tendencies of the idea; so that the notion that truth could fall altogether inside of the thinker's private experience and be something purely psychological, is absurd. It is *between* the idea and the object that the truth-relation is to be sought and it involves both terms.

But the 'intellectualistic' position, if I understand Mr. Pratt rightly, is that, altho we can use this *fundamentum*, this mass of go-between experience, for *testing* truth, yet the truth-relation in itself remains as something apart. It means, in Mr. Pratt's words, merely "this simple thing, *that the object of which one is thinking is as one thinks it.*"

It seems to me that the word 'as,' which qualifies the relation here, and bears the whole 'epistemological' burden, is anything but simple. What it most immediately suggests is that the idea should be *like* the object; but most of our ideas, being abstract concepts, bear almost no resemblance to their objects. The 'as' must therefore, I should say, be usually interpreted functionally, as meaning that the idea shall lead us into the same quarters of experience *as* the object would. Experience leads ever on and on, and objects and our ideas of objects may both lead to the same goals. The ideas being in that case shorter cuts, we *substitute* them more and more for their objects; and we habitually waive direct verification of each one of them, as their train passes through our mind, because if an idea leads *as* the object would lead, we can say, in Mr. Pratt's words, that in so far forth the object is *as* we think it, and that the idea, verified thus in so far forth, is true enough.

Mr. Pratt will undoubtedly accept most of these facts, but he will deny that they spell pragmatism. Of course, definitions are free to everyone; but I have myself never meant by the pragmatic view of truth anything different from what I now describe; and inasmuch as my use of the term came earlier than my friend's, I think it ought to have the right of way. But I suspect that Professor Pratt's contention is not solely as to what one must think in order to be called a pragmatist. I am sure that he believes that the truth-relation has something *more* in it than the *fundamentum* which I assign can account for. Useful to test truth by, the matrix of circumstance, he thinks, cannot found the truth-relation *in se*, for that is trans-empirical and 'saltatory.'

Well, take an object and an idea, and assume that the latter is true of the former—as eternally and absolutely true as you like. Let the object be as much 'as' the idea thinks it, as it is possible for one thing to be 'as' another. I now formally ask of Professor Pratt to tell what this 'as'-ness in itself *consists* in—for it seems to me that it ought to consist in something assignable and describable, and not remain a pure mystery, and I promise that if he can assign any determination of it whatever which I cannot successfully refer to some specification of what in this article I have called the empirical *fundamentum*, I will confess my stupidity cheerfully, and will agree never to publish a line upon this subject of truth again.

II

Professor Pratt has returned to the charge in a whole book,[2] which for its clearness and good temper deserves to supersede all the rest of the anti-pragmatistic literature. I wish it might do so; for its author admits all *my* essential contentions, simply distinguishing my account of truth as 'modified' pragmatism from Schiller's and Dewey's, which he calls pragmatism of the 'radical' sort. As I myself understand Dewey and Schiller, our views absolutely agree, in spite of our different modes of statement; but I have enough trouble of my own in life without having to defend my friends, so I abandon them provisionally to the tender mercy of Professor Pratt's interpretations, utterly erroneous tho I deem these to be. My reply as regards myself can be very short, for I prefer to consider only essentials, and Dr. Pratt's whole book hardly takes the matter farther than the article to which I retort in Part I of the present paper.

He repeats the 'as'-formula, as if it were something that I, along

[2] J. B. Pratt: *What is Pragmatism?* New York, The Macmillan Company, 1909.— The comments I have printed were written in March, 1909, after some of the articles printed later in the present volume.

with other pragmatists, had denied,[3] whereas I have only asked those who insist so on its importance to do something more than merely utter it—to explicate it, for example, and tell us what its so great importance consists in. I myself agree most cordially that for an idea to be true the object must be 'as' the idea declares it, but I explicate the 'as'-ness as meaning the idea's verifiability.

Now since Dr. Pratt denies none of these verifying 'workings' for which I have pleaded, but only insists on their inability to serve as the *fundamentum* of the truth-relation, it seems that there is really nothing in the line of *fact* about which we differ, and that the issue between us is solely as to how far the notion of workableness or verifiability is an essential part of the notion of 'trueness'—'trueness' being Dr. Pratt's present name for the character of as-ness in the true idea. I maintain that there is no meaning left in this notion of as-ness or trueness if no reference to the possibility of concrete working on the part of the idea is made.

Take an example where there can be no possible working. Suppose I have an idea to which I give utterance by the vocable 'skrkl,' claiming at the same time that it is true. Who now can say that it is *false*, for why may there not be somewhere in the unplumbed depths of the cosmos some object with which 'skrkl' can agree and have trueness in Dr. Pratt's sense? On the other hand who can say that it is *true*, for who can lay his hand on that object and show that it and nothing else is what I *mean* by my word? But yet again, who can gainsay anyone who shall call my word utterly *irrelative* to other reality, and treat it as a bare fact in my mind, devoid of any cognitive function whatever. One of these three alternatives must surely be predicated of it. For it not to be irrelevant (or not-cognitive in nature), an object of some kind must be provided which it may refer to. Supposing that object provided, whether 'skrkl' is true or false of it, depends, according to Professor Pratt, on no intermediating condition whatever. The trueness or the falsity is even now immediately, absolutely, and positively there.

I, on the other hand, demand a cosmic environment of some

[3] *Op. cit.*, pp. 77–80.

kind to establish which of them is there rather than utter irrelevancy.[4] I then say, first, that unless some sort of a natural path exists between the 'skrkl' and *that* object, distinguishable among the innumerable pathways that run among all the realities of the universe, linking them promiscuously with one another, there is nothing there to constitute even the *possibility of its referring* to that object rather than to any other.

I say furthermore that unless it have some *tendency to follow up that path,* there is nothing to constitute its *intention* to refer to the object in question.

Finally, I say that unless the path be strown with possibilities of frustration or encouragement, and offer some sort of terminal satisfaction or contradiction, there is nothing to constitute its *agreement* or *disagreement* with that object, or to constitute the as-ness (or 'not-as-ness') in which the trueness (or falseness) is said to consist.

I think that Dr. Pratt ought to do something more than repeat the name 'trueness,' in answer to my pathetic question whether that there be not some *constitution* to a relation as important as this. The pathway, the tendency, the corroborating or contradicting progress, need not in every case be experienced in full, but I don't see, if the universe doesn't contain them among its possibilities of furniture, what *logical material for defining* the trueness of my idea is left. But if it do contain them, they and they only are the logical material required.

I am perplexed by the superior importance which Dr. Pratt attributes to abstract trueness over concrete verifiability in an idea, and I wish that he might be moved to explain. It is prior to veri-

---

[4] Dr. Pratt, singularly enough, disposes of this primal postulate of all pragmatic epistemology, by saying that the pragmatist "unconsciously surrenders his whole case by smuggling in the idea of a conditioning environment which determines whether or not the 'experience' *can* work, and which cannot itself be identified with the experience or any part of it" (pp. 167–168). The 'experience' means here of course the idea, or belief; and the expression 'smuggling in' is to the last degree diverting. If any epistemologist could dispense with a conditioning environment, it would seem to be the anti-pragmatist, with his immediate saltatory trueness, independent of work done. The mediating pathway which the environment supplies is the very essence of the pragmatist's explanation.

fication, to be sure, but so is the verifiability for which I contend prior, just as a man's 'mortality' (which is nothing but the possibility of his death) is prior to his death, but it can hardly be that this abstract priority of all possibility to its correlative fact is what so obstinate a quarrel is about. I think it probable that Dr. Pratt is vaguely thinking of something concreter than this. The trueness of an idea must mean *something definite in it that determines its tendency to work,* and indeed towards this object rather than towards that. Undoubtedly there is something of this sort in the idea, just as there is something in man that accounts for his tendency towards death, and in bread that accounts for its tendency to nourish. What that something is in the case of truth psychology tells us: the idea has associates peculiar to itself, motor as well as ideational; it tends by its place and nature to call these into being, one after another; and the appearance of them in succession is what we mean by the 'workings' of the idea. According to what they are, does the trueness or falseness which the idea harbored come to light. These tendencies have still earlier conditions which, in a general way, biology, psychology and biography can trace. This whole chain of natural causal conditions produces a resultant state of things in which new relations, not simply causal, can now be found, or into which they can now be introduced—the relations namely which we epistemologists study, relations of adaptation, of substitutability, of instrumentality, of reference and of truth.

The prior causal conditions, altho there could be no knowing of any kind, true or false, without them, are but preliminary to the question of what makes the ideas true or false when once their tendencies have been obeyed. The tendencies must exist in some shape anyhow, but their fruits are truth, falsity, or irrelevancy, according to what they concretely turn out to be. They are not 'saltatory' at any rate, for they evoke their consequences contiguously, from next to next only; and not until the final result of the whole associative sequence, actual or potential, is in our mental sight, can we feel sure what its epistemological significance, if it have any, may be. True knowing is, in fine, not substantially, in itself, or 'as such,' inside of the idea from the first, any more than mortality *as such* is inside of the man, or nourishment *as such* inside of the bread. Something else is there first, that practically *makes for* knowing, dying or nourishing, as the case may be. That something is the 'nature' namely of the first term, be it idea, man, or bread, that operates to start the causal chain of processes which, when completed, is the complex fact to which we give whatever functional name best fits the case. Another nature, another chain of cognitive workings; and then either another object known or the same object known differently, will ensue.

Dr. Pratt perplexes me again by seeming to charge Dewey and Schiller[5] (I am not sure that he charges me) with an account of truth which would allow the object believed in not to exist, even if the belief in it were true. "Since the truth of an idea," he writes, "means merely the fact that the idea works, that fact is all you mean when you say the idea is true" (p. 206). *"When you say the idea is true"*—does that mean true for *you*, the critic, or true for the believer whom you are describing? The critic's trouble over this seems to come from his taking the word 'true' irrelatively, whereas the pragmatist always means 'true for him who experiences the workings.' "But is the object *really* true or not?"—the critic then seems to ask—as if the pragmatist were bound to throw in a whole ontology on top of his epistemology and tell us what realities indubitably exist. "One world at a time," would seem to be the right reply here.

One other trouble of Dr. Pratt's must be noticed. It concerns the 'transcendence' of the object. When our ideas have worked so as to bring us flat up against the object, *next* to it, "is our relation to it then ambulatory or saltatory?" Dr. Pratt asks. If *your* headache be my object, "*my* experiences break off where yours begin," Dr. Pratt writes, and "this fact is of great importance, for it bars out the sense of transition and fulfillment which forms so important an element in the pragmatist description of knowledge,—the sense of fulfillment due to a continuous passage from the original idea to the known object. If this comes at all when I know your head-

---

[5] Page 200.

97

ache, it comes not with the object but quite on my side of the 'epistemological gulf.' The gulf is still there to be transcended" (p. 158).

Some day of course, or even now somewhere in the larger life of the universe, different men's headaches may become confluent or be 'co-conscious.' Here and now, however, headaches do transcend each other and, when not felt, can be known only conceptually. My idea is that you really have a headache; it works well with what I see of your expression, and with what I hear you say; but it doesn't put me in possession of the headache itself. I am still at one remove, and the headache 'transcends' me, even tho it be in nowise transcendent of human experience generally. But the 'gulf' here is that which the pragmatist epistemology itself fixes in the very first words it uses, by saying there must be an object and an idea. The idea however doesn't immediately leap the gulf, it only works from next to next so as to bridge it, fully or approximately. If it bridges it, in the pragmatist's vision of his hypothetical universe, it can be called a 'true' idea. If it only *might* bridge it, but doesn't, or if it throws a bridge distinctly *at* it, it still has, in the onlooking pragmatist's eyes, what Professor Pratt calls 'trueness.' But to ask the pragmatist thereupon whether, when it thus fails to coalesce bodily with the object, it is *really* true or has *real* trueness—in other words whether the headache he supposes, and supposes the thinker he supposes, to believe in, be a real headache or not—is to step from his hypothetical universe of discourse into the altogether different world of natural fact.

VIII

The Pragmatist Account of Truth and its Misunderstanders[1]

The account of truth given in my volume entitled *Pragmatism*, continues to meet with such persistent misunderstanding that I am tempted to make a final brief reply. My ideas may well deserve refutation, but they can get none till they are conceived of in their proper shape. The fantastic character of the current misconceptions shows how unfamiliar is the concrete point of view which pragmatism assumes. Persons who are familiar with a conception move about so easily in it that they understand each other at a hint, and can converse without anxiously attending to their P's and Q's. I have to admit, in view of the results, that we have assumed too ready an intelligence, and consequently in many places used a language too slipshod. We should never have spoken elliptically. The critics have boggled at every word they could boggle at, and refused to take the spirit rather than the letter of our discourse. This seems to show a genuine unfamiliarity in the whole point of view. It also shows, I think, that the second stage of opposition, which has already begun to express itself in the stock phrase that 'what is new is not true, and what is true not new,' in pragmatism, is insincere. If we said nothing in any degree new,

[1] Reprint from the *Philosophical Review*, January, 1908 (vol. xvii, p. 1).

why was our meaning so desperately hard to catch? The blame cannot be laid wholly upon our obscurity of speech, for in other subjects we have attained to making ourselves understood. But recriminations are tasteless; and, as far as I personally am concerned, I am sure that some of the misconception I complain of is due to my doctrine of truth being surrounded in that volume of popular lectures by a lot of other opinions not necessarily implicated with it, so that a reader may very naturally have grown confused. For this I am to blame—likewise for omitting certain explicit cautions, which the pages that follow will now in part supply.

First misunderstanding: Pragmatism is only a re-editing of positivism.

This seems the commonest mistake. Scepticism, positivism, and agnosticism agree with ordinary dogmatic rationalism in presupposing that everybody knows what the word 'truth' means, without further explanation. But the former doctrines then either suggest or declare that real truth, absolute truth, is inaccessible to us, and that we must fain put up with relative or phenomenal truth as its next best substitute. By scepticism this is treated as an unsatisfactory state of affairs, while positivism and agnosticism are cheerful about it, call real truth sour grapes, and consider phenomenal truth quite sufficient for all our 'practical' purposes.

In point of fact, nothing could be farther from all this than what pragmatism has to say of truth. Its thesis is an altogether previous one. It leaves off where these other theories begin, having contented itself with the word truth's *definition*. "No matter whether any mind extant in the universe possess truth or not," it asks, "what does the notion of truth signify *ideally?*" "What kind of things would true judgments be *in case* they existed?" The answer which pragmatism offers is intended to cover the most complete truth that can be conceived of, 'absolute' truth if you like, as well as truth of the most relative and imperfect description. This question of what truth would be like if it did exist, belongs obviously to a purely speculative field of inquiry. It is not a psychological, but rather a logical question. It is not a theory about any sort of reality, or about what kind of knowledge is actually possible; it abstracts from particular terms altogether, and defines the nature of a possible relation between two of them.

As Kant's question about synthetic judgments had escaped previous philosophers, so the pragmatist question is not only so subtle as to have escaped attention hitherto, but even so subtle, it would seem, that when openly broached now, dogmatists and sceptics alike fail to apprehend it, and deem the pragmatist to be treating of something wholly different. He insists, they say (I quote an actual critic), "that the greater problems are insoluble by human intelligence, that our need of knowing truly is artificial and illusory, and that our reason, incapable of reaching the foundations of reality, must turn itself exclusively towards *action.*" There could not be a worse misapprehension.

Second misunderstanding: Pragmatism is primarily an appeal to action.

The name 'pragmatism,' with its suggestions of action, has been an unfortunate choice, I have to admit, and has played into the hands of this mistake. But no word could protect the doctrine from critics so blind to the nature of the inquiry that, when Dr. Schiller speaks of ideas 'working' well, the only thing they think of is their immediate workings in the physical environment, their enabling us to make money, or gain some similar 'practical' advantage. Ideas do work thus, of course, immediately or remotely; but they work indefinitely inside of the mental world also. Not crediting us with this rudimentary insight, our critics treat our view as offering itself exclusively to engineers, doctors, financiers, and men of action generally, who need some sort of a rough and ready *weltanschauung,* but have no time or wit to study genuine philosophy. It is usually described as a characteristically american movement, a sort of bobtailed scheme of thought, excellently fitted for the man on the street, who naturally hates theory and wants cash returns immediately.

It is quite true that, when the refined theoretic question that pragmatism begins with is once answered, secondary corollaries of a practical sort follow. Investigation shows that, in the function called truth, previous realities are not the only independent variables. To a certain extent our ideas, being realities, are also independent variables, and, just as they follow other reality and fit it, so, in a measure, does other reality follow and fit them. When they add themselves to being, they partly redetermine the existent, so that reality as a whole appears incompletely definable unless ideas also are kept account of. This pragmatist doctrine, exhibiting our ideas as complemental factors of reality, throws open (since our ideas are instigators of our action) a wide window upon human action, as well as a wide license to originality in thought. But few things could be sillier than to ignore the prior epistemological edifice in which the window is built, or to talk as if pragmatism began and ended at the window. This, nevertheless, is what our critics do almost without exception. They ignore our primary step and its motive, and make the relation to action, which is our secondary achievement, primary.

Third misunderstanding: Pragmatists cut themselves off from the right to believe in ejective realities.

They do so, according to the critics, by making the truth of our beliefs consist in their verifiability, and their verifiability in the way in which they do work for us. Professor Stout, in his otherwise admirable and helpful review of Schiller in *Mind* for October, 1907, considers that this ought to lead Schiller (could he sincerely realize the effects of his own doctrine) to the absurd consequence of being unable to believe genuinely in another man's headache, even were the headache there. He can only 'postulate' it for the sake of the working value of the postulate to himself. The postulate guides certain of his acts and leads to advantageous consequences; but the moment he understands fully that the postulate is true *only* (!) in this sense, it ceases (or should cease) to be true for him that the other man really *has* a headache. All that makes the postulate most precious then evaporates: his interest in his fellow-man "becomes a veiled form of self-interest, and his world becomes cold, dull and heartless."

Such an objection makes a curious muddle of the pragmatist's universe of discourse. Within that universe the pragmatist finds someone with a headache or other feeling, and someone else who postulates that feeling. Asking on what condition the postulate is 'true,' the pragmatist replies that, for the postulator at any rate, it is true just in proportion as to believe in it works in him the fuller sum of satisfactions. What is it that is satisfactory here? Surely to *believe* in the postulated object, namely, in the really existing feeling of the other man. But how (especially if the postulator were himself a thoroughgoing pragmatist) could it ever be satisfactory to him *not* to believe in that feeling, so long as, in Professor Stout's words, disbelief "made the world seem to him cold, dull, and heartless"? Disbelief would seem, on pragmatist principles, quite out of the question under such conditions, unless the heartlessness of the world were made probable already on other grounds. And since the belief in the headache, true for the subject assumed in the pragmatist's universe of discourse, is also true for the pragmatist who for his epistemologizing purposes has assumed that entire universe, why is it not true in that universe absolutely? The headache believed in is a reality there, and no extant mind disbelieves it, neither the critic's mind nor his subject's! Have our opponents any better brand of truth in this real universe of ours that they can show us?[2]

[2] I see here a chance to forestall a criticism which someone may make on Lecture III of my *Pragmatism*, where, on pp. 96–100 [*ed.*, 50.20–52.21], I said that 'God' and 'Matter' might be regarded as synonymous terms, so long as no differing future consequences were deducible from the two conceptions. The passage was transcribed from my address at the California Philosophical Union, reprinted in the *Journal of Philosophy*, vol. i, p. 673. I had no sooner given the address than I perceived a flaw in that part of it; but I have left the passage unaltered ever since, because the flaw did not spoil its illustrative value. The flaw was evident when, as a case analogous to that of a godless universe, I thought of what I called an 'automatic sweetheart,' meaning a soulless body which should be absolutely indistinguishable from a spiritually animated maiden, laughing, talking, blushing, nursing us, and performing all feminine offices as tactfully and sweetly as if a soul were in her. Would anyone regard her as a full equivalent? Certainly not, and why? Because, framed as we are, our egoism craves above all things inward sympathy and recognition, love and admiration. The outward treatment is valued mainly as an expression, as a manifestation of the accompanying consciousness believed in. Pragmatically, then, belief in the automatic sweetheart would not *work*, and in point of fact no one treats it as a serious hypothesis. The godless universe would be exactly similar. Even if matter could do every outward thing that God does, the idea of it would not work as satisfactorily, because the chief call for a God on modern men's part is for a being who will inwardly recognize them and judge them sympathetically. Matter disappoints this craving of our ego, so God remains for most men the truer hypothesis, and indeed remains so for definite pragmatic reasons.

So much for the third misunderstanding, which is but one specification of the following still wider one.

Fourth misunderstanding: No pragmatist can be a realist in his epistemology.

This is supposed to follow from his statement that the truth of our beliefs consists in general in their giving satisfaction. Of course satisfaction *per se* is a subjective condition; so the conclusion is drawn that truth falls wholly inside of the subject, who then may manufacture it at his pleasure. True beliefs become thus wayward affections, severed from all responsibility to other parts of experience.

It is difficult to excuse such a parody of the pragmatist's opinion, ignoring as it does every element but one of his universe of discourse. The terms of which that universe consists positively forbid any non-realistic interpretation of the function of knowledge defined there. The pragmatizing epistemologist posits there a reality and a mind with ideas. What, now, he asks, can make those ideas true of that reality? Ordinary epistemology contents itself with the vague statement that the ideas must 'correspond' or 'agree'; the pragmatist insists on being more concrete, and asks what such 'agreement' may mean in detail. He finds first that the ideas must point to or lead towards *that* reality and no other, and then that the pointings and leadings must yield satisfaction as their result. So far the pragmatist is hardly less abstract than the ordinary slouchy epistemologist; but as he defines himself farther, he grows more concrete. The entire quarrel of the intellectualist with him is over his concreteness, intellectualism contending that the vaguer and more abstract account is here the more profound. The concrete pointing and leading are conceived by the pragmatist to be the work of other portions of the same universe to which the reality and the mind belong, intermediary verifying bits of experience with which the mind at one end, and the reality at the other, are joined. The 'satisfaction,' in turn, is no abstract satisfaction *überhaupt*, felt by an unspecified being, but is assumed to consist of such satisfactions (in the plural) as concretely existing men actually do find in their beliefs. As we humans are constituted in point of fact, we find that to believe in other men's minds, in independent physical realities, in past events, in eternal logical relations, is satisfactory. We find hope satisfactory. We often find it satisfactory to cease to doubt. Above all we find *consistency* satisfactory, consistency between the present idea and the entire rest of our mental equipment, including the whole order of our sensations, and that of our intuitions of likeness and difference, and our whole stock of previously acquired truths.

The pragmatist, being himself a man, and imagining in general no contrary lines of truer belief than ours about the 'reality' which he has laid at the base of his epistemological discussion, is willing to treat our satisfactions as possibly really true guides to it, not as guides true solely for *us*. It would seem here to be the duty of his critics to show with some explicitness why, being our subjective feelings, these satisfactions can *not* yield 'objective' truth. The beliefs which they accompany 'posit' the assumed reality, 'correspond' and 'agree' with it, and 'fit' it in perfectly definite and assignable ways, through the sequent trains of thought and action which form their verification, so merely to insist on using these words abstractly instead of concretely is no way of driving the pragmatist from the field—his more concrete account virtually includes his critic's. If our critics have any definite idea of a truth more objectively grounded than the kind we propose, why do they not show it more articulately? As they stand, they remind one of Hegel's man who wanted 'fruit,' but rejected cherries, pears, and grapes, because they were not fruit in the abstract. We offer them the full quart-pot, and they cry for the empty quart-capacity.

But here I think I hear some critic retort as follows: "If satisfactions are all that is needed to make truth, how about the notorious fact that errors are so often satisfactory? And how about the equally notorious fact that certain true beliefs may cause the bitterest dissatisfaction? Isn't it clear that not the satisfaction which it gives, but the relation of the belief *to the reality* is all that makes it true? Suppose there were no such reality, and that the satisfactions yet remained: would they not then effectively work falsehood? Can they consequently be treated distinctively as the truth-builders? It is the *inherent relation to reality* of a belief that gives us that specific *truth*-satisfaction, compared with which all other satisfactions are the hollowest humbug. The satisfaction of *knowing truly* is thus the only one which the pragmatist ought to have considered. As a *psychological sentiment*, the anti-pragmatist gladly concedes it to him, but then only as a concomitant of truth, not as a constituent. What *constitutes* truth is not the sentiment, but the purely logical or objective function of rightly cognizing the reality, and the pragmatist's failure to reduce this function to lower values is patent."

Such anti-pragmatism as this seems to me a tissue of confusion. To begin with, when the pragmatist says 'indispensable,' it confounds this with 'sufficient.' The pragmatist calls satisfactions indispensable for truth-building, but I have everywhere called them insufficient unless reality be also incidentally led to. If the reality assumed were cancelled from the pragmatist's universe of discourse, he would straightway give the name of falsehoods to the beliefs remaining, in spite of all their satisfactoriness. For him, as for his critic, there can be no truth if there is nothing to be true about. Ideas are so much flat psychological surface unless some mirrored matter gives them cognitive lustre. This is why as a pragmatist I have so carefully posited 'reality' *ab initio*, and why, throughout my whole discussion, I remain an epistemological realist.[3]

The anti-pragmatist is guilty of the further confusion of imagining that, in undertaking to give him an account of what truth formally means, we are assuming at the same time to provide a warrant for it, trying to define the occasions when he can be sure of materially possessing it. Our making it hinge on a reality so 'independent' that when it comes, truth comes, and when it goes, truth goes with it, disappoints this naive expectation, so he deems our description unsatisfactory. I suspect that under this confusion lies the still deeper one of not discriminating sufficiently between the two notions, truth and reality. Realities are not *true*, they *are*; and beliefs are true *of* them. But I suspect that in the anti-pragmatist

---

[3] I need hardly remind the reader that both sense-percepts and percepts of ideal relation (comparisons, etc.) should be classed among the realities. The bulk of our mental 'stock' consists of truths concerning these terms.

mind the two notions sometimes swap their attributes. The reality itself, I fear, is treated as if 'true,' and conversely. Whoso tells us of the one, it is then supposed, must also be telling us of the other; and a true idea must in a manner *be*, or at least *yield* without extraneous aid, the reality it cognitively is possessed of.

To this absolute-idealistic demand pragmatism simply opposes its *non possumus*. If there is to be truth, it says, both realities and beliefs about them must conspire to make it; but whether there ever is such a thing, or how anyone can be sure that his own beliefs possess it, it never pretends to determine. That truth-satisfaction *par excellence* which may tinge a belief unsatisfactory in other ways, it easily explains as the feeling of consistency with the stock of previous truths, or supposed truths, of which one's whole past experience may have left one in possession.

But are not all pragmatists sure that their own belief is right? their enemies will ask at this point; and this leads me to the

Fifth misunderstanding: What pragmatists say is inconsistent with their saying so.

A correspondent puts this objection as follows: "When you say to your audience, 'pragmatism is the truth concerning truth,' the first truth is different from the second. About the first you and they are not to be at odds; you are not giving them liberty to take or leave it according as it works satisfactorily or not for their private uses. Yet the second truth, which ought to describe and include the first, affirms this liberty. Thus the *intent* of your utterance seems to contradict the *content* of it."

General scepticism has always received this same classic refutation. "You have to dogmatize," the rationalists say to the sceptics, "whenever you express the sceptical position; so your lives keep contradicting your thesis." One would suppose that the impotence of so hoary an argument to abate in the slightest degree the amount of general scepticism in the world might have led some rationalists themselves to doubt whether these instantaneous logical refutations are such fatal ways, after all, of killing off live mental attitudes. General scepticism is the live mental attitude of refusing to conclude. It is a permanent torpor of the will, renewing itself in detail towards each successive thesis that offers, and you can no more kill it off by logic than you can kill off obstinacy or practical joking. This is why it is so irritating. Your consistent sceptic never puts his scepticism into a formal proposition—he simply chooses it as a habit. He provokingly hangs back when he might so easily join us in saying yes, but he is not illogical or stupid—on the contrary, he often impresses us by his intellectual superiority. This is the *real* scepticism that rationalists have to meet, and their logic does not even touch it.

No more can logic kill the pragmatist's behavior: his act of utterance, so far from contradicting, accurately exemplifies the matter which he utters. What is the matter which he utters? In part, it is this, that truth, concretely considered, is an attribute of our beliefs, and that these are attitudes that follow satisfactions. The ideas around which the satisfactions cluster are primarily only hypotheses that challenge or summon a belief to come and take its stand upon them. The pragmatist's idea of truth is just such a challenge. He finds it ultra-satisfactory to accept it, and takes his own stand accordingly. But, being gregarious as they are, men seek to spread their beliefs, to awaken imitation, to infect others. Why should not *you* also find the same belief satisfactory? thinks the pragmatist, and forthwith endeavors to convert you. You and he will then believe similarly; you will hold up your subject-end of a truth, which will be a truth objective and irreversible if the reality holds up the object-end by being itself present simultaneously. What there is of self-contradiction in all this I confess I cannot discover. The pragmatist's conduct in his own case seems to me on the contrary admirably to illustrate his universal formula; and of all epistemologists, he is perhaps the only one who is irreproachably self-consistent.

Sixth misunderstanding: Pragmatism explains not what truth is, but only how it is arrived at.

In point of fact it tells us both, tells us what it is incidentally to telling us how it is arrived at—for what *is* arrived at except just what the truth is? If I tell you how to get to the railroad station, don't I implicitly introduce you to the *what*, to the being and nature of that edifice? It is quite true that the abstract *word* 'how' hasn't the same meaning as the abstract *word* 'what,' but in this universe of concrete facts you cannot keep hows and whats asunder. The reasons why I find it satisfactory to believe that any idea is true, the *how* of my arriving at that belief, may be among the very reasons why the idea *is* true in reality. If not, I summon the anti-pragmatist to explain the impossibility articulately.

His trouble seems to me mainly to arise from his fixed inability to understand how a concrete statement can possibly mean as much, or be as valuable, as an abstract one. I said above that the main quarrel between us and our critics was that of concreteness *versus* abstractness. This is the place to develope that point farther.

In the present question, the links of experience sequent upon an idea, which mediate between it and a reality, form and for the pragmatist indeed *are*, the *concrete* relation of truth that may obtain between the idea and that reality. They, he says, are all that we mean when we speak of the idea 'pointing' to the reality, 'fitting' it, 'corresponding' with it, or 'agreeing' with it—they or other similar mediating trains of verification. Such mediating events *make* the idea 'true.' The idea itself, if it exists at all, is also a concrete event: so pragmatism insists that truth in the singular is only a collective name for truths in the plural, these consisting always of series of definite events; and that what intellectualism calls *the* truth, the *inherent* truth, of any one such series is only the abstract name for its truthfulness in act, for the fact that the ideas there do lead to the supposed reality in a way that we consider satisfactory.

The pragmatist himself has no objection to abstractions. Elliptically, and 'for short,' he relies on them as much as anyone, finding upon innumerable occasions that their comparative emptiness makes of them useful substitutes for the overfulness of the facts he meets with. But he never ascribes to them a higher grade of reality. The full reality of a truth for him is always some process of verification, in which the abstract property of connecting ideas with objects truly is workingly embodied. Meanwhile it is endlessly serviceable to be able to talk of properties abstractly and apart from their working, to find them the same in innumerable cases, to take them 'out of time,' and to treat of their relations to other similar abstractions. We thus form whole universes of platonic ideas *ante rem,* universes *in posse,* tho none of them exists effectively except *in rebus.* Countless relations obtain there which nobody experiences as obtaining—as, in the eternal universe of musical relations, for example, the notes of Aennchen von Tharau were a lovely melody long ere mortal ears ever heard them. Even so the music of the future sleeps now, to be awakened hereafter. Or, if we take the world of geometrical relations, the thousandth decimal of π sleeps there, tho no one may ever try to compute it. Or, if we take the universe of 'fitting,' countless coats 'fit' backs, and countless boots 'fit' feet, on which they are not practically *fitted*; countless stones 'fit' gaps in walls into which no one seeks to fit them actually. In the same way countless opinions 'fit' realities, and countless truths are valid, tho no thinker ever thinks them.

For the anti-pragmatist these prior timeless relations are the presupposition of the concrete ones, and possess the profounder dignity and value. The actual workings of our ideas in verification-processes are as naught in comparison with the 'obtainings' of this discarnate truth within them.

For the pragmatist, on the contrary, all discarnate truth is static, impotent, and relatively spectral, full truth being the truth that energizes and does battle. Can anyone suppose that the sleeping quality of truth would ever have been abstracted or have received a name, if truths had remained forever in that storage-vault of essential timeless 'agreements' and had never been embodied in any panting struggle of men's live ideas for verification? Surely no more than the abstract property of 'fitting' would have received a name, if in our world there had been no backs or feet or gaps in walls to be actually fitted. *Existential* truth is incidental to the actual competition of opinions. *Essential* truth, the truth of the intellectualists, the truth with no one thinking it, is like the coat that fits tho no one has ever tried it on, like the music that no ear has listened to. It is less real, not more real, than the verified article; and to attribute a superior degree of glory to it seems little more than a piece of perverse abstraction-worship. As well might a pencil insist that the outline is the essential thing in all pictorial representation, and chide the paint-brush and the camera for omitting it, forgetting that *their* pictures not only contain the whole outline, but a hundred other things in addition. Pragmatist truth contains the whole of intellectualist truth and a hundred other things in addition. Intellectualist truth is then only pragmatist truth *in posse*. That on innumerable occasions men do substitute truth *in posse* or verifiability, for verification or truth in act, is a fact to which no one attributes more importance than the pragmatist: he emphasizes the practical utility of such a habit. But he does not on that account consider truth *in posse*—truth not alive enough ever to have been asserted or questioned or contradicted—to be the metaphysically prior thing, to which truths in act are tributary and subsidiary. When intellectualists do this, pragmatism charges them with inverting the real relation. Truth in posse *means* only truths in act; and he insists that these latter take precedence in the order of logic as well as in that of being.

Seventh misunderstanding: Pragmatism ignores the theoretic interest.

This would seem to be an absolutely wanton slander, were not a certain excuse to be found in the linguistic affinities of the word 'pragmatism,' and in certain offhand habits of speech of ours which assumed too great a generosity on our reader's part. When we spoke of the meaning of ideas consisting in their 'practical' consequences, or of the 'practical' differences which our beliefs make to us; when we said that the truth of a belief consists in its 'working' value, etc.; our language evidently was too careless, for by 'practical' we were almost unanimously held to mean *opposed* to theoretical or genuinely cognitive, and the consequence was punctually drawn that a truth in our eyes could have no relation to any independent reality, or to any other truth, or to anything whatever but the acts which we might ground on it or the satisfactions they might bring. The mere existence of the idea, all by itself, if only its results were satisfactory, would give full truth to it, it was charged, in our absurd pragmatist epistemology. The solemn attribution of this rubbish to us was also encouraged by two other

111

circumstances. First, ideas *are* practically useful in the narrow sense, false ideas sometimes, but most often ideas which we can verify by the sum total of all their leadings, and the reality of whose objects may thus be considered established beyond doubt. That these ideas should be true in advance of and apart from their utility, that, in other words, their objects should be really there, is the very condition of their having that kind of utility—the objects they connect us with are so important that the ideas which serve as the objects' substitutes grow important also. This manner of their practical working was the first thing that made truths good in the eyes of primitive men; and buried among all the other good workings by which true beliefs are characterized, this kind of subsequential utility remains.

The second misleading circumstance was the emphasis laid by Schiller and Dewey on the fact that, unless a truth be relevant to the mind's momentary predicament, unless it be germane to the 'practical' situation—meaning by this the quite particular perplexity—it is no good to urge it. It doesn't meet our interests any better than a falsehood would under the same circumstances. But why our predicaments and perplexities might not be theoretical here as well as narrowly practical, I wish that our critics would explain. They simply assume that no pragmatist *can* admit a genuinely theoretic interest. Having used the phrase 'cash-value' of an idea, I am implored by one correspondent to alter it, "for everyone thinks you mean only pecuniary profit and loss." Having said that the true is 'the expedient in our thinking,' I am rebuked in this wise by another learned correspondent: "The word expedient has no other meaning than that of self-interest. The pursuit of this has ended by landing a number of officers of national banks in penitentiaries. A philosophy that leads to such results must be unsound."

But the word 'practical' is so habitually loosely used that more indulgence might have been expected. When one says that a sick man has now practically recovered, or that an enterprise has practically failed, one usually means just the opposite of practically in the literal sense. One means that, altho untrue in strict practice, what one says is true in theory, true virtually, *certain to be* true.

Again, by the practical one often means the distinctively concrete, the individual, particular, and effective, as opposed to the abstract, general, and inert. To speak for myself, whenever I have emphasized the practical nature of truth, this is mainly what has been in my mind. 'Pragmata' are things in their plurality; and in that early California address, when I described pragmatism as holding that "the meaning of any proposition can always be brought down to some particular consequence, in our future practical experience, whether active or passive," I expressly added these qualifying words: "the point lying rather in the fact that the experience must be particular, than in the fact that it must be active"—by 'active' meaning here 'practical' in the narrow literal sense.[4] But particular consequences can perfectly well be of a theoretic nature. Every remote fact which we infer from an idea is a particular theoretic consequence which our mind practically works towards. The loss of every old opinion of ours which we see that we shall have to give up if a new opinion be true, is a particular theoretic as well as a particular practical consequence. After man's interest in breathing freely, the greatest of all his interests (because it never fluctuates or remits, as most of his physical interests do) is his interest in *consistency*, in feeling that what he now thinks goes with what he thinks on other occasions. We tirelessly compare truth with truth for this sole purpose. Is the present candidate for belief perhaps contradicted by principle number one? Is it compatible with fact number two? and so forth. The particular operations here are the purely logical ones of analysis, deduction, comparison, etc.; and altho general terms may be used *ad libitum*, the satisfactory *practical working* of the candidate-idea consists in the consciousness

[4] The ambiguity of the word 'practical' comes out well in these words of a recent would-be reporter of our views: "Pragmatism is an Anglo-Saxon reaction against the intellectualism and rationalism of the Latin mind. . . . Man, each individual man, is the measure of things. He is able to conceive none but relative truths, that is to say, illusions. What these illusions are worth is revealed to him, not by general theory, but by individual practice. Pragmatism, which consists in experiencing these illusions of the mind and obeying them by acting them out, is a *philosophy without words*, a philosophy of *gestures and of acts*, which abandons what is general and holds only to what is *particular*." (Bourdeau, in *Journal des Débats*, October 29, 1907.)

yielded by each successive theoretic consequence in particular. It is therefore simply idiotic to repeat that pragmatism takes no account of purely theoretic interests. All it insists on is that verity in act means *verifications,* and that these are always particulars. Even in exclusively theoretic matters, it insists that vagueness and generality serve to verify nothing.

Eighth misunderstanding: Pragmatism is shut up to solipsism.

I have already said something about this misconception under the third and fourth heads, above, but a little more may be helpful. The objection is apt to clothe itself in words like these: "You make truth to consist in every value except the cognitive value proper; you always leave your knower at many removes (or, at the uttermost, at one remove) from his real object; the best you do is to let his ideas carry him towards it; it remains forever outside of him," etc.

I think that the leaven working here is the rooted intellectualist persuasion that, to know a reality, an idea must in some inscrutable fashion possess or be it.[5] For pragmatism this kind of coalescence is inessential. As a rule our cognitions are only processes of mind off their balance and in motion towards real termini; and the reality of the termini, believed in by the states of mind in question, can be *guaranteed* only by some wider knower.[6]

[5] Sensations may, indeed, possess their objects or coalesce with them, as common sense supposes that they do; and intuited differences between concepts may coalesce with the 'eternal' objective differences; but to simplify our discussion here we can afford to abstract from these very special cases of knowing.

[6] The transcendental idealist thinks that, in some inexplicable way, the finite states of mind are identical with the transfinite all-knower which he finds himself obliged to postulate in order to supply a *fundamentum* for the relation of knowing, as he apprehends it. Pragmatists can leave the question of identity open; but they cannot do without the wider knower any more than they can do without the reality, if they want to *prove* a case of knowing. They themselves play the part of the absolute knower for the universe of discourse which serves them as material for epistemologizing. They warrant the reality there, and the subject's true knowledge, there, of it. But whether what they themselves say about that whole universe is objectively true, *i.e.*, whether the pragmatic theory of truth is true *really,* they cannot warrant—they can only believe it. To their hearers they can only *propose* it, as I propose it to my readers, as something to be verified *ambulando,* or by the way in which its consequences may confirm it.

But if there is no reason extant in the universe why they should be doubted, the beliefs are true in the only sense in which anything can be true anyhow: they are practically and concretely true, namely. True in the mystical mongrel sense of an *identitäts-philosophie* they need not be; nor is there any intelligible reason why they ever need be true otherwise than verifiably and practically. It is reality's part to possess its own existence; it is thought's part to get into 'touch' with it by innumerable paths of verification.

I fear that the 'humanistic' developments of pragmatism may cause a certain difficulty here. We get at one truth only through the rest of truth; and the reality, everlastingly postulated as that which all our truth must keep in touch with, may never be given to us save in the form of truth other than that which we are now testing. But since Dr. Schiller has shown that all our truths, even the most elemental, are affected by race-inheritance with a human coefficient, reality *per se* thus may appear only as a sort of limit; it may be held to shrivel to the mere *place* for an object, and what is known may be held to be only matter of our psyche that we fill the place with.

It must be confessed that pragmatism, worked in this humanistic way, is *compatible* with solipsism. It joins friendly hands with the agnostic part of kantism, with contemporary agnosticism, and with idealism generally. But worked thus, it is a metaphysical theory about the matter of reality, and flies far beyond pragmatism's own modest analysis of the nature of the knowing function, which analysis may just as harmoniously be combined with less humanistic accounts of reality. One of pragmatism's merits is that it is so purely epistemological. It must assume realities; but it prejudges nothing as to their constitution, and the most diverse metaphysics can use it as their foundation. It certainly has no special affinity with solipsism.

As I look back over what I have written, much of it gives me a queer impression, as if the obvious were set forth so condescendingly that readers might well laugh at my pomposity. It may be, however, that concreteness as radical as ours is not so obvious. The whole originality of pragmatism, the whole point in it, is its use of the concrete way of seeing. It begins with concreteness, and returns and ends with it. Dr. Schiller, with his two 'practical' aspects of truth, (1) relevancy to situation, and (2) subsequential utility, is only filling the cup of concreteness to the brim for us. Once seize that cup, and you cannot misunderstand pragmatism. It seems as if the power of imagining the world concretely *might* have been common enough to let our readers apprehend us better, as if they might have read between our lines, and, in spite of all our infelicities of expression, guessed a little more correctly what our thought was. But alas! this was not on fate's program, so we can only think, with the german ditty:

> "Es wär' zu schön gewesen,
> Es hat nicht sollen sein."

IX

The Meaning of the Word Truth[1]

My account of truth is realistic, and follows the epistemological dualism of common sense. Suppose I say to you "The thing exists"—is that true or not? How can you tell? Not till my statement has developed its meaning farther is it determined as being true, false, or irrelevant to reality altogether. But if now you ask "what thing?" and I reply "a desk"; if you ask "where?" and I point to a place; if you ask "does it exist materially, or only in imagination?" and I say "materially"; if moreover I say "I mean that desk," and then grasp and shake a desk which you see just as I have described it, you are willing to call my statement true. But you and I are commutable here; we can exchange places; and as you go bail for my desk, so I can go bail for yours.

This notion of a reality independent of either of us, taken from ordinary social experience, lies at the base of the pragmatist definition of truth. With some such reality any statement, in order to be counted true, must agree. Pragmatism defines 'agreeing' to mean certain ways of 'working,' be they actual or potential. Thus, for my statement "the desk exists" to be true of a desk recognized as

[1] Remarks at the meeting of the American Philosophical Association, Cornell University, December, 1907.

117

real by you, it must be able to lead me to shake your desk, to explain myself by words that suggest that desk to your mind, to make a drawing that is like the desk you see, etc. Only in such ways as this is there sense in saying it agrees with *that* reality, only thus does it gain for me the satisfaction of hearing you corroborate me. Reference then to something determinate, and some sort of adaptation to it worthy of the name of agreement, are thus constituent elements in the definition of any statement of mine as 'true.'

You cannot get at either the reference or the adaptation without using the notion of the workings. *That* the thing is, *what* it is, and *which* it is (of all the possible things with that what) are points determinable only by the pragmatic method. The 'which' means a possibility of pointing, or of otherwise singling out the special object; the 'what' means choice on our part of an essential aspect to conceive it by (and this is always relative to what Dewey calls our own 'situation'); and the 'that' means our assumption of the attitude of belief, the reality-recognizing attitude. Surely for understanding what the word 'true' means as applied to a statement, the mention of such workings is indispensable. Surely if we leave them out the subject and the object of the cognitive relation float—in the same universe, 'tis true—but vaguely and ignorantly and without mutual contact or mediation.

Our critics nevertheless call the workings inessential. No functional possibilities 'make' our beliefs true, they say; they are true inherently, true positively, born 'true' as the Count of Chambord was born 'Henri-Cinq.' Pragmatism insists, on the contrary, that statements and beliefs are thus inertly and statically true only by courtesy: they practically pass for true; but you *cannot define what you mean* by calling them true without referring to their functional possibilities. These give its whole *logical content* to that relation to reality on a belief's part to which the name 'truth' is applied, a relation which otherwise remains one of mere coexistence or bare withness.

The foregoing statements reproduce the essential content of the lecture on Truth in my book *Pragmatism*. Schiller's doctrine of 'humanism,' Dewey's *Studies in logical theory*, and my own 'radical empiricism,' all involve this general notion of truth as 'working,' either actual or conceivable. But they envelope it as only one detail in the midst of much wider theories that aim eventually at determining the notion of what 'reality' at large is in its ultimate nature and constitution.

X

The Existence of Julius Cæsar[1]

My account of truth is purely logical and relates to its definition only. I contend that you cannot tell what the *word* 'true' *means*, as applied to a statement, without invoking the *concept of the statement's workings*.

Assume, to fix our ideas, a universe composed of two things only: imperial Cæsar dead and turned to clay, and me, saying "Cæsar really existed." Most persons would naively deem truth to be thereby uttered, and say that by a sort of *actio in distans* my statement had taken direct hold of the other fact.

But have my words so certainly denoted *that* Cæsar?—or so certainly connoted *his* individual attributes? To fill out the complete measure of what the epithet 'true' may ideally mean, my thought ought to bear a fully determinate and unambiguous 'one-to-one-relation' to its own particular object. In the ultra-simple universe imagined the reference is uncertified. Were there two Cæsars we shouldn't know which was meant. The conditions of truth thus seem incomplete in this universe of discourse so that it must be enlarged.

Transcendentalists enlarge it by invoking an absolute mind

[1] Originally printed under the title of 'Truth versus Truthfulness,' in the *Journal of Philosophy*.

which, as it owns all the facts, can sovereignly correlate them. If it intends that my statement *shall* refer to that identical Cæsar and that the attributes I have in mind *shall* mean his attributes, that intention suffices to make the statement true.

I, in turn, enlarge the universe by admitting finite intermediaries between the two original facts. Cæsar *had*, and my statement *has*, effects; and if these effects in any way run together, a concrete medium and bottom is provided for the determinate cognitive relation, which, as a pure *actio in distans*, seemed to float too vaguely and unintelligibly.

The real Cæsar, for example, wrote a manuscript of which I see a real reprint and say "the Cæsar I mean is the author of *that*." The workings of my thought thus determine both its denotative and its connotative significance more fully. It now defines itself as neither irrelevant to the real Cæsar nor false in what it suggests of him. The absolute mind, seeing me thus working towards Cæsar through the cosmic intermediaries, might well say: "Such workings only specify in detail what I meant myself by the statement being true. I decree the cognitive relation between the two original facts to mean that just that kind of concrete chain of intermediaries exists or can exist."

But the chain involves facts prior to the statement the logical conditions of whose truth we are defining, and facts subsequent to it; and this circumstance, coupled with the vulgar employment of the terms truth and fact as synonyms, has laid my account open to misapprehension. "How," it is confusedly asked, "can Cæsar's existence, a truth already 2000 years old, depend for its truth on anything about to happen now? How can my acknowledgment of it be made true by the acknowledgment's own effects? The effects may indeed confirm my belief, but the belief was made true already by the fact that Cæsar really did exist."

Well, be it so, for if there were no Cæsar, there could, of course, be no positive truth about him—but then distinguish between 'true' as being positively and completely so established, and 'true' as being so only 'practically,' elliptically, and by courtesy, in the sense of not being positively irrelevant or *un*true. Remember also that Cæsar's having existed in fact may make a present statement false or irrelevant as well as it may make it true, and that in neither case does it itself have to alter. It being given, whether truth, untruth, or irrelevancy shall be also given depends on something coming from the statement itself. What pragmatism contends for is that you cannot adequately *define* the something if you leave the notion of the statement's functional workings out of your account. Truth meaning agreement with reality, the mode of the agreeing is a practical problem which the subjective term of the relation alone can solve.

NOTE. This paper was originally followed by a couple of paragraphs meant to conciliate the intellectualist opposition. Since you love the word 'true' so, and since you despise so the concrete working of our ideas, I said, keep the word 'truth' for the saltatory and incomprehensible relation you care so much for, and I will say of thoughts that know their objects in an intelligible sense that they are 'truthful.'

Like most offerings, this one has been spurned, so I revoke it, repenting of my generosity. Professor Pratt, in his recent book, calls any objective state of *facts* 'a truth,' and uses the word 'trueness' in the sense of 'truth' as proposed by me. Mr. Hawtrey (see below, page 281 [*ed.*, 150.15–29]) uses 'correctness' in the same sense. Apart from the general evil of ambiguous vocabularies, we may really forsake all hope, if the term 'truth' is officially to lose its status as a property of our beliefs and opinions, and become recognized as a technical synonym for 'fact.'

XI

The Absolute and the Strenuous Life[1]

Professor W. A. Brown, in the *Journal* for August 15, approves my pragmatism for allowing that a belief in the absolute may give holidays to the spirit, but takes me to task for the narrowness of this concession, and shows by striking examples how great a power the same belief may have in letting loose the strenuous life.

I have no criticism whatever to make upon his excellent article, but let me explain why 'moral holidays' were the only gift of the absolute which I picked out for emphasis. I was primarily concerned in my lectures with contrasting the belief that the world is still in process of making with the belief that there is an 'eternal' edition of it ready-made and complete. The former, or 'pluralistic' belief, was the one that my pragmatism favored. Both beliefs confirm our strenuous moods. Pluralism actually demands them, since it makes the world's salvation depend upon the energizing of its several parts, among which we are. Monism permits them, for however furious they may be, we can always justify ourselves in advance for indulging them by the thought that they *will have been* expressions of the absolute's perfect life. By escaping from your finite perceptions to the conception of the eternal whole, you

[1] Reprinted from the *Journal of Philosophy, etc.*, 1906.

can hallow any tendency whatever. Tho the absolute *dictates* nothing, it will *sanction* anything and everything after the fact, for whatever is once there will have to be regarded as an integral member of the universe's perfection. Quietism and frenzy thus alike receive the absolute's permit to exist. Those of us who are naturally inert may abide in our resigned passivity; those whose energy is excessive may grow more reckless still. History shows how easily both quietists and fanatics have drawn inspiration from the absolutistic scheme. It suits sick souls and strenuous ones equally well.

One cannot say thus of pluralism. Its world is always vulnerable, for some part may go astray; and having no 'eternal' edition of it to draw comfort from, its partisans must always feel to some degree insecure. If, as pluralists, we grant ourselves moral holidays, they can only be provisional breathing-spells, intended to refresh us for the morrow's fight. This forms one permanent inferiority of pluralism from the pragmatic point of view. It has no saving message for incurably sick souls. Absolutism, among its other messages, has that message, and is the only scheme that has it necessarily. That constitutes its chief superiority and is the source of its religious power. That is why, desiring to do it full justice, I valued its aptitude for moral-holiday giving so highly. Its claims in that way are unique, whereas its affinities with strenuousness are less emphatic than those of the pluralistic scheme.

In the last lecture of my book I candidly admitted this inferiority of pluralism. It lacks the wide indifference that absolutism shows. It is bound to disappoint many sick souls whom absolutism can console. It seems therefore poor tactics for absolutists to make little of this advantage. The needs of sick souls are surely the most urgent; and believers in the absolute should rather hold it to be great merit in their philosophy that it can meet them so well.

The pragmatism or pluralism which I defend has to fall back on a certain ultimate hardihood, a certain willingness to live without assurances or guarantees. To minds thus willing to live on possibilities that are not certainties, quietistic religion, sure of salvation *any how*, has a slight flavor of fatty degeneration about it which has caused it to be looked askance on, even in the church. Which side is right here, who can say? Within religion, emotion is apt to be tyrannical; but philosophy must favor the emotion that allies itself best with the whole body and drift of all the truths in sight. I conceive this to be the more strenuous type of emotion; but I have to admit that its inability to let loose quietistic raptures is a serious deficiency in the pluralistic philosophy which I profess.

XII

Professor Hébert on Pragmatism[1]

Professor Marcel Hébert is a singularly erudite and liberal thinker (a seceder, I believe, from the Catholic priesthood) and an uncommonly direct and clear writer. His book *Le Divin* is one of the ablest reviews of the general subject of religious philosophy which recent years have produced; and in the small volume the title of which is copied above he has, perhaps, taken more pains not to do injustice to pragmatism than any of its numerous critics. Yet the usual fatal misapprehension of its purposes vitiates his exposition and his critique. His pamphlet seems to me to form a worthy hook, as it were, on which to hang one more attempt to tell the reader what the pragmatist account of truth really means.

M. Hébert takes it to mean what most people take it to mean, the doctrine, namely, that whatever proves subjectively expedient in the way of our thinking is 'true' in the absolute and unrestricted sense of the word, whether it corresponds to any objective state of things outside of our thought or not. Assuming this to be the pragmatist thesis, M. Hébert opposes it at length. Thought that proves itself to be thus expedient may, indeed, have every

[1] Reprint from the *Journal of Philosophy* for December 3, 1908 (vol. v, p. 689), of a review of *Le Pragmatisme; étude de ses diverses formes anglo-américaines*, by Marcel Hébert. (Paris: Librairie critique Emile Nourry. 1908. Pp. 105.)

other kind of value for the thinker, he says, but cognitive value, representative value, *valeur de connaissance proprement dite*, it has not; and when it does have a high degree of general-utility value, this is in every case derived from its previous value in the way of correctly representing independent objects that have an important influence on our lives. Only by thus representing things truly do we reap the useful fruits. But the fruits follow on the truth, they do not constitute it; so M. Hébert accuses pragmatism of telling us everything about truth except what it essentially is. He admits, indeed, that the world is so framed that when men have true ideas of realities, consequential utilities ensue in abundance; and no one of our critics, I think, has shown as concrete a sense of the variety of these utilities as he has; but he reiterates that, whereas such utilities are secondary, we insist on treating them as primary, and that the *connaissance objective* from which they draw all their being is something which we neglect, exclude, and destroy. The utilitarian value and the strictly cognitive value of our ideas may perfectly well harmonize, he says— and in the main he allows that they do harmonize—but they are not logically identical for that. He admits that subjective interests, desires, impulses may even have the active 'primacy' in our intellectual life. Cognition awakens only at their spur, and follows their cues and aims; yet, when it *is* awakened, it is objective cognition proper and not merely another name for the impulsive tendencies themselves in the state of satisfaction. The owner of a picture ascribed to Corot gets uneasy when its authenticity is doubted. He looks up its origin and is reassured. But his uneasiness does not make the proposition false, any more than his relief makes the proposition true, that the actual Corot was the painter. Pragmatism, which, according to M. Hébert, claims that our sentiments *make* truth and falsehood, would oblige us to conclude that our minds exert no genuinely cognitive function whatever.

This subjectivist interpretation of our position seems to follow from my having happened to write (without supposing it necessary to explain that I was treating of cognition solely on its subjective side) that in the long run the true is the expedient in the way of our thinking, much as the good is the expedient in the way of our behavior! Having previously written that truth means 'agreement with reality,' and insisted that the chief part of the expediency of any one opinion is its agreement with the rest of acknowledged truth, I apprehended no exclusively subjectivistic reading of my meaning. My mind was so filled with the notion of objective reference that I never dreamed that my hearers would let go of it; and the very last accusation I expected was that in speaking of ideas and their satisfactions, I was denying realities outside. My only wonder now is that critics should have found so silly a personage as I must have seemed in their eyes, worthy of explicit refutation.

The object, for me, is just as much one part of reality as the idea is another part. The truth of the idea is one relation of it to the reality, just as its date and its place are other relations. All three relations *consist* of intervening parts of the universe which can in every particular case be assigned and catalogued, and which differ in every instance of truth, just as they differ with every date and place.

The pragmatist thesis, as Dr. Schiller and I hold it—I prefer to let Professor Dewey speak for himself—is that the relation called 'truth' is thus concretely *definable*. Ours is the only articulate attempt in the field to say positively what truth actually *consists of*. Our denouncers have literally nothing to oppose to it as an alternative. For them, when an idea is true, it *is* true, and there the matter terminates, the word 'true' being indefinable. The relation of the true idea to its object, being, as they think, unique, it can be expressed in terms of nothing else, and needs only to be named for anyone to recognize and understand it. Moreover it is invariable and universal, the same in every single instance of truth, however diverse the ideas, the realities, and the other relations between them may be.

Our pragmatist view, on the contrary, is that the truth-relation is a definitely experienceable relation, and therefore describable as well as namable; that it is not unique in kind, and neither invariable nor universal. The relation to its object that makes an idea true in any given instance, is, we say, embodied in intermediate details of reality which lead towards the object, which vary in every instance, and which in every instance can be concretely traced. The chain of workings which an opinion sets up *is* the opinion's truth, falsehood, or irrelevancy, as the case may be. Every idea that a man has works some consequences in him, in the shape either of bodily actions or of other ideas. Through these consequences the man's relations to surrounding realities are modified. He is carried nearer to some of them and farther from others, and gets now the feeling that the idea has worked satisfactorily, now that it has not. The idea has put him into touch with something that fulfils its intent, or it has not.

This something is the *man's object*, primarily. Since the only realities we can talk about are such *objects-believed-in*, the pragmatist, whenever he says 'reality,' means in the first instance what may count for the man himself as a reality, what he believes at the moment to be such. Sometimes the reality is a concrete sensible presence. The idea, for example, may be that a certain door opens into a room where a glass of beer may be bought. If opening the door leads to the actual sight and taste of the beer, the man calls the idea true. Or his idea may be that of an abstract relation, say of that between the sides and the hypothenuse of a triangle, such a relation being, of course, a reality quite as much as a glass of beer is. If the thought of such a relation leads him to draw auxiliary lines and to compare the figures they make, he may at last, perceiving one equality after another, *see* the relation thought of, by a vision quite as particular and direct as was the taste of the beer. If he does so, he calls *that* idea, also, true. His idea has, in each case, brought him into closer touch with a reality felt at the moment to verify just that idea. Each reality verifies and validates its own idea exclusively; and in each case the verification consists in the satisfactorily-ending consequences, mental or physical, which the idea was able to set up. These 'workings' differ in every single instance, they never transcend experience, they consist of particulars, mental or sensible, and they admit of concrete description in every individual case. Pragmatists are unable to see what you can possibly *mean* by calling an idea true, unless you mean that between it as a *terminus a quo* in someone's mind and some particular reality as a *terminus ad quem*, such concrete workings do or may intervene. Their direction constitutes the idea's reference to that reality, their satisfactoriness constitutes its adaptation thereto, and the two things together constitute the 'truth' of the idea for its possessor. Without such intermediating portions of concretely real experience the pragmatist sees no materials out of which the adaptive relation called truth can be built up.

The anti-pragmatist view is that the workings are but evidences of the truth's previous inherent presence in the idea, and that you can wipe the very possibility of them out of existence and still leave the truth of the idea as solid as ever. But surely this is not a counter-theory of truth to ours. It is the renunciation of all articulate theory. It is but a claim to the right to call certain ideas true anyhow; and this is what I meant above by saying that the anti-pragmatists offer us no real alternative, and that our account is literally the only positive theory extant. What meaning, indeed, can an idea's truth have save its power of adapting us either mentally or physically to a reality?

How comes it, then, that our critics so uniformly accuse us of subjectivism, of denying the reality's existence? It comes, I think, from the necessary predominance of subjective language in our analysis. However independent and ejective realities may be, we can talk about them, in framing our accounts of truth, only as so many objects believed-in. But the process of experience leads men so continually to supersede their older objects by newer ones which they find it more satisfactory to believe in, that the notion of an *absolute* reality inevitably arises as a *grenzbegriff*, equivalent to that of an object that shall never be superseded, and belief in which shall be *endgültig*. Cognitively we thus live under a sort of rule of three: as our private concepts represent the sense-objects to which they lead us, these being public realities independent of the individual, so these sense-realities may, in turn, represent realities of a hypersensible order, electrons, mind-stuff, God, or what not, existing independently of all human thinkers. The notion of such final realities, knowledge of which would be absolute truth, is an outgrowth of our cognitive experience from which neither pragmatists nor anti-pragmatists escape. They form an inevitable regulative postulate in everyone's thinking. Our notion of them is the most abundantly suggested and satisfied of all our beliefs, the last to suffer doubt. The difference is that our critics use this belief as their sole paradigm, and treat anyone who talks of human realities as if he thought the notion of reality 'in itself' illegitimate. Meanwhile, reality-in-itself, so far as by them *talked of*, is only a human object; they postulate it just as we postulate it; and if we are subjectivists they are so no less. Realities in themselves can be there *for* anyone, whether pragmatist or anti-pragmatist, only by being believed; they are believed only by their notions appearing true; and their notions appear true only because they work satisfactorily. Satisfactorily, moreover, for the particular thinker's purpose. There is no idea which is *the* true idea, of anything. Whose is *the* true idea of the absolute? Or to take M. Hébert's example, what is *the* true idea of a picture which you possess? It is the idea that most satisfactorily meets your present interest. The interest may be in the picture's place, its age, its 'tone,' its subject, its dimensions, its authorship, its price, its merit, or what not. If its authorship by Corot have been doubted, what will satisfy the interest aroused in you at that moment will be to have your claim to own a Corot confirmed; but, if you have a normal human mind, merely calling it a Corot will not satisfy other demands of your mind at the same time. For *them* to be satisfied, what you learn of the picture must make smooth connexion with what you know of the rest of the system of reality in which the actual Corot played his part. M. Hébert accuses us of holding that the proprietary satisfactions of themselves suffice to make the belief true, and that, so far as we are concerned, no actual Corot need ever have existed. Why we should be thus cut off from the more general and intellectual satisfactions, I know not; but whatever the satisfactions may be, intellectual or proprietary, they belong to the subjective side of the truth-relation. They found our beliefs; our beliefs are in realities; if no realities are there, the beliefs are false; but if realities are there, how they can ever be *known* without first being *believed*; or how *believed* except by our first having ideas of them that work satisfactorily, pragmatists find it impossible to imagine. They also find it impossible to imagine what makes the anti-pragmatists' dogmatic 'ipse dixit' assurance of reality more credible than the pragmatists' conviction based on concrete verifications. M. Hébert will probably agree to this, when put in this way, so I do not see our inferiority to him in the matter of *connaissance proprement dite.*

Some readers will say that, altho *I* may possibly believe in realities beyond our ideas, Dr. Schiller, at any rate, does not. This is a great misunderstanding, for Schiller's doctrine and mine are identical, only our expositions follow different directions. He starts from the subjective pole of the chain, the individual with his beliefs, as the more concrete and immediately given phenomenon. "An individual claims his belief to be true," Schiller says, "but what does he mean by true? and how does he establish the claim?" With these questions we embark on a psychological inquiry. To be true, it appears, means, *for that individual*, to work satisfactorily for him; and the working and the satisfaction, since they vary from case to case, admit of no universal description. What works is true and represents a reality, for the individual for whom it works. If he is infallible, the reality is 'really' there; if mistaken it is not there, or not there as he thinks it. We all believe, when our ideas work satisfactorily; but we don't yet know who of us is infallible; so that the problem of truth and that of error are *ebenbürtig* and arise out of the same situations. Schiller, remaining with the fallible individual, and treating only of reality-for-him, seems to many of his readers to ignore reality-in-itself altogether. But that is because he seeks only to tell us how truths are attained, not what the content of those truths, when attained, shall be. It may be that the truest of all beliefs shall be that in trans-subjective realities. It certainly *seems* the truest, for no rival belief is as voluminously satisfactory, and it is probably Dr. Schiller's own belief; but he is not required, for his immediate purpose, to profess it. Still less is he obliged to assume it in advance as the basis of his discussion.

I, however, warned by the ways of critics, adopt different tactics. I start from the object-pole of the idea-reality chain and follow it in the opposite direction from Schiller's. Anticipating the results of the general truth-processes of mankind, I begin with the abstract notion of an objective reality. I postulate it, and ask on my own account, *I vouching for this reality*, what would make anyone else's idea of it true for me as well as for him. But I find no different answer from that which Schiller gives. If the other man's idea leads him, not only to believe that the reality is there, but to use it as the reality's temporary substitute, by letting it evoke adaptive thoughts and acts similar to those which the reality itself would provoke, then it is true in the only intelligible sense, true through its particular consequences, and true for me as well as for the man.

My account is more of a logical definition; Schiller's is more of a psychological description. Both treat an absolutely identical matter of experience, only they traverse it in opposite ways.

Possibly these explanations may satisfy M. Hébert, whose little book, apart from the false accusation of subjectivism, gives a fairly instructive account of the pragmatist epistemology.

XIII

Abstractionism and 'Relativismus'

Abstract concepts, such as elasticity, voluminousness, disconnected-ness, are salient aspects of our concrete experiences which we find it useful to single out. Useful, because we are then reminded of other things that offer those same aspects; and, if the aspects carry consequences in those other things, we can return to our first things, expecting those same consequences to accrue.

To be helped to anticipate consequences is always a gain, and such being the help that abstract concepts give us, it is obvious that their use is fulfilled only when we get back again into concrete particulars by their means, bearing the consequences in our minds, and enriching our notion of the original objects therewithal.

Without abstract concepts to handle our perceptual particulars by, we are like men hopping on one foot. Using concepts along with the particulars, we become bipedal. We throw our concept forward, get a foothold on the consequence, hitch our line to this, and draw our percept up, traveling thus with a hop, skip and jump over the surface of life at a vastly rapider rate than if we merely waded through the thickness of the particulars as accident rained them down upon our heads. Animals have to do this, but men raise their heads higher and breathe freely in the upper conceptual air.

The enormous esteem professed by all philosophers for the conceptual form of consciousness is easy to understand. From Plato's time downwards it has been held to be our sole avenue to essential truth. Concepts are universal, changeless, pure; their relations are eternal; they are spiritual, while the concrete particulars which they enable us to handle are corrupted by the flesh. They are precious in themselves, then, apart from their original use, and confer new dignity upon our life.

One can find no fault with this way of feeling about concepts so long as their original function does not get swallowed up in the admiration and lost. That function is of course to enlarge mentally our momentary experiences by *adding* to them the consequences conceived; but unfortunately, that function is not only too often forgotten by philosophers in their reasonings, but is often converted into its exact opposite, and made a means of diminishing the original experience by *denying* (implicitly or explicitly) all its features save the one specially abstracted to conceive it by.

This itself is a highly abstract way of stating my complaint, and it needs to be redeemed from obscurity by showing instances of what is meant. Some beliefs very dear to my own heart have been conceived in this viciously abstract way by critics. One is the 'will to believe,' so called; another is the indeterminism of certain futures; a third is the notion that truth may vary with the standpoint of the man who holds it. I believe that the perverse abuse of the abstracting function has led critics to employ false arguments against these doctrines, and often has led their readers too to false conclusions. I should like to try to save the situation, if possible, by a few counter-critical remarks.

Let me give the name of 'vicious abstractionism' to a way of using concepts which may be thus described: We conceive a concrete situation by singling out some salient or important feature in it, and classing it under that; then, instead of adding to its previous characters all the positive consequences which the new way of conceiving it may bring, we proceed to use our concept privatively; reducing the originally rich phenomenon to the naked suggestions of that name abstractly taken, treating it as a case of 'nothing but' that concept, and acting as if all the other characters from out of which the concept is abstracted were expunged.[1] Abstraction, functioning in this way, becomes a means of arrest far more than a means of advance in thought. It mutilates things; it creates difficulties and finds impossibilities; and more than half the trouble that metaphysicians and logicians give themselves over the paradoxes and dialectic puzzles of the universe may, I am convinced, be traced to this relatively simple source. *The viciously privative employment of abstract characters and class names* is, I am persuaded, one of the great original sins of the rationalistic mind.

To proceed immediately to concrete examples, cast a glance at the belief in 'free will,' demolished with such specious persuasiveness recently by the skilful hand of Professor Fullerton.[2] When a common man says that his will is free, what does he mean? He means that there are situations of bifurcation inside of his life in which two futures seem to him equally possible, for both have their roots equally planted in his present and his past. Either, if realized, will grow out of his previous motives, character and circumstances, and will continue uninterruptedly the pulsations of his personal life. But sometimes both at once are incompatible with physical nature, and then it seems to the naive observer as if he made a choice between them *now*, and that the question of which future is to be, instead of having been decided at the foundation of the world, were decided afresh at every passing moment in which fact seems livingly to grow, and possibility seems, in turning itself towards one act, to exclude all others.

He who takes things at their face-value here may indeed be deceived. He may far too often mistake his private ignorance of what is predetermined for a real indetermination of what is to be. Yet, however imaginary it may be, his picture of the situation offers no appearance of breach between the past and future. A train is the same train, its passengers are the same passengers, its momentum is the same momentum, no matter which way the

---

[1] Let not the reader confound the fallacy here described with legitimately negative inferences such as those drawn in the mood 'celarent' of the logic-books.

[2] *Popular Science Monthly*, N.Y., vols. lviii and lix.

switch which fixes its direction is placed. For the indeterminist there is at all times enough past for all the different futures in sight, and more besides, to find their reasons in it, and whichever future comes will slide out of that past as easily as the train slides by the switch. The world, in short, is just as *continuous with itself* for the believers in free will as for the rigorous determinists, only the latter are unable to believe in points of bifurcation as spots of really indifferent equilibrium or as containing shunts which there—and there only, *not before*—direct existing motions without altering their amount.

Were there such spots of indifference, the rigorous determinists think, the future and the past would be separated absolutely, for, *abstractly taken, the word 'indifferent' suggests disconnexion solely.* Whatever is indifferent is in so far forth unrelated and detached. Take the term thus strictly, and you see, they tell us, that if any spot of indifference is found upon the broad highway between the past and the future, then *no* connexion of any sort whatever, no continuous momentum, no identical passenger, no common aim or agent, can be found on both sides of the shunt or switch which there is moved. The place is an impassable chasm.

Mr. Fullerton writes—the italics are mine—as follows:

"In so far as my action is 'free,' what I have been, what I am, what I have always done or striven to do, what I most earnestly wish or resolve to do at the present moment—these things can have *no more to do with its future realization than if they had no existence. . . .* The possibility is a hideous one; and surely even the most ardent 'free-willist' will, when he contemplates it frankly, excuse me for hoping that, if I am 'free,' I am at least not very 'free,' and that I may reasonably expect to find *some* degree of consistency in my life and actions. . . . Suppose that I have given a dollar to a blind beggar. Can *I*, if it is really an act of 'free-will,' be properly said to have given the money? Was it given because I was a man of tender heart, etc., etc.? . . . What has all this to do with acts of 'free-will'? If they are 'free,' they must not be conditioned by antecedent circumstances of *any* sort, by the misery of the beggar, by the pity in the heart of the passer-by. They must be causeless, not determined. They must drop from a clear sky out of the void, for just in so far as they can be accounted for they are not 'free.'"[3]

Heaven forbid that I should get entangled here in a controversy about the rights and wrongs of the free-will question at large, for I am only trying to illustrate vicious abstractionism by the conduct of some of the doctrine's assailants. The moments of bifurcation, as the indeterminist seems to himself to experience them, are moments both of re-direction and of continuation. But because in the 'either—or' of the re-direction we hesitate, the determinist abstracts this little element of discontinuity from the superabundant continuities of the experience, and cancels in its behalf all the connective characters with which the latter is filled. Choice, for him, means henceforward *dis*connexion pure and simple, something undetermined in advance *in any respect whatever,* and a life of choices must be a raving chaos, at no two moments of which could we be treated as one and the same man. If Nero were 'free' at the moment of ordering his mother's murder, Mr. McTaggart[4] assures us that no one would have the right at any other moment to call him a bad man, for he would then be an absolutely other Nero.

A polemic author ought not merely to destroy his victim. He ought to try a bit to make him feel his error—perhaps not enough to convert him, but enough to give him a bad conscience and to weaken the energy of his defence. These violent caricatures of men's beliefs arouse only contempt for the incapacity of their authors to see the situations out of which the problems grow. To treat the negative character of one abstracted element as annulling all the positive features with which it coexists, is no way to change any actual indeterminist's way of looking on the matter, tho it may make the gallery applaud.

Turn now to some criticisms of the 'will to believe,' as another example of the vicious way in which abstraction is currently employed. The right to believe in things for the truth of which

[3] *Loc. cit.,* vol. lviii, pp. 189, 188.
[4] *Some Dogmas of Religion,* p. 179.

complete objective proof is yet lacking is defended by those who apprehend certain human situations in their concreteness. In those situations the mind has alternatives before it so vast that the full evidence for either branch is missing, and yet so significant that simply to wait for proof, and to doubt while waiting, might often in practical respects be the same thing as weighing down the negative side. Is life worth while at all? Is there any general meaning in all this cosmic weather? Is anything being permanently bought by all this suffering? Is there perhaps a transmundane experience in Being, something corresponding to a 'fourth dimension,' which, if we had access to it, might patch up some of this world's *zerrissenheit* and make things look more rational than they at first appear? Is there a superhuman consciousness of which our minds are parts, and from which inspiration and help may come? Such are the questions in which the right to take sides practically for yes or no is affirmed by some of us, while others hold that this is methodologically inadmissible, and summon us to die professing ignorance and proclaiming the duty of everyone to refuse to believe.

I say nothing of the personal inconsistency of some of these critics, whose printed works furnish exquisite illustrations of the will to believe, in spite of their denunciations of it as a phrase and as a recommended thing. Mr. McTaggart, whom I will once more take as an example, is sure that "reality is rational and righteous" and "destined *sub specie temporis* to become perfectly good"; and his calling this belief a result of necessary logic has surely never deceived any reader as to its real genesis in the gifted author's mind. Mankind is made on too uniform a pattern for any of us to escape successfully from acts of faith. We have a lively vision of what a certain view of the universe would mean for us. We kindle or we shudder at the thought, and our feeling runs through our whole logical nature and animates its workings. It *can't* be that, we feel; it *must* be this. It must be what it *ought* to be, and it *ought* to be this; and then we seek for every reason, good or bad, to make this which so deeply ought to be, seem objectively the probable thing. We show the arguments against it to be insufficient, so that it *may* be true; we represent its appeal to be to our whole nature's loyalty and not to any emaciated faculty of syllogistic proof. We reinforce it by remembering the enlargement of our world by music, by thinking of the promises of sunsets and the impulses from vernal woods. And the essence of the whole experience, when the individual swept through it says finally "I believe," is the intense concreteness of his vision, the individuality of the hypothesis before him, and the complexity of the various concrete motives and perceptions that issue in his final state.

But see now how the abstractionist treats this rich and intricate vision that a certain state of things must be true. He accuses the believer of reasoning by the following syllogism:

All good desires must be fulfilled;

The desire to believe this proposition is a good desire;

Ergo, this proposition must be believed.

He substitutes this abstraction for the concrete state of mind of the believer, pins the naked absurdity of it upon him, and easily proves that anyone who defends him must be the greatest fool on earth. As if any real believer ever thought in this preposterous way, or as if any defender of the legitimacy of men's concrete ways of concluding ever used the abstract and general premise "All desires must be fulfilled"! Nevertheless Mr. McTaggart solemnly and laboriously refutes the syllogism in sections 47 to 57 of the above-cited book. He shows that there is no fixed link in the dictionary between the abstract concepts 'desire,' 'goodness' and 'reality'; and he ignores all the links which in the single concrete case the believer feels and perceives to be there! He adds:

"When the reality of a thing is uncertain, the argument encourages us to suppose that our approval of a thing can determine its reality. And when this unhallowed link has once been established, retribution overtakes us. For when the reality is independently certain, we [then] have to admit that the reality of a thing should determine our approval of that thing. I find it difficult to imagine a more degraded position."

One here feels tempted to quote ironically Hegel's famous equation of the real with the rational to his english disciple, who ends his chapter with the heroic words:

"For those who do not pray, there remains the resolve that, so far as their strength may prevail, neither the pains of death nor the pains of life shall drive them to any comfort in that which they hold to be false, or drive them from any comfort [discomfort?] in that which they hold to be true."

How can so ingenious-minded a writer fail to see how far over the heads of the enemy all his arrows pass? When Mr. McTaggart himself believes that the universe is run by the dialectic energy of the absolute idea, his insistent desire to have a world of that sort is felt by him to be no chance example of desire in general, but an altogether peculiar *insight-giving passion* to which, in this if in no other instance, he would be *stupid* not to yield. He obeys its concrete singularity, not the bare abstract feature in it of being a 'desire.' His situation is as particular as that of an actress who resolves that it is best for her to marry and leave the stage, of a priest who becomes secular, of a politician who abandons public life. What sensible man would seek to refute the concrete decisions of such persons by tracing them to abstract premises, such as that 'all actresses must marry,' 'all clergymen must be laymen,' 'all politicians should resign their posts'? Yet this type of refutation, absolutely unavailing tho it be for purposes of conversion, is spread by Mr. McTaggart through many pages of his book. For the aboundingness of our real reasons he substitutes one narrow point. For men's real probabilities he gives a skeletonized abstraction which no man was ever tempted to believe.

The abstraction in my next example is less simple, but is quite as flimsy as a weapon of attack. Empiricists think that truth in general is distilled from single men's beliefs; and the so-called pragmatists 'go them one better' by trying to define what it consists in when it comes. It consists, I have elsewhere said, in such a working on the part of the beliefs as may bring the man into satisfactory relations with objects to which these latter point. The working is of course a concrete working in the actual experience of human beings, among their ideas, feelings, perceptions, beliefs and acts, as well as among the physical things of their environment, and the relations must be understood as being possible as well as actual. In the chapter on truth of my book *Pragmatism* I have taken pains to defend energetically this view. Strange indeed have been the misconceptions of it by its enemies, and many have these latter been. Among the most formidable-sounding onslaughts on the attempt to introduce some concreteness into our notion of what the truth of an idea may mean, is one that has been raised in many quarters to the effect that to make truth grow in any way out of human opinion is but to reproduce that protagorean doctrine that the individual man is 'the measure of all things,' which Plato in his immortal dialogue, the Theætetus, is unanimously said to have laid away so comfortably in its grave two thousand years ago. The two cleverest brandishers of this objection to make truth concrete, Professors Rickert and Münsterberg, write in German,[5] and 'relativismus' is the name they give to the heresy which they endeavor to uproot.

The first step in their campaign against 'relativismus' is entirely in the air. They accuse relativists—and we pragmatists are typical relativists—of being debarred by their self-adopted principles, not only from the privilege which rationalist philosophers enjoy, of believing that these principles of their own are truth impersonal and absolute, but even of framing the abstract notion of such a truth, *in the pragmatic sense, of an ideal opinion in which all men might agree, and which no man should ever wish to change.* Both charges fall wide of their mark. I myself, as a pragmatist, believe in my own account of truth as firmly as any rationalist can possibly believe in his. And I believe in it for the very reason that I *have* the idea of truth which my learned adversaries contend that no pragmatist can frame. I expect, namely, that the more fully men discuss and test my account, the more they will agree that it *fits*, and the less will they desire a change. I may of course be premature in this confidence, and the glory of being truth final and absolute may fall upon some later revision and correction of my scheme, which latter will then be judged untrue in just the measure in which it departs from that finally satisfactory formulation. To admit, as we pragmatists do, that we are liable to correction (even tho we may not expect it) *involves* the use on our part of an ideal standard. Rationalists themselves are, as individuals, sometimes sceptical enough to admit the abstract possibility of their own present opinions being corrigible and revisable to some degree, so the fact that the mere *notion* of an absolute standard should seem

[5] Münsterberg's book has just appeared in an english version: *The Eternal Values*, Boston, 1909.

to them so important a thing to claim for themselves and to deny to us is not easy to explain. If, along with the notion of the standard, they could also claim its exclusive warrant for their own fulminations now, it would be important to them indeed. But absolutists like Rickert freely admit the sterility of the notion, even in their own hands. Truth is what we *ought* to believe, they say, even tho no man ever did or shall believe it, and even tho we have no way of getting at it save by the usual empirical processes of testing our opinions by one another and by facts. Pragmatically, then, this part of the dispute is idle. No relativist who ever actually walked the earth[6] has denied the regulative character in his own thinking of the notion of absolute truth. What is challenged by relativists is the pretence on anyone's part to have found for certain at any given moment what the shape of that truth is. Since the better absolutists agree in this, admitting that the proposition 'There *is* absolute truth' is the only absolute truth of which we can be sure,[7] further debate is practically unimportant, so we may pass to their next charge.

It is in this charge that the vicious abstractionism becomes most apparent. The anti-pragmatist, in postulating absolute truth, refuses to give any account of what the words may mean. For him they form a self-explanatory term. The pragmatist, on the contrary, articulately defines their meaning. Truth absolute, he says, means an ideal set of formulations towards which all opinions may in the long run of experience be expected to converge. In this definition of absolute truth he not only postulates that there is a tendency to

---

[6] Of course the bugaboo creature called 'the sceptic' in the logic-books, who dogmatically makes the statement that no statement, not even the one he now makes, is true, is a mere mechanical toy-target for the rationalist shooting-gallery—hit him and he turns a summersault—yet he is the only sort of relativist whom my colleagues appear able to imagine to exist.

[7] Compare Rickert's *Gegenstand der Erkenntnis*, pp. 137, 138. Münsterberg's version of this first truth is that "Es gibt eine Welt"—see his *Philosophie der Werte*, pp. 38 and 74. And, after all, both these philosophers confess in the end that the primal truth of which they consider our supposed denial so irrational is not properly an insight at all, but a dogma adopted by the will which anyone who turns his back on duty may disregard! But if it all reverts to 'the will to believe,' pragmatists have that privilege as well as their critics.

such convergence of opinions, to such ultimate consensus, but he postulates the other factors of his definition equally, borrowing them by anticipation from the true conclusions expected to be reached. He postulates the existence of opinions, he postulates the experience that will sift them, and the consistency which that experience will show. He justifies himself in these assumptions by saying that they are not postulates in the strict sense but simple inductions from the past extended to the future by analogy; and he insists that human opinion has already reached a pretty stable equilibrium regarding them, and that if its future development fails to alter them, the definition itself, with all its terms included, will be part of the very absolute truth which it defines. The hypothesis will, in short, have worked successfully all round the circle and proved self-corroborative, and the circle will be closed.

The anti-pragmatist, however, immediately falls foul of the word 'opinion' here, abstracts it from the universe of life, and uses it as a bare dictionary-substantive, to deny the rest of the assumptions which it coexists withal. The dictionary says that an opinion is "what some one thinks or believes." This definition leaves everyone's opinion free to be autogenous, or unrelated either to what anyone else may think or to what the truth may be. Therefore, continue our abstractionists, we must conceive it *as essentially thus unrelated,* so that even were a billion men to sport the same opinion, and only one man to differ, we could admit no collateral circumstances which might presumptively make it more probable that he, not they, should be wrong. Truth, they say, follows not the counting of noses, nor is it only another name for a majority vote. It is a relation, that antedates experience, between our opinions and an independent something which the pragmatist account ignores, a relation which, tho the opinions of individuals should to all eternity deny it, would still remain to qualify them as false. To talk of opinions without referring to this independent something, the anti-pragmatist assures us, is to play Hamlet with Hamlet's part left out.

But when the pragmatist speaks of opinions, does he mean any such insulated and unmotived abstractions as are here supposed? Of course not, he means men's opinions in the flesh, as they have really formed themselves, opinions surrounded by their grounds and the influences they obey and exert, and along with the whole environment of social communication of which they are a part and out of which they take their rise. Moreover the 'experience' which the pragmatic definition postulates *is* the independent something which the anti-pragmatist accuses him of ignoring. Already have men grown unanimous in the opinion that such experience is 'of' an independent reality, the existence of which all opinions must acknowledge, in order to be true. Already do they agree that in the long run it is useless to resist experience's pressure; that the more of it a man has, the better position he stands in, in respect of truth; that some men, having had more experience, are therefore better authorities than others; that some are also wiser by nature and better able to interpret the experience they have had; that it is one part of such wisdom to compare notes, discuss, and follow the opinion of our betters; and that the more systematically and thoroughly such comparison and weighing of opinions is pursued, the truer the opinions that survive are likely to be. *When the pragmatist talks of opinions, it is opinions as they thus concretely and livingly and interactingly and correlatively exist that he has in mind*; and when the anti-pragmatist tries to floor him because the word 'opinion' can also be taken abstractly and as if it had no environment, he simply ignores the soil out of which the whole discussion grows. His weapons cut the air and strike no blow. No one gets wounded in the war against caricatures of belief and skeletons of opinion of which the german onslaughts upon 'relativismus' consist. Refuse to use the word 'opinion' abstractly, keep it in its real environment, and the withers of pragmatism remain unwrung.

That men do exist who are 'opinionated,' in the sense that their opinions are self-willed, is unfortunately a fact that must be admitted, no matter what one's notion of truth in general may be. But that this fact should make it impossible for truth to form itself authentically out of the life of opinion is what no critic has yet proved. Truth may well consist of certain opinions, and does indeed consist of nothing but opinions, tho not every opinion need be true. No pragmatist needs to *dogmatize* about the consensus of opinion in the future being right—he need only *postulate* that it will probably contain more of truth than anyone's opinion now.

XIV

Two English Critics

Mr. Bertrand Russell's article, entitled 'Transatlantic Truth,'[1] has all the clearness, dialectic subtlety, and wit which one expects from his pen, but it entirely fails to hit the right point of view for apprehending our position. When, for instance, we say that a true proposition is one the consequences of believing which are good, he assumes us to mean that anyone who believes a proposition to be true must first have made out clearly that its consequences *are* good, and that his belief must primarily be in that fact—an obvious absurdity, for that fact is the deliverance of a new proposition, quite different from the first one and is, moreover, a fact usually very hard to verify, it being "far easier," as Mr. Russell justly says, "to settle the plain question of fact: 'Have Popes always been infallible?' than to settle the question whether the effects of thinking them infallible are on the whole good."

We affirm nothing as silly as Mr. Russell supposes. Good consequences are not proposed by us merely as a sure sign, mark, or criterion, by which truth's presence is habitually ascertained, tho they may indeed serve on occasion as such a sign; they are proposed rather as the lurking *motive* inside of every truth-claim, whether

---

[1] In the *Albany Review* for January, 1908.

the 'trower' be conscious of such motive, or whether he obey it blindly. They are proposed as the *causa existendi* of our beliefs, not as their logical cue or premise, and still less as their objective deliverance or content. They assign the only intelligible practical *meaning* to that difference in our beliefs which our habit of calling them true or false comports.

No truth-claimer except the pragmatist himself need ever be aware of the part played in his own mind by consequences, and he himself is aware of it only abstractly and in general, and may at any moment be quite oblivious of it with respect to his own beliefs.

Mr. Russell next joins the army of those who inform their readers that according to the pragmatist definition of the word 'truth' the belief that A exists may be 'true,' even when A does *not* exist. This is the usual slander, repeated to satiety by our critics. They forget that in any concrete account of what is denoted by 'truth' in human life, the word can only be used relatively to some particular trower. Thus, I may hold it true that Shakespere wrote the plays that bear his name, and may express my opinion to a critic. If the critic be both a pragmatist and a baconian, he will in his capacity of pragmatist see plainly that the workings of my opinion, I being what I am, make it perfectly true for me, while in his capacity of baconian he still believes that Shakespere never wrote the plays in question. But most anti-pragmatist critics take the word 'truth' as something absolute, and easily play on their reader's readiness to treat his own truths as the absolute ones. If the reader whom they address believes that A does not exist, while we pragmatists show that those for whom the belief that it exists works satisfactorily will always call it true, he easily sneers at the naiveté of our contention, for is not then the belief in question 'true,' tho what it declares as fact has, as the reader so well knows, no existence? Mr. Russell speaks of our statement as an "attempt to get rid of 'fact' " and naturally enough considers it "a failure" (p. 410). "The old notion of truth reappears," he adds—that notion being, of course, that when a belief is true, its object does exist.

It is, of course, *bound* to exist, on sound pragmatic principles.

Concepts signify consequences. How is the world made different for me by my conceiving an opinion of mine under the concept 'true'? First, an object must be findable there (or sure signs of such an object must be found) which shall agree with the opinion. Second, such an opinion must not be contradicted by anything else of which I am aware. But in spite of the obvious pragmatist requirement that when I have said truly that something exists, it *shall* exist, the slander which Mr. Russell repeats has gained the widest currency.

Mr. Russell himself is far too witty and athletic a ratiocinator simply to repeat the slander dogmatically. Being nothing if not mathematical and logical, he must prove the accusation *secundum artem,* and convict us not so much of error as of absurdity. I have sincerely tried to follow the windings of his mind in this procedure, but for the life of me I can only see in it another example of what I have called (above, p. 249 [*ed.,* 135.29–30]) vicious abstractionism. The abstract world of mathematics and pure logic is so native to Mr. Russell that he thinks that we describers of the functions of concrete fact must also mean fixed mathematical terms and functions. A mathematical term, as a, b, c, x, y, sin., log., is self-sufficient, and terms of this sort, once equated, can be substituted for one another in endless series without error. Mr. Russell, and also Mr. Hawtrey, of whom I shall speak presently, seem to think that in our mouth also such terms as 'meaning,' 'truth,' 'belief,' 'object,' 'definition,' are self-sufficients with no context of varying relation that might be further asked about. What a word means is expressed by its definition, isn't it? The definition claims to be exact and adequate, doesn't it? Then it can be substituted for the word—since the two are identical—can't it? Then two words with the same definition can be substituted for one another, *n'est-ce pas?* Likewise two definitions of the same word, *nicht wahr,* etc., etc., till it will be indeed strange if you can't convict someone of self-contradiction and absurdity.

The particular application of this rigoristic treatment to my own little account of truth as working seems to be something like what follows. I say 'working' is what the 'truth' of our ideas means, and call it a definition. But since meanings and things meant, definitions and things defined, are equivalent and interchangeable, and nothing extraneous to its definition can be meant when a term is used, it follows that whoso calls an idea true, and means by that word that it works, cannot mean anything else, can believe nothing but that it does work, and in particular can neither imply nor allow anything about its object or deliverance. "According to the pragmatists," Mr. Russell writes, "to say 'it is true that other people exist' *means* 'it is useful to believe that other people exist.' But if so, then these two phrases are merely different words for the same proposition; therefore when I believe the one, I believe the other" (p. 400). [Logic, I may say in passing, would seem to require Mr. Russell to believe them both at once, but he ignores this consequence, and considers that 'other people exist' and 'it is useful to believe that they do *even if they don't*,' must be identical and therefore substitutable propositions in the pragmatist mouth.]

But may not real terms, I now ask, have accidents not expressed in their definitions? and when a real value is finally substituted for the result of an algebraic series of substituted definitions, do not all these accidents creep back? Beliefs have their objective 'content' or 'deliverance' as well as their truth, and truth has its implications as well as its workings. If anyone believe that other men exist it is both a content of his belief and an implication of its truth, that they should exist in fact. Mr. Russell's logic would seem to exclude, 'by definition,' all such accidents as contents, implications, and associates, and would represent us as translating all belief into a sort of belief in pragmatism itself—of all things! If I say that a speech is eloquent, and explain 'eloquent' as meaning the power to work in certain ways upon the audience; or if I say a book is original, and define 'original' to mean differing from other books, Mr. Russell's logic, if I follow it at all, would seem to doom me to agreeing that the speech is about eloquence, and the book about other books. When I call a belief true, and define its truth to mean its workings, I certainly do not mean that the belief is a belief *about* the workings. It is a belief about the object, and I who talk about the workings am a different subject, with a different universe of discourse, from that of the believer of whose concrete thinking I profess to give an account.

The social proposition 'other men exist' and the pragmatist proposition 'it is expedient to believe that other men exist' come from different universes of discourse. One can believe the second without being logically compelled to believe the first; one can believe the first without having ever heard of the second; or one can believe them both. The first expresses the object of a belief, the second tells of one condition of the belief's power to maintain itself. There is no identity of any kind, save the term 'other men' which they contain in common, in the two propositions; and to treat them as mutually substitutable, or to insist that *we* shall do so, is to give up dealing with realities altogether.

Mr. Ralph Hawtrey, who seems also to serve under the banner of abstractionist logic, convicts us pragmatists of absurdity by arguments similar to Mr. Russell's.[2]

As a favor to us and for the sake of the argument, he abandons the word 'true' to our fury, allowing it to mean nothing but the fact that certain beliefs are expedient; and he uses the word 'correctness' (as Mr. Pratt uses the word 'trueness') to designate a fact, not about the belief, but about the belief's object, namely that it is as the belief declares it. "When, therefore," he writes, "I say 'it is correct to say that Cæsar is dead,' I mean 'Cæsar is dead'. . . . This must be regarded as the *definition* of correctness." And Mr. Hawtrey then goes on to demolish me by the conflict of the definitions. What is 'true' for the pragmatist cannot be what is 'correct,' he says, for the definitions are not logically interchangeable; or if we interchange them, we reach the tautology: " 'Cæsar is dead' means 'it is expedient to believe that Cæsar is dead.' But *what* is it expedient to believe? Why, that 'Cæsar is dead.' A precious definition indeed of 'Cæsar is dead!' "

Mr. Hawtrey's conclusion would seem to be that the pragmatic definition of the truth of a belief in no way implies—what?—that the believer shall believe in his own belief's deliverance?—or that the pragmatist who is talking about him shall believe in that deliverance? The two cases are quite different. For the believer,

[2] See *The New Quarterly*, for March, 1908.

Cæsar must of course really exist; for the pragmatist critic he need not, for the pragmatic deliverance belongs, as I have just said, to another universe of discourse altogether. When one argues by substituting definition for definition one needs to stay in the same universe.

The great shifting of universes in this discussion occurs when we carry the word 'truth' from the subjective into the objective realm, applying it sometimes to a property of opinions, sometimes to the facts which the opinions assert. A number of writers, as Mr. Russell himself, Mr. G. E. Moore, and others, favor the unlucky word 'proposition,' which seems expressly invented to foster this confusion, for they speak of truth as a property of 'propositions.' But in naming propositions it is almost impossible not to use the word 'that.' *That* Cæsar is dead, *that* virtue is its own reward, are propositions.

I do not say that for certain logical purposes it may not be useful to treat propositions as absolute entities, with truth or falsehood inside of them respectively, or to make of a complex like 'that-Cæsar-is-dead' a single term and call it a 'truth.' But the 'that' here has the extremely convenient ambiguity for those who wish to make trouble for us pragmatists, that sometimes it means the *fact* that, and sometimes the *belief* that, Cæsar is no longer living. When I then call the belief true, I am told that the truth means the fact; when I claim the fact also, I am told that my definition has excluded the fact, being a definition only of a certain peculiarity in the belief—so that in the end I have no truth to talk about left in my possession.

The only remedy for this intolerable ambiguity is, it seems to me, to stick to terms consistently. 'Reality,' 'idea' or 'belief,' and the 'truth of the idea or belief,' which are the terms I have consistently held to, seem to be free from all objection.

Whoever takes terms abstracted from all their natural settings, identifies them with definitions, and treats the latter *more algebraico*, not only risks mixing universes, but risks fallacies which the man in the street easily detects. To prove 'by definition' that the statement 'Cæsar exists' is identical with a statement about 'expediency' because the one statement is 'true' and the other is about 'true statements,' is like proving that an omnibus is a boat because both are vehicles. A horse may be defined as a beast that walks on the nails of his middle digits. Whenever we see a horse we see such a beast, just as whenever we believe a 'truth' we believe something expedient. Messrs. Russell and Hawtrey, if they followed their anti-pragmatist logic, would have to say here that we see *that it is* such a beast, a fact which notoriously no one sees who is not a comparative anatomist.

It almost reconciles one to being no logician that one thereby escapes so much abstractionism. Abstractionism of the worst sort dogs Mr. Russell in his own trials to tell positively what the word 'truth' means. In the third of his articles on Meinong, in *Mind*, vol. xiii, p. 509 (1904), he attempts this feat by limiting the discussion to three terms only, a proposition, its content, and an object, abstracting from the whole context of associated realities in which such terms are found in every case of actual knowing. He puts the terms, thus taken in a vacuum, and made into bare logical entities, through every possible permutation and combination, tortures them on the rack until nothing is left of them, and after all this logical gymnastic, comes out with the following portentous conclusion as what he believes to be "the correct view: that there is no problem at all in truth and falsehood; that some propositions are true and some false, just as some roses are red and some white; that belief is a certain attitude towards propositions, which is called knowledge when they are true, error when they are false"—and he seems to think that when once this insight is reached the question may be considered closed forever!

In spite of my admiration of Mr. Russell's analytic powers, I wish, after reading such an article, that pragmatism, even had it no other function, might result in making him and other similarly gifted men ashamed of having used such powers in such abstraction from reality. Pragmatism saves us at any rate from such diseased abstractionism as those pages show.

P. S. Since the foregoing rejoinder was written an article on Pragmatism which I believe to be by Mr. Russell has appeared in the *Edinburgh Review* for April, 1909. As far as his discussion of the truth-problem goes, altho he has evidently taken great pains to be fair, it seems to me that he has in no essential respect improved upon his former arguments. I will therefore add nothing further, but simply refer readers who may be curious to pp. 272–280 of the said article.

XV

A Dialogue

After correcting the proofs of all that precedes I imagine a residual
state of mind on the part of my reader which may still keep him
unconvinced, and which it may be my duty to try at least to dispel.
I can perhaps be briefer if I put what I have to say in dialogue
form. Let then the anti-pragmatist begin:

ANTI-PRAGMATIST:—You say that the truth of an idea is constituted by its workings. Now suppose a certain state of facts, facts
for example of antediluvian planetary history, concerning which
the question may be asked: 'Shall the truth about them ever be
known?' And suppose (leaving the hypothesis of an omniscient
absolute out of the account) that we assume that the truth is never
to be known. I ask you now, brother pragmatist, whether according
to you there can be said to be any truth at all about such a state of
facts. Is there a truth, or is there not a truth, in cases where at any
rate it never comes to be known?

PRAGMATIST:—Why do you ask me such a question?

ANTI-PRAG:—Because I think it puts you in a bad dilemma.

PRAG:—How so?

ANTI-PRAG:—Why, because if on the one hand you elect to say
that there is a truth, you thereby surrender your whole pragmatist
theory. According to that theory, truth requires ideas and workings

to constitute it; but in the present instance there is supposed to be no knower, and consequently neither ideas nor workings can exist. What then remains for you to make your truth of?

PRAG:—Do you wish, like so many of my enemies, to force me to make the truth out of the reality itself? I cannot: the truth is something known, thought or said about the reality, and consequently numerically additional to it. But probably your intent is something different; so before I say which horn of your dilemma I choose, I ask you to let me hear what the other horn may be.

ANTI-PRAG:—The other horn is this, that if you elect to say that there is *no* truth under the conditions assumed, because there are no ideas or workings, then you fly in the face of common sense. Doesn't common sense believe that every state of facts must in the nature of things be truly stateable in some kind of a proposition, even tho in point of fact the proposition should never be propounded by a living soul?

PRAG:—Unquestionably common sense believes this, and so do I. There have been innumerable events in the history of our planet of which nobody ever has been or ever will be able to give an account, yet of which it can already be said abstractly that only one sort of possible account can ever be true. The truth about any such event is thus already generically predetermined by the event's nature; and one may accordingly say with a perfectly good conscience that it virtually pre-exists. Common sense is thus right in its instinctive contention.

ANTI-PRAG:—Is this then the horn of the dilemma which you stand for? Do you say that there is a truth even in cases where it shall never be known?

PRAG:—Indeed I do, provided you let me hold consistently to my own conception of truth, and do not ask me to abandon it for something which I find impossible to comprehend.—You also believe, do you not, that there is a truth, even in cases where it never shall be known?

ANTI-PRAG:—I do indeed believe so.

PRAG:—Pray then inform me in what, according to you, this truth regarding the unknown consists.

ANTI-PRAG:—Consists?—pray what do you mean by 'consists'?

It consists in nothing but itself, or more properly speaking it has neither consistence nor existence, it obtains, it *holds*.

PRAG:—Well, what relation does it bear to the reality of which it holds?

ANTI-PRAG:—How do you mean, 'what relation'? It holds *of* it, of course; it knows it, it represents it.

PRAG:—Who knows it? what represents it?

ANTI-PRAG:—The truth does; the truth knows it; or rather not exactly that, but anyone knows it who *possesses* the truth. Any true idea of the reality *represents* the truth concerning it.

PRAG:—But I thought that we had agreed that no knower of it, nor any idea representing it was to be supposed.

ANTI-PRAG:—Sure enough!

PRAG:—Then I beg you again to tell me in what this truth consists all by itself, this *tertium quid* intermediate between the facts *per se*, on the one hand, and all knowledge of them, actual or potential, on the other. What is the shape of it in this third estate? Of what stuff, mental, physical, or 'epistemological,' is it built? What metaphysical region of reality does it inhabit?

ANTI-PRAG:—What absurd questions! Isn't it enough to say that it *is true* that the facts are so-and-so, and false that they are otherwise?

PRAG:—'*It*' is true that the facts are so-and-so—I won't yield to the temptation of asking you *what* is true; but I do ask you whether your phrase that 'it is true that' the facts are so-and-so really means anything really additional to the bare *being* so-and-so of the facts themselves.

ANTI-PRAG:—It seems to mean more than the bare being of the facts. It is a sort of mental equivalent for them, their epistemological function, their value in noetic terms.

PRAG:—A sort of spiritual double or ghost of them, apparently! If so, may I ask you *where* this truth is found.

ANTI-PRAG:—Where? where? There is no 'where'—it simply obtains, absolutely obtains.

PRAG:—Not in anyone's mind?

ANTI-PRAG:—No, for we agreed that no actual knower of the truth should be assumed.

PRAG:—No actual knower, I agree. But are you sure that no notion of a potential or ideal knower has anything to do with forming this strangely elusive idea of the truth of the facts in your mind?

ANTI-PRAG:—Of course if there be a truth concerning the facts, that truth is what the ideal knower would know. To that extent you can't keep the notion of it and the notion of him separate. But it is not him first and then it; it is it first and then him, in my opinion.

PRAG:—But you still leave me terribly puzzled as to the status of this so-called truth, hanging as it does between earth and heaven, between reality and knowledge, grounded in the reality, yet numerically additional to it, and at the same time antecedent to any knower's opinion and entirely independent thereof. Is it as independent of the knower as you suppose? It looks to me terribly dubious, as if it might be only another name for a potential as distinguished from an actual knowledge of the reality. Isn't your truth, after all, simply what any successful knower *would* have to know *in case he existed*? and in a universe where no knowers were even conceivable would any truth about the facts there as something numerically distinguishable from the facts themselves find a place to exist in? To me such truth would not only be non-existent, it would be unimaginable, inconceivable.

ANTI-PRAG:—But I thought you said a while ago that there *is* a truth of past events, even tho no one shall ever know it.

PRAG:—Yes, but you must remember that I also stipulated for permission to define the word in my own fashion. The truth of an event, past, present, or future, is for me only another name for the fact that *if* the event ever *does* get known, the nature of the knowledge is already to some degree predetermined. The truth which precedes actual knowledge of a fact means only what any possible knower of the fact will eventually find himself necessitated to believe about it. He must believe something that will bring him into satisfactory relations with it, that will prove a decent mental substitute for it. What this something may be is of course partly fixed already by the nature of the fact and by the sphere of its associations.

This seems to me all that you can clearly mean when you say that truth pre-exists to knowledge. It is knowledge anticipated, knowledge in the form of possibility merely.

ANTI-PRAG:—But what does the knowledge know when it comes? Doesn't it know the *truth*? And if so, mustn't the truth be distinct from either the fact or the knowledge?

PRAG:—It seems to me that what the knowledge knows is the fact itself, the event, or whatever the reality may be. Where you see three distinct entities in the field, the reality, the knowing, and the truth, I see only two. Moreover, I can see what each of my two entities is *known-as*, but when I ask myself what your third entity, the truth, is known-as, I can find nothing distinct from the reality on the one hand, and the ways in which it may be known on the other. Are you not probably misled by common language, which has found it convenient to introduce a hybrid name, meaning sometimes a kind of knowing and sometimes a reality known, to apply to either of these things interchangeably? And has philosophy anything to gain by perpetuating and consecrating the ambiguity? If you call the object of knowledge 'reality,' and call the manner of its being cognized 'truth,' cognized moreover on particular occasions, and variously, by particular human beings who have their various businesses with it, and if you hold consistently to this nomenclature, it seems to me that you escape all sorts of trouble.

ANTI-PRAG:—Do you mean that you think you escape from my dilemma?

PRAG:—Assuredly I escape. For if truth and knowledge are terms correlative and interdependent, as I maintain they are, then wherever knowledge is conceivable truth is conceivable, wherever knowledge is possible truth is possible, wherever knowledge is actual truth is actual. Therefore when you point your first horn at me, I think of truth *actual*, and say it doesn't exist. It doesn't; for by hypothesis there is no knower, no ideas, no workings. I agree, however, that truth *possible* or *virtual* might exist, for a knower might possibly be brought to birth; and truth *conceivable* certainly exists, for, abstractly taken, there is nothing in the nature of antediluvian events that should make the application of knowledge to them inconceivable. Therefore when you try to impale me on your second horn, I think of the truth in question as a mere abstract possibility, so I say it does exist, and side with common sense.

Do not these distinctions rightly relieve me from embarrassment? and don't you think it might help you to make them yourself?

ANTI-PRAG:—Never!—so avaunt with your abominable hair-splitting and sophistry! Truth is truth; and never will I degrade it by identifying it with low pragmatic particulars in the way you propose.

PRAG:—Well, my dear antagonist, I hardly hoped to convert an eminent intellectualist and logician like you; so enjoy, as long as you live, your own ineffable conception. Perhaps the rising generation will grow up more accustomed than you are to that concrete and empirical interpretation of terms in which the pragmatic method consists. Perhaps they may then wonder how so harmless and natural an account of truth as mine could have found such difficulty in entering the minds of men far more intelligent than I can ever hope to become, but wedded by education and tradition to the abstractionist manner of thought.

Notes

Notes

The William James Collection is housed in the Houghton Library of Harvard University. It can be identified by the call number 'MS Am 1092', with either 'b' or 'f' as a prefix and, sometimes, a decimal following the numeral '2'. Many books from James's library are also preserved there; most of these are sufficiently identified by their call numbers which begin with 'WJ'. Other books from his library are in Harvard's Widener Library and elsewhere, and in such cases their location is stated. Still others were sold and have not been located. However, Ralph Barton Perry made a list, noting markings and annotations; this unpublished list can be consulted at Houghton.

James was a very active reader who filled his books with annotations and markings. The term 'markings' refers to underlining, vertical lines in margins, and the notation 'N.B.' His style is distinctive: the N.B.'s are usually written so that the same vertical stroke serves for both the 'N' and the 'B', while his underlining often has a distinctive waver. Further evidence is provided by the indexes with which James habitually filled the flyleaves of his books. Pages singled out in this fashion usually have markings. Thus, for books protected in Houghton, the risk of error in attributing a given marking to James is slight, except where there are signs that others had owned or handled the book. The risk is greater for materials in open stacks such as those in Widener, where the only claim made is that the book was owned by James and that there are markings. Any conclusions that might be drawn for these books are subject to error; although markings are noted only where the evidence points to James. Where the books have been sold, we are totally dependent upon Perry's reports.

3.1 *Pragmatism*] William James, *Pragmatism: A New Name for Some Old Ways of Thinking* (first published, New York: Longmans, Green, 1907); all references to *Pragmatism* are to the volume in the present edition (Cambridge, Mass.: Harvard University Press, 1975), identified as WORKS.

3.3 "Truth"] *Pragmatism* (WORKS, 96.3).

3.8 "Where] *Pragmatism* (WORKS, 96.23).

3.10 'Grant] *Pragmatism* (WORKS, 97.1).

3.20 "The truth] *Pragmatism* (WORKS, 97.12).

4.4 "To 'agree'] *Pragmatism* (WORKS, 102.15).

4.13 " 'The true'] *Pragmatism* (Works, 106.29).

4.22 Dewey] In *Pragmatism* (WORKS, p. 5), James singled out John Dewey (1859–1952) and others, *Studies in Logical Theory* (Chicago: University of Chicago Press, 1903) (WJ 417.93), as well as a number of Dewey's other essays. For a note on James's recognition of Dewey as a pragmatist, see *Pragmatism* (WORKS, note to 5.18).

4.22 Schiller] Ferdinand Canning Scott Schiller (1864–1937), British philosopher; in *Pragmatism* (WORKS, p. 6), James mentioned Schiller's *Studies in Humanism* (London: Macmillan, 1907). For the relations between James and Schiller see Ralph Barton Perry, *The Thought and Character of William James*, 2 vols. (Boston: Little, Brown, 1935), II, ch. 80.

4.33 But] *Pragmatism* (WORKS, 99.36).

5.6 *Pragmatism*] James's treatment of the pragmatic meaning of the Absolute can be found in *Pragmatism* (WORKS, pp. 40–41, 43).

5.27 'some] Not a quotation from *Pragmatism,* but a summary of the results of the discussion of the absolute.

5.35 'God'] These three topics are discussed primarily in Lecture III of *Pragmatism,* "Some Metaphysical Problems Pragmatically Considered."

6.30 radical] The most extensive statement of James's radical empiricism can be found in a series of essays he published in the *Journal of*

Philosophy, Psychology, and Scientific Methods in 1904 and 1905. These are included in the posthumous *Essays in Radical Empiricism* (New York: Longmans, Green, 1912). James used the term 'radical empiricism' in the preface to *The Will to Believe* (New York: Longmans, Green, 1897), p. vii.

8.36 distinction] James Bissett Pratt (1875–1944), American philosopher, in his *What is Pragmatism?* (New York: Macmillan, 1909), draws a distinction between the radical pragmatism of Dewey and Schiller and the moderate pragmatism of James. Pratt writes: "The most obvious difference is the recognition found in the more moderate view that it is indispensable for the trueness of an idea that its object should really 'be there' " (p. 99). James returns to this point in the present volume, see p. 93. In his review of Schiller's *Humanism: Philosophical Essays*, *Nation*, 78 (1904), 175–176, reprinted in part in *Collected Essays and Reviews* (New York: Longmans, Green, 1920), pp. 448–452, James placed the problem of the reality of objects among the unsolved problems of humanism.

9.29 Read] Carveth Read (1848–1931), British philosopher, *The Metaphysics of Nature*, 2nd edition with appendixes (London: Adam and Charles Black, 1908) (WJ 575.2). Appendix A, pp. 357–359, is entitled "Of Truth." Writing to H. V. Knox, Jan. 22, 1909, James says that this appendix marks Read as a humanist (Marjorie R. Kaufman, "William James's Letters to a Young Pragmatist," *Journal of the History of Ideas*, 24 (1963), 415). In a letter to James, Nov. 2, 1909, Read states that James should not say that Read has become a pragmatist, for he has been a pragmatist for forty years (bMS Am 1092, letter 784).

9.32 Johnson] Francis Howe Johnson (1835–1920), American philosopher, *What is Reality?* (Boston and New York: Houghton, Mifflin, 1891). Perry lists a copy of this book among those sold from James's library and notes that the remark "commonsense humanism 110+; 167" appeared on the flyleaf.

9.34 Miller] Irving Elgar Miller (1869–1962), American educator, *The Psychology of Thinking* (New York: Macmillan, 1909).

9.38 Knox] Howard Vincenté Knox (1868–1960), British military officer and philosopher, "Pragmatism; The Evolution of Truth," *Quarterly Review*, 210 (1909), 379–407; reprinted in *The Evolution of Truth and Other Essays* (London: Constable, 1930), pp. 40–81. This collection contains other papers on pragmatism by Knox: "Review of J. B. Pratt, *What is Pragmatism?*," "The Philosophy of William

James," and "The Letters of William James." Knox also wrote a book on James, *The Philosophy of William James* (London: Constable, 1914). For an account of the relations between James and Knox, including their letters, see Kaufman, "William James's Letters to a Young Pragmatist," pp. 413–421.

10.10 Taylor] Alfred Edward Taylor (1869–1945), British philosopher. On pp. 57–58 of this volume, James comments on Taylor's "Some Side Lights on Pragmatism," *University Magazine* (McGill), 3 (1903–1904), 44–66. In a letter to Bradley, June 16, 1904 (Perry, II, 488), James remarks that this essay is a "farcical interpretation" of *The Will to Believe*. Taylor also attacked pragmatism in "Truth and Practice," *Philosophical Review*, 14 (1905), 265–289; and in "Truth and Consequences," *Mind*, n.s. 15 (1906), 81–93.

10.10 Lovejoy] Arthur Oncken Lovejoy (1873–1962), American philosopher, "The Thirteen Pragmatisms," *Journal of Philosophy, Psychology, and Scientific Methods*, 5 (1908), 5–12, 29–39; reprinted in *The Thirteen Pragmatisms and Other Essays* (Baltimore: Johns Hopkins Press, 1963). A proof of this article with James's annotations can be found among the letters from Lovejoy to James (bMS Am 1092). For correspondence between James and Lovejoy concerning Lovejoy's article, see Perry, II, 480–484.

10.11 Gardiner] Harry Norman Gardiner (1855–1927), English-born American philosopher, "The Problem of Truth," *Philosophical Review*, 17 (1908), 113–137. This was given as the presidential address to the American Philosophical Association meeting at Cornell, Dec. 26–28, 1907, the same meeting at which James made the remarks which appear in the present volume as "The Meaning of the Word Truth." For a letter from James to Gardiner, Jan. 9, 1908, on Gardiner's address, see Perry, II, 484–485.

10.11 Bakewell] Charles Montague Bakewell (1867–1957), American philosopher, "On the Meaning of Truth," *Philosophical Review*, 17 (1908), 579–591, part of the discussion of James's remarks, mentioned above. Writing to Schiller, Jan. 4, 1908 (Perry, II, 509), James described the discussion as "abortive."

10.11 Creighton] James Edwin Creighton (1861–1924), American philosopher, made three contributions to the pragmatism controversy in the *Philosophical Review*: "Purpose as a Logical Category," 13 (1904), 284–297; "Experience and Thought," 15 (1906), 482–493; "The Nature and Criterion of Truth," 17 (1908), 592–605. The first two

papers are reprinted in Creighton's *Studies in Speculative Philosophy*
(New York: Macmillan, 1925), pp. 93–109 and 110–123. The third
paper was part of the discussion of James's remarks, mentioned above.

10.11 Hibben] John Grier Hibben (1861–1933), American philosopher,
"The Test of Pragmatism," *Philosophical Review*, 17 (1908), 365–382,
part of the discussion of James's remarks, mentioned above.

10.11 Parodi] Dominque Parodi (1870–1955), Italian-born philosopher, wrote primarily in French, "Le Pragmatisme d'après Mm. W.
James et Schiller," *Revue de Métaphysique et de Morale*, 16 (1908),
93–112; reprinted in Parodi's *Du Positivisme à l'idéalisme*, 2nd ser.
(Paris: J. Vrin, 1930), pp. 48–49. Parodi's book also contains "La
Signification du pragmatisme," delivered in 1908, but apparently not
published at that time.

10.11 Salter] William Mackintire Salter (1853–1931), American ethical
culture lecturer and writer, "Pragmatism: A New Philosophy," *Atlantic Monthly*, 101 (1908), 657–663. Salter was the brother-in-law of
James's wife.

10.11 Carus] Paul Carus (1852–1919), German-born American philosopher, Carus published three articles on pragmatism in the *Monist*:
"Pragmatism," 18 (1908), 321–362; "The Philosophy of Personal Equation," 19 (1909), 78–84; "A Postscript on Pragmatism," 19 (1909), 85–94.

10.12 Lalande] André Lalande (1867–1963), French philosopher, contributed two articles on pragmatism to the *Revue Philosophique de la
France et de l'Etranger*: "Pragmatisme et pragmaticisme," 61 (1906),
121–146; "Pragmatisme, humanisme, et vérité," 65 (1908), 1–26.

10.12 Mentré] Francois Mentré (1877–1950), French philosopher, contributed two articles on pragmatism to the *Revue de Philosophie*:
"Note sur la valeur pragmatique du pragmatisme," 11 (1907), 5–22;
"Complément à la note sur la valeur pragmatique du pragmatisme,"
11 (1907), 591–594.

10.12 McTaggart] John McTaggart Ellis McTaggart (1866–1925), British philosopher. McTaggart reviewed *Pragmatism* in *Mind*, n.s. 17
(1908), 104–109. In Chapter 13 of this volume, James criticizes
McTaggart's *Some Dogmas of Religion* (London: Edward Arnold,
1906), in particular, chapter II, "The Inadequacy of Certain Common
Grounds of Belief." James's annotated copy (WJ 553.15) provides
ample evidence that he took this chapter as a criticism of *The Will to
Believe*. Thus, his index on the back flyleaf has the entries "Against

faith + the W. to B. 52–76" and "56+ abstract treatment of Will to Believe," while the pages he mentions constitute the bulk of McTaggart's chapter 2. In his book McTaggart nowhere mentions James, but it is probable that James is one of his targets. McTaggart had read *The Will to Believe*. According to G. Lowes Dickinson, *J. McT. E. McTaggart* (Cambridge, England: University Press, 1931), p. 36, the following entry occurs in McTaggart's diary: "*1st April, 1898. Will to Believe*, pp. 221–328, which finishes it, thank goodness. I never realised before how true Entweder Spinozismus oder keine Philosophie is, because I never saw how low a clever man could fall for want of Spinozism."

10.12 Moore] George Edward Moore (1873–1958), British philosopher, "Professor James' 'Pragmatism'," *Proceedings of the Aristotelian Society*, n.s. 8 (1907–1908), 33–77.

10.12 Ladd] George Trumbull Ladd (1842–1921), American philosopher and psychologist, "The Confusion of Pragmatism," *Hibbert Journal*, 7 (1908–1909), 784–801. On p. 789 Ladd refers to James's remark in *Pragmatism* (WORKS, p. 16). For a letter from James to Ladd, July 21, 1909, on this article, see Eugene S. Mills, *George Trumbull Ladd: Pioneer American Psychologist* (Cleveland: Press of Case Western Reserve University, 1969), p. 257. Ladd reviewed *The Meaning of Truth* in the *Philosophical Review*, 19 (1910), 63–69.

10.13 Schinz] Albert Schinz (1870–1943), Swiss-born philosopher, taught in the United States, *Anti-Pragmatisme* (Paris: Félix Alcan, 1909), English translation, *Anti-Pragmatism; an Examination into the Respective Rights of Intellectual Aristocracy and Social Democracy* (Boston: Small, Maynard, ᶜ1909). Two letters from Schinz to James are at Houghton. The later one (bMS Am 1092, letter 984), Nov. 25, 1909, comments upon James's remark. From this letter it is clear that James had sent a copy of *The Meaning of Truth* to Schinz.

13.2 Hodgson] Shadworth Hollway Hodgson (1832–1912), English philosopher, *The Two Senses of "Reality"* (Printed for Private Circulation, 1883), p. 4: "By conditions of essence, I may remind you, I mean the members of analysis of anything, which are an answer to the question *what it is;* and by conditions of existence I mean the concomitants and antecedents upon which it depends, and which answer the question *how it comes* to be what it is, or, more precisely, how a particular content, being what it is, has come to exist when and where it does exist." This passage is not marked in James's copy, preserved in a collection of Hodgson pamphlets from James's library (WJ 539.18). Perry devotes three chapters, I, 611–653, to relations between Hodgson and James.

13.12 'feeling'] James discusses the term 'feeling' in "On Some Omissions of Introspective Psychology," *Mind*, 9 (1884), 19n. See also *The Principles of Psychology* (New York: Henry Holt, 1890), I, 185–187.

13.18 Lockian] John Locke, *An Essay Concerning Human Understanding*, ed. Alexander Campbell Fraser, 2 vols. (Oxford: Clarendon, 1894), I, 32. Houghton preserves James's annotated copy of the 31st edition (London: William Tegg, 1853) (WJ 551.13). It is dated in James's hand, September 1876.

14.14 Condillac] Etienne Bonnot, Abbé de Condillac, *Traité des sensations*; English translation, *Condillac's Treatise on the Sensations*, trans. Geraldine Carr (London: Favil Press, 1930). Condillac uses the statue throughout his book to illustrate the process of sensation. The statue is internally like ourselves, but initially has no contact with an outside world. The senses are then opened one by one.

14.30 *semper*] In *The Principles of Psychology* (1890), II, 9–13, James has a section entitled " 'The Relativity of Knowledge'." In the text, he quotes Carl Stumpf and in a note, pp. 11–12, mentions works by John Stuart Mill, James Mill, and Alexander Bain. A Latin phrase, very much like the one here, is attributed to Hobbes. The complete sentence, translated from the Latin, is as follows: "I might perhaps say he were astonished, and looked upon it; but I should not say he saw it; it being almost all one for a man to be always sensible of one and the same thing, and not to be sensible at all of any thing," *Elements of Philosophy. The First Section, Concerning Body*, in *The English Works of Thomas Hobbes*, ed. William Molesworth (London: John Bohn, 1839), I, 394 (pt. IV, ch. 25, sec. 5).

17.17 Green] Thomas Hill Green (1836–1882), English philosopher. James refers to Green on sensation also in *The Principles of Psychology* (1890), II, 10–11 and *A Pluralistic Universe* (New York: Longmans, Green, 1909), p. 279. Perry lists volume I of the *Works of Thomas Hill Green* (1885) among books sold from James's library and notes that the entry "Criticism of sensation 410–419" appears on the flyleaf. James's copy of Green's *Prolegomena to Ethics*, ed. A. C. Bradley (Oxford: Clarendon, 1883), is preserved (WJ 535.22). The quotations come from Green's Introduction to Hume's *Treatise of Human Nature*, *Works of Thomas Hill Green*, ed. R. L. Nettleship (London: Longmans, Green, 1885), I, 259; I, 16; and *Prolegomena to Ethics*, p. 23 (p. 27 of the 4th edition).

17.36 Grote] John Grote (1813–1866), British philosopher, *Exploratio Philosophica: Rough Notes on Modern Intellectual Science*, Part I

(Cambridge, England: Deighton, Bell; London: Bell and Dalby, 1865), p. 60. James's copy is preserved (WJ 535.67).

18.36 Green's] Thomas Hill Green, "Introduction" to David Hume, *A Treatise of Human Nature*, ed. T. H. Green and T. H. Grose, 2 vols. (London: Longmans, Green, 1874), I, 36. James's copy is preserved (WJ 540.54.2). In Green's *Works* also, this discussion can be found in I, 36.

20.36 Bowne's] Borden Parker Bowne (1847–1910), American philosopher, *Metaphysics* (New York: Harper & Brothers, 1882). Perry records *Metaphysics* (1882) among books sold from James's library. Several letters from James to Bowne can be found in Francis John McConnell, *Borden Parker Bowne* (New York: Abingdon, ᶜ1929).

20.37 Lotze] Rudolph Hermann Lotze (1817–1881), German philosopher, *Logic*, trans. B. Bosanquet (Oxford: Clarendon, 1884), pp. 424–426 (sec. 308). James's copy is preserved (WJ 751.88.10). Also preserved is the more heavily annotated copy of the German edition, *Logik* (Leipzig: S. Hirzel, 1874) (WJ 751.88.8).

23.29 Royce] Josiah Royce (1855–1916), James's colleague at Harvard and one of his closer personal friends. Royce's *The Religious Aspect of Philosophy* (Boston: Houghton, Mifflin) was published early in 1885. James's copy is preserved (WJ 477.98.4). His unsigned review appeared in the *Atlantic Monthly*, 55 (1885), 840–843, and was reprinted in *Collected Essays* (1920), pp. 276–284. James is referring to Royce's chapter 11, "The Possibility of Error." For an account of the relations between James and Royce see Perry, I, 778–824.

23.38 Miller] Dickinson Sergeant Miller (1868–1963), American philosopher, "The Meaning of Truth and Error," *Philosophical Review*, 2 (1893), 408–425. James's p. 403 is not correct. Miller's essay contains references to Royce. For relations between James and Miller, who sometimes published under the name R. E. Hobart, see Perry, II, 240–244.

26.32 Ferrier] James Frederick Ferrier (1808–1864), Scottish philosopher, *Institutes of Metaphysic*, 2nd ed. (Edinburgh and London: Wm. Blackwood and Sons, 1856). Proposition III, p. 105, reads: "The objective part of the object of knowledge, though distinguishable, is not separable in cognition from the subjective part, or the ego; but the objective part and the subjective part do together constitute the unit or *minimum* of knowledge."

30.25 Thackeray] William Makepeace Thackeray, *The History of Pendennis*, p. 184, in the *Oxford Thackeray*, ed. George Saintsbury (London: Oxford University Press, 1908): "Ah, sir,—a distinct universe walks about under your hat and under mine—all things in nature are different to each—the woman we look at has not the same features, the dish we eat from has not the same taste to the one and the other— you and I are but a pair of infinite isolations, with some fellow-islands a little more or less near to us."

31.37 Peirce] Charles Sanders Peirce (1839–1914), "How to Make Our Ideas Clear," *Popular Science Monthly*, 12 (1878), 293; reprinted with corrections and notes in the *Collected Papers of Charles Sanders Peirce*, ed. Charles Hartshorne and Paul Weiss (Cambridge, Mass.: Harvard University Press, 1934), V, 257, 258 (secs. 400, 402). James usually credits Peirce with the founding of pragmatism, see *Pragmatism* (WORKS, p. 10).

33.11 Hodgson's] In his pamphlet *The Method of Philosophy* (Printed for Private Circulation, 1882), p. 19, Hodgson writes: "what do we know it as"; while in *Philosophy and Experience* (London: Williams and Norgate, 1885), p. 20, Hodgson has: "what Being is *known as.*" In James's copies (WJ 539.18), there are markings in both places. Writing to Hodgson, Jan. 1, 1910 (Perry, I, 653), James stated that Peirce and Hodgson's question what things are "known-as" are the two sources of his pragmatism.

33.20 Extracts] The complete address was published as "The Knowing of Things Together," *Psychological Review*, 2 (1895), 105–124, and reprinted in *Collected Essays* (1920), pp. 371–400. An abstract appears as an appendix to the present volume. The association met at Princeton, N.J., Dec. 27–28, 1894.

34.27 loose] David Hume, *An Enquiry Concerning Human Understanding*, in volume II of *Essays Moral, Political, and Literary*, ed. T. H. Green and T. H. Grose (London: Longmans, Green, 1875), p. 60 (sec. VII, pt. 2). For James's copies of Hume see *Pragmatism* (WORKS, note to 47.32).

35.4 Miller] Miller presented a paper, "The Confusion of Content and Function in the Analysis of Ideas," at the second annual meeting of the American Psychological Association, at Columbia College, New York, Dec. 27–28, 1893. This paper was published as "The Confusion of Function and Content in Mental Analysis," *Psychological Review*, 2 (1895), 535–550. The other paper did appear in the *Philosophical Review*; see above, note to 23.38.

37.1 Bradley's] Francis Herbert Bradley (1846–1924), English philosopher, "On Truth and Practice," *Mind*, n.s. 13 (1904), 309–335;
reprinted with changes in Bradley's *Essays on Truth and Reality* (Oxford: Clarendon, 1914), pp. 65–106. Writing to Bradley, July 16, 1904,
James notes that he had received from George Frederick Stout (1860–
1944), British philosopher and psychologist, then editor of *Mind*, advance proofs of Bradley's article and had just posted the reply (J. C.
Kenna, "Ten Unpublished Letters from William James, 1842–1910,
to Francis Herbert Bradley, 1846–1924," *Mind*, n.s. 75 (1966), 318).
This was written in reply to Bradley's letter of July 4, 1904 (fMS Am
1092, vol. 16), which James received "about ten days after" the proofs
from Stout. Bradley wrote to explain that his article "gives or may
give a very mistaken view" of what he thinks about James's work.
Writing to James, Aug. 19, 1904, Stout remarks that James's manuscript, together with a reply by Schiller, has just gone to the printers
(bMS Am 1092, letter 1041). Schiller's reply is titled "In Defense of
Humanism" and appeared in *Mind*, n.s. 13 (1904), 525–542; reprinted
with changes as "Truth and Mr. Bradley," in Schiller's *Studies in
Humanism*, pp. 114–140. For relations between James and Bradley,
see Perry, II, ch. 88.

37.10 Peirce] This appears to be James's own restatement of the Peirce
passages quoted above, p. 31n.

38.8 Schiller's] For discussion between James and Schiller on what to
call their movement see *Pragmatism* (WORKS, note to 37.24).

38.18 Schiller] James tried to persuade Schiller to tone down his reply
to Bradley; see especially James's letter of Aug. 9, 1904 (Perry, II, 503).
Schiller's letter to James, Sept. 4, 1904 (bMS Am 1092, letter 890),
indicates that James had appealed also to Stout.

39.4 'too] Probably this is James's recollection of the line "Too full for
sound and foam" from Tennyson's "Crossing the Bar"; Alfred Lord
Tennyson, *Poems and Plays* (London: Oxford University Press, 1965),
p. 831.

40.16 *Barbara*] Mnemonic names of syllogisms. William Kneale and
Martha Kneale, *The Development of Logic* (Oxford: Clarendon, 1962),
p. 231, trace them to the work of William of Shyreswood in the thirteenth century.

40.35 'Energetics'] James usually associated the science of energetics
with Wilhelm Ostwald (1853–1932), German chemist; see James's review of Schiller's *Humanism: Philosophical Essays*.

41:11 Salisbury] Robert Arthur Talbot Gascoyne Cecil, third Marquis of Salisbury (1830–1903), British statesman, *Evolution: A Retrospect* (London: Roxburghe Press, 1894), pp. 28–29: "When, nearly a century ago, Young and Fresnel discovered that the motions of an incandescent particle were conveyed to our eyes by undulation, it followed that between our eyes and the particle there must be something to undulate. In order to furnish that something the notion of the ether was conceived, and for more than two generations the main, if not the only, function of the word ether has been to furnish a nominative case to the verb 'to undulate.' "

42.25 *denkmittel*] For James's definition of this term see *Pragmatism* (WORKS, p. 84).

43.6 ejective] An eject is an entity the existence of which is inferred and which can never be present to the one making the inference. Usually, the term is used to refer to other minds and is traced to the writings of William Kingdon Clifford (1845–1879), English philosopher; see the *Dictionary of Philosophy and Psychology*, ed. James Mark Baldwin (New York: Macmillan, 1901), I, 312–313.

43.6 Berkeley] James makes a similar claim about Berkeley in *Pragmatism* (WORKS, p. 47), see note to 47.12.

43.6 Mill] The view that matter is only a "permanent possibility of sensation" is stated by John Stuart Mill in chapter 11, "The Psychological Theory of the Belief in an External World," of his *An Examination of Sir William Hamilton's Philosophy*. Perry in his list of books sold from James's library lists two editions of this work, one in two volumes dated 1865, with marginal annotations "apparently by H[enry] J[ames]," the other, a copy of the 4th edition, dated 1872. Widener has a copy of volume I from James's library (Boston: William V. Spencer, 1865) (Phil. 2138.30[1]). Some of the many annotations appear to be by James, while the origin of others is uncertain.

43.6 Cornelius] Hans Cornelius (1863–1947), Monacan-born philosopher. Cornelius devotes most of his *Einleitung in die Philosophie* (Leipzig: B. G. Teubner, 1903) to the problem of the existence of an external world. James's copy (WJ 714.77), is dated Chocorua, July 1903.

43.27 Bradley's] The term 'encounters' appears frequently in Bradley's *The Principles of Logic* (London: Kegan, Paul, Trench, 1883). James's heavily annotated copy is preserved (WJ 510.2.2).

44.5 Royce] James is probably referring to Royce's "The Eternal and the Practical," *Philosophical Review*, 13 (1904), 113–142, where Royce states that he can be thought of as an "Absolute Pragmatist." In a letter to Bradley, July 16, 1904 (Kenna, "Ten Unpublished Letters," pp. 318–320), James refers to this essay by Royce and suggests that Bradley likewise could adopt humanism and "throw" his Absolute around it.

44.5 Bergson] Henri Bergson (1859–1941). James has two essays on Bergson, "The Philosophy of Bergson," *Hibbert Journal*, 7 (1909), 562–577, reprinted in an abridged form in *A Pluralistic Universe*; and "Bradley or Bergson?", *Journal of Philosophy, Psychology, and Scientific Methods*, 7 (1910), 29–33. Perry, II, 599–636, discusses the relations between James and Bergson.

44.6 Wilbois] Joseph Wilbois (b. 1874), French physicist and writer. In a letter to Schiller, Nov. 27, 1902 (Perry, II, 498), James remarks that he has been reading articles by Wilbois and others in the *Revue de Métaphysique et de Morale*. Two articles by Wilbois had appeared in the *Revue*: "La Méthode des sciences physiques," 7 (1899), 579–615, 8 (1900), 291–322; "L'Esprit positif," 9 (1901), 154–209, 579–645, 10 (1902), 69–105, 334–370, 565–612.

44.6 Leroy] In the preface to *Pragmatism* (WORKS, p. 6), James mentions Edouard Le Roy (1870–1954), French philosopher, and lists several articles by him; see note to 6.7.

44.7 Milhaud] In the preface to *Pragmatism* (WORKS, p. 6), James mentions Gaston Samuel Milhaud (1858–1918), French philosopher; see note to 6.6.

44.8 Poincaré] In *Pragmatism* (WORKS, p. 34), James includes Henri Poincaré (1854–1912), French scientist, in the "wave of scientific logic" which has led to the work of Dewey and Schiller; see note to 34.3.

44.9 Simmel] Georg Simmel (1858–1918), German philosopher. On March 16, 1905 (Perry, II, 469–470), James wrote to Hugo Münsterberg that he has not read any of Simmel's longer works, "only his original pragmatistic article (which seemed to me rather crude, though essentially correct)." According to Perry, the article was "Über eine Beziehung der Selektionslehre zur Erkenntnistheorie," *Archiv für Systematische Philosophie*, 1 (1895), 34–45.

44.10 Mach] James mentions Ernst Mach (1838–1916), Austrian physicist and philosopher, in *Pragmatism* (WORKS, p. 34); see note 34.2.

44.10 Hertz] It is likely that James is referring to Heinrich Rudolph Hertz (1857–1894), German physicist, whose *Die Prinzipien der Mechanik* was published in 1894 and translated into English in 1899. Hertz emphasized simplicity in scientific theories.

44.11 Ostwald] James quotes Ostwald in *Pragmatism* (WORKS, pp. 29, 30).

44.15 Royce] Royce's first published criticism of pragmatism, "The Eternal and the Practical," appeared in March 1904, and it is this essay that James could have had in mind. On the other hand, James could be thinking of Royce's work as a whole, inasmuch as the relation of idea and object was a major problem in Royce's thought. In his review of Royce's *The Religious Aspect of Philosophy*, echoed in the note on p. 23, above, James praised Royce's analysis of the problem.

44.20 *adæquatio*] *A Lexicon of St. Thomas Aquinas* (Washington: Catholic University of America Press, ᶜ1948), pp. 1144–1145, gives a number of St. Thomas' definitions of truth, among them, "veritas est adaequatio rei et intellectus." James could have been familiar with numerous similar formulations in scholastic writings. For a note on James's scholastic sources, see *Pragmatism* (WORKS, note to 62.2).

44.21 Bradley's] "On Truth and Practice," p. 311; *Essays on Truth and Reality*, p. 76.

46.15 Dewey's] James's account of Dewey's *Studies in Logical Theory*, "The Chicago School," *Psychological Bulletin*, 1 (1904), 1–5, reprinted in part in *Collected Essays* (1920), pp. 445–447, was originally given at a conference organized by Royce. See James's letter to Schiller, Nov. 15, 1903 (Perry, II, 501–502). James's notes for his Seminary of 1903–1904 have survived. In connection with the notes for Dec. 1, 1903, in the margin, James wrote in the following: " 'How can pragmatism distinguish betw. bluff & sincerity?' R. Cabot" (bMS Am 1092, Box L, notebook Nⁱⁱ, fol. 23). James could be referring to Richard Clarke Cabot (1868–1939), American physician and writer on social ethics.

46.17 Royce] The quotation seems to be not a direct quotation, but James's own summary of the argument in Royce's "The Eternal and the Practical." Royce used the term 'pure' rather than 'mere'.

46.17 Bradley] Bradley, "On Truth and Practice," p. 322; *Essays on Truth and Reality*, p. 90.

46.19 Taylor] In his "Some Side Lights on Pragmatism," Taylor does not describe pragmatism in these words. However, several of his criticisms do seem to suppose that pragmatism is simply a proposal to ignore evidence. Taylor summarizes his objections as follows: "Hence, in philosophy at any rate, which aims at being a reasoned system of true beliefs, the appeal to the 'will to believe' can never take the place of unbiassed examination of the objective grounds of belief" (p. 64).

48.5 colleague] In his notes for his Seminary of 1903–1904, notes for Dec. 1, 1903 (fol. 22–23), James refers to a paper by Santayana on Schiller and to Royce's objections to Schiller's account of truth. Royce is said to have objected that, on Schiller's view, a person cannot "meet others with his truth." Thus, James could be referring to some seminar discussion with Royce. In "The Eternal and the Practical," Royce did argue that a pure pragmatist, if he were consistent, could not try to convert opponents. In his "The Problem of Truth," p. 137, Harry Norman Gardiner refers to Royce with approval on this point.

49.26 "Autant] Madame Emile Duclaux (Agnes Mary Frances née Robinson, widow of James Darmesteter) (1857–1944), English poet and critic, *La Vie de Emile Duclaux* (Laval: L. Barnéaud, 1906), pp. 243, 247–248. Emile Duclaux (1840–1904), French biochemist, active in behalf of Alfred Dreyfus.

50.27 Eucken's] Rudolf Eucken (1846–1926), German philosopher, *Geistige Strömungen der Gegenwart*, 3rd ed. (Leipzig: Veit, 1904), p. 36, "ein Erhöhen des vorgefundenen Daseins." James's copy, where this passage is marked, is preserved in Widener (Phil. 179.3.5).

50.31 Lotze] Rudolph Hermann Lotze (1817–1881), German philosopher. James makes the same claim in *Pragmatism* (WORKS, p. 123); see note to 123.8 for a quotation from Lotze's *Outlines of Logic and of Encyclopædia of Philosophy* and for information about James's copies of Lotze. In his *Outlines of Metaphysic*, trans. George T. Ladd (Boston: Ginn, 1886) (WJ 751.88.16), pp. 143–144 (sec. 85), Lotze writes: "It is a prejudice, that the World exists, without the kingdom of spirits, ready-made and completed in effective consistence of its own; and that the life of mental representation which spirits lead is simply a kind of half-idle appendage, by means of which the content of the World is not increased, but only its ready-made content once more copied in miniature. The rather is the fact, that the world of ideas is awakened within these spirits by means of the influence of Things upon them, in itself one of the most significant events in the entire course of the world;—an event, without which the content of the world would not simply be imperfect, but would straightway lack what is most essential to its completion."

51.9 Spencer] In his *The Principles of Psychology,* Herbert Spencer (1820–1903) includes a chapter entitled "The Law of Intelligence." James's copy of the work was a reprint of the drastically altered second edition, 2 vols. (New York: D. Appleton, 1871–1873) (WJ 582.24.6); in this edition, the chapter is found in vol. I, pp. 407–417 (secs. 182–187). This portion in James's copy is heavily annotated.

52.3 Jevons's] William Stanley Jevons (1835–1882), English logician and economist. For many years James used Jevons' *Elementary Lessons in Logic* as a text in introductory courses. His copy is preserved (London: Macmillan, 1870) (WJ 542.25). Perry mentions Jevons' *Treatise on Logic* (1874) among the books sold from James's library, presumably meaning thereby *The Principles of Science: A Treatise on Logic and Scientific Method* (1874). Both works contain some discussions of George Boole (1815–1864). Jevons is considered a follower of Boole and introduced some improvements into the system of notation Boole had proposed; see Kneale, p. 422.

52.23 *Principles*]. *The Principles of Psychology* (1890), II, ch. 28, "Necessary Truths and the Effects of Experience."

52.35 Locke] James seems to be referring to Locke's chapter on the "Reality of Knowledge," in which Locke claims that "all our complex ideas, *except those of substances,* being archetypes of the mind's own making, not intended to be copies of anything, nor referred to the existence of anything, as to their originals, cannot want any conformity necessary to real knowledge." *Essay Concerning Human Understanding,* II, 230, (bk. IV, ch. IV, sec.5).

57.15 Taylor] In his "Some Side Lights on Pragmatism," Taylor criticizes a view which James had expressed in *The Will to Believe* that beliefs may help to bring about their objects. Taylor concludes: "Hence, if I have to accept them as a pre-condition of their becoming true, then, when I first accept them, I shall be believing what is not yet true; that is, what actually is false" (pp. 58–59). Taylor also rejects the argument from the "magnitude of the issues at stake." "We may perhaps, in our loyalty to logic, have to do without some convictions which the future will yet show to be well-founded, but at least we have not the 'lie in the soul,' we have not blinded ourselves to the distinction between what we can prove and what we cannot, between what we know and what we merely surmise or hope" (p. 65).

62.7 'Does] "Does 'Consciousness' Exist?" *Journal of Philosophy, Psychology, and Scientific Methods*, 1 (1904), 477–491; reprinted in *Essays in Radical Empiricism* (1912).

62.25 Harvard] The Harvard Delta is a delta-shaped plot of land where Memorial Hall is located.

64.17 Lotze] In *Essays in Radical Empiricism* (1912), p. 59, Perry adds the footnote "Cf. H. Lotze: *Metaphysik*, §§ 37–39, 97, 98, 243." In James's copy of the English translation, *Metaphysic*, trans. B. Bosanquet (Oxford: Clarendon, 1884) (WJ 751.88.12), p. 39 (sec. 37), the following passage is marked: " 'It is not in virtue of a substance contained in them that Things are; they are, when they are qualified to produce an appearance of there being a substance in them.' " The same passage is marked in James's copy of the German text, *Metaphysik* (Leipzig: S. Hirzel, 1879) (WJ 751.88.8), p. 84. Lotze is quoting from an earlier work and he repeats the same quotation several times in the *Metaphysic*. After one such repetition, Lotze adds: "For my only definition of the idea of substance was this,—that it signifies everything which possesses the power of producing and experiencing effects, in so far as it possesses that power" (p. 426 [sec. 243]).

67.4 *salto*] In his notes for Philosophy 9, 1905–1906, James makes the following remark: "Where the terminus is not reached, but an ideal, Cohen says the *salto mortale* exists. There is transcendence" (bMS Am 1092, Box L, notebook N^v, fol. 7v). This appears to be a record of a discussion with a student, since Morris Raphael Cohen (1880–1947), Russian-born American philosopher, who in 1906 received his doctorate from Harvard, was enrolled in that course, according to a list of students preserved with James's notebook. However, there are no indications of the occasion and no philosophers or writings are mentioned as sources. At 81.37 James attributes the same phrase to Ladd; see note to 81.37.

69.29 Lotze] This view has not been located in Lotze's writings. In *Essays in Radical Empiricism* (1912), p. 167, James attributes a similar view to Lotze, but instead of 'valid', uses its German equivalent '*gelten*'. To this text Perry added a note referring the reader to another of his notes, the reference to Lotze's *Metaphysik* quoted above, note to 64.17.

70.16 Baldwin] James Mark Baldwin (1861–1934), American philosopher and psychologist, "On Selective Thinking," *Psychological Review*, 5 (1898), 1–24, reprinted in *Development and Evolution* (New

York: Macmillan, 1902); "The Limits of Pragmatism," *Psychological Review*, 11 (1904), 30–60. Of the many letters from James to Baldwin, eighteen are included in Baldwin's autobiography, *Between Two Wars* (Boston: Stratford, 1926), II, 204–220.

71.30 Dewey's] James lists the following articles by Dewey: in the *Psychological Review*, "The Significance of Emotions," 2 (1895), 13–32, is the second of two articles on "The Theory of Emotion," the first of which, "Emotional Attitudes," appeared in 1 (1894), 553–569; "The Reflex Arc Concept in Psychology," 3 (1896), 357–370; "Psychology and Social Practice," 7 (1900), 105–124; "Interpretation of Savage Mind," 9 (1902), 217–230; in the *Philosophical Review*, "Green's Theory of the Moral Motive," 1 (1892), 593–612; "Self-Realization as the Moral Ideal," 2 (1893), 652–664; "The Psychology of Effort," 6 (1897), 43–56; "The Evolutionary Method as Applied to Morality," 11 (1902), 107–124, 353–371; in the *Monist*, "Evolution and Ethics," 8 (1898), 321–341.

72.14 span] Especially in Lecture 3 of *The World and the Individual*, 2nd series (New York: Macmillan, 1901), Royce developed the view that the absolute consciousness has a time-span of infinite extent. The time-spans of finite beings are limited, ranging from fractions of a second to whole eons. Royce's view is a development of James's own doctrine of the specious present, stated by James in *The Principles of Psychology* (1890), I, 642.

73.6 Woodbridge] Frederick James Eugene Woodbridge (1867–1940), American philosopher, an editor of the *Journal of Philosophy, Psychology, and Scientific Methods*. "The Field of Logic," *Science*, n.s. 20 (1904), 599: "The point from which knowledge starts and to which it ultimately returns, is always some portion of reality where there is consciousness, the things, namely, which, we are wont to say, are in consciousness. These things are not ideas representing other things outside of consciousness, but real things, which, by being in consciousness, have the capacity of representing *each other*, of standing for or implying each other."

73.33 This] "Does 'Consciousness' Exist?" and "A World of Pure Experience" appeared in the *Journal of Philosophy, Psychology, and Scientific Methods*, 1 (1904), 477–491; 533–543, 561–570; both were reprinted in *Essays in Radical Empiricism* (1912).

78.15 Miller] "The Meaning of Truth and Error," see above, note to 23.38; "The Confusion of Function and Content in Mental Analysis," see above, note to 35.4.

78.16 Strong] Charles Augustus Strong (1862–1940), American philosopher and psychologist, "A Naturalistic Theory of the Reference of Thought to Reality," *Journal of Philosophy, Psychology, and Scientific Methods*, 1 (1904), 253–260. "The James-Miller theory of cognition" is not a direct quotation, although Strong does refer to the "James-Miller theory." Strong concludes that "the James-Miller theory is simply . . . the correct analysis of the experiencing." But in his letters to James, Strong is critical. For example, on July 20, 1907, he writes: "You say that cognition is essentially a process of leading, and that it would find its perfect fulfilment in confluence with the objects. I cannot admit either of these propositions" (Perry, II, 539), and on Aug. 6, 1907: "In the present account you leave out of consideration the whole element of *agreement* and *correspondence* between idea and object" (Perry, II, 542). Strong took part in the Cornell discussion, see above, note to 10.11. An abstract of his remarks appears in the *Philosophical Review*, 17 (1908), 184–186. Strong also published two papers, one written before and the other after the Cornell discussion, under the single title "Pragmatism and Its Definition of Truth," *Journal of Philosophy, Psychology, and Scientific Methods*, 5 (1908), 256–264.

79.14 Strong] The distinction has been located only in an unpublished manuscript which Strong sent to James in 1907. James annotated the manuscript and prepared a synopsis. Strong writes: "In the first place, there are two kinds of relations, which I shall call, till I can think of a better pair of words, ambulatory and saltatory relations. In the saltatory relations we pass directly from one term to the other, and consider simply the impression which the second term makes on us in coming from the first; no third term, or intervening existence between the terms, is requisite to the relation. Of these similarity is an example. In the ambulatory relations we make our way from the first term to the second over a medium of the same kind as the terms it unites, and this middle existence is an indispensable implicate of the relation. So different times and places are connected by intervening time and space. . . . Now only the ambulatory relations are existential, and serve to connect experiences. The saltatory relations are logical" (bMS Am 1092, Box F, env. 8, fol. 27–28).

79.21 disciples] Max H. Fisch, "Philosophical Clubs in Cambridge and Boston," *Coranto* (University of Southern California), vol. 2, no. 2 (1965), p. 16, identifies the disciple of Green as James Elliot Cabot (1821–1903), a participant with James in several philosophical clubs. James's "The Spatial Quale," *Journal of Speculative Philosophy*, 13 (1879), 64–87, is a reply to Cabot's "Some Considerations on the Notion of Space," *Journal of Speculative Philosophy*, 12 (1878), 225–236.

James begins his criticism of Cabot by stating that because for Cabot space "forms a system of relations, it cannot be given in any one sensation." According to James, Cabot concludes that space "is a symbol of the general relatedness of objects constructed by thought from data which lie below consciousness" (p. 64).

79.28 spaces] James is referring to the section "Space-relations" of chapter 20, "The Perception of Space," originally published in *Mind*, 12 (1887), 1–30, 183–211, 321–353, 516–548.

81.37 Ladd] This phrase has not been located in Ladd's writings. In his *The Philosophy of Mind* (New York: Charles Scribner's Sons, 1895), p. 105, and elsewhere, Ladd claims that knowledge involves a "leap to reality." In his copy (WJ 448.17.2), James repeatedly marked passages of this kind.

83.36 This] *A Pluralistic Universe* (1909), p. 60: "*The treating of a name as excluding from the fact named what the name's definition fails positively to include, is what I call 'vicious intellectualism.'* "

84.1 *Pragmatism*] The squirrel illustration is found in *Pragmatism* (WORKS, pp. 27–28).

90.1 paper] "Truth and Its Verification," *Journal of Philosophy, Psychology, and Scientific Methods*, 4 (1907), 320–324.

90.10 He] In part, Pratt argues that we must distinguish between verification and verifiability and that verifiability is transcendent of experience and, thus, that the notion of verifiability is not available to the pragmatist.

93.1 Useful] Pratt ends his article as follows: "The usefulness of an hypothesis is indeed an excellent test of its truth. . . . But to identify the truth of a thought with the process of its own verification can hardly lead to anything but intellectual confusion" (p. 324).

93.20 'modified'] See above, note to 8.36.

93.31 'as'-formula] In *What is Pragmatism?* Pratt states that truth means that "*the object of which one is thinking is as one thinks it*" (p. 67). In James's copy (WJ 471.5) this passage is marked 'N.B.'

94.7 'workings'] "Successful working is therefore the tag or ear-mark by which we distinguish the true idea. But . . . this only leads us to the more fundamental and difficult question as to what we mean by the idea's being true, the question of the nature of the thing tagged or marked," Pratt, *What is Pragmatism?*, p. 62. In James's copy there are several markings at this point.

94.12 'trueness'] In *What is Pragmatism?* Pratt gives the following as one of the three senses in which the word truth is used: "as the relation or quality belonging to an 'idea' which makes it '*true*'—its *trueness*" (p. 52). The definition quoted above, note to 93.31, is intended by Pratt as an explanation of 'trueness'.

95.29 Pratt] In James's copy of *What is Pragmatism?* the passage James quotes is marked by six exclamation points.

97.10 Pratt] On p. 200 of *What is Pragmatism?* Pratt quotes Schiller's remark that to say that the Absolute is false is to say that it is useless. Accordingly, Pratt infers, even true claims about God are only useful and do not mean "*that there really is* a God." After stating that Dewey too is committed to this result, to show how Schiller and Dewey differ from James, Pratt quotes from p. 509 of *The Varieties of Religious Experience* (New York: Longmans, Green, 1902), to the effect that from religious beliefs we want more than a "subjective way of feeling things," we want to know "the objective truth of their content."

97.26 'transcendence'] Pratt, *What is Pragmatism?*, pp. 137–138: "Opinion is *about* something, it means or points to something not itself, and hence involves 'transcendence.' This of course is a terrifying term, and the pragmatist (who denies transcendence) makes capital out of its terrors." In James's copy, part of this passage is marked with an exclamation point.

97.27 "is] Pratt, *What is Pragmatism?*, p. 155.

102.19 Stout] George Frederick Stout (1860–1944), English philosopher and psychologist, review of F. C. S. Schiller, *Studies in Humanism*, *Mind*, n.s. 16 (1907), 579–588. James is referring to the following: "My sympathy with my neighbour's headache presupposes that he is actually feeling it. But according to Mr. Schiller's theory, my belief in other minds might be as true as truth can be, even though there were no emotions, feelings, desires, purposes, etc., experienced by any one except myself. All that, in his view, is required to constitute truth, is that I should postulate experiences other than mine, and that this postulate should enable me to control my own experiences" (p. 587).

102.31 "becomes] Stout, p. 587.

103.20 Lecture] The text of Lecture III, "Some Metaphysical Problems Pragmatically Considered," in which 'God' and 'matter' are discussed, is taken from "Philosophical Conceptions and Practical Results," which appears as an appendix in the *Pragmatism* volume of this edition. This essay, with changes, was reprinted as "The Pragmatic Method" in the *Journal of Philosophy, Psychology, and Scientific Methods*, 1 (1904), 673–687.

105.24 Hegel's] Georg Wilhelm Friedrich Hegel, *The Logic of Hegel*, trans. William Wallace (Oxford: Clarendon, 1874), pp. 18–19 (sec. 13). In James's copy (*AC 85.J2376.Zz874h), in Houghton, this passage is marked.

110.6 Aennchen] *Aennchen von Tharau*, an opera by Heinrich Hofmann (1842–1902), German composer, first produced in 1878.

113.37 Bourdeau] Jean Bourdeau (1848–1928), French journalist, contributed a series of articles on pragmatism to the *Journal des Débats*, reprinted in book form as *Pragmatisme et Modernisme* (Paris: Alcan, 1909). The series was also reprinted in the weekly edition of the *Journal* and the reference given below is to that edition: "Une Sophistique du Pragmatisme," *Revue Hebdomadaire du Journal des Débats*, 14 (Nov. 8, 1907), 880. According to Perry, II, 468, James received the articles from Thomas Sergeant Perry (1845–1928), American critic. James's date, "October 29, 1907," could be an indication that he saw the articles in their original form of publication.

115.14 Schiller] This can be understood as a summary of the view Schiller developed in his "Axioms as Postulates," in *Personal Idealism: Philosophical Essays by Eight Members of the University of Oxford*, ed. Henry Sturt (London: Macmillan, 1902). James makes several references to Schiller's conception of reality in *Pragmatism*; see WORKS, pp. 117, 120.

116.2 Schiller] In "The Ambiguity of Truth," *Studies in Humanism*, p. 152, Schiller summarizes his reply to the question how we distinguish truth from falsity: "If we can take the answers as relevant to our questions and conducive to our ends, they will yield 'truth'; if we cannot, 'falsehood.' "

116.12 "Es] Josef Victor von Scheffel (1826–1886), German poet and novelist, *Der Trompeter von Säkkingen*, in *J. V. von Scheffels Werke*, ed. Karl Siegen and Max Mendheim (Berlin: Bong, 1917[?]), I, 164:
> Behüt' dich Gott! es wär' zu schön gewesen,
> Behüt' dich Gott, es hat nicht sollen sein! —

An opera of the same name by Victor Nessler (1841–1890), German composer, was based upon this poem. The aria in which the quoted words appear is said to have been very popular.

118.25 Count] Henri Charles Ferdinand Marie Dieudonné d'Artois, Count of Chambord (1820–1883), heir to the French throne in the Bourbon line and often styled Henri V by French legitimists. The present paper appeared in the "Proceedings of the American Philosophical Association: the Seventh Annual Meeting, Cornell University, Dec. 26–28, 1907," *Philosophical Review*, 17 (1908), 180–181, where the passage reads: "much as the Count of Chambord was supposed to be born King of France, though he never exercised regal functions, —no need of functioning in either case!"

122.10 This] James's decision to withdraw these concluding paragraphs could have been influenced by Dewey. In a letter to James, Feb. 24, 1909 (Perry, II, 529–530), Dewey writes: "In view of what you told me about reprinting your essays on truth, I am going to be impertinent enough to ask about one essay, *viz.*, that on 'Truth versus Truthfulness'; provided, that is, you are thinking of reprinting that as it stands. My remarks have to do with the two closing paragraphs. For a pragmatist to say that the question is 'almost purely academic' gives the unbeliever too much chance to blaspheme, doesn't it? Or, on the other hand, if this is an almost purely academic question, how can it be admitted that 'truthfulness' is so much the more important idea, as the last paragraph indicates?" Dewey goes on to say that this is a "stumbling-block" to the undecided and a "cause of congratulation" to those opposed. He further points out that some opponents, such as Strong, do make this distinction.

122.17 Pratt] *What is Pragmatism?*, pp., 51–52: "The three different ways in which the word truth is commonly used are, then, the following: (1) as a synonym for 'reality'; (2) as a synonym for known 'fact' or verified and accepted belief; (3) as the relation or quality belonging to an 'idea' which makes it '*true*'—its *trueness*." According to Pratt, the first sense, common among absolutists, leads to confusion and the pragmatists have done well to attack it. The second sense, however, is "justifiable" (p. 55). For a definition of "trueness" see above, note to 94.12.

123.1 Brown] William Adams Brown (1865–1943), American theologian, "The Pragmatic Value of the Absolute," *Journal of Philosophy, Psychology, and Scientific Methods*, 4 (1907), 459–464: "It would seem, then, that the formula in which Professor James has expressed the pragmatic value of the absolute is too narrow a one. Important as has been the function of the idea as an inducer of rest, it is not to be compared with that which it has exerted as an inspirer of action" (p. 463).

126.1 Hébert] Marcel Hébert (1851–1916), French educator, *Le Pragmatisme; étude de ses diverses formes Anglo-Américaines, Francaises, Italiennes et de sa valeur religieuse* (Paris: E. Nourry, 1908); a French translation of James's review together with Hébert's reply appears in the second edition (Paris: E. Nourry, 1910), pp. 139–153. According to Hébert's note, James saw and corrected the translation. Hébert left the priesthood of the Roman Catholic church in 1903.

126.3 *Le Divin*] *Le Divin. Expériences et hypothèses* (Paris: Alcan, 1907). According to James's letter to Hébert, preserved in the Bibliothèque Nationale, Paris, dated July 27, 1907, James had received a letter from Hébert on June 24, 1907, and as a result had "at last" read *Le Divin* carefully.

127.2 *valeur*] Hébert, *Le Pragmatisme*, p. 29: "De ce que nos idées ont une *valeur d'usage* (pragmatique) s'ensuit-il qu'elles n'aient pas aussi une *valeur de connaissance* proprement dite?"

127.15 *connaissance*] Hébert, *Le Pragmatisme*, pp. 32–33: "M. W. James admet-il que la sensation est un simple état de conscience purement subjectif? Si, conformément au sens commun, il y reconnaît quelque chose, si peu que ce soit, d'objectif, la sensation deviendra un rapport qui n'a de sens que par ses deux termes: objectif et subjectif, aussi essentiels l'un que l'autre. Mais c'est admettre par là même la possibilité d'une certaine valeur *de connaissance* objective."

131.15 Hébert's] Hébert, *Le Pragmatisme*, p. 60: "Je répondrai: le possesseur du faux Corot est troublé dans sa quiétude; il cherche à sortir de ce trouble par une enquête; il retrouve son calme . . . Tout cela est exact, mais on s'obstine alors à confondre deux questions parallèles: les dispositions, les émotions subjectives avec la question de vérité objective. Ce n'est point *parce que* le possesseur est troublé dans ses tendances qu'*il n'est pas vrai* que le tableau *soit* de Corot, ni *parce qu'il* a recouvré le calme et l'équilibre de ses tendances qu'*il est vrai* que le tableau est d'un autre peintre."

132.12 "An] This passage is apparently James's summary of Schiller's view. In "The Ambiguity of Truth," in *Studies in Humanism*, Schiller emphasizes the contrast between a claim to truth and the establishing of that claim.

136.12 Fullerton] George Stuart Fullerton (1859–1925), American philosopher, "Freedom and 'Free-Will'," *Popular Science Monthly*, 58 (1900), 183–192; " 'Free-Will' and the Credit for Good Actions," *Popular Science Monthly*, 59 (1901), 526–533.

137.21 Fullerton] The quotation is a composite of three excerpts from "Freedom and 'Free-Will' "; 137.22 to 137.30 comes from pp. 189–190; 137.30 to 137.33 from p. 188; 137.33 to 138.2 from pp. 188–189.

138.17 McTaggart] *Some Dogmas of Religion*, p. 179: "When the volition is over, it has ceased to exist, and it has not, on the indeterminist theory, left a permanent cause behind it. For, according to that theory, it has no permanent cause at all. Directly Nero has ceased to think of a murder, nothing at all connected with it remains in his moral nature, except the mere abstract power of undetermined choice, which is just as likely to be exercised on the next occasion in an utterly different way. How then can the indeterminist venture to call Nero a wicked man between his crimes?" In James's copy, most of this passage is marked with a vertical line and an exclamation point.

139.22 McTaggart] *Studies in the Hegelian Dialectic* (Cambridge, England: University Press, 1869) (WJ 553.15.4), p. 255: "all reality is rational and righteous"; p. 256: all facts are *"sub specie temporis,* destined to become perfectly good."

140.11 All] From here to the direct quotation at 140.26, James is giving his interpretation of McTaggart's position in *Some Dogmas of Religion*. The topic is treated in sections 44–54, and James's "sections 47 to 57" appears to be an error.

140.26 "When] McTaggart, *Some Dogmas of Religion*, p. 66.

140.33 Hegel's] *The Logic of Hegel*, p. 7 (sec. 6): "What is rational is actual; and, What is actual is rational." Later editions have 'reasonable' instead of 'rational'. Hegel is quoting from the preface to his *The Philosophy of Right.*

140.36 "For] McTaggart, *Some Dogmas of Religion*, p. 76. In his copy, line 18, James wrote 'dis' with a guideline to 'comfort'. But McTaggart has 'comfort' not only in the book, but also in the earlier version, "The Inadequacy of Certain Common Grounds of Belief," *Hibbert Journal*, 4 (1905–1906), 140.

142.4 Plato] In "From Plato to Protagoras," in *Studies in Humanism*, Schiller claims that Protagoras was not a skeptic but a humanist and that Plato did not refute him.

142.8 Rickert] Heinrich Rickert (1863–1936), German philosopher, *Der Gegenstand der Erkenntnis*, 2nd ed. (Tübingen and Leipzig: J. C. B. Mohr [Paul Siebeck], 1904) (WJ 776.13). "Relativismus" is the title of one chapter. James refers to Rickert in *Pragmatism* (WORKS, pp. 109, 113).

142.8 Münsterberg] Hugo Münsterberg (1863–1916), German-born psychologist, James's colleague at Harvard, *Philosophie der Werte* (Leipzig: Johann Ambrosius Barth, 1908). James's copy is preserved at Houghton (*AC 85.J2376.Zz908m). The discussion of 'relativismus' can be found on pp. 29–37. In James's copy, there are many marginal comments in this section, usually critical.

143.5 Rickert] James makes the same claim in *Pragmatism* (WORKS, p. 113n).

143.11 regulative] The change from 'constitutive' to 'regulative' seems to have been prompted by Schiller. Writing to James, Oct. 26, 1909 (bMS Am 1092, letter 958), Schiller asks whether James meant to write 'regulative'. James replied, Nov. 6, 1909 (Stanford University Library, Educators and Librarians Collection, M130, folder 18), that his "mind groped for regulative, but blindly took up the other term of the Kantian pair." But on Dec. 4, 1909 (M130, folder 18), while stating that the change has been made, James wrote that "humanly speaking" the two terms are "synonyms" and that he was not "thinking of Kantian terminology" when he wrote 'constitutive'.

143.32 Münsterberg's] *Philosophie der Werte*, pp. 38, 74: "dass es eine Welt gibt." In James's copy, in both cases, this phrase is underlined.

146.1 Russell's] Bertrand Russell (1872–1970), "Transatlantic 'Truth',", *Albany Review*, 2 (1908), 393–410; reprinted as "William James's Conception of Truth," *Philosophical Essays* (London: Longmans, Green, 1910; rev. ed. London: George Allen & Unwin, 1966). For documents concerning this controversy, see Appendix IV.

146.4 we] Russell, p. 399: "Let us consider for a moment what it means to say that a belief 'pays.' We must suppose that this means that the consequences of entertaining the belief are better than those of rejecting it. In order to know this, we must know what are the consequences of entertaining it, and what are the consequences of rejecting it; we must know also what consequences are good, what bad, what consequences are better, and what worse."

146.11 Russell] Russell, p. 399.

147.12 Russell] Russell, p. 403: "The pragmatic account of truth assumes, so it seems to me, that no one takes any interest in facts, and
that the truth of the proposition that your friend exists is an adequate
substitute for the fact of his existence."

147.32 Russell] Russell, p. 410: "The attempt to get rid of 'fact' turns
out to be a failure, and thus the old notion of truth reappears."

150.12 Hawtrey] Ralph George Hawtrey (b. 1879), English economist,
"Pragmatism," *New Quarterly*, 1 (1908), 197–210. The copy preserved
from James's library (WJ 500.5) has no marginalia and only a few
markings of uncertain origin.

150.15 abandons] Hawtrey, p. 201: "A certain amount of confusion
will be avoided if, in criticising Professor James, the words 'true' and
'truth' be limited to the meaning which he assigns to them. And therefore I propose for the present to use the word 'correct' to describe the
idea represented by 'true' to the ordinary man."

150.20 "When] Hawtrey, p. 201. The text James quotes follows directly
that quoted above, note to 150.15, and actually reads as follows:
"When, therefore, I say 'it is correct that Cæsar is dead,' I mean
'Cæsar is dead,' and similarly if any other statement whatever be substituted for 'Cæsar is dead.' This must be regarded as the *definition*
of correctness."

150.24 'true'] Hawtrey, p. 201: "Now 'correctness' *cannot* be identical
with the Pragmatist's truth. 'It is true that Cæsar is dead' means 'It
is expedient to believe that Cæsar is dead.' If truth is only another
name for 'correctness,' then 'It is true that Cæsar is dead' means simply
'Cæsar is dead.' It follows, therefore, that 'Cæsar is dead' means 'it
is expedient to believe that Cæsar is dead.' But *what* is it expedient
to believe? Why, that 'Cæsar is dead.' A precious definition indeed of
'Cæsar is dead!' Thus, 'it is true that—' unlike 'it is correct that—'
adds something new to 'Cæsar is dead.' And whatever may be the
legitimate use of the word 'true,' it is at any rate clear that we have
here two distinct ideas."

151.10 Russell] In his *Principles of Mathematics* (Cambridge, England: University Press, 1903), I, ix, Russell writes: "Holding, as I do,
that what is true or false is not in general mental, I require a name
for the true or false as such, and this name can scarcely be other than
proposition." In James's copy, preserved at Houghton (*AC 85.J2376.-
Zz903r), there are no marks at this point.

151.10 Moore] Moore explicitly says that truth is a property of what he calls propositions; see in particular "Truth" in Baldwin's *Dictionary*, II, 716–718; also, "The Nature of Judgment," *Mind*, n.s. 8 (1899), 176–193.

152.11 Russell] "Meinong's Theory of Complexes and Assumptions," *Mind*, n.s. 13 (1904), 204–219; 336–354; 509–524; reprinted in *Essays in Analysis*, ed. Douglas Lackey (London: George Allen & Unwin, 1973).

152.21 correct] Russell, "Meinong's Theory," p. 523.

152.35 Russell] "Pragmatism," *Edinburgh Review*, 209 (1909), 363–388; reprinted in *Philosophical Essays*. In a letter to Russell, May 14, 1909 (710.051466 in the Russell Archives at McMaster University, Hamilton, Ontario, Canada), James states that he has just received the article, has read it, and thinks it useless to reply. It is far simpler, James writes, to challenge Russell himself to state what truth is.

I.K.S.

A Note on the Editorial Method
The Text of *The Meaning of Truth*

A Note on the Editorial Method

These volumes of *The Works of William James* offer the critical text of a definitive edition of his published and unpublished writings (letters excepted). A text may be called 'critical' when an editor intervenes to correct the errors and aberrations of the copy-text[1] on his own responsibility or by reference to other authoritative documents, and also when he introduces authoritative revisions from such documents into the basic copy-text. An edition may be called 'definitive' (a) when the editor has exhaustively determined the authority, in whole or in part, of all preserved documents for the text; (b) when the text is based on the most authoritative documents produced during the work's formulation and execution and then during its publishing history; and (c) when the complete textual data of all authoritative documents are recorded, together with a full account of the edited text's divergences from the document chosen as copy-text, so that the user may reconstruct these sources in complete detail as if they were before him. When backed by this data, a critical text in such a definitive edition may be called 'established' if from the fully recorded documentary evidence it attempts to reconstruct the author's true and latest intention, even though in some details the restoration of intention from imperfect sources is conjectural and subject to differing opinion.

Not only every different printed version of a work, as between journal

---

[1] The copy-text is that early document, whether a manuscript or a printed edition, chosen by the editor as the most authoritative basis for his text, and therefore one which is reprinted in the present edition subject only to recorded editorial emendations, and to substitution or addition of readings from other authoritative documents, judged to be necessary or desirable for completing James's final intentions.

and book publication, but every printing of a book during the author's lifetime carries within itself the possibility of authoritative correction and revision which an editor must take into account. Hence, after preserved manuscripts and journal publications have been identified, the definitive form of the book text itself is established by the mechanical collation of the first printing on the Hinman Collator against some posthumous printing from the same plates, followed by the identification of the precise impression in which each alteration in the plates was made, with a view to determining its date and authority. Moreover, the James Collection in the Houghton Library of Harvard University contains various examples of article offprints and personal copies of his books annotated with corrections and revisions, valuable evidence of his post-publication intentions to improve the texts. The richness of the James Collection in James's working manuscripts, including various examples of the actual printer's copy, offers an unusual opportunity for an editor to secure documentary evidence not usually available to assist in the many critical and bibliographical decisions required in the formulation of a critical text.

The most important editorial decision for any work edited without modernization[2] is the choice of its copy-text, that documentary form on which the edited text will be based. Textual theorists have long distinguished two kinds of authority: first, the authority of the words themselves—the *substantives*; second, the authority of the punctuation, spelling, capitaliza-

---

[2] By 'modernization' one means the exact presentation of the words (or substantives) of the copy-text as emended, but the silent substitution for the author's of an entirely new system of punctuation, spelling, capitalization, and word-division in order to bring these original old-fashioned 'accidentals' of the text thoroughly up to date for the benefit of a current reader. It is the theory of the present edition, however, that James's turn-of-the-century 'accidentals' offer no difficulty to a modern scholar or general reader and that to tamper with them by 'modernization' would not only destroy some of James's unique and vigorous flavor of presentation but would also risk distortion of his meaning. The annotations in his private copies after publication, as well as his alterations in proof, indicate clearly that he was conscious of the importance of punctuation for his meaning and that he could alter such punctuation—presumably more the printer's house-styling than his own first thoughts—when he noticed that it did not agree with his ultimate intentions. In short, since there is every evidence that, in his books at least, James was concerned to control the texture of presentation and made numerous nonverbal as well as verbal changes in preparing printer's copy, and later in proof, for an editor to interfere with James's specific, or even general, wishes by modernizing his system of 'accidentals' would upset on many occasions the designedly subtle balances of his meaning. Moreover, it would be pointless to change his various idiosyncrasies of presentation, such as his increasing use of 'reform' spellings and his liking for the reduction of the capitals in words like *darwinism*. Hence in the present edition considerable pains have been devoted to reprinting the authoritative accidentals of the copy-text and also by emendation to purifying them, so far as documentary evidence extends, from the house-styling to which they were subjected in print, one not entirely weeded out in proof. For a further discussion, see below under the question of copy-text and its treatment.

tion, word-division, paragraphing, and devices of emphasis—the *accidentals* so-called—that is, the texture in which the substantives are placed but itself often a not unimportant source of meaning. In an unmodernized edition like the present, an attempt is made to present not only the substantives but also their 'accidental' texture, each in its most authoritative form. The most authoritative substantives are taken to be those that reflect most faithfully the author's latest intentions as he revised to perfect the form and meaning of his work. The most authoritative accidentals are those which are preferential, and even idiosyncratic, in the author's usage even though not necessarily invariable in his manuscripts. These characteristic forms convey something of an author's flavor, but their importance goes beyond aesthetic appreciation since they may become important adjuncts to meaning. It is precisely these adjuncts, however, that are most susceptible to compositorial and editorial styling away from authorial characteristics and toward the uniformity of whatever contemporary system the printing or publishing house fancied. Since few authors are in every respect so firm in their 'accidental' intentions as to demand an exact reproduction of their copy, or to attempt systematically to restore their own system in proof from divergent compositorial styling, their 'acceptance' of printing-house styling is meaningless as an indication of intentions. Thus, advanced editorial theory agrees that in ordinary circumstances the best authority for the accidentals is that of a holograph manuscript or, when the manuscript is not preserved, whatever typed or printed document is closest to it, so that the fewest intermediaries have had a chance to change the text and its forms. Into this copy-text—chosen on the basis of its most authoritative accidentals—are placed the latest revised substantives, with the result that each part of the resulting eclectic text is presented in its highest documentary form of authority.[3] It is recognized, however, that an author may be so scrupulous in supervising each stage of the production of a work that the accidentals of its final version join with the substantives in representing his latest intentions more faithfully than in earlier forms of the text. In such special cases a document removed by some stages from a preserved manuscript or from an early intermediary may in practical terms compose the best copy-text.

Each work, then, must be judged on its merits. In general, experience shows that whereas James accepted journal styling without much objection even though he read proof and had the chance to alter within reason

---

[3] The use of these terms, and the application to editorial principles of the divided authority between both parts of an author's text, was chiefly initiated by W. W. Greg, "The Rationale of Copy-Text," *Studies in Bibliography*, 3 (1950–51), 19–36. For extensions of the principle, see Fredson Bowers, "Current Theories of Copy-Text," *Modern Philology*, 68 (1950), 12–20; "Multiple Authority: New Concepts of Copy-Text," *The Library*, 5th ser., 27 (1972), 81–115; "Remarks on Eclectic Texts," *Essays in Bibliography, Text, and Editing* (1975).

what he wished, he was more seriously concerned with the forms of certain of his accidentals in the books, not only by his marking copy pasted up from journal articles for the printer but more particularly when he received the galley proofs. Indeed, it is not too much to state that James sometimes regarded the copy that he submitted for his books (especially when it was manuscript) as still somewhat in a draft state, to be shaped by proof-alterations to conform to his ultimate intentions. The choice of copy-texts in this edition, therefore, rests on the evidence available for each document, and the selection will vary according to the circumstances of 'accidental' authority as superior either in the early or in the late and revised forms of the text.

On the other hand, although James demonstrably made an effort to control the forms of certain of his accidentals in the proofs, even when he had been relatively careless about their consistency in his manuscript printer's copy, he was not always equally attentive to every detail of the house-styling that printers imposed on his work. In some cases he simply did not observe anomalies even in his own idiosyncratic practices; in others he may have been relatively indifferent when no real clash of principles was involved. Thus, when an editor is aware that certain 'accidental' printing-house stylings have been substituted for James's own practices as established in manuscripts and marked copy, or have been substituted for relatively neutral journal copy that seems to approximate James's usual practice, he may feel justified in emending to recover by the methods of textual criticism as much of the purity of the Jamesian accidentals as of the substantives—both ultimately contributing to the most complete and accurate expression of James's meaning. On the contrary, although the texture of a book copy-text may be accepted in general detail over earlier documents, not every book variant is to be thought of as the direct result of James's own marking whether of copy or of proof. Most are taken to have derived from this actual authority, but a decision on such grounds is impossible to make comma for comma, say, and unless contrary evidence is present the general authority of the copy-text is likely to hold so long as it conforms on the whole to James's practices: whether inadvertently or by his direction can often be determined with no assurance.

Except for the small amount of silent alteration listed below, every editorial change in the copy-text has been recorded, with the identification of its immediate source and the record of the rejected copy-text reading. An asterisk prefixed to the page-line reference (always to this edition) indicates that the alteration is discussed in a Textual Note. The formulas for notation are described in the headnote to the list of Emendations, but it may be well to mention here the use of the term *stet* to call attention in special cases to the retention of the copy-text reading. Textual Notes discuss certain emendations or refusals to emend. The Historical Collation lists all readings in the collated authoritative documents that differ from the edited text except for the 'accidental' alterations recorded in the list of Emendations, which are not repeated in the Historical Collation even though the substantive emendations will be repeated because of their special interest. The principles for the recording of variants are described in the headnote to this Collation. When manuscripts are preserved in the textual transmission their rejected variants will be recorded in the Historical Collation according to the finally inscribed readings of the text. However, James's manuscripts are likely to be considerably rewritten both during the course of composition and in the process of review, and these variants created while he was struggling to give shape to his thought are of particular concern to the scholar. Since this edition is bound to the principle that its apparatus should substitute for all authoritative documents, special provision is made in a list of Alterations to the Manuscripts for the analysis and description of every variant between the initial inscription and the final revision within each manuscript. The formulas for transcription and recording are found in the headnote to this section.

A special section of the apparatus treats hyphenated word-compounds, listing the correct copy-text form of those broken between lines in the present edition and indicating those in the present text, with the form adopted, that were broken between lines in the copy-text and partake of the nature of emendations. Consultation of the first list will enable any user to quote from the present text with the correct hyphenation of the copy-text.

Manuscripts that are printed in this edition are transcribed in diplomatic form,[4] ordinarily without emendation, except for a single feature. As with many writers, James's placement of punctuation in relation to quotation marks was erratic, sometimes appearing within the quotes as in the standard American system for commas and periods, sometimes outside according to the sense as in the British system, and sometimes carelessly placed immediately below the quotation mark. To attempt to determine the exact position of each mark would often be impossible; hence all such punctuation is transcribed placed as it would be by an American printer, the system which James in fact seems generally to have employed himself when he thought of it. According to convenience, manuscripts may be transcribed in their final form, with all variants recorded systematically in an apparatus list, or on occasion they may be transcribed with a record of their variants placed within the text.

---

[4] A diplomatic transcript reproduces exactly the original, insofar as type can represent script, but with no attempt to follow the lining of the original or visually—by typographical devices—to reproduce deletions, interlineations, additions, or substitutions. It follows that ordinarily no emendation whatever is attempted in such a transcript and all errors in the text are allowed to stand without correction.

A Note on the Editorial Method

In this edition of the WORKS OF WILLIAM JAMES an attempt has been made to identify the exact edition used by James for his quotations from other authors and ordinarily to emend his carelessnesses of transcription so that the quotation will reproduce exactly what the author wrote. All such changes are noted in the list of Emendations. On some occasions, however, James altered quotations for his own purposes in such a manner that his version should be respected. Such readings are retained in the text but recorded in the list of Emendations (with the signal *stet*), and the original form is provided for the information of the consulting scholar. Although James's own footnotes are preserved in the text as he wrote them (the only footnotes allowed in the present edition), the citations have been expanded and corrected as necessary in Professor Skrupskelis' Notes to provide the full bibliographical detail required by a scholar, this ordinarily having been neglected in James's own sketchy notation. The Notes also provide full information about quotations in the text that James did not footnote.

Silent alterations in the text concern themselves chiefly with mechanical presentation. For instance, heading capitals are normalized in the first line of any chapter or section, headings may have their final periods removed, the headlines of the originals may be altered for the purposes of the present edition, anomalous typographical conventions or use of fonts may be normalized including roman or italic syntactical punctuation made to conform to a logical system. When unusual features call for unusual treatment, special notice is always given.

The intent of the editorial treatment both in large and in small matters, and in the recording of the textual information, has been to provide a clean reading text for the general user, with all specialized material isolated for the convenience of the scholar who wishes to consult it. The result has been to establish in the wording James's latest intentions in their most authoritative form, divorced from verbal corruption whether in the copy-text or in subsequent printings or editions. To this crucial aim has been added the further attempt to present James's final verbal intentions within a logically contrived system of his own accidentals that in their texture are as close to their most authoritative form as controlled editorial theory can establish from the documentary evidence that has been preserved for each work.

The aid offered by this edition to serious scholars of William James's writings is not confined to the presentation of a trustworthy, purified, and established text. Of equal ultimate importance are the apparatuses and appendixes devoted to the facts about the progress of James's thought from its earliest known beginnings to final publication in journal and book, and continuing to annotation in his private copies, recording alterations that were usually never made public except when practicable in a few plate-changes. Most of the materials here made available for close study of the development and refinement of James's ideas—almost literally in the workshop—have not previously been seen by scholars except in the James Collection of the Houghton Library, and then they could not be studied in detail without tiresome collation (here fully recorded in the apparatus). The refinements of thought between journal articles and book collection are of particular interest; but scholars may find more fascinating and fruitful for study the record of the manuscripts which—as they are reprinted in this edition or can be reconstructed from its apparatus—offer material for scholarly analysis of the way in which James shaped the thought itself as well as its expression, if the two can indeed ever be separated. As this edition progresses, the entire collection of manuscripts and of annotated journals and books at Harvard will be brought to philosophers, wherever they may live, for analysis and research in the privacy and convenience of their own studies.

It is the belief of the editors of the WORKS, as well of the Board, that this living historical record of the development of James's philosophical ideas and their expression, as found in the apparatus and appendixes, is as significant a part of the proposed 'definitive edition' for the purposes of scholarly research as is the establishment of a text closer to James's own intentions than is customarily represented by any single preserved document, including even his carefully worked-over books.

F.B.

The Text of *The Meaning of Truth*

I. THE DOCUMENTS

The earliest known record that James intended to collect the series of essays that became *The Meaning of Truth* and had started preparing them for the press is a diary entry for February 28, 1909, "Workt over 'Nature of Truth' book." However, this jotting seems to have been made relatively late in the process of collecting and revising the first twelve journal articles (proof for the thirteenth had not yet been returned) that precede the two previously unpublished Chapters XIV and XV, the last of which was added in proof. For example, little more than a week later, on March 9, he noted that he began to write on Russell: this would represent the first draft of Chapter XIV, "Two English Critics," which, according to his diary, he continued on March 10. On March 12 he busied himself with proof of the *Popular Science Monthly* article which later became Chapter XIII. On March 16 he "Finisht 'the Meaning of Truth'," perhaps a reference to a late stage of Chapter XIV. More work was needed, of course. On March 24, "House finisht copying my Nature of Truth." Unlike the manuscripts of Lectures VII and VIII of *Pragmatism* which were used as printer's copy—although one would have thought under the Riverside Press's protest—the manuscript of Chapter XV, written when James had finished correcting the proofs for the book, is like its predecessor, Chapter XIV, in not being consecutively numbered as book copy but more important in also showing no marks by the printer. It seems possible, then, to associate this note about the unknown House with professional typescript copies of the addendum to Chapter VII on Pratt and of Chapter XIV. (Whether a draft of the Preface could have been typed at this time is much more speculative and need not be pressed.) James may still have concerned himself with revising the book copy, for it was not until April 7 that he recorded carrying the manuscript to the Riverside Press in Cambridge. According to his diary he began to correct 'new proofs' on May 8; the reference may be to some other work, but the date would be suitable for the start of the first proofs for *The Meaning of Truth*. Curiously, it was as late as June 15 that he wrote to F. J. E. Woodbridge, editor of the *Journal of Philosophy, Psychology, and Scientific Methods*, for permission to reprint 'my polemic and other articles' in the collection about truth (which he first wrote as 'Nature of truth' and then altered to ' "meaning of truth, a sequel to pragmatism" ' to appear in September.[1] The 'Nature of Truth' seems to have been his originally conceived title, as found in the diary entry on February 28; although on March 16 he called it the 'Meaning', it was 'Nature' again on March 24. When on April 7 he brought the copy to the printer, his title was ambiguous and might be taken to represent still some uncertainty: "Took the MS of my new book Sequel to P-m to the Riverside press." In this sequence, a diary entry on March 11 "Finisht Preface, 18 pp.!" may not apply to *The Meaning of Truth*, since in the book the Preface is dated August, 1909. Nonetheless, it is difficult to think what other preface he could have been writing at this date, and the importance of the prefatory statement about his philosophic position does not suggest a late and hurried analysis written when the body of the book was in proof and ready for printing. The Preface is of approximately 3,200 words. The word count in James's manuscripts for Chapters XIV and XV may vary considerably from page to page, but about 145 words to the page is a fair average, which for eighteen pages would total 2,600 words, a close enough approximation given the probability of some expansion in a revision before August. Hence it is at least conjecturable that in the interval between his diary entry on March 10, "Wrote on Russell & Hawtrey" (which just possibly may have marked the first revision of the brief early draft of Chapter XIV begun the previous day), and the next entry about the book on March 15, "Wrote very well against B. Russell," he may have written a draft of the Preface before returning to Chapter XIV on March 15 and "Finisht 'the Meaning of Truth' " on March 16. Since the Preface would not have been given to the printer on April 7 with the rest of the copy, James would be certain to rework it, and thus he may have dated it in its final form when he sent it to the Press in August.

The publication history is relatively straightforward. The first American edition may be described as follows:

[1] *Journal of Philosophy, Psychology, and Scientific Methods* Collection, Columbia University Library, Special Collections. Woodbridge's reply of June 18 granting permission is in Harvard bMS Am 1092, letter 1178. The articles in question were the copy for Chapters IV–VII, X–XII.

title: THE MEANING OF TRUTH | A SEQUEL TO 'PRAGMATISM' | BY | WILLIAM JAMES | LONGMANS, GREEN, AND CO. | 91 AND 93 FIFTH AVENUE, NEW YORK | LONDON, BOMBAY AND CALCUTTA | 1909

collation: [unsigned: 1–20⁸ 21⁴], 164 leaves, pp. [2], [i–iv] v–xix [xx] xxi [xxii–xxiv], 1–302 (42, 50, 101, 120, 135, 161, 179, 216, 220, 225, 229, 245, 271, 286, 298–302 unnumbered)

contents: p. ᵖ1: blank; p. ᵖ2: advert. for 10 WJ books within a rule-frame; p. i: hf. tit., 'THE MEANING OF TRUTH'; p. ii: blank; p. iii: title; p. iv: 'COPYRIGHT, 1909, BY WILLIAM JAMES | ALL RIGHTS RESERVED'; p. v: 'PREFACE', subscribed on p. xx, '95 IRVING ST., CAMBRIDGE (MASS.), | August, 1909.'; p. xxi: 'CONTENTS'; p. xxiii: hf. tit., 'THE MEANING OF TRUTH'; p. xxiv: blank; p. 1: text, headed 'I | THE FUNCTION OF COGNITION¹'; p. 43: 'II | THE TIGERS IN INDIA¹'; p. 51: 'III | HUMANISM AND TRUTH¹'; p. 102: 'IV | THE RELATION BETWEEN KNOWER | AND KNOWN¹'; p. 121: 'V | THE ESSENCE OF HUMANISM¹'; p. 136: 'VI | A WORD MORE ABOUT TRUTH¹'; p. 162: 'VII | PROFESSOR PRATT ON TRUTH'; p. 180: 'VIII | THE PRAGMATIST ACCOUNT OF | TRUTH AND ITS MISUNDER-|STANDERS¹'; p. 217: 'IX | THE MEANING OF THE WORD | TRUTH¹'; p. 221: 'X | THE EXISTENCE OF JULIUS CÆSAR¹'; p. 226: 'XI | THE ABSOLUTE AND THE | STRENUOUS LIFE¹'; p. 230: 'XII | PROFESSOR HÉBERT ON | PRAGMATISM¹'; p. 246: 'XIII | ABSTRACTIONISM AND | RELATIVISMUS'; p. 272: 'XIV | TWO ENGLISH CRITICS'; p. 287: 'XV | A DIALOGUE'; p. 299: blank; p. 300: '𝕿𝖍𝖊 𝕽𝖎𝖛𝖊𝖗𝖘𝖎𝖉𝖊 𝕻𝖗𝖊𝖘𝖘 | CAMBRIDGE · MASSACHUSETTS | U·S·A'; pp. 301–302: blank.

paper and binding: white wove unwatermarked paper, leaf measuring 214 x 133 mm., trimmed gilt top edge, uncut fore and bottom edges; endpapers heavy white stock, free endpaper acting as flyleaf. Gray-green buckram with dark green buckram spine, spine paper label in black, '[double rule] | THE MEANING | OF TRUTH | BY | WILLIAM JAMES | [double rule]'. In the Bodleian Library, Oxford University, is preserved a copy of the first edition (2657.e.311) with the spine of the original dust jacket of buff paper pasted in, reading '[double rule] | THE MEANING | OF TRUTH | BY | WILLIAM JAMES | [double rule] | Price $1.25 net | LONGMANS'

copies consulted: Harvard (*AC85.J2376.909m[A] & [B]; AC9.Sa591.Zz909j); University of South Carolina; Seattle Public Library; Bodleian Library.

The first English edition consisted of the American sheets of the first printing except for the variant imprint on the conjugate title-page: 'LONGMANS, GREEN, AND CO. | 39 PATERNOSTER ROW, LONDON | NEW YORK, BOMBAY, AND CALCUTTA | 1909'. All records of this book in the Longmans, Green archives were destroyed during the 1940 air-raids, but the book was presumably published like *Pragmatism* before it, that is to say, with the imported American sheets bound in England in a casing identical with that in the United States. The statutory copy deposited in the then British Museum for copyright (223.b.13) is date-stamped November 5, 1909. The London Library owns a copy of the second printing in 1909 and the fourth in 1911.

The book had three printings in 1909 in the United States. The first was copyrighted on October 11, and the two copyright copies were received by the Library of Congress on October 14 (A 248528). The second and third printings followed in November, the latter with its title-page dated 1910. The fourth was called for in January 1911 but the fifth not until February 1914. Although published in 1919, the sixth continues the 1914 date on its title and the same printing notice on the verso but can be distinguished from the fifth printing by the addition of 'New Impression' on the title and the change of address of the publisher to Fourth Avenue and 30th Street, New York. A regular seventh printing appeared in 1927 and an eighth in March 1932. In 1943 parts of the book were detached and joined with *Pragmatism* to create a 'Combined Edition'.

The James Collection at Harvard University contains James's private marked copy of the first printing (*AC85.J2376.909m[B]). The upper two-fifths of the front free endpaper are torn off. On the verso of the back free endpaper are six page numbers in a column: 105 (heavy black ink), 249 (light black ink), 275 (light black ink), 255 (pencil), 265 (heavy black ink), 269 (pencil). A pencil brace and 'Corrected' appear to the right of the column. At the time of each of these entries, the appropriate correction or revision was made in the text in the same medium as the columnar notations. On page 105.14 of the book James deleted the final 's' in 'others' (62.37); on page 249.12 he altered 'privately' to 'privatively' (135.35); on page 255.20 'may' was inserted after 'it' (138.29); on page 265.18 'constitutive' was altered to 'regulative' (143.11); on page 269.12 'causes' was deleted and 'grounds' substituted (144.38); and, finally, on page 275.19 'else' was inserted after 'anything' (148.6). Of these six alterations, all but the change of 'causes' to 'grounds' were later made in the plates; this was the last on the list and may have been entered in the copy after the alteration of the other readings had been requested. The first error to be detected was 'privately', which is marked in ink to 'privatively' in the copy James presented to the Harvard Library on October 11, 1909 (*AC85.J2376.909m[A]), and thus must have been detected almost immediately, on the evidence of an erratum slip inserted in some copies of the first printing, including one that James presented to George Santayana[2] (*AC9.Sa591.Zz909j), tipped in before page 1. F. C. S. Schiller was responsible for the change from 'constitutive' to 'regulative'. On October 20 he thanked James for the receipt of a copy and on October 26 asked whether James had not meant to write 'regulative' instead of 'constitutive' on page 265.[3] On November 6 James replied that Schiller was right and

---

[2] Santayana made extensive pencil annotations in this copy.
[3] Houghton Library bMS Am 1092, letters 957–958.

that 'regulative' was the term of the 'Kantian pair' that he ought to have selected (Stanford M130, folder 18). In the second printing, the first of the two in November 1909, the plate for page 249 was altered to read 'privatively';[4] the other four changes were made in the plates of pages 105, 255, 265, and 275 in the third printing, the second in November; in the process of inserting 'else' on page 275 the printer was forced to change the text unauthoritatively from 'of which I am aware' to 'I am aware of' (see Textual Note to 148.6).[5] Thereafter, as established by collation on the Hinman Machine of the first printing against the seventh of 1927, no further alterations were made.[6] James's revision to 'grounds' (144.38) on page 269 enters the text for the first time in the present edition. So far as is known, no other authorial corrections exist in the book text, although the present edition adopts some present in marked copies of a few articles even though these had not found their way to James's annotated first printing of the book.

Except for Chapters XIV–XV, *The Meaning of Truth* consists of a collection of previously published journal articles, some only lightly touched up but a few considerably rearranged and rewritten. The exact details of the documents relating to the text that bear on the publication in book form are as follows:

Preface.
Manuscript or typescript (not preserved).

Chapter I. The Function of Cognition.
Annotated printed copy (not preserved): "On the Function of Cognition," *Mind*, 10 (Jan. 1885), 27–44 (McDermott 1885–1). The place of honor in this book is not only chronologically appropriate but structurally so, for in a letter of September 17, 1907, to Charles A. Strong, James asserted that this essay was the *'fons et origo'* of all his pragmatism as a theory of truth (Perry, *Thought and Character*, II, 548). An offprint is present in the James Collection, envelope 9 of Box O, containing only one annotation: the deletion in pencil of 'we' and the marginal substitution of 'he', the corrected reading found in the book (24.34). This alteration is repeated in James's marked file of *Mind* in the Houghton Library at Harvard (Phil.22.4.6*), which contains in addition the underlining of roman 'feeling' (16.8), the insertion 'Cf. Leibnitz I, 70' after footnote 4 (19.38), the shift of the double quotation marks (single in the book and in the present edition) at 28.30–31 to enclose 'about' instead of the

---

[4] As checked in the University of Virginia copy.
[5] As checked in the University of Georgia copy.
[6] The first printing in the Seattle Public Library was machined against the University of South Carolina copy of the 1927 printing.

phrase 'about realities', and the deletion at 31.8 of the journal 'latter' and the substitution of 'former' (the book reading is 'substitute'), for which see the Textual Note. In James's 1907 holograph table of contents for his proposed *Essays in Radical Empiricism* volume (bMS Am 1092, folder F7), "The Function of Cognition" is the first in order, but R. B. Perry did not reprint the essay in his 1912 collection of the *Essays*, no doubt because of its appearance, complete, in *The Meaning of Truth*.

Chapter II. The Tigers in India.

Annotated printed copy (not preserved): "The Knowing of Things Together," *Psychological Review*, 2 (March 1895), 105–124 (McD 1895–4). "The Tigers in India" is an extract from pages 107–110 of the journal article.[7] In the James Collection is preserved an annotated copy of the article in envelope 11 of Box O, but none of the markings affects the extract. Box O, envelope 14ª, preserves a combination of journal pages and typescript copy made from the journal which is without variation in the area covered by the extract. However, in James's annotated set of the *Psychological Review* (WJ 110.72) three revisions are present: the substitution of 'may be' for 'is' at 35.29 and again at 35.32, and the substitution of a comma and 'for' for a dash at 35.34–35. The article in this set is headed by James's pencil note, "Philosophy 3 [*written over* '9'] men may also refer to my article on the function of cognition in Mind, vol X p 27 (1885) W.J." This article originated as James's presidential address on December 27, 1894, at the meeting of the American Psychological Association at Princeton University. (On December 1, 1894, James admitted to J. M. Baldwin: "I haven't written a line yet, and imagine that nothing may come at all ... and I am disposed to think, if my paper does materialize, that since it will be wholly technical in form, it will be better to give it as one of the common communications and not as a presidential address" [J. M. Baldwin, *Between Two Wars* (1926), II, 207].) A summary was printed following the text in the *Psychological Review*, 2 (March 1895), 152–153, as the first of the abstracts of papers at the meeting. This was reprinted without substantive change in the summaries of articles section of the *Philosophical Review*, 4 (May 1895), 336–337, where it was subscribed as Author's Summary. The notation is confirmed by a letter on March 20 from James to J. E. Creighton, editor of the *Review*, saying that he is welcome to print 'my summary' (fMS Am 1092, vol. 18). Since the summary is thus authenticated as of James's own composition, it has an interest in connection with the article and is reprinted from the original *Psychological Review* text as Appendix I of the present volume, where it may be helpful in relating the passages of "The Tigers

---

[7] The complete article will be reprinted in the volume *Essays in Philosophy and Religion* in the WORKS.

in India" to the whole. In James's holograph table of contents for his proposed collection *Essays in Radical Empiricism*, "The Knowing of Things Together" is listed as second but is followed by the notation '(partly)', this perhaps being the reason why Perry omitted it from his collection of the *Essays* in 1912.

Chapter III. Humanism and Truth.

Annotated printed copy (not preserved): "Humanism and Truth," *Mind*, n.s. 13 (Oct. 1904), 457–475 (McD 1904–11) with brief additions from "Humanism and Truth Once More," *Mind*, n.s. 14 (April 1905), 190–198 (McD 1905–5). The text drawn from this latter article appears at 39.2–23, 39.29–40.9, and 58.6–59.21. An offprint of "Humanism and Truth" is not preserved in the James Collection, but in James's marked file set of *Mind* he drew a line against 44.21–24 and jotted in the margin the word 'suggestion', apparently in reference to his use of the word at 44.21; at 57.34 he deleted journal 'object' and substituted 'purpose' in the margin (the book reading is 'motive'). An unannotated offprint of "Humanism and Truth Once More" is in Box O, envelope 8, in the James Collection; the file set of *Mind* has one alteration but not in the portion used in *The Meaning of Truth*. A reference to the main article appears in a letter from James to Dickinson S. Miller, dated September 8, 1904, remarking that he has written three articles on the 'new philosophy', "Humanism and Truth," "Does 'Consciousness' Exist?" and "A World of Pure Experience" (bMS Am 1092.1). Although "Humanism and Truth" is listed as seventh in James's proposed table of contents for *Essays in Radical Empiricism*, Perry did not include it in his collection but he did add "Humanism and Truth Once More" which does not appear in James's contents list. This latter essay is reprinted in the collection *Essays in Radical Empiricism* in the WORKS.

Chapter IV. The Relation between Knower and Known.

Annotated printed copy (not preserved): "A World of Pure Experience," *Journal of Philosophy, Psychology, and Scientific Methods*, 1 (Sept. 29, 1904), 533–543; (Oct. 13, 1904), 561–570 (McD 1904–10). The chapter is extracted, with excisions, from the *Journal* part 1, pages 538.4–543.24, and part 2, pages 561.1–564.32. This includes most of sections III "The Cognitive Relation," IV "Substitution," and V "What Objective Reference Is"; omitted are sections I–II, VI–VII, which appeared in the reprint of the complete article in *Essays in Radical Empiricism* in Perry's collection and will be found in that volume in the WORKS. In the present volume, however, the excisions made in Chapter IV within the range of sections III–V from which the chapter is drawn are provided in the Historical Collation so that the continuous text of these sections may be followed as in the published article.

In a letter to F. J. E. Woodbridge, editor of the *Journal*, sent from Chocorua on August 7, 1904, James states that he ought to settle down to the second article (i.e., "The World of Pure Experience"). On August 17 he writes Woodbridge from Chocorua that he cannot send the article until September 5 or thereabouts. In an undated letter, perhaps only a few days later, he tells Woodbridge that his second paper ("A World of Pure Experience") should be cut into two parts and so he is sending the first half, hoping to post the rest in ten days. According to the letter to D. S. Miller mentioned above in the discussion of Chapter III, he had apparently finished the second part by September 8. On September 25 it is possible that the whole was in type, for James writes Woodbridge from Chocorua repeating a request that it be reprinted as a single article. An offprint in the James Collection, Box O, envelope 5, is preserved in this special form, which gives the second part continuous page numbers and rearranges the type into different pages to take account of the omission of the heading to the second section. A normal reprint of the two parts is preserved in the James Collection, Box O, envelope 8, unannotated; the file of the *Journal* in WJ 110.42 is not marked for this article. A manuscript of three chapters from a proposed book is found in Box F, envelope 3, first entitled "A World of Pure Experience" and then altered to "Radical Empiricism," but the manuscript appears to be later than the article and to have no intimate connection with it.

Chapter V. The Essence of Humanism.

Annotated printed copy (not preserved): "The Essence of Humanism," *Journal of Philosophy, Psychology, and Scientific Methods*, 2 (March 2, 1905), 113–118 (McD 1905–3 [dated June 8 in error]). Box O, envelope 6, contains a clipping without markings; the article is not annotated in James's file of the *Journal*. On February 3, 1905, James wrote to Woodbridge: "Here's another statement of my radical empiricism, prompted by 'Joseph's' review of me in the January Mind. . . . I venture to hope that this particular article may lead you to see that humanism can perfectly well house both the 'epistemological' realism, and the pragmatic empiricism which you so stoutly stand for jointly in your 'field of Logic' address. [¶] I have taken passage for Naples on the 25th, meaning to be gone 3 months, so if you are to publish at any proximate date I should have proof ere then." On February 6, in a letter offering Woodbridge what must be "How Two Minds Can Know One Thing," which the *Journal* published on March 30, 1905 (see *Essays in Radical Empiricism*), James added: "Meanwhile I have postponed my departure from Feb 25th to March 11th. so there seems no reason why I might not correct both proofs [*period del.*] before I go. I think, on the whole, that though the present article directly hitches on to the last words of my last article, the Thing and its relations, the article ['of' *del.*] called the Essence of Humanism had better appear before it."

"The Essence of Humanism" was listed as sixth in James's proposed table of contents for *Essays in Radical Empiricism* and was reprinted in Perry's edition, a procedure followed in the WORKS since the essay is a key document in James's discussion of empiricism.

Chapter VI. A Word More about Truth.

Annotated printed copy (not preserved) : "A Word More about Truth," *Journal of Philosophy, Psychology, and Scientific Methods,* 4 (July 18, 1907), 396–406 (McD 1907–7). Box O, envelope 5, contains a clipping but without markings; no annotations appear in James's file of the journal. The article is not mentioned specifically by name in the diary, but three entries may refer to it: on May 28, 1907, James noted, "Wrote article on Truth ('last word')"; on May 29 he "Revised article"; and on May 30 he "Finish^t & mailed article." As "One word more about truth" the essay is listed in tenth place in James's proposed table of contents for *Essays in Radical Empiricism* but it was not reprinted in Perry's edition and has also been omitted in the WORKS.

Chapter VII. Professor Pratt on Truth.

Annotated printed copy (not preserved) : "Professor Pratt on Truth," *Journal of Philosophy, Psychology, and Scientific Methods,* 4 (Aug. 15, 1907), 464–467 (McD 1907–8). Box O, envelope 7, contains an offprint without markings; the article is not annotated in James's file of the journal. The diary records on June 30, 1907, "Writing all a day a reply to Pratt's attack on Pragmatism's theory of truth," and on July 1, "Mailed reply to Pratt." On February 21, 1909, the diary note "Pratts 'What is Pragmatism?'" seems to refer either to James's receipt of a copy of Pratt's new book or else to his starting to read it, an entry that is of interest as applying to his writing the second part of this chapter in March 1909 according to his footnote statement (95.29–38). The copy for this addition in the book would have been either a manuscript or a typescript. A discarded note in pencil and in ink on Pratt's book written on L. L. Brown typewriter paper was kept and its blank verso used to inscribe fol. 3 of the manuscript for "Two English Critics"; in addition, an ink draft of some text for Chapter VII, also deleted, was used for the inscription of fol. 6, this written on the punched notebook paper that was the original stock for Chapter XIV and therefore presumably the paper used for the otherwise lost manuscript for the Chapter VII addition. The texts of these two fragments are transcribed after the Historical Collation for Chapter VII. In his table of contents for the proposed collection of *Essays in Radical Empiricism* James later inserted as his eleventh entry, below no. 10, 'Pratt on Truth'; however, Perry did not reprint the article in his edition and it has been omitted in the WORKS.

Chapter VIII. The Pragmatist Account of Truth and its Misunderstanders.

Annotated printed copy (not preserved) : "The Pragmatist Account of

Truth and Its Misunderstanders," *Philosophical Review*, 17 (Jan. 1908), 1–17 (McD 1908–1). Box O, envelope 15, no. 3, contains an offprint annotated in black ink and in blue pencil: at 100.35–36 after 'inquiry' James inserted in ink 'It is not a psychological, but rather a logical question.'; at 105.25 he corrected in ink the misprint 'peas' to the book reading 'pears'; at 111.12 after 'been' he inserted in blue pencil 'asserted,' (the book reads 'been asserted or questioned') and corrected in blue pencil the misprint 'even' to 'ever' in the line above (111.12), the reading of the book; finally, at 116.13 he altered 'können' to 'sollen' in blue pencil, also the reading of the book. A note on the cover of this offprint, signed 'H J' identifies these alterations and remarks that other notations, made in black pencil, are not James's. These are confined to an occasional marginal vertical stroke opposite some passages and to two comments: (1) at 106.14 the words 'unless reality' are underlined and a marginal query reads 'how do we know it'; (2) at 113.11 the word 'particular' is underlined and a marginal note inserted 'Prag 46'. The hand has not been identified but presumably it was some friend to whom James had lent the offprint, for James wrote on the cover 'Please return to' before his rubber-stamped name and address. James's diary records on November 10, 1907, "Work hard over article for Phil. Review"; on November 12, "Writing on Truth till late"; and on November 15, "Finisht & mailed my article for Phil. Rev." These are undoubtedly to be connected with "The Pragmatist Account of Truth," published the following January in the *Philosophical Review*.

Chapter IX. The Meaning of the Word Truth.

Annotated printed copy (not preserved): The exact printed copy that James marked up for the book is not altogether certain, although it was probably his privately printed pamphlet "The Meaning of the Word Truth" (McD 1908–4). The paper was given before the American Philosophical Association, meeting at Cornell University on December 26–28, 1907. On January 1, 1908, James noted in his diary that he was "Writing abstract on 'truth'." and on January 2 that he "finisht writing abstract about truth." These entries apply to the untitled abstract of his Association paper which was printed in the *Philosophical Review*, 17 (March 1908), 180–181, heading the Discussion section entitled "The Meaning and Criterion of Truth." On January 7, 1908, James wrote the Association's president, Harry N. Gardiner: "The *enclosures ['ures' *above del.* 'ed'] may perhaps entertain you. The larger type-writing is my remarks (or the remarks I would have made had there been a chance) at the "symposium" at Cornell. I am sending them to the Secretary for his report of proceedings. *I must ask you for *this [alt. from 'the'] *copy back.* I sent them to Strong, & *replied to [*above del.* 'enclosed'] his response. Then I sent both to Santayana, and I now enclose *his* response. Of course the doctrine is the one exprest in my lecture on Truth in "Pragmatism" without a hairs' variation. But it is so skeletonized that apparently people think it different" (MS fAm 1092, vol. 5). The abstract, typewritten, seems to have been the main enclosure, and the remainder the responses of Strong and Santayana. Another letter, on January 9, refers once more to this typed copy. It is clear that the abstract (P[28]) printed under the general heading for the discussion papers of "The Meaning and Criterion of Truth" represents an early state of the article before revision, and it is probably closer to the form of James's remarks at the meeting than any other preserved document. From James's use of the word 'abstract' to denote it, the typescript form as printed may have been briefer than the orally delivered paper, or the remarks from notes that James proposed to deliver but (according to his letter to Gardiner) was unable to speak in full.[8] At any rate, James adopted its essential content and structure for his revised version later printed in *Mind*.

On January 5, 1908, the diary records that he "Recopied truth paper." Although the reference may be to the abstract sent to Gardiner on January 7, it is also possible to speculate that in fact this was the revision of the abstract that he privately printed in a four-page fold as "The Meaning of the Word Truth,"[9] probably in early February. The *terminus ad quem* is a letter of February 12, in which he promised to send Horace M. Kallen a copy the next day. (P[24]) "The Meaning of the Word 'Truth'," *Mind*, n.s. 17 (July 1908), 455–456 (McD 1908–4) was probably set from an unmarked copy of the privately printed pamphlet (PPr) and not from, say, the carbon of a hypothetical typescript, the ribbon copy of which had been used to set the pamphlet—or from the recovered ribbon copy (or holograph) used by the printer of PPr. That P[24] and PPr were set from the same copy, or else P[24] from PPr, is clear enough; but the text is too brief to demonstrate the exact nature of the transmission, whether linear or else radiating from common copy. Both share readings in common that were altered by James in the printer's copy for the book or else in proof,[10] although no reading (whether variant or shared) can be inter-

[8] It is true, however, that by omitting the conclusion of the revised version ('These give ... constitution' [118.30–119.5]), James in some sort could have justified the word 'abstract' unless, however, the conclusion were added in the revision.

[9] 'THE MEANING OF THE WORD TRUTH.* | [short rule]' with footnote '*Remarks at the meeting of the American Philosophical | Association, Cornell University, December, 1907.', subscribed 'WILLIAM JAMES' on p. 4; 4 pp. [1] 2–4, wove paper watermarked BOND LINEN LEDGER, 216 x 138.5 mm. Copy in Houghton Library *AC85.J2376.907m; another copy as no. 9 in envelope 1 of Box O. Neither copy is annotated.

[10] As, for instance, PPr, P[24] 'thing' but (I) 'desk' at [1]117.18. Other common variants against (I) occur at 117.11, 117.18–118.1, 118.8, 118.18, 118.25, and 119.4. Of these, the abstract under "The Meaning and Criterion of Truth" (P[28]) agrees with PPr and P[24] against (I) in the substitute readings at 117.18, 117.18–118.1, and 118.8; but since it has different text P[28] offers no evidence in the case of the agreement of PPr and P[24] in 'Reality' at 119.4 versus (I) 'reality'.

preted to indicate the exact relationship. If it is true that, as early as January 5, James had written out the revised copy for the privately printed pamphlet,[11] one may assume without much doubt that the *Mind* publication was the later, but whether James would have sent a typescript duplicate to *Mind* (if one existed) or the pamphlet itself is not to be demonstrated, even though probability might suggest the latter course.

This problem is independent of the next, however, which is whether the printer's copy for the book was the pamphlet or an offprint from *Mind*. Here again the text is too brief for demonstration, and the evidence is slightly conflicting because James's revisions in the book copy or in proof tend to obscure the question of which document was marked up. For instance, the book (I) and *Mind* (P[24]) agree at 118.4 in italic *'that'* for roman 'that' in PPr, the pamphlet, and in the setting of *'Pragmatism'* in italics at 118.35 instead of the single quotation marks of PPr. It is interesting that the abstract (P[28]) agrees with (I) and P[24] in the first; its omission of the text of the conclusion prevents it from being a witness to the second. These straws in the wind might suggest that P[24] was the book copy, but the evidence is too slight for any certainty; for example, the use of italics in (I) as in P[24] for the book title *Pragmatism* versus single quotation marks in PPr is not evidential since it appears to have been only a part of the styling given the book in the printing-house.[12] On the other hand, the agreement of (I) and PPr in the correct reading 'withness' versus the P[24] misprint 'witness' (118.33) has no particular significance, either, for if P[24] had been the book copy the error would have been corrected as a matter of course. The one piece of evidence that may be significant is the agreement of (I) and PPr in no punctuation after 'you' at 117.2 introduc-

---

The book and P[28] agree in placing quotation marks about 'true' at 118.18 versus no quotes in PPr and P[24]. Another variant occurs at 117.11 in which the book (with P[28]) puts a semicolon after 'places' without omitting the comma after 'and' as does P[28], whereas PPr and P[24] read 'places∧ and,'—but this variant is also non-evidential.

[11] The question naturally arises why—if this hypothesis is true—James permitted the original 'abstract' form to go to the *Philosophical Review* (through the Association's secretary) in a mailing two days later than the writing of the revised version. Here we may only speculate, but it would not seem unreasonable to suggest that James could scarcely publish the identical revised form in two different philosophical journals, whereas the *Mind* editor would (seemingly) not object to reprinting a privately printed version. The differences between the 'abstract' in P[28] and the revised form in P[24] are sufficient to prevent the charge of double publication. Moreover, from his letter James shows that he is conscious that this paper marked no advance on the thinking of *Pragmatism* and he may have felt the full form not suitable for publication in the United States as a consequence.

[12] James usually surrounded book titles by quotation marks. The same use of italics for *'Pragmatism'* in the book versus single quotes and roman in the journal copy occurs at 84.1. At 79.34 (I) puts *Principles of Psychology* into italics from the journal single quotes, and at 126.3 and 143.33 the titles of books by other men are similarly italicized in (I) although printed in roman between quotation marks in the journal copy.

ing a quotation, as against the conventional P^{24} comma (and the P^{28} colon). In six similar cases that cluster immediately following between 117.5–9 and repeat the lack of punctuation, both PPr and P^{24} agree with (I) in this occasional characteristic of James's style; hence it could be argued that in marking copy for the printer James could have removed the comma from P^{24} for consistency, so that this also does not constitute evidence for a direct relationship of one or other document with (I). The argument is a valid one but it is applicable to almost any piece of evidence (except overlooked mechanical error) bearing on the transmission of a text when the author has intervened by correcting and revising copy. Thus, all one can say is that a small matter like this was hypothetically less liable to be altered by James than the lack of emphasis italics as in '*that*' which represents a kind of change he frequently made in copy. If probability is to tilt the beam, the unique evidence of this comma would seem to be more trustworthy than the contrary evidence of the italic word in the *Mind* offprint,[13] although the choice must remain always a matter of conjecture. Fortunately in this particular case the question of the exact copy between the two possibilities has no effect on the final edited text.

It is the present editor's working hypothesis that the abstract under "The Meaning and Criterion of Truth" was set from the typescript James mentioned as sent to the *Philosophical Review* on January 7. The interest in this document justifies reprinting it as Appendix II, in part because it seems to reflect more closely than the later revision in the pamphlet text the actual remarks delivered by James, and in part because it was either of his own typing or else typed directly from holograph even though the *Review* heavily restyled it. For reference, also, its substantive variants from the revised form are included in the Historical Collation where they may be seen at a glance. It is furthermore the working hypothesis—although a less certain one—that an annotated example of the privately printed pamphlet was the actual printer's copy for the book. Since it is also the working hypothesis that the text in *Mind* derived from the pamphlet, without authorial alteration, the *Mind* text is taken as having no authority, in contrast to the texts of the pamphlet and of the *Review* 'abstract.' James's file set of *Mind* has not been annotated.

Chapter X. The Existence of Julius Cæsar.

Annotated printed copy (not preserved): " 'Truth' versus 'Truthfulness'," *Journal of Philosophy, Psychology, and Scientific Methods*, 5 (March 26, 1908), 179–181 (McD 1908–3). In the James Collection,

[13] For instance, in *The Meaning of Truth* the book follows such punctuation or lack of punctuation in journal copy regularly and never removes a mark preceding a quotation in the copy. For what it is worth, also, although the James Collection contains two copies of the pamphlet, it has not preserved any example of a *Mind* offprint for this article. Such evidence—although not in an entirely similar situation —was useful in assisting the determination of book copy between two possibilities in *Pragmatism*; see WORKS, pp. 188–189.

envelope 7 of Box O contains an unannotated reprint; no markings appear in James's file of the *Journal*. The latter part of the journal text is omitted in the book, which substitutes the "Note" at 122.10–22. (The original *Journal* text for this section is reprinted at the end of the Historical Collation for Chapter X.) In the Miscellaneous Manuscripts Collection, the Joseph Regenstein Library of the University of Chicago, is preserved a five-page typescript, the ribbon copy, on wove paper watermarked DIXIE BOND (279 x 216 mm.) double-spaced, headed 'W. JAMES'S STATEMENT.' Autograph corrections and revisions appear, chiefly in ink but some in pencil. On the back of the last leaf is the note in another hand, 'Presented to F S B by William James. Published in Jr. of Phil., Psych, & Sci Meth., under title *Truth and "Truthfulness,"* 1908.'[14] The text is that of the *Journal* article, complete, but in a considerably earlier state, perhaps even the original. The typing is amateurish and some signs of composition during the course of the typing suggest that James himself was the typist, but whether he composed it on the typewriter or copied an antecedent manuscript draft is not to be determined. On the first page James wrote '1 Cop.' The carbon copy to which this seems to refer is preserved in the Special Collections (Manuscript Division) of the Stanford University Library, the paper being the same. The use of this Dixie Bond paper suggests that the Statement was typed in Cambridge, for the stock appears—although rarely—in James's manuscripts.[15] The Stanford carbon was a presentation from James to his close friend F. C. S. Schiller, and forms a part of the Schiller collection of letters bequeathed by his widow and now kept in the Educators and Librarians Collection.

Using a pencil, James wrote in eight corrections and revisions, perhaps while the paper was still in the typewriter or before the next page was

---

[14] The 'F S B' is Frederick Stephen Breed, Associate Professor of Philosophy at the University of Chicago, whose widow gave the typescript in 1962 to the University of Chicago Library with an accompanying letter: "This manuscript was presented to my husband (Dr. Frederick S. Breed) when he was a student of Dr. William James at Harvard, about 1908 or '09. He completed his doctorate at Harvard in Philosophy and had a very fine relationship with Dr. James. He was also interested in fine writing and cherished this as a 'working copy' of a great master in both fields." F. S. Breed is recorded in the 1907–1908 Harvard University Catalogue as in his second year of graduate school; he received his doctorate in 1910. In the same catalogue James is listed as Emeritus, and seems to have taught no courses after Philosophy D in 1906–1907. The date of presentation, then, is uncertain and does not bear on the date of the typescript's composition or the order of the annotations in the two copies.

[15] This paper is uncommon in the preserved James manuscripts, but three leaves of holograph (one dated July 30, 1906) occur among the loose papers in bMS Am 1092 Mounted MSS "From Notebooks on Truth, Reality, Unity, Will to Believe"; in the typescript "Preliminary Report on Mrs. Piper's Hodgson-Control" (also in Mounted MSS), eight leaves occur in the first nineteen sheets.

typed, as attested by the carbon impressions in the Stanford copy. Subsequently, he made the major part of his revision in ink in both copies, and later independently revised both without reference to each other. These separate revisions overlap in only one place: the fourth paragraph had been typed to end '& that the attributes I have in mind shall be his.' In the revision of the two copies together, James interlined 'mean' above deleted 'be' and altered the original ending after 'his.' by adding handwritten 'attributes, that fact is enough.' to end the first page. The second page began with a new paragraph, 'I enlarge it by admitting finite intermediaries', itself revised by hand. In the Chicago typescript only the original ink addition 'fact' is crossed through and 'statute' interlined in pencil. However, in the Stanford carbon the whole of the addition after 'attributes, that' is deleted and a new ending substituted, reading 'intention suffices to make it true;'. Probably because of the turn of the page, James did not delete the paragraph indention beginning page 2, before 'I enlarge'; however, the semicolon of the revision at the foot of the preceding page sufficiently indicates his altered intention. One might conjecture that the complete change in the sentence ending, and indeed in the sentence structure that links it to the next paragraph, in the Stanford carbon is perhaps more likely to come later than the less drastic Chicago alteration, and thus that the Stanford revisions made after the initial general round and independent of the Chicago separate alterations could represent James's later preferences. An analogy would be the marginalia to "Transatlantic Truth" which are more copious in the copy sent to his student Kallen than in his own private copy. Thus it is possible that for Schiller's benefit James revised the carbon more thoroughly than he had done the original in his possession (always assuming that the annotations were not made for Breed at a later time). The order of annotation turns out to be basically undemonstrable, whatever one's opinions about probability; nevertheless, without regard for the actual history, this typescript is a valuable textual document and hence it has been reproduced in Appendix III in an eclectic text that contains all the revisions in both typescripts conflated. In the Historical Collation to Chapter X the typescript variants from the printed text have been included in their respective finally revised forms, the differences distinguished; but a separate list of Alterations is attached to the Appendix III text, keyed to its lineation in the present edition, that makes clear the original typescript readings and the changes that James made in both documents.

At least two entries in James's diary may refer to his rewriting of the Statement into the form of the *Journal* article. On January 8, 1908, within a few days of his work on the privately printed form of "The Meaning of the Word Truth," he noted, "Writing about 'truth'," with the same entry ("Writing about 'truth' etc.") the next day. Since the article appeared in the March 26 number of the *Journal of Philosophy, Psychology, and Scientific Methods,* the time would be about right to associate these entries with " 'Truth' versus 'Truthfulness'."[16] Some part of the revision of the article in the book seems to have resulted from a letter to James from John Dewey on February 24, 1909, taking exception to certain of its statements, for which see Professor Skrupskelis' Notes.

Chapter XI. The Absolute and the Strenuous Life.

Annotated printed copy (not preserved) : "The Absolute and the Strenuous Life," *Journal of Philosophy, Psychology, and Scientific Methods,* 4 (Sept. 26, 1907), 546–548 (McD 1907–9), printed in the Discussion section. In the James Collection, Box O, envelope 5, contains an unannotated offprint; no markings are present in James's file of the *Journal.* No diary entry seems to refer to the writing of this note.

Chapter XII. Professor Hébert on Pragmatism.

Annotated printed copy (not preserved) : Review of Marcel Hébert, *Le Pragmatisme; étude de ses diverses formes,* printed in the review section of the *Journal of Philosophy, Psychology, and Scientific Methods,* 5 (Dec. 3, 1908), 689–694 (McD 1908–8). No offprints are found in the James Collection and there are no markings in his file of the *Journal.* During James's visit to his brother Henry in England, the diary records on August 10, 1908, "Wrote on my review of Hebert on truth," and again on August 13, "Wrote on my review of Hebert's pragmatism all the morning." In a letter to F. J. E. Woodbridge, the editor of the *Journal,* James writes on August 14 that he encloses "one more attempt at 'truth'," almost certainly this review.

Chapter XIII. Abstractionism and 'Relativismus'.

Annotated proof or printed copy (not preserved) : "On a Very Prevalent Abuse of Abstraction," *Popular Science Monthly,* 74 (May 1909), 485–493 (McD 1909–4). In envelope 10 of Box O an offprint is preserved without annotation. On February 12, 1909, James's diary records, "Finisht article on Abstractionism for Pop. Sci." and on March 12, "Proof of Pop. Sci. article on Relativismus."

Chapter XIV. Two English Critics.

Typescript (not preserved) : The original manuscript (McD 1909–8)[17]

[16] The particular terms of the January 5, 1908, entry, 'Recopied truth paper' appear to associate this with the preparation of "The Meaning of the Word Truth" revised from its abstract form instead of with the January 8–9 entries conjecturally related to " 'Truth' versus 'Truthfulness'." See above under Chapter IX.

[17] The McDermott checklist number 1908–9 was assigned in error under the misapprehension that "Two English Critics" was the title of a James article in the *Albany Review* for January 1908. Instead, the reference is to Bertrand Russell's review of James's *Pragmatism,* entitled "Transatlantic 'Truth'," pp. 393–410. The number must be corrected to 1909–8 to be brought under *The Meaning of Truth* instead.

is found in the James Collection in bMS Am 1092 under Mounted Manuscripts with the heading " 'Meaning of Truth'." Unlike the manuscripts
of Lectures VII and VIII of *Pragmatism*, the pages have not been renumbered in a book series for printer's copy nor do printer's markings appear,
signs that the Riverside Press was not given the manuscripts of Chapters
XIV and XV to set, just possibly because difficulties with the similarly
revised manuscripts for *Pragmatism* may have persuaded James not to
submit such heavily worked-over copy.

On February 13, 1908, James's diary notes that he annotated Russell's
article (*i.e.*, "Transatlantic 'Truth' " in the January *Albany Review*) and
sent it to his graduate student Horace M. Kallen, who was studying at
Oxford and had sent James the reprint. The letter of February 12 in which
the annotated copy was returned has been preserved (see Appendix IV).
Not only was Kallen writing a doctoral dissertation "Notes on the Nature
of Truth" (which James had criticized in draft form in a letter of August 15
[fMS Am 1092]) but he was also in touch with Russell. This copy of the
annotated offprint is now at Harvard (WJ 500.5) ; a more extensively annotated copy is preserved in the Russell Archives at McMaster University.
The marginalia in both copies are transcribed in Appendix IV.

James's diary for February 21, 1909, records the title of Pratt's *What
is Pragmatism?*, on which he began to make notes, two of which are preserved deleted on the versos of fols. 3 and 6 of the manuscript of Chapter
XIV. (See under Chapter VII and the discussion below.) James then
worked on revising the journal articles for chapters of *The Meaning of
Truth*, if that is the meaning of the February 28 entry "Workt over 'Nature of Truth' book," and it was not until March 9 that he noted "Began
to write on Bertrand Russell's transatlantic truth," with an additional entry
on March 10, "Wrote on Russell & Hawtrey," and on March 15, "Wrote
very well against B. Russell." When on March 16 he records "Finisht 'the
Meaning of Truth'," it would seem that Chapter XIV was substantially
completed, or at least in an advanced stage. The entry on March 24,
"House finisht copying my Nature of Truth" may corroborate what is suggested by the lack of printer's marks in the manuscript—that a typescript
of Chapter XIV had been completed for James on this date. (Chapter
XV, by James's statement, was written after he had read proofs for the
book.) Since a typescript of the one chapter (and even of the second section of Chapter VII if this had been included) would scarcely have taken
eight days to prepare, it seems probable that more work was devoted to
the manuscript between March 16 and a few days before March 24. Even
so, the delay between March 24 and the delivery of the book's copy to the
Riverside Press on April 7 remains unaccounted for, except by further
possible revision of the earlier journal articles, perhaps accompanied by a revision of the Chapter XIV typescript to something intermediate between
the manuscript and the book text. It is certain, however, that this interval
could not have been devoted to any of the revision represented in the

present manuscript, at least: this document must have been complete shortly before March 24 at the latest. The postscript in the book is not found in the manuscript since James did not receive Russell's *Edinburgh Review* article until May 14, 1909 (see the Note on 152.34–153.5 and Appendix IV); hence the postscript was added in proof at no inconvenience to the printer since it fitted below the text on the last page of the chapter and required no repaging.

The essay appears to have been written out, at first, as a relatively brief note of five pages concerned only with Bertrand Russell's "Transatlantic Truth" but then expanded to eighteen with more material, including a discussion of Hawtrey. The original paper James used was a rather heavy grayish wove unwatermarked paper (267 x 203 mm.) punched with two holes for notebook use. For his late revisions he used a white wove typewriter paper (267 x 203 mm.) manufactured by the L. L. Brown Paper Co., Adams, Massachusetts, and watermarked G in a shield with an arm brandishing a scimitar above, the countermark being L L Brown Paper Co.

The revision was so extensive and its history so complex that the following synopsis of its leaves may act as a reference for the verbal description. In this synopsis N stands for the original punched notebook paper and B for the L. L. Brown typewriter paper; page-line references are to the present edition and its text.

Fol. 1 [N] (*lightly numbered 1 in pencil upper left*): 'TWO ... says, "to' (146.0–12).

2 [N] (*numbered R.² black ink upper right*): 'settle the ... proposed as the' (146.12–147.2), *ending with deleted* 'only ration reasonable ... pragmatist critic,' | ['the high valu' *independ. del.*] [*cont. on del. fol. 4ᵛ false start; the undeleted text then continued on fol. 4, the connecting text being deleted later at the head of 4 when fol. 3 inserted*].

3 [B] (*numbered 3 black ink centered*): 'causa ... comports.' (147.2–6). [6 *lines written on blank verso of deleted pencil and ink note for Ch. VII now constituting 3ᵛ; this inserted leaf replaces deleted text at head of fol. 4*].

4 [N] (*numbered 4 light ink upper left to right of pencil 4 over pencil 3 deleted in black ink*): [*begins with space at left and then deleted* 'distinction between ... No'] 'No truth-claimer ... exist.' (147.7–15), *ending with deleted* 'at all ... accus-' *continued by deleted text head of fol. 10.*

5 [B] (*numbered 5 black ink upper left*): 'This is ... easily' (147.15–26), *last word with space at right.*

6 [N] (*numbered 6 black ink upper left over black ink 5*): [*begins deleted* 'or Mr. Hawtrey.' *then deleted* 'This is the usual ... make out that'] 'play on ... 'true' though' (147.26–31).

7 [B] (*numbered 7 black ink upper left to left of black ink deleted 6*):
'what it declares . . . exist. [*insert 7½*] Mr. Russell . . . pure logic'
(147.31–36, 148.10–17).

7½ [B] (*numbered 7½ black ink upper left*): 'It is . . . currency.'
(147.37–148.9).

8 [B] (*numbered 8 black ink upper left*): 'is so native . . . Then' (148.17–
30).

9 [B] (*numbered 9 black ink upper left*): 'two words . . . deliverance.'
(148.30–149.6).

10 [N] (*numbered 10 black ink upper left to left of pencil 6 over pencil
5 deleted black ink*): [*deleted* 'tomed to think . . . belief.'] [*no* ¶] ' "According . . . pragmatist mouth.' (149.6–15) [*deleted* 'for the pragmatist
. . . reality!'].

11 [B] (*numbered 11 black ink upper left*): 'But may not . . . if I'
(149.16–30) [*deleted* 'under-'].

12 [B] (*numbered 12 black ink upper left*): 'follow it . . . 'men', which'
(149.30–150.9).

13 [B] (*part page numbered 13 black ink upper left*): 'which they . . .
the word' (150.9–16); *at foot is false start* 'which' *deleted when James
stopped and turned page end for end (as usual when writing on the
back of a discarded leaf)*.

14 [N] (*numbered 14 light ink upper left over pencil* 11): 'the word . . .
Why that Cæsar is' (150.16–28).

15 [N] (*numbered 15 black ink upper left over pencil* 12): 'is dead.' . . .
for definition' (150.28–151.4).

16 [N] (*numbered 16 black ink upper left over pencil* 13): 'one needs . . .
propositions.' (151.4–15) [*deleted* 'But the . . . for those' *continued with
deleted text head of fol.* 17].

16½ [B] (*numbered 16½ black ink upper left*): 'I do not say . . . belief's
quality' [='in the belief'] (151.16–26).

17 [N] (*numbered 17 black ink upper left to left of ink-deleted pencil*
14): [*deleted* 'who wish to . . . not a fact'] 'so that . . . objection.'
(151.26–31) [*deleted* 'In'].

18 [N] (*numbered 18 light ink upper left*): [*deleted* 'any case . . . discussing.'] 'Whoever takes . . . beast,' (151.32–152.4) [*deleted* 'but does he
see . . . would say' *continued with deleted text head of fol.* 20].

19 [B] (*part page numbered 19 black ink upper left*): 'just as . . . anatomist.' (152.4–8).

20 [B] (*part page numbered 20 light ink upper left*): [*deleted* 'it seems
. . . beast!'] 'It almost . . . entities, through' (152.9–18).

21 [N] (*numbered 21 black ink upper left to right of deleted light ink
doubtful 9*): [*deleted* 'and taken in a vacuum . . . through'] 'every possible . . . exhibits.' [='show.'] (152.18–33). [P. S. *wanting*].

deleted versos

3ᵛ [B] (*unnumbered*) : 'Pratt seems . . . does exist.', *part page notes for Ch.* VII.

4ᵛ [N] (*unnumbered*) : 'am in the position . . . at large;', *false start continuing fol.* 2.

6ᵛ [N] (*unnumbered*) : 'Since he himself . . . experience,' *part page draft for text in Ch.* VII.

13ᵛ [B] (*unnumbered*) : 'substitutable. But when you . . . workings.' [*deleted* 'It is an . . . truth of the'], *continues text foot of deleted fol.* 19ᵛ *and is continued head of fol.* 20ᵛ.

19ᵛ [B] (*unnumbered*) : 'Such a definition . . . mutually', *begins deleted passage continued on fol.* 13ᵛ.

20ᵛ: [B] (*unnumbered part page*) : [*deleted* 'belief that Caesar . . . exist,'] 'That Caesar does exist . . . definition.', *continued from fol.* 13ᵛ.

Text in deleted passages is found in the Alterations list in the apparatus; the text of deleted versos is added at the end of that list, except for fols. 3ᵛ and 6ᵛ which are appended to the Historical Collation for Chapter VII.

On March 9, 1909, James began to write the text for fol. 1 below some penciled notes at the head, preceded by a pencil 1, 'boat = vehicle = omnibus | book is eloquent .˙. is about eloquence.', the first words of which refer to material at 151.35–152.8 on fol. 18, notebook paper, and the second group to a passage at 149.27–32 on fol. 11, Brown's typewriter paper. At some later time after the decision to include Hawtrey in the discourse —and perhaps as the final operation of renumbering the leaves—the title 'Two English Critics' was written in black ink over these pencil lines. After completing unnumbered(?) fol. 1, James proceeded to fol. 2, which he numbered 'R.²' in ink in the right-hand corner, this evidently an identification for a piece on Russell. He then started to write his third page, now 4ᵛ, unnumbered, but after two lines he abandoned and deleted it, deleted some text at the foot of fol. 2 and proceeded to write a new unnumbered third leaf (now fol. 4) on its back, beginning 'the *meaning* which the word truth comports' ('distinction between truth and falsehood in' in the line above seems to be a discarded later insertion). He completed this leaf and carried on to his next leaf, also unnumbered (now fol. 10), concluding the initial inscription on his unnumbered fifth leaf, now fol. 21.

In the next stage, probably starting with March 10, James decided to include Hawtrey (or at least to expand what on the evidence of the deleted start of fol. 6 could have been only a brief mention in an early revision), and he added after what is now fol. 10 (his original fourth leaf) five pages of manuscript—now lost—on the notebook paper before coming to what is preserved as the sequence on present fols. 14–18, less 16½, still on the notebook paper, and then carried on to one or perhaps two lost leaves that would have led into the original conclusion on present fol. 21. At the same time, or very close to it, he added a now lost leaf of notebook paper between present fol. 4 and present 10 of his original sequence, and it would seem that at this time he numbered in pencil the pages of what he thought might be his essay.[18] Folio 2 had already been numbered R² in ink but the other pages were now numbered for the first time. Present fol. 4 was 3, the lost intervening leaf conjecturally 4, and fol. 10 was 5. Then there would have been 6–10 in the lost leaves before the preserved leaves numbered 11–14 (present 14–17), at which point although the foliation stopped temporarily, the revision carried on to connect with what would have been fol. 19 (original 5, now 21). The evidence of the subsequent renumbering suggests that James next inserted present fol. 3 on the Brown typewriter paper to replace deletion of text at the foot of fol. 2 and the head of fol. 4. It then seems that he foliated this insert 3 in ink when he wrote it and later altered his earlier fol. 3 to 4 in pencil; fol. 10—first numbered 5 in pencil—was changed in pencil to 6 to accommodate the added fol. 3.

The initial use for fol. 3 of the Brown typewriter paper (later to be used exclusively for the manuscript of Chapter XV) has its points of interest, for it was a discarded leaf containing eight lines on an unnumbered page of a note on Pratt's *What Is Pragmatism?* The first sentence of the note consists of six pencil lines with an ink interlineation; the second sentence is inscribed in ink as an afterthought, and the vertical deleting line for the page is also in ink. The case of fol. 3 and its verso has some relation to the curious circumstances involving the appearance of fol. 6 (notebook paper) written on the back of a discarded draft of material in Chapter VII, "Profesor Pratt on Truth," covered roughly by 94.7–16, 95.26–96.5, 97.26–29, material in part referred to in the jotting on fol. 3ᵛ. However, this material occurs only in the second part of the chapter on Pratt, which was added to the original journal article, James tells us in a footnote at 93.33–35, when he read Pratt's *What Is Pragmatism?*: "The comments I have printed were written in March, 1909, after some of the articles printed later in the present volume." Chapters VIII–XII appeared in journals in 1907–8, and only Chapter XIII, "Abstractionism and 'Relativismus'," came out in 1909, finished on February 12, according to the diary, and proofread on March 12. Thus, James's statement would mean that the addition to Chapter VII was made before Chapters XIV and XV, since no other parts of the book would qualify for exclusion by the word 'some'. On February 21 James's diary contains the simple note "Pratt's 'What is Pragmatism?'," which one may assume signifies that he had received or perhaps had started to read the book on that date. On February 28 he

---

[18] The figure 1 comes nearly on the line to the left of the first line of the pencil notes and could easily be a key to them, not a foliation. James did not ordinarily number the first pages of his manuscripts.

"Workt over 'Nature of Truth' book," and on March 9 "Began to write on Bertrand Russell's transatlantic truth." On March 16 the entry "Finisht 'the Meaning of Truth'" would suggest that Chapter XIV (at least in some form, perhaps not the final one) had been completed and presumably what at the time he felt was the necessary annotation of the journal articles for the printer. It is impossible to estimate whether Chapter XIV took a week to write and revise, and thus it is likely that he set to work on the addendum to Chapter VII shortly after he had read *What Is Pragmatism?* sometime between February 21 and March 9 when Chapter XIV was started. Whether the February 28 diary entry about working on the book refers to this second part of Chapter VII or to revision of journal articles cannot be determined. What can be conjectured with confidence, however, is that the second part of the Pratt essay had been written—almost certainly on the same notebook paper as the original form of Chapter XIV— before the stage of revision represented by the insertion of fol. 6 on the blank verso of the discarded draft, and even earlier as indicated by the insertion of fol. 3 on the blank verso of a note on the book that seems to have been jotted down on the L. L. Brown typewriter paper while he was reading or marking *What Is Pragmatism?*

Whether the expansion of Chapter VII came in an interval between the writing of the first draft of Chapter XIV on notebook paper and its subsequent revision on the same paper, or preceded it, is unknown; but only a matter of days at best could have intervened between the two so that James had to hand two discarded leaves from the second part of Chapter VII when he came to the early revision of XIV. However, the original start of fol. 6 text with its mention of Hawtrey that relates to the first stage of revision does not follow continuously with any preserved text in the manuscript; thus it must have completed some sentence (before a deletion at the foot) in the notebook leaf that has been hypothesized as once existing as an addition after present fol. 4, one that would have been numbered 4 in pencil in the first foliation. The start of fol. 6 ('or Mr. Hawtrey.') has been independently deleted before the beginning of the text (now deleted) that runs 'This is the usual slander . . . .' However, on fol. 6 the undeleted text does not continue the deleted opening seven lines but joins with the text at the foot of present (inserted) fol. 5. Thus the deletion at the head of 6 (at the time when it was numbered 5) must have been made as a part of a revision during composition, and James then continued the text of lost fol. 4 above its deleted foot with the new text on present 6 (then 5), reading 'play on their reader's readiness' (147.26). Later, present fol. 5 was written on Brown's typewriter paper to substitute for this lost fol. 4 and to restore the originally deleted material about the critics' slander. Present fol. 6 was originally numbered 5 in the text ink, but the number was changed to the final 6 after the insertion of fol. 5. If the original foliation of 6 as 5 had been in pencil, one could have conjectured that the leaf was added at the time the hypothetical fol. 4 was inserted after fol. 3 (now 4). But instead the insertion of present 6 seems to have been related to the addition of the succeeding leaf on typewriter paper which has continuous text with it and was originally numbered 6 in dark ink, then altered to 7 probably at the time 5 was changed to 6 on the preceding insert. Hence the punched paper of fol. 6 (since it came from a discarded leaf from Chapter VII) was not a part of the early revision on punched paper but instead takes its place in the revisory sequence on Brown's typewriter paper.

This fol. 7 (altered from 6) is followed in turn by an added 7½ marked for insertion within the text of 7. That this number was never altered means only that it was written after fol. 7 had been renumbered. More important, perhaps, is the fact that fol. 8, on typewriter paper, is not altered, nor is any number thereafter except for the changes needed to bring the earlier numbered notebook leaves into the series of the final foliation. It would seem, then, that fol. 6 was first inserted, numbered 5, with continuous text after a lost pencil-numbered fol. 4 and was immediately followed by the inscription of fol. 7, first numbered 6, and then by fol. 8. When the conjectured fourth leaf was removed and fol. 5 (revising the text at the start of 6) was inserted, the numbering 5 on fol. 6 was altered to 6, and 6 on fol. 7 to 7.

It does not follow, necessarily, that fol. 8 succeeded without delay the inscription of fol. 7. The last sentence of fol. 7 'The abstract world of mathematics & pure logic' was deleted so that the leaf was made to end with the sentence concluding 'another example of what I have called (above, p. 000) vicious abstractionism.'[19] The deleted phrase was marked *stet* before fol. 8 was written, but it may seem more probable that the last sentence was deleted to precede the excision of some matter on a following now lost leaf before the sentence was restored and continued on fol. 8, the more especially since 8 is numbered in a lighter ink also used originally to number fol. 13 (touched up later in black ink), and 16 (numbered 13 in light ink and renumbered 16 in black), as well as 18–20, an ink that was also used for the text of inserted fol. 19 written on the back of an un-numbered leaf that is the first in a long passage of deleted text found on fols. 19^v, 13^v, and 20^v. In fact, after the deletion of the start of the sentence at the foot of fol. 7, the text of fol. 10 could follow quite appropriately. On the other hand, the long discarded unnumbered passage beginning on fol. 19^v, continuing on 13^v, and ending halfway down on 20^v (transcribed at the end of the list of Alterations in the Manuscript) seems originally to have carried the argument from the foot of fol. 7 (above the deleted start of the last sentence on the page) to join with the fourth line on original leaf fol. 10 following the deletion at the top of 10's initial continuation of fol. 4. It follows that present fols. 8–9 are later substitutes for these three

---

[19] This is a reference to Chapter XIII.

leaves, and that the *stet* at the foot of fol. 7 restored its part sentence only when revised fol. 8 was written as the start of two substitute leaves.

We have now progressed to the stage of revision represented by the incorporation in the final text of the original fourth leaf of the first draft, now numbered 10. Folios 11–12 and the half page fol. 13 now follow in order to expand the text between 10 and the second-stage insertion of notebook leaves 14–18 that had been added between the originally continuous text of fols. 10 and 21. An insertion 16½ on typewriter paper was made between notebook leaves 16 and 17. Folio 20 on typewriter paper then followed notebook leaf 18, but a small amount of text at the foot of 18 and the head of 20 was deleted to admit the revision found in the six lines that constitute inserted fol. 19. After the deletion at the head of notebook leaf 21 (which had originally followed the undeleted text at the foot of 10), the final leaf 20 on typewriter paper was fitted in and the revision of the whole essay was complete.[20]

Chapter XV. A Dialogue.

Typescript (not preserved): The original manuscript (McD 1909–8) entitled "Postscript," of sixteen leaves, is found in the James Collection in bMS Am 1092 under Mounted Manuscripts with the heading " 'Meaning of Truth'." The first sentence states that the chapter was not written until James had completed the proofs 'of all that precedes', which of course would include Chapter XIV. The date could have been as late as August, when final copy for the Preface seems to have been sent to the printer, according to its subscription. Otherwise, nothing is known of the history of the chapter except that the interval was short enough so that the same stock of L. L. Brown typewriter paper was used for its sixteen leaves as for the later revised sheets of Chapter XIV. Like Chapter XIV, this manuscript shows no printer's markings, and it is probable that a typescript was made from it for the press. Consecutive numbering as part of the book's copy would not have been found in any case, for it was not submitted at the same time as the rest of the copy. The leaves contain text as follows, numbered in ink [1] 2–16 centered:

Fol. 1 (*unnumbered*): 'A DIALOGUE [= MS 'Postscript'] ... question may' (154.0–9).
2 'be asked: ... if on the' (154.9–19).
3 (*numbered* 3 *over* 2): 'one hand ... because there' (154.19–155.11).
4 (*numbered* 4 *over* 3): 'are no ideas ... predetermined by' (155.11–22).
5 'the event's ... what do' (155.22–37).
6 'you mean by ... intermediate between' (155.37–156.15).

---

[20] The notes and the draft for the text of Chapter VII found on fols. 3ᵛ and 6ᵛ are transcribed after the Historical Collation for that chapter.

7 'the facts . . . noetic *value*.' [= 'value in noetic terms.'] (156.15–30) [*deleted* 'for intelligence'].

8 'PRAG:—A sort of . . . sure that' (156.31–157.1) [*deleted* 'your notion of . . . nothing to do with', *continued on fol.* 9].

9 'no [*deleted* 'the'] notion . . . name for a' (157.1–16).

10 'potential as . . . only another' (157.16–28).

11 'name for . . . knowledge know' (157.28–158.3) [*deleted* 'when it comes becomes actual.'] *cont. on fol.* 12.

12 'when it comes? . . . correlative' (158.3–27).

13 'and interdependent . . . when you' (158.27–30) [*deleted* 'ask me whether . . . from the dilemma'].

14 'point your first . . . make them yourself?' (158.30–159.6).

15 (*numbered* 15 *to right of deleted* 14 *over* 13 *over* 12): [*deleted* 'word truth, . . . pragmatist view.'] 'ANTI-PRAG:—Never! . . . conception' (159.7–13).

16 (*numbered* 16 *to right of deleted* 14 *over* 13): 'of truth. [= 'conception. Perhaps'] . . . men.' [='of thought.'] (159.13–20).

deleted versos

1ᵛ (*unnumbered*): 'but that neither ideas . . . to give it.'

5ᵛ (*unnumbered*): 'Probably the idea . . . in question,' [*deleted* 'but that it unfor which unfortunately'], *continued on fol.* 6ᵛ *after a trial start on fol.* 1ᵛ

6ᵛ (*unnumbered*): 'or that there . . . in advance determines' [*deleted* 'unequivocally']

9ᵛ (*part page numbered* 9): 'defining the notion . . . there being a', *continues deleted text foot of fol.* 8.

13ᵛ (*numbered* 11½): 'name for the fact . . . possibility merely.'

The order of all the revisions and expansions is not entirely clear, but it would seem that the essay was at first planned in standard expository form and not as a dialogue. What may perhaps be the original first page is now found deleted on the verso of fol. 5, initially continued on what is now the verso of fol. 1, but this continuation was discarded after about half a page and a revised substitute was written on what is now fol. 6ᵛ to follow the text on fol. 5ᵛ. The extended trial beginning ends in mid-sentence near the foot of fol. 6ᵛ where the original plan seems to have been abandoned and James made a new start—in the form of a dialogue—on a now lost fol. 1. This revised beginning was then continued on what are now fols. 3–4 and perhaps into the inscription of part of fol. 5 (not yet numbered)[21] before

---

[21] James's practice in numbering leaves seems to have been erratic. In Chapter XIV the unnumbered sequence of fols. 19ᵛ, 13ᵛ, 20ᵛ with continuous discarded text indicates that at least when he thought he was writing drafts James could inscribe a whole series of pages without numbering them until he felt he had it completed;

James again broke off, this time to expand the original first leaf (no longer preserved) into the present fols. 1–2, in the process renumbering original fols. 2–3 as 3–4 before completing and numbering fol. 5. This earliest form of the chapter is transcribed in the section of discarded verso texts at the end of the list of Alterations in the Manuscript. Although the case is not demonstrable, it would seem that in the revised fol. 1 James retained the original title "Postscript," and altered it to the book's "A Dialogue" (perhaps spelled 'A Dialog') either in the printer's copy or in proof.

The next extensive revision covers the major excision of the lower half of fol. 8, 'your notion of truth . . . nothing to do with'. Originally this text (now deleted) was continued on the next leaf (numbered 9 before inscription), but then the seven lines of this continuation ('defining the notion . . . these being') were halted in mid-sentence, the lower half of fol. 8 and this aborted start of 9 deleted,[22] and the leaf turned over (reversed) to continue the upper half of fol. 8 with a revision on what is now fol. 9 recto beginning 'no notion of a potential' (157.1–2). It is clear that present fols. 15–16 concluded the original form of the essay, numbered 12–13. Before these last two leaves there are signs of marked disruption. Evidently the deleted text numbered 11½ now preserved on the verso of fol. 13 was written before the almost identical material now found on fol. 11; moreover, the fact that fol. 11 joins the text of fol. 10 but only after a space to the right of the last word 'another' at the foot of fol. 10 indicates that after normally written fol. 9 two now lost leaves of text numbered 10–11 intervened before the addition now found as deleted 11½ was written for insertion before the start of the undeleted text on original fol. 12 (now 15). Yet no text in the essay leads into the deleted text ('word truth as you use it . . . pragmatist view') that heads early fol. 12 (now 15); hence it must be said that present fols. 10–14 are revised text and that the original fols. 10–11 (which led presumably into what is now fol. 15) have been lost although perhaps partially represented by the text on discarded 11½. The successive renumberings of fols. 15–16 first as 12–13, then as 13–14, then 14–[*unchanged*], and finally as 15–16 must mark stages in this revision now found on fols. 1–14. One of these intermediate stages appears to be fol. 13, which has its deleted lower two-thirds reworked as

---

see also his numbering of the first form of the note that became Chapter XIV only after it had been expanded and revised. Such holding off of numbering was, of course, a precaution against the need to keep on changing the foliation whenever he expanded a manuscript on which he was working. In Chapter XV this reluctance to number at an early stage is seen in the two continuous leaves of text now found on fols. 5[v] and 6[v], unnumbered. On other occasions he may not have numbered the leaf until he had finished the page; yet fol. 9, a part-page discard of only seven lines, was numbered before inscription.

[22] The deleted text on fol. 8 and its original continuation on what is now deleted fol. 9[v] may be found in the list of Alterations at 157.1 with the lemma 'that'.

fol. 14. (Possibly at one time the new beginning on fol. 15 after the deleted material was intended to follow immediately after the now deleted text on fol. 13.)

The variants in the finally revised manuscript of Chapter XV from the accepted book copy-text have been recorded in the Historical Collation. All internal variation and revision as the manuscript was written are described in the list of Alterations, at the end of which is placed the independent text on deleted versos transcribed in a descriptive system that simultaneously shows the revisions.

II. The Editorial Problem

The materials on which a text of *The Meaning of Truth* must be based have been detailed in the first section. It remains to describe the editorial treatment suitable for dealing with the special problems raised by the transmission of the text of each lecture when its basic antecedent documents have been preserved. As sketched in "A Note on the Editorial Method," the classic theory of copy-text calls for a text to be based on the *accidentals*—that is, the spelling, punctuation, capitalization, paragraphing, word-division, and emphasis methods—of the preserved document closest to the author's holograph. Any authorial revisions in these accidentals or in the *substantives*—that is, the words themselves—established from preserved documents, or to be conjectured as occurring in intermediate lost documents, are then inserted in the generally authoritative accidental texture by emendation. If this procedure were followed, the holograph manuscripts of Chapters XIV and XV and the typescript "W. James's Statement" for Chapter X would be the most authoritative copytexts; for the remainder, the journal articles which were the printer's copy for the book would be one step closer to James's lost manuscripts and hence would normally be taken as copy-texts even though their annotated versions have not been preserved. Only for the second part of Chapter VII, the substituted final note in Chapter X, and the postscript to Chapter XIV is the book the sole authority in lieu of any other document. Since the first thirteen chapters were originally discrete publishing ventures, written and printed at different times before collection in a book, the resulting varieties of accidental texture from five different journals would be of less textual concern than the methodical attempt to recover and unite for each separate unit the two parts of authority—accidentals and substantives—with maximum fidelity according to the evidence of the preserved documents.

Fortunately this complex theory—perhaps disturbing in its implications to the usual reader despite its classic textual purity—need not be applied here, for the copious evidence that James revised his journal articles for book publication with considerable care in accidentals as well as in substantives, and then devoted further attention to both in the book proofs, throws the weight of general authority and final intentions very strongly on the side of the book as copy-text.[23] Since in classic theory it is the authority of the accidentals that governs the choice of copy-text (not that of the substantives), the evidence is clear in *The Meaning of Truth*, as it is in *Pragmatism* (1907), that whereas James was relatively content to have his articles published according to the particular journal's house-styling, when he marked the journal copy and read proof for his book he regularly (although not entirely consistently) wrote in certain of his favorite spelling-reform characteristics[24] and was concerned with the whole range of other accidentals. On the whole, then, the cumulative evidence suggests that although some changes in the accidentals from copy represent com-

---

[23] The evidence is particularly strong in *Pragmatism*, where a fragment of revised journal copy for the book has been preserved. But *The Meaning of Truth* displays the same differences between journals and book as in *Pragmatism* and gives every sign of having been put together according to the same system. For example, the variants in the book from the manuscripts of Chapters XIV and XV result only in small part from the printer's house-styling (combined with the conjectural typist) and in the main are to be attributed to James. Just as in *Pragmatism*, whether in journal or in manuscript text—but particularly in the latter—*The Meaning of Truth* evidence suggests that James regarded his printer's copy and the resulting first proofs as providing him only with some further basis for continued and extensive revision. For a general discussion, with evidence, see "The Text of *Pragmatism*," WORKS, pp. 198–199.

[24] This idiosyncrasy explains the presence in the book of spellings like 'tho' and 'altho', even if James did not insist on the printer's following the spellings of his manuscripts in words like 'thru' and 'publisht'. Ordinarily he did not alter the printer's division of his characteristic 'everyone' or 'anyone' or 'cannot' and the like from the Riverside Press (and sometimes the journals' styling 'every one', 'any one', and 'can not'). However, he certainly corrected words like 'connection' to 'connexion', hyphenated compounds according to his own ideas, and tinkered with the punctuation as part of his concern with meaning. The large number of accidental changes among the seventy-eight corrections and revisions made in his private copy of *Pragmatism* are not matched by the six alterations (all substantive) noted in his private copy of *The Meaning of Truth*. It may be that he was more satisfied with the texture of *The Meaning of Truth*, or it may be that he recognized in 1909 the impossibility of what he could have contemplated in 1907, either the wholesale alteration of plates or else resetting the type for a second and improved edition. There may be signs that he learned something from the publication of *Pragmatism* not only in respect to the unwillingness of a publisher to alter plates for less than positive error but also to the unwillingness of a printer to set from such extraordinarily marked-up manuscript copy as that for Lectures VII and VIII. The apparent submission of typescripts instead of manuscripts for Chapters XIV and XV may have resulted from his experiences with *Pragmatism*. To explain the relatively few revisions that he marked in his copy of *The Meaning of Truth* as against the earlier volume one may also speculate that perhaps by 1909 the high hopes he had held of revolutionizing philosophical thought with *Pragmatism* had flickered and he was less concerned with making notes of improvements for another edition.

positorial styling (more consistent in *The Meaning of Truth* than in the Riverside Press's setting of *Pragmatism*) that James overlooked in proof, or did not trouble to alter, perhaps a majority of the variants may be assessed as authorial. This being so, the usual approach to the problem of the most authoritative copy-text is altered, for the evidence is certain that the book represents James's own accidental texture more closely than the journal printer's copy. Under these circumstances the book, and not the antecedent documents (even the manuscripts), may be accepted as the superior copy-text to embody both branches of authority. Emendation from the sources, therefore, reverses the usual progression. Instead of incorporating the book's revised substantives in the earliest texture of the accidentals, emendation is chiefly drawn from the original source documents in an attempt to restore the accidentals and substantives of the book copy-text from the conjectured departures from copy unauthoritatively produced by the book's compositorial styling or typesetting error.

In addition to this purification of the book copy-text, three other ranges of emendation are found in the present edition. The first covers a small amount of controlled normalization of accidentals. Advanced textual theory permits normalization of variant accidentals within bibliographical units (which would here be the chapters) according to the norms of the author's own established characteristics in order to bring such variants into conformity with authorial style whenever examples of these norms are also present in the same unit. On the other hand, in certain of the briefer chapters not every different form variant from James's marked characteristics may have the opportunity to be paired with his usual norm; moreover, the close attention that he gave in marking printer's copy and proof on an even basis throughout the book suggests that in this case the definition of bibliographical unit should be expanded to cover the whole collection of essays. Hence, even when no documentary evidence is present in any single chapter, an editor may rely on the evidence elsewhere in the book, and particularly in the manuscripts of Chapters XIV and XV, to engage in the normalization to James's established and most marked preferences and thus to recover from the ministrations of the compositors the forms that he customarily wrote in his manuscripts and, on many occasions, himself altered in the book from the styled journal copy. Second, the purity of the sources that James quoted from (often with considerable carelessness in details) has ordinarily been restored by reference to the book or article he was utilizing. The emendation of quotations is always recorded with their source, or else James's departures that are retained for special reasons are noticed in the list of Emendations and emphasized by the use of *stet*. Third, autograph revisions and corrections that James made in offprints of his journal articles are ordinarily adopted in the present text—as well as the six alterations that he marked in his own copy of the book—which thus approaches more nearly than any previous edition to his revised intentions, not all of which found their way into the book.[25] When adopted, these revisions are specially keyed to the sigil WJ in the Emendations list and are again emphasized in the Historical Collation, which will also contain a complete record of annotations that have been rejected in the present text, principally because of later though variant revision in the book.

Since the authorially revised form of the text as represented by the book's first edition, first printing, has been accepted as copy-text, this reversal of the usual editorial procedure causes some change in the use of the apparatus. The list of Emendations is considerably reduced since it is confined to independent editorial alterations (marked as H) or else to changes from source documents that in each individual case have been taken to represent superior authority to the copy-text. Under these conditions the main evidence for the transmission of the text is moved from the Emendations list to the Historical Collation. For instance, in Chapters XIV and XV the Historical Collation contains those variant readings of the final form of the manuscripts which have been rejected as less authoritative than the altered forms accepted from the copy-text in the present edition of the book. The earliest and intermediate forms of the texts in manuscript as represented by their progressive revision during and after composition are recorded in full in the list of Alterations in the Manuscripts. A reader who wishes to recover the exact forms of the manuscript texts as they are found in the James Collection at Harvard can do so by the use of these two sections of the apparatus. Correspondingly, the record of what is accepted in the present edition as the alterations that James made in copy and in proof between the journal articles and the book

---

[25] A certain number of the corrections he made in private copies of offprints or else in his files of journals he remembered and altered in the exemplars used as printer's copy. The evidence on the whole suggests, however, that he did not systematically consult his files to ensure that his earlier second thoughts were all entered in the book copy. Often the book may leave untouched words or phrases with which he had shown dissatisfaction when reading over and annotating the journal articles as they appeared or as he revised them for the use of his philosophy classes. On various occasions his sense of dissatisfaction remained and he revised the copy but in a different manner from that of his earlier annotations, whether consciously or not. In such cases his latest intentions as found in the book have been respected in the present text. But the evidence is too copious that he did not consult his files for any argument to hold that when the book reprints the original journal text that he had revised earlier in his file copies, the book version must represent his considered return to the original readings. Under these circumstances it has seemed editorially appropriate to incorporate almost all of his revisory annotations of this sort in the present text. How James could revise on different occasions without memory of his earlier annotations is clearly illustrated by the different revisions (following the first stage) that he made in the two typescripts of his "Statement" as illustrated by the apparatus for Chapter X and especially for the eclectic typescript text in Appendix III.

appears in the Historical Collation, including in Chapter X the variants from both revised forms of the typescript that is the earliest record of the text. The conventions of the different sections of apparatus are described in their headnotes. James's own footnotes are keyed in his manuscripts by asterisks or crosses. According to standard printing style the Riverside Press numbered these freshly for each page. For convenience this unauthoritative system has been rejected in the present edition for consecutive footnote numbering within each chapter. Finally, for technical reasons accents above capital letters have been omitted except in bibliographical descriptions.

FREDSON BOWERS

Addendum

Chapter XIII. Abstractionism and 'Relativismus' (p. 216).

On January 22, 1909, James McKeen Cattell, the editor of the *Popular Science Monthly*, wrote to James apparently in response to James's suggestion that he might print an article on pragmatism (Thomas M. Shackleford, "What Pragmatism Is As I Understand It," *Popular Science Monthly*, 75 [December 1909], 571–585) : "I fear that I ought not to print the article in THE POPULAR SCIENCE MONTHLY. Since you let us print your two lectures there have been articles on and for pragmatism by Papini and by Bawden, and I have the general impression that the judge's article does not clear matters up very much, except in so far as this is done by the quotations. I will, however, agree to print this article, if you will agree to print an article in the MONTHLY within a reasonable time." To this James responded in a note at the foot of the sheet: "O.K., if you will let it be an article on 'relativismus,' pitching into Munsterberg's and Rickerts attempt to rule out individual opinion from the truth-forum. I think I can make it quite untechnical. W. J." On June 15, 1909, he wrote to Cattell: "I am about to publish—in September—a collection of my articles about 'truth' ('The meaning of truth, a sequel to Pragmatism') and should like to include the pages on 'Abstraction' etc. which appeared in the April [actually May] Pop. Sci. I suppose you have no objection!" (James McKeen Cattell Papers, Library of Congress).

Apparatus

Emendations

Every editorial change from the copy-text is recorded for the substantives, and every change in the accidentals as well save for such silent typographical adjustments as are remarked in "A Note on the Editorial Method." The reading to the left of the bracket represents the form chosen in the present edition, usually as an emendation of the copy-text. (A prefixed superior [1] or [2] indicates which of the two identical words in the same line is intended.) The sigil immediately following the bracket is the identifying symbol for the earliest source of the emendation. If there is an intermediary between this earliest source and the rejected reading of the copy-text, the sigil for that document will also appear, provided it is an authoritative document and one in the direct line of textual transmission. Readings in parentheses after sigla indicate a difference in the accidental form of the source from that of the emended reading to the left of the bracket. A semicolon follows the last of the sigla for emending sources. To the right of this semicolon then appears the rejected reading of the copy-text followed by its sigil. The copy-text is (I), the first-edition typesetting as represented by the first printing from the plates. If no indication of printing is given, the assumption is that the reading is invariant in all impressions from the original plates. A superior number identifies the exact printing in case of need, as I^1 for October 1909 or I^3 for the third printing (the second in November). Emendations marked as H are editorial and are not drawn from any authoritative document. The word *stet* after the bracket calls special attention to the retention of a copy-text reading. It may be employed when a plausible reading in another source has been rejected and the crux is discussed in a Textual Note, as indicated by the asterisk before the page-line number. Occasionally, however, this *stet* may be used in a quotation to indicate to the reader that James's version (differing from the source in some respect) has been retained in the edited text. In all such uses, the source reading will also be supplied so that a reader can always reconstruct from this list both the quoted source and James's own version of it. For convenience, certain shorthand symbols familiar in textual notation are employed. A wavy dash ($\sim$) represents the same word that appears before the bracket and is used exclusively in recording punctuation or other accidental variants. An inferior caret ($_\wedge$) indicates the absence of a punctuation mark when a difference in the punctuation constitutes the variant being recorded, or is a part of the variant. A vertical stroke ($|$) represents a line ending, sometimes noted as bearing on the cause of an error or fault. Asterisked readings are discussed in the Textual Notes. Quotations within the text are identified in Professor Skrupskelis' Notes. The sigil WJ/I identifies James's revisions in his private marked copy at Harvard; WJ/P (with identification) indicates James's revisions in copies of journal offprints or file sets of journals at Harvard.

PREFACE

The copy-text for the Preface is (I), the October 1909 first printing of *The Meaning of Truth*. The quotations from *Pragmatism* are identified and given in their first-edition form (1907).

3.3-4.20 "Truth," . . . formulas."]
  H; *all single quotes in* I
3.5 'agreement,'] *Prag.*; ∧ ∼ ,∧ I
3.5 'reality.'] *Prag.*; ∧ ∼ . ∧ I
3.7 course. . . .] H; ∼ . I
3.9 Pragmatism] *stet* I; Pragmatism,
  on the other hand, *Prag.*
3.10-14 'Grant . . . terms?'] H; *all
  double quotes in* I
3.11 anyone's] H; any one's *Prag.*, I
3.11 life?] *stet* I; life? How will the
  truth be realized? *Prag.*
3.13 How . . . realized?] *stet* I; *omit
  Prag.* (*see above, note to line* 15)
3.14 The (*no* ¶)] *stet* I; ¶ *Prag.*
3.16 corroborate∧] *Prag.*; ∼ , I
3.17 cannot] *stet* I; can not *Prag.*
3.18 , therefore,] *Prag.*; ∧ ∼ ∧ I
3.19 known-as] *Prag.*; ∼ ∧ ∼ I
3.20 "The] *stet* I (' ∼); This thesis
  is what I have to defend. The *Prag.*
4.1 process:] *Prag.*; ∼ , I

4.2 veri-*fication*] *Prag.*; veri*fication* I
4.3 valid-*ation*] *Prag.*; valid*ation* I
4.4 'agree'] *Prag.*; ∧ ∼ ∧ I
4.4-7 can . . . disagreed.] *Prag.*; *roman* I
4.8 practically!] *Prag.*; ∼ . I
4.8 deal] *Prag.*; deal I
4.12 hold] *Prag.*; be I
4.13 '*The true,*'] *Prag.*; ∧ ∼ ∼ , ∧ I
4.13 to . . . briefly,] *stet* I; *italic Prag.*
4.14 'the right'] *Prag.*; ∧ ∼ ∼ ∧ I
4.15 fashion;] *Prag.*; ∼ , I
4.33 "verifi*ability*,"] *Prag.*
  (∧Verifi*ability*∧∧); '*verifiability*,' I
4.33-37 "is . . . happens."] H;
  ' ∼ . . . ∼ .' I
4.33-34 completed∧] *Prag.*; ∼ , I
4.35 turn] *Prag.*; lead I
4.35 towards] *Prag.*; towards I
4.35 surroundings] *Prag.*; surroundings I
4.35 objects] *Prag.*; object I
5.28 universe∧'] H; ∼, ' I
6.6;8.7 tho] H; though I

CHAPTER I. The Function of Cognition

The copy-text for Chapter I is (I), the October 1909 first printing of *The Meaning of Truth*, which is a revision of (P²⁴) "On the Function of Cognition," *Mind*, 10 (January 1885), 27–44 (McD 1885:1). James's annotations in his set of *Mind* (Harvard Phil. 22.4.6*) are noted as WJ/P²⁴ⁱ, and the annotation in his private offprint of the article in Box O, envelope 9 as P²⁴ⁱⁱ. The quotations from Green, Grote, Thackeray, and Peirce are identified in the Notes. References to *Mind* do not take account of English spellings or placement of punctuation in respect to quotation marks. See the headnote to Chapter I of the Historical Collation.

14.8 "How . . . possible?"]
  P²⁴; ' ∼ . . . ∼ ? ' I
14.9-12 "How . . . rest?"]
  H; ∧ ∼ . . . ?∧ P²⁴; ' ∼ . . . ∼ ?' I
14.13 psychology∧—] H; ∼ ,— P²⁴,I
15.2-3 befals . . . befal] P²⁴;
  befalls . . . befall I
15.4 life∧—] H; ∼ ,— P²⁴,I
15.6-8 universe∧— . . . account∧—]
  H; ∼ ,— . . . ∼ ,— P²⁴,I
15.11 "the . . . q."] P²⁴;
  ' ∼ . . . ∼ .' I
15.18;16.32;22.29 anyone] P²⁴;
  any one I
15.38 -about∧—] H; ∼ ,— P²⁴,I
16.6;30.17,32;31.9 tho] H;
  though P²⁴,I

16.29 "How . . . feeling?"] P²⁴;
  ' ∼ . . . ∼ ?' I
16.34-35 feeling∧— . . . one∧—]
  H; ∼ ,— . . . ∼ ,— P²⁴,I
17.8-15 "A . . . left."] P²⁴; *all single
  external quotes in* I
17.8 detached] *stet* P²⁴, I; *detached
  Green*
17.8 ∧left . . . 'heap] Green;
  ' ∼ . . . ∧ ∼ P²⁴; " ∼ . . . ∧ ∼ I
17.9 which] Green; *omit* P²⁴,I
17.9 mind,'] Green, P²⁴; ∼, " I
17.10 'consider'] Green; ∧ ∼ ∧ P²⁴,I
17.11 itself—] Green; ∼ ∧ P²⁴,I
17.12 because, . . . it,] Green;
  ∼ ∧ . . . ∼∧ P²⁴ I
17.13 same] Green; very same P²⁴,I

18.1-22 "Our ... both."] P²⁴;
  all single external quotes in I
18.3 'object'] P²⁴; " ~ " I
18.4 ¹thus:] *stet* P²⁴,I; ~ , Grote
18.4 etc.;] *stet* P²⁴,I; ~. : Grote
18.8 noscere ... connaître] Grote;
  italic P²⁴,I
18.9 scire ... savoir] Grote; *italic* P²⁴,I
18.11 acquaintance] *stet* P²⁴,I; *roman*
  Grote
18.11 known:] Grote; ~ ; P²⁴,I
18.13 other:] Grote; ~ ; P²⁴,I
18.15-16 'vorstellung'.] Grote;
  ∧*Vorstellung*∧. P²⁴,I
18.17 'begriffe'] Grote; *Begriffe* P²⁴,I
18.19 *intellectual*] Grote; intellectual
  P²⁴,I
18.19 There (*no* ¶)] *stet* P²⁴,I; ¶ Grote
18.19 ∧however∧] Grote; , ~ , P²⁴,I
18.30 hegelian] H; Hegelian P²⁴,I
19.32-33 "Didn't ... brother"] P²⁴;
  all single quotes in I
21.15 exactly∧—] H; ~ ,— P²⁴,I
22.25 neighbors∧—] H; ~ ,— P²⁴,I
23.3 action∧—] H; ~ ,— P²⁴,I
23.15-16 "I ... suffer!"] P²⁴;
  ' ~ ... ~ !' I
23.39 2,] H; ~ ∧ I
24.15 them∧—] H;"~ ,— P²⁴,I
24.18 it∧—] H; ~ ,— P²⁴,I

24.34 he] WJ/P²⁴ⁱ⁻ⁱⁱ,I; we P²⁴
25.1 connexion] P²⁴; connection I
25.11 Everyone] P²⁴; Every one I
25.33 experience∧—] H; ~ ,— P²⁴,I
26.20(*twice*), 22 criticized] H;
  criticised P²⁴,I
27.10 know,] P²⁴; ~ ∧ | I
28.1 thought,] P²⁴ (*Thought*,); ~ ∧ I
28.2 on∧] P²⁴; ~ , I
28.7 thereto∧—] H; ~ ,— P²⁴,I
28.11-13 "Newton ... kingdom."]
  P²⁴; ' ~ ... ~ .' I
28.22 Zoology] P²⁴; Zoölogy I
*28.30-31 'about' realities∧] WJ/P²⁴ⁱ
  (" ~ " ~ ∧); " ~ ∧ ~ " P²⁴;
  ' ~ ∧ ~ ' I
29.3 for∧—] H; ~ ,— P²⁴,I
29.15 develope] H; develop P²⁴,I
30.4 someone] P²⁴; some one I
30.25-31.37 "My ... object."] P²⁴;
  all single quotes in I
30.25-26 My ... walk] *stet* I; My
  friend, a different universe walks P²⁴;
  Ah, sir,—a distinct universe walks
  Thackeray
*31.8 substitute] *stet* I; former
  WJ/P²⁴ⁱ; latter P²⁴
31.34 [highest]] *stet* P²⁴,I; third Peirce
32.4 asserted:∧] H; ~ :— I
32.18 are:∧] H; ~ :— I

CHAPTER II. The Tigers in India

The copy-text for Chapter II is (I), the October 1909 first printing of *The Meaning of Truth*, a revision of 107.22–111.1 of (P³⁴) "The Knowing of Things Together," *Psychological Review*, 2 (March 1895), 105–124 (McD 1895:4). James's annotations in his file set of the *Review* (WJ 110.72) at Harvard are noted as WJ/P³⁴.

35.29,32 **may be**] WJ/P³⁴; is P³⁴,I
35.30 someone] H; some one P³⁴,I
35.34-35 again, for,] WJ/P³⁴; again—
  P³⁴,I

36.11 connexions] H; connections
  P³⁴,I
36.31 naif] H; naïf I

CHAPTER III. Humanism and Truth

The copy-text for Chapter III is (I), the October 1909 first printing of *The Meaning of Truth*, which is a revision of (P²⁴) "Humanism and Truth," *Mind*, n.s. 13 (October 1904), 457–475 (McD 1904:11) with additions from (HTOM [P²⁴]) "Humanism and Truth Once More," *Mind*, n.s. 14 (April 1905), 190–198 (McD 1905:5). The quotations from Tennyson, Bradley, and Duclaux are identified in the Notes. References to *Mind* do not take account of English spellings or placement of punctuation in respect to quotation marks. See the headnote to Chapter III of the Historical Collation.

37.11 someone] H; some one P²⁴,I
39.2-23 Humanism . . . argument.]
added from HTOM (P²⁴)
39.4 deep] *stet* I; full Tennyson,
HTOM (P²⁴)
39.29-40.9 The . . . belief.] *added
from* HTOM (P²⁴)
39.31-33 "In . . . word."] P²⁴; *all
single quotes in* I
39.33 replyʌ—] H; ～ ,— HTOM
(P²⁴),I
40.12 "God geometrizes,"] P²⁴
(geometrises); ' ～ ～ , ' I
40.22;53.33 everyone] H; every one
P²⁴,I
41.30 program] H; programme P²⁴,I
42.21;52.36 connexions] P²⁴; connections I
43.7 criticize] H; criticise P²⁴,I
44.20 *adæquatio*] P²⁴; *adæquatio* I
44.22-23 "must . . . make,"] P²⁴;
' ～ . . . ～ , ' I
45.5-6 altho] H; although P²⁴,I
45.20 tho] H; though P²⁴,I
45.34 *itself*ʌ] P²⁴; ～ , I
46.13-19 "How . . . so."] P²⁴; *all
single quotes in* I
46.18 he "must] H; "he must P²⁴;
'he must I
46.18 hold . . .] H; ～ ʌ P²⁴,I
46.18-19 ideaʌ . . . madʌ . . . truthʌ]
Bradley; ～ , . . . ～ , . . . ～ , P²⁴,I
46.19 any one] *stet* P²⁴,I; only some
one is resolved that he Bradley
47.20-21 "Parliament . . . it,"] P²⁴;
' ～ . . . ～ , ' I
48.11-13 "Truth . . . agree."] P²⁴;
all single quotes in I
48.21-29 "But . . . goods?"] P²⁴; *all
single quotes in* I
49.26-39 "Autant . . . *importe.*"] H;
' ～ . . . ～ . ' I

49.26 la Révolution] *stet* I; les révolu-
tions des deux derniers siècles Duclaux
49.26 ʌl'Affaireʌ] Duclaux;"l'Affaire"
I
49.26 'origines'.] H; " ～ ." Duclaux
(" ～ ".), I
49.27 gouffre, . . .] H; ～ , ʌ I
49.28 préparé] Duclaux; preparé I
49.29-31 *la* . . . *examen*] *stet* I; *roman*
Duclaux
49.29-30 *traditionalistes,*] Duclaux;
～ ʌ I
49.30-31 a priori] Duclaux; *à priori* I
49.33 périsseʌ] Duclaux; ～ , I
49.33 fût] Duclaux; fut I
49.35 préférât] Duclaux; préferât I
49.35 bien] Duclaux; *omit* I
49.38-39 *C'étaient . . . importe.*] *stet* I;
roman Duclaux
49.38 *C'étaient*] Duclaux; *C'etaient* I
49.39 *Emile . . .* Em.] *stet* I; [*acute
accents*] Duclaux
50.22-25 "the . . . not."] P²⁴; *all
single quotes in* I
50.28 "*Die . . . daseins,*"] P²⁴
(*Erhöhung . . . Daseins*); ' ～ . . . ～ ,' I
52.6 hindoo] H; Hindoo P²⁴,I
55.1-2 "the . . . Ocean,"] P²⁴;
' ～ . . . ～ ,' I
56.13 anyone] H; any one P²⁴,I
57.12 trustʌ—] H; ～ ,— P²⁴,I
57.13 effortʌ—] P²⁴; ～ ,— I
57.34 "Even . . . numbered."] P²⁴;
' ～ . . . ～ .' I
57.36 criticizing] H; criticising P²⁴,I
58.3-8 "Has . . . all?"] H;
' ～ . . . ～ ?' I
58.6-59.21 crowd . . . criterion]
added from HTOM (P²⁴)
*58.11 known-as] H; ～ ʌ ～ HTOM
(P²⁴),I
59.28 these:ʌ] H; ～ :— P²⁴,I

CHAPTER IV. The Relation between Knower and Known

The copy-text for Chapter IV is (I), the October 1909 first printing of *The Meaning of Truth*, which is a revision of (P²⁰) "A World of Pure Experience," *Journal of Philosophy, Psychology, and Scientific Methods*, 1 (September 29, 1904), 533–543, and 1 (October 13, 1904), 561–570 (McD 1904:10), abstracted from pp. 538.3–543.24, and 561.1–562.20, 562.38–564.32. A correction in James's marked copy of the first edition at Harvard (*AC85.J2376.909m[B]), which also appears in the plates of the third printing in November 1909, is recorded as WJ/I and as I³.

62.37 other] WJ/I,I³; others P²⁰,I¹⁻²	*66.32 partly common and] H; partly continuous and P²⁰; partly shared and common I
63.10-11 cannot] H; can not P²⁰,I	
63.17 develope] H; develop P²⁰,I	68.20 developes] H; develops P²⁰,I
63.34-64.5 "Mere ... still."] P²⁰; *all single quotes in* I	68.30 already,] P²⁰; ~ ; I
	*69.6 knowledge-about] H; ~ ∧ ~ P²⁰,I
64.1 'apprehension'] P²⁰; " ~ " I	
64.12 predication] P²⁰; prediction I	69.36 anyone] H; any one P²⁰,I
66.27 tho] H; though P²⁰,I	

CHAPTER V. The Essence of Humanism

The copy-text for Chapter V is (I), the October 1909 first printing of *The Meaning of Truth*, which is a revision of (P²⁰) "The Essence of Humanism," *Journal of Philosophy, Psychology, and Scientific Methods*, 2 (March 2, 1905), 113–118 (McD 1905:3).

70.6 tho] H; though P²⁰,I	76.1 *identitätsphilosophie*] H; Identitätsphilosophie P²⁰,I
71.7 programs] P²⁰; programmes I	
71.23; 73.34 Anyone] H; Any one P²⁰,I	76.29-30 connexion] H; connection P²⁰,I
72.11 develope] H; develop P²⁰,I	

CHAPTER VI. A Word More about Truth

The copy-text for Chapter VI is (I), the October 1909 first printing of *The Meaning of Truth*, which is a revision of (P²⁰), "A Word More about Truth," *Journal of Philosophy, Psychology, and Scientific Methods*, 4 (July 18, 1907), 396–406 (McD 1907:7).

79.23-25 "Yes ... nature?"] P²⁰; ' ~ ... ~ ?' I	84.9 english] H; English P²⁰,I
	85.14-18 "I ... truth."] H; *all single quotes in* P²⁰,I
80.23 it∧—] H; ~ ,— P²⁰,I	
84.5 'going-round.'] H; ' ~ ∧ ~.' P²⁰,I	86.5 anyone] H; any one P²⁰,I
	87.33 criticized] P²⁰; criticised I

CHAPTER VII. Professor Pratt on Truth

The copy-text for Chapter VII is (I), the October 1909 first printing of *The Meaning of Truth*, which is an expansion of (P²⁰), "Professor Pratt on Truth," *Journal of Philosophy, Psychology, and Scientific Methods*, 4 (August 15, 1907), 464–467 (McD 1907:8), which ends at 93.15. The quotations from Pratt are identified in the Notes.

90.6-9 "altogether ... psychology,"] H; *all single quotes in* P²⁰,I	92.12 this simple thing,] Pratt; *this simple thing*∧ P²⁰,I
92.12-13 "this ... it."] H; ' ~ ... ~ .' P²⁰,I	92.31 everyone] H; every one P²⁰,I [*end* P²⁰]

93.33 *Pragmatism?*] H; $\sim$. I
94.25 anyone] H; any one I
95.30-33 "unconsciously . . . it"] H;
' $\sim$ . . . $\sim$ ' I
95.30 surrenders] *stet* I; surrendering
Pratt
95.32 'experience'] Pratt (" $\sim$ ");
$_\wedge \sim {_\wedge}$ I
95.32 *can*] Pratt; can I
96.22 introduced$_\wedge$—] H; $\sim$,— I
97.13-30 "Since . . . "this] H; *all
single quotes in* I
97.14 all] Pratt; all that I
97.21 ask$_\wedge$—] H; $\sim$,— I

97.27-28 is . . . saltatory?] *stet* I; Is
this relation ambulatory or saltatory?
Pratt
97.29 experiences . . . begin] *stet* I;
italic Pratt
97.31,33 fulfillment] Pratt; fulfilment I
97.32 knowledge,—] Pratt; $\sim$ $_\wedge$— I
98.1 object$_\wedge$] Pratt; $\sim$, I
98.2 'epistemological gulf.'] H;
" $\sim$ $\sim$." Pratt, I
98.2 transcended$_\wedge$] *stet* I; transcended.
Pratt
98.23-25 trueness$_\wedge$— . . . not$_\wedge$—] H;
$\sim$,— . . . $\sim$,— I

CHAPTER VIII. The Pragmatist Account of Truth and Its Misunderstanders

The copy-text for Chapter VIII is (I), the October 1909 first printing of *The Meaning of Truth*, which is a revision of (P[28]), "The Pragmatist Account of Truth and Its Misunderstanders," *Philosophical Review*, 17 (January 1908), 1–17 (McD 1908:1). Annotations in an offprint preserved in the James Collection at Harvard, Box O, envelope 15, no. 3, are distinguished as WJ/P[28] either in black ink or in blue pencil. According to a note on the cover, signed 'H.J.' annotations in black pencil are by 'someone else' and thus have not been listed. Quotations from Stout and Bourdeau are identified in the Notes. Reference is made to (UC) "Philosophical Conceptions and Practical Results," *University Chronicle* (of the University of California at Berkeley), 1 (September 1898), 287–310.

100.9 blame$_\wedge$—] H; $\sim$,— P[28],I
100.27-30 "No . . . existed?"] P[28];
all single quotes in I
100.35-36 It . . . question.] WJ/P[28]
ink; omit P[28],I
101.9-12 "that . . . action."] P[28];
' $\sim$ . . . $\sim$.' I
101.29 american] H; American P[28],I
102.20 helpful] P[28]; hopeful I
102.21 1907] H; *omit* P[28]; 1897 I
102.31-32 "becomes . . . heartless."]
P[28]; ' $\sim$ . . . $\sim$.' I
102.31 his] *stet* P[28],I; my Stout
102.32 becomes] Stout; grows P[28],I
102.32 dull$_\wedge$] Stout; $\sim$, P[28],I
102.35 *et seq. this chap.* someone]
P[28]; some one I
103.8-9 "made . . . heartless"] P[28];
' $\sim$ . . . $\sim$ ' I
103.14 epistemologizing] P[28];
epitemologizing I
103.31-32;109.29;110.24 anyone] H;
any one P[28],I

105.21 field$_\wedge$—] H; $\sim$,— P[28],I
105.25 pears] WJ/P[28] *ink*,I; peas P[28]
105.28-106.9 "If . . . patent."] P[28];
' $\sim$ . . . $\sim$.' I
106.30 naive] H; *naïve* P[28],I
107.19-30 "When . . . thesis."] P[28];
all single external quotes in I
107.20 'pragmatism . . . truth,'] P[28];
" $\sim$ . . . $\sim$," I
108.4 proposition$_\wedge$—] H; $\sim$,— P[28],I
108.6 stupid$_\wedge$—] H; $\sim$,— P[28],I
108.34 at$_\wedge$—] H; $\sim$,— P[28],I
109.12 develope] H; develop P[28],I
109.18 it$_\wedge$—] H; $\sim$ — P[28],I
110.5 obtaining$_\wedge$—] H; $\sim$,— P[28],I
111.11-12 *posse$_\wedge$*— . . . contra-
dicted$_\wedge$—] H; $\sim$,— . . . $\sim$,— P[28],I
111.12 ever] WJ/P[28] *blue pencil*,I;
even P[28]
111.12 asserted$_\wedge$ or] *stet* I; asserted,
WJ/P[28] *blue pencil; omit* P[28]
112.7 utility$_\wedge$—] H; $\sim$,— P[28],I
112.17-18 situation$_\wedge$— . . . perplex-

ityʌ—] H; ~ ,— ... ~ ,— P²⁸,I
112.24-25 "for ... loss."] P²⁸;
' ~ ... ~ .' I
112.24-25 everyone] P²⁸; every one I
112.27-31 "The ... unsound."] P²⁸;
' ~ ... ~ .' I
113.7-11 "the ... active"] P²⁸; *all
single quotes in* I
113.7 meaning ... proposition]
stet P²⁸,I; effective meaning ...
philosophic proposition UC
113.8 consequence,] UC; ~ ʌ P²⁸,I
113.9 active or passive] UC; passive
or active P²⁸,I
113.11 particular,] UC; ~ ʌ P²⁸,I

113.20 do) ʌ] P²⁸; ~), I
113.30-37 "Pragmatism ... *particular*."] P²⁸; ' ~ ... ~ .' I
113.31 man,] H; ~ ʌ P²⁸,I
114.10-15 "You ... him,"] P²⁸;
' ~ ... ~ ,' I
114.37 warrantʌ—] H; ~ ,— P²⁸,I
115.4-5 *identitätsphilosophie*] H;
Identitätsphilosophie P²⁸,I
115.16 coefficient] P²⁸; co-|efficient I
116.10 program] P²⁸; programme I
116.11 german] H; German P²⁸,I
116.11 ditty:ʌ] P²⁸; ~ :— I
116.13 sollen] WJ/P²⁸ *blue pencil*, I;
können P²⁸

CHAPTER IX. The Meaning of the Word Truth

The copy-text for Chapter IX is (I), the October 1909 first printing of *The Meaning of Truth*, which is a revision of (P²⁴) "The Meaning of the Word 'Truth'," *Mind*, 17 (July 1908), 455-456 (McD 1908:4); emendations from an earlier private printing (PPr) in 1908 of the journal article are included, as is a record of the forms of the emended readings in (P²⁸) under "The Meaning and Criterion of Truth," *Philosophical Review*, 17 (March 1908), 180-181. References to *Mind* do not take account of English spellings or placement of punctuation in respect to quotation marks. See the headnote to the Historical Collation for Chapter IX.

117.2-9 "The ... desk,"] PPr,P²⁴,²⁸;
all single quotes in I
117.11 andʌ] PPr; ~ , P²⁴,²⁸,I
117.18 "the desk existsʌ"] P²⁸
("The ... exists,"); ' ~ ... ~ ʌ'

PPr,P²⁴,I
118.36 ʌ*Studies ... theory*,ʌ] P²⁴
(*initial caps*); '*Studies ... theory*,'
PPr,I
119.2 envelope] PPr; envelop P²⁴,I

CHAPTER X. The Existence of Julius Cæsar

The copy-text for Chapter X is (I), the October 1909 first printing of *The Meaning of Truth*, which is abstracted from (P²⁰) " 'Truth' versus 'Truthfulness'," *Journal of Philosophy, Psychology, and Scientific Methods*, 5 (March 26, 1908), 179-181 (McD 1908:3). In turn, P²⁰ is based on (TMs) "W. James's Statement," ribbon copy of a typescript in the University of Chicago Library and the carbon in the Stanford University Library.

120.7 "Cæsar ... existed."] TMs,P²⁰;
' ~ ... ~ .' I
120.7 naively] TMs; naïvely P²⁰,I
121.2,15 Cæsarʌ] TMs; ~ , P²⁰,I
121.12 reprintʌ] TMs; ~ , P²⁰,I

121.12 "the ... *that*."] TMs,P²⁰;
' ~ ... ~ .' I
121.17-31 "Such ... exist."] TMs,P²⁰;
all single quotes in I

CHAPTER XI. The Absolute and the Strenuous Life

The copy-text for Chapter XI is (I), the October 1909 first printing of *The Meaning of Truth*, which is a revision of (P²⁰) "The Absolute and the Strenuous

Life," *Journal of Philosophy, Psychology, and Scientific Methods*, 4 (September 26, 1907), 546–548 (McD 1907:9).

No emendations

CHAPTER XII.   Professor Hébert on Pragmatism

The copy-text for Chapter XII is (I), the October 1909 first printing of *The Meaning of Truth*, which is a revision of (P[20]), a review of Marcel Hébert's *Le Pragmatisme; étude de ses diverses formes* in *Journal of Philosophy, Psychology, and Scientific Methods*, 5 (December 3, 1908), 689–694 (McD 1908:8).

126.20   *Le . . . ses*] H; *Le pragmatisme et ses* I
127.3   general-utility] P[20]; ~ ∧|~ I
128.20-21   it∧— . . . himself∧—] P[20] (. . . pages∧–); ~ ,— . . . ~ ,— I
128.29;131.4,9;133.3   anyone] H; any one P[20],I

129.37   someone's] H; some one's P[20],I
131.1   everyone's] H; everybody's P[20]; every one's I
131.24-25   connexion] H; connection P[20],I
132.12-14   "An . . . claim?"] P[20]; *all single quotes in* I

CHAPTER XIII.   Abstractionism and 'Relativismus'

The copy-text for Chapter XIII is (I), the October 1909 first printing of *The Meaning of Truth*, which is a revision of (P[29]) "On a Very Prevalent Abuse of Abstraction," *Popular Science Monthly*, 74 (May 1909), 485–493 (McD 1909:4). Annotations in James's private copy preserved in the James Collection at Harvard (*AC85.J2376.909m[B]) are distinguished as WJ/I. The quotations from Fullerton and McTaggart are identified in the Notes.

134.16   traveling] P[29]; travelling I
135.35   privatively] P[29], WJ/I,I[2] (+I[1] *errata slip*); privately I[1]
136.20   naive] H; naïve P[29],I
137.13   *disconnexion*] H; *disconnection* P[29],I
137.17   connexion] H; connection P[29],I
137.21   follows:∧] P[29]; ~ :— I
137.22-138.2   "In . . . free.'"] H; ∧ ~ . . . ~ .∧∧ P[29] (*inset passage*); ' ~ . . . ~ .∧' I
137.22   "In . . . 'free,'] *stet* I; *italics* Fullerton
137.22   my] *stet* P[29],I; *any* Fullerton
137.22,28,29,34;138.2   'free,'] Fullerton; ∧ ~ ,∧ P[29],I
137.25-26   *no . . . existence*] *stet* P[29],I; *roman* Fullerton
137.27   'free-willist'] Fullerton; ∧ ~ - ~ ∧ P[29],I
137.28   that, . . . free,] Fullerton; ~ ∧ . . . ~ ∧ P[29],I
137.29   *some*] *stet* P[29],I; some Fullerton

137.31   I] *stet* Fullerton, P[29],I
137.31   'free-will,'] Fullerton; ∧ ~ ∧ ~ ,∧ P[29]; ∧ ~ - ~ ,∧ I
137.32   I] *stet* P[29],I; *I* Fullerton
137.33   etc., etc.] *stet* P[29],I; *omit* Fullerton
137.33   What] *stet* P[29],I; what Fullerton
137.34   'free-will'] Fullerton; ∧ ~ - ~ ∧ P[29],I
137.35   *any*] *stet* P[29],I; any Fullerton
138.1   for∧] Fullerton; ~ , P[29],I
138.13   *disconnexion*] H; *disconnection* P[29],I
138.29   may] P[29],WJ/I,I[3]; *omit* I[1-2]
139.18   everyone] H; every one P[29],I
139.23-24   "reality . . . good"] P[29]; *all single quotes in* I
140.4   "I believe,"] P[29]; ' ~ ~ ,' I
140.10   syllogism:∧] P[29]; ~ :— I
140.16;143.13,36;144.21;145.38   anyone] H; any one P[29],I
140.19   premise∧] P[29]; ~ , I
140.19-20   "All . . . fulfilled"] P[29]; ' ~ . . . ~ ' I

140.20 Nevertheless∧] P²⁹; ∼ , I
140.25 adds:∧] P²⁹ (says:) ; ∼ :— I
140.26-32 "When ... position."] H;
  ∧ ∼ ... ∼ .∧ P²⁹ (*inset passage*);
  ' ∼ ... ∼ .' I
140.29 reality] McTaggart; reality
  of the thing P²⁹,I
140.30 a thing] McTaggart; the
  thing P²⁹,I
140.35 words:∧] P²⁹; ∼ :— I
140.36-141.2 "For ... true."] H;
  ∧ ∼ ... ∼ .∧ P²⁹ (*inset passage*);
  ' ∼ ... ∼ .' I
140.36 For] *stet* P²⁹,I; And for
  McTaggart
140.37 prevail] McTaggart; permit

P²⁹,I
141.18 tho] H; though P²⁹,I
142.5 Theætetus] H; Thæatetus P²⁹,I
143.11 regulative] WJ/I,I³; constitutive P²⁹,I¹⁻²
143.32 *Erkenntnis*] H; *Erkentniss* P²⁹, I
143.33 "Es ... Welt∧"—] P²⁹;
  ' ∼ ... ∼ ,'— I
144.19 "what ... believes."] P²⁹;
  ' ∼ ... ∼ .' I
144.19-20 everyone's] H; every one's
  P²⁹,I
144.28 relation,] P²⁹; ∼ ∧ I
144.38 grounds] WJ/I; causes P²⁹,I
145.25 german] H; German P²⁹,I
145.26 consist] P²⁹; consists I

CHAPTER XIV. Two English Critics

The copy-text for Chapter XIV is (I), the October 1909 first printing of *The Meaning of Truth*, which derives from (MS), the holograph manuscript preserved in the Houghton Library, probably through a lost typescript. Annotations in James's private copy preserved in the James Collection at Harvard (*AC85. J2376.909m[B]) are distinguished as WJ/I. The quotations from Russell and Hawtrey are identified in the Notes.

146.1 article,] MS; ∼ ∧ I
146.6;149.21 anyone] MS; any one I
146.8 fact—] H; ∼ ,— I
146.11 "far easier,"] H; ' ∼ ∼ ,'
  MS,I
146.12-14 "to ... good."] H;
  ' ∼ ... ∼ .' MS,I
146.12 Popes] Russell, MS; popes I
146.12-13 'Have ... infallible?'] H;
  " ∼ ... ∼ ," MS; " ∼ ... ∼ ?" I
147.30 naiveté] H; naivetè MS;
  naiveté I
147.33 "attempt ... 'fact' "] Russell;
  ' ∼ ... ∧ ∼ ∧' MS,I
147.34 "a failure"] H; ' ∼ ∼ ' MS,I
147.34-35 "The ... reappears,"] H;
  ' ∼ ... ∼ ,' MS,I
*148.6 else] WJ/I,I³; *omit* MS,I¹⁻²
148.31 *n'est-ce pas*] H; *roman* MS,I
148.33 someone] MS; some one I
149.6-7 "According ... pragmatists,"]
  H; ' ∼ ... ∼ ,∧ MS; ' ∼ ... ∼ ,' I
149.7-11 "to ... other"] H;
  ' ∼ ... ∼ ∧ (p. 400)." MS;
  ' ∼ ... ∼ ' I
149.7-8 'it ... exist'] H; " ∼ ... ∼ "
  Russell,MS,I
149.8 *means*] Russell, MS; means I

149.8 'it ... exist.'] H; " ∼ ... ∼ .∧
  MS; " ∼ ... ∼ ." Russell,I
149.10 one,] Russell; ∼ ∧ MS,I
149.22 exist∧] MS; ∼ , I
*149.30 Mr.] MS; *omit* I
150.20 "When, therefore,"] Hawtrey;
  " ∼ ∧ ∼ ', MS; ' ∼ ∧ ∼ ,' I
150.21-22 "I ... correctness."] H;
  ' ∼ ... ∼ .' MS,I
150.21 'it ... dead,'] Hawtrey, MS;
  ∧ ∼ ... ∼ ,∧ I
150.21 to say] *stet* I; *omit* Hawtrey,
  MS
150.21-22 'Cæsar is dead'. ...] H;
  "Cæsar is dead," and similarly if
  any other statement whatever be
  substituted for "Cæsar is dead."
  Hawtrey; ' ∼ ∼ ∼ '. MS;
  " ∼ ∼ ∼ " I
150.22 *definition*] Hawtrey; definition
  MS,I
150.25 ∧for] MS; ' ∼ I
150.27 " 'Cæsar is dead'] Hawtrey,
  MS; " ∧ ∼ ∼ ∼ " I
150.27-28 'it ... dead.'] Hawtrey,
  MS; " ∼ ... ∼ ." I
150.28 *what*] Hawtrey, MS; what I
150.28-29 ∧that 'Cæsar is dead.']

Hawtrey; ∧∼∧∼∼∼.' MS;
" ∼∧∼∼∼." ' I
150.29 dead!' "] Hawtrey; ∼ ! ∧ "
MS; ∼.'∧ I
151.4 ²definition∧] MS; ∼ , I

152.21-26 "the . . . false"] MS;
' ∼ . . . ∼ ' I
152.21 view:] *stet* I; ∼ — Russell, MS
152.22 falsehood;] Russell; ∼ , MS,I
152.24 white;] Russell; ∼ , MS,I

CHAPTER XV. A Dialogue

The copy-text for Chapter XV is (I), the October 1909 first printing of *The
Meaning of Truth*, which derives from (MS) the holograph manuscript preserved
in the Houghton Library, probably through a lost typescript. The treatment of
speech-prefixes is described in the Textual Notes to 154.6, 154.16.

154.5 begin: ∧] H; ∼ :— MS,I
*154.6 ANTI-PRAGMATIST] H (*up to*
155.26; *thereafter* MS); *Anti-pragmatist*
MS (*up to* 155.26); *Anti-Pragmatist*
I. *See Textual Note for details of
these speech-prefixes and their abbreviation*
*154.16 PRAGMATIST] H (*up to* 155.29;
· *thereafter* MS); *Pragmatist* MS (*up to*
155.29); *Pragmatist* I. *See Textual Note
for details of these speech-prefixes and
their abbreviation*
155.14 stateable] MS; statable I

*155.22 thus] *stet* I; then MS
*156.2 obtains] *stet* I; *obtains* MS
156.7 what] MS; What I
156.9,35 anyone] MS; any one I
156.14-15 consists∧] MS (*comma del.*);
∼ , I
157.19 and] MS; And I
*157.21 themselves∧] H; ∼ , MS,I
158.4 And∧] MS; ∼ , I
158.26 escape. For] MS; ∼ ; for I
159.5 and∧] MS; And, I

Textual Notes

28.30-31 'about' realities] In his file set of *Mind* James altered the quotation marks that had enclosed the phrase 'about realities' to apply, instead, only to the single word 'about'. That this was a sound correction may be seen from the text of 17.29-32 discussing the need to say something *about* objects of knowledge. However, in annotating a spare offprint of the journal article as printer's copy for his book, James overlooked the earlier change, with the result that book and journal agree in surrounding 'about realities' with the quotation marks; moreover, James did not observe the desirable alteration when he was annotating his private copy of the book. Nevertheless, the improvement in sense is manifest and the change has his authority in the marking of the article in his file set; hence it has been adopted in the present edition.

31.8 substitute] The journal here read 'latter', changed to 'substitute' in (I). However, in his file set of *Mind* James deleted 'latter' and added 'former' in the margin. The book reading 'substitute' makes more precise the autograph revision in the file set, for the 'former' is indeed the substitute, whereas in the journal text 'latter' had referred to the rejected percept that had been replaced. Even so, the passage is not marked by James's usual clarity of expression. It would seem that at 30.20-21 his tacit association of concepts as 'higher modes of thought' than percepts is not fully approving in view of his praise of percepts in 30.27ff. as the only salvation from 'the chaos of mutually repellent solipsisms' resulting from this conceptual 'higher mode of thought'. In his fifth criticism of the early article on which this chapter is based, he specifically lists as among its defects the treatment in this passage of 'percepts as the only realm of reality. I now treat concepts as a co-ordinate realm' (32.29-30). It may be that the change from 'latter' to 'former' and then to 'substitute' was a part of this raising in importance of concepts, but, if so, the retention of the word 'reduction' for the transfer of the substituting percept to 'the status of a conceptual sign' takes some of the bloom off any possible approval of what happens to this new percept once it has been established as the substitute. For the substitution of one experience for another, see James's discussion at 65.14ff.

58.11 known-as] For James's characteristic hyphenating of this technical phrase, see 33.11, 34.5.

66.32 partly common and] Since P20 read 'partly continuous and', it seems clear that in his revision James first substituted 'shared' for 'continuous' so that the intended reading was 'partly shared and partly discrete'. He then seems to have changed his mind and substituted 'common' for 'shared'. The printer in some manner mistook the intention and thought that 'common' was to be added without the deletion of 'shared'. In this manner 'common' got itself inserted after the 'and' instead of before it.

69.6'knowledge-about'] The hyphenation as a technical phrase is James's characteristic, as seen also at 15.38, 31.3, 62.9.

148.6 else . . . aware.] James's annotation of his private copy was confined to the addition of 'else' in the phrase 'anything of which I am aware.' In order to make this change, the printer of I³ (the third printing of the book and the second in November 1909) had to adjust the lines to avoid excessive resetting and an expensive plate-alteration. On his own hook, therefore, he modified James's phrasing in line 6 of page 148 to read 'anything else I am aware of.' The present edition, of course, ignores this mechanical and unauthoritative difference and reads, according to James's intentions, 'anything else of which I am aware.'

149.30 Mr.] As a consequence of what must have been James's revisions in proof in

245

the same line by which MS 'as' was changed to 'to mean' and 'previous' to 'other', the printer seems to have accommodated the expansion in the line without rearranging the type of following lines by omitting MS 'Mr.' Otherwise, in the book as in the manuscript, Russell is invariably addressed as 'Mr.'; one cannot believe that James omitted the courtesy intentionally by a marked proof-revision.

154.6 ANTI-PRAGMATIST] James began his manuscript with a single underline (italics) for all speech-prefixes, but at 155.26 and 155.29 respectively he shifted to a double underline to indicate small capitals with a heading capital. Whether it was the typist or the printer, some agent retained the early italic marking of the prefixes for consistency after he had come to the changed copy. However, James's final intention in his manuscript was clearly to use small capitals in these prefixes; hence they have been restored in the present edition throughout. Furthermore, the manuscript is regular in the lower-case form '-pragmatist' in these prefixes save at 154.19 where in a prefix not underlined in error the form is inconsistently capitalized as 'Anti-Prag'. The book form is consistently capitalized as 'Anti-Pragmatist', abbreviated to 'Anti-Prag', but the present edition follows the manuscript preference for lower case. Both manuscript and book have the full form of the prefix followed by a colon and dash on the first appearance of each character, at 154.6 and 154.16 respectively. Thereafter the manuscript continues with the full form on the next occurrence at 154.17 (abbreviated in [I]); but for the rest both manuscript and book agree in abbreviated prefixes. In the manuscript the first abbreviation of 'Prag' at 154.18 has a semicolon (in error) before the dash but thereafter only colons. On the other hand, the book regularly places a period for the abbreviation before the colon and dash, an unnecessary refinement which has been altered in the present edition to the manuscript usage. These minutiae of variation are not recorded in the Historical Collation.

154.16 See Textual Note to 154.6 above.

155.22 thus] The slight possibility exists that MS 'then', not written very clearly, was misread by the typist as 'thus' and the change not detected before copy was sent to the printer. However, the book reading 'thus' is sufficiently good not to be alterable for such speculative considerations. James added 'generically' only two words later, probably in proof, and thus must have scrutinized the line with some care; hence the odds seem to favor 'thus' as an intentional alteration of MS 'then'.

156.2 obtains] The possibility here of a typist's misreading is stronger than in 155.22 above, for in the interlineation of MS 'It *obtains*, it *holds*' the underline of '*obtains*' could readily have been mistaken as part of the guideline bringing the interlineation down and so the word could have been typed by mistake in roman. However, the removal of emphasis from 'obtains' adds to that of 'holds', and James ordinarily being so extremely careful about his italics for emphasis, the temptation to assume a misreading is perhaps better laid aside.

157.21 themselves_] Presumably in proof when the MS comma after 'there' (157.20) was removed to make the phrase 'as . . . themselves' restrictive, the remaining comma was overlooked in error.

Historical Collation

This list comprises the substantive and accidental variant readings that differ from the edited text in the authoritative documents noted for each chapter. The reading to the left of the bracket is that of the present edition. The rejected variants in the authoritative documents follow in chronological order to the right of the bracket. Any collated texts not recorded are to be taken as agreeing with the edition-reading to the left of the bracket: only variation appears to the right, except for the special case of emphasis when the origin of an accepted reading to the left is a James annotation in his marked private copy at Harvard University, indicated as WJ/I, or in annotated offprints or file sets of journals at Harvard, indicated as WJ/P (P for periodical), with identification. The listing of variant readings is complete for the substantives without regard for the records in the list of Emendations. The accidental variations are also complete, except for one special circumstance: to save space, they are omitted in this Historical Collation whenever the copy-text has been emended in respect to the accidentals and thus when the details may be found recorded in the list of Emendations. For conventions of notation, see the headnote for the Emendations list. One special convention appears in the Historical Collation. When the phrase *et seq. this chapter* occurs, all subsequent readings within the chapter are to be taken as agreeing with the particular feature of the reading being recorded unless specifically noted to the contrary, as by listing within the chapter headnote or by *stet* within the apparatus.

CHAPTER I.   The Function of Cognition

The copy-text for Chapter I is (I), the first edition of *The Meaning of Truth,* with reference to (P²⁴) "On the Function of Cognition," *Mind,* 10 (January 1885), 27–44 (McD 1885:1). James's annotations in his file of *Mind* (Harvard Phil.22.4.6*) are recorded as WJ/P²⁴ⁱ and the annotation in his private offprint of this article in Box O, envelope 9, as P²⁴ⁱⁱ. English spellings in *Mind* which have been Americanized in (I) to James's usual practice are not recorded as variants in this collation. Also not recorded save for exceptions is the rejection of double quotation marks in *Mind* which are ordinarily present when (I) (and the present edition) uses single quotes. The formula '&c.' *vs.* 'etc.' is not recorded as a variation, nor is the difference in English and American typography in the placement of punctuation in respect to quotation marks.

13.9   implies.] implies. In other words, our task is a purely analytic and introspective one; less important, possibly, than would be a successful research into the *causes* of cognition, but still interesting enough in its way. P²⁴

13.12   elsewhere] in MIND XXXIII. P²⁴

13.12   'feeling'] "Feeling" P²⁴

13.16-14.2   [If . . . instead.]]
    ∧ ∼ . . . ∼ .∧ P²⁴

13.17   'feeling,'] ∧ ∼ ,∧ P²⁴

13.19-21   ¹Read . . . redundancy]
    ¹Read before the Aristotelian Society on December 1st P²⁴

14.5   subjective,] ∼ ∧ P²⁴

14.20   *in*] in P²⁴

14.27 which] *omit* P²⁴

14.33 sense,] ~ ∧ P²⁴

14.36 days∧] ~ , P²⁴

15.13 feeling] feeling itself P²⁴

15.13 dirempted itself] been discriminated P²⁴

15.17-18 so . . . pocket] in its pocket, so to speak, endogenously P²⁴

15.29-30 *create . . . it*] *roman* P²⁴

15.38 condition.] condition. (Since writing this note I have read with the greatest pleasure Stumpf's demolition of the Relativity-doctrine in §1 of his *Tonpsychologie*, and beg leave to urge the study of it upon all readers.) P²⁴

16.4 reality?] reality? *Quis custodiet custodem ipsum?* P²⁴

16.4-5 present critic∧] psychologist, critic, P²⁴

16.13 assumptions.] ~ . Psychologists and P²⁴

16.18-19 *The . . . say*] *roman* P²⁴

16.21 the reality of] *omit* P²⁴

16.27 later] later on P²⁴

16.28 Some persons] Followers of Berkeley and Reid P²⁴

16.29 resemble] *resemble* P²⁴

17.3 ∧feeling∧∧ consciousness] " ~ "- ~ P²⁴

17.9 which] *omit* P²⁴

17.13 same] very same P²⁴,I

17.16 Altho] Although P²⁴

17.16 writings of] late P²⁴

17.17 they] it P²⁴

17.18 of collection] *omit* P²⁴

17.35 seldom] seldon P²⁴

18.1 knowledge," writes Grote, "may] knowledge may P²⁴

18.27 unjust, . . . failure,] ~ ∧ . . . ~ ∧ P²⁴

19.1 sign] *sign* P²⁴

19.7 -*about*,] ~ , of things into their relations P²⁴

19.8 about . . . knowledge] between which the relations P²⁴

19.9 situation] relations also P²⁴

19.10 ∧about∧] "about" P²⁴

19.17 *whats*∧] ~ , P²⁴

19.19 ∧speechless∧] " ~ " P²⁴

19.21 reality∧] fact, P²⁴

19.21 *extra*∧] ~ , P²⁴

19.28 ∧first intention,∧] " ~ ~ ," P²⁴

20.3 may have] has P²⁴

20.5 would be] is P²⁴

20.6 would oblige] obliges P²⁴

20.9 *so . . . resemble*] *roman* P²⁴

20.10 *of*] of P²⁴

20.11 fact] truth P²⁴

20.23 *blaue*] *Blaue* P²⁴

20.25+ *space*] *no space* P²⁴

20.27 odd] paradoxical P²⁴

20.38 ['Unmediated . . . 1909.]] *omit* P²⁴

21.24 platonic] Platonic P²⁴

21.28 all.] all. Of our quality, resembling the feeling, and supposed to form the only reality in the world, we can say, however, that it is known to the feeling as much as in the nature of things it can possibly be known to any cognitive agency whatever, however perfect, —the feeling knowing of it all there is to be known, and standing for it and discriminating it as much as it admits of being discriminated and stood-for at all. P²⁴

22.14 'society . . . research'] "Society for Psychical Research" P²⁴

22.24 *acting*] acting P²⁴

22.24 'the start'] *stet* P²⁴,I

22.25 instructed] informed P²⁴

22.25-26 in all probability] probably all P²⁴

23.9 performed] brought about P²⁴

23.16 tell . . . remedy,] ask me, "Do you know a remedy?" P²⁴

23.25 harmony] Leibnizian harmony P²⁴

23.33-41 [I . . . would.]] *omit* P²⁴

24.4 of much] a great part P²⁴

24.12,13 action] actions P²⁴

24.15 ∧*überhaupt*,∧] " ~ , " P²⁴

24.29 *grübelsucht*] *Grübelsucht* P²⁴

24.31 my body resembled] our two bodies resemble P²⁴

24.34 he] WJ/P²⁴ⁱ⁻ⁱⁱ,I; we P²⁴

24.35 by me] *omit* P²⁴

24.36 term] certain ejective term P²⁴

24.36 we trace] *omit* P²⁴

24.36 happen] happen in our two bodies point P²⁴

25.1 body] two bodies P²⁴

25.2 another that is not] others that are no objects of P²⁴

25.4 body] bodies P²⁴

25.14,15,20,23,24,27,29,32 ∧Ivanhoes∧] " ~ " P²⁴

25.24 make] *make* P²⁴
25.26 author] *author* P²⁴
25.34 Ivanhoe∧] ~ , P²⁴
25.39 same] *same* P²⁴
27.4-5 —in . . . course—] *omit* P²⁴
27.7 realities.] realities. As Reid says, "every man knows that he can relate the pain he suffered, not only without pain, but with pleasure; and that to suffer pain and think of it, are things which differ totally in kind and not in degree only". P²⁴
27.11-12 that . . . degree] out of which an image of them might be framed P²⁴
27.13 no] no substantive P²⁴
27.20-21 terminal *more*] *terminus* P²⁴
27.22 might . . . yet] might, but do not, lead P²⁴
27.23 towards] *towards* P²⁴
27.28 tho] though P²⁴
27.36 *percept*] *Percept* P²⁴
27.37-28.1 *conceptual . . . thought*] *Conceptual Feeling, or Thought* P²⁴
28.1 *knows*] *refers to, and takes cognisance of,* P²⁴
28.3-4 , or . . . context] *omit* P²⁴
28.4 latter] *omit* P²⁴
28.6 must] must be aware of the percept in one of those dim ways

described in a former article,[2] that it must consciously look in the direction thereof, and | [fn] ²*Ibid.*, pp. 14-17, 19, 23-24. P²⁴
28.30-31 'about' realities] WJ/P²⁴ⁱ; " ~ ∧ ~ " P²⁴; ' ~ ∧ ~ ' I
28.34 knowledge] knowledges P²⁴
28.36 etc.] &c. See MIND XXXIII. 23. P²⁴
29.11 working] moving P²⁴
29.22 -century∧] - ~ - P²⁴
29.23 'Newton'] ∧ ~ ∧ P²⁴
29.25 of the] of P²⁴
30.1-2 *we . . . PERCEPTS . . . common*] roman (except 'percepts' *italic*) P²⁴
30.4 I . . . you] you mean by me P²⁴
30.13-14 *erkenntnisstheoretiker*] *Erkenntnisstheoretiker* P²⁴
30.25-26 two . . . walk] a different universe walks P²⁴
30.30 resemblance] *resemblance* P²⁴
30.30 perceptual] *omit* P²⁴
30.31 power] strange power P²⁴
30.31 one another] each other P²⁴
30.36-37 physical] *omit* P²⁴
31.8 substitute] former WJ/P²⁴ⁱ; latter P²⁴
31.29-30 ∧*Nirgends . . . Sohlen*∧—] " ~ . . . ~ ": P²⁴
32.1-32 NOTE.— . . . part.] *omit* P²⁴

CHAPTER II.   The Tigers in India

The copy-text for Chapter II is (I), with reference to (P³⁴) "The Knowing of Things Together," *Psychological Review*, 2 (March 1895), 105-124 (McD 1895:4), the extracts in (I) being drawn from pp. 107-110. James's annotations in his file set of the *Review* (WJ 110.72) are noted as WJ/P³⁴.

33.3 Altho] Although P³⁴
33.20-21 ¹Extracts . . . (1895).] ¹Read as the President's Address before the American Psychological Association at Princeton, December, 1894, and reprinted with some unimportant omissions, a few slight revisions, and the addition of some explanatory notes. P³⁴
34.23 *taken by themselves*] roman P³⁴
34.24 phenomenal] physical P³⁴
34.25 intra-experiential] physical P³⁴
34.26 *if . . . there*] roman P³⁴
34.35,37 *may*] may P³⁴
35.4 D.S. Miller] Miller, of Bryn

Mawr, P³⁴
35.20 being,] ~ ∧ P³⁴
35.29,32 may be] WJ/P³⁴; is P³⁴,I
35.31-32 far, again,] ~ ∧ ~ ∧ P³⁴
35.34-35 again, for,] WJ/P³⁴; again— P³⁴,I
35.36-37 See . . . 1895.] See also Dr. Miller's article on Truth and Error, in the *Philosophical Review*, July, 1893. P³⁴
36.17-18 philosophers . . . men.⁵] common men and of philosophers.∧ P³⁴
36.31-32 ⁵[The . . . controversy.]] *omit* P³⁴

CHAPTER III. Humanism and Truth

The copy-text for Chapter III is (I), with reference to (P²⁴) "Humanism and Truth," *Mind*, n.s. 13 (October 1904), 457–475 (McD 1904:11) and the additions from (P²⁴) "Humanism and Truth Once More," *Mind*, n.s. 14 (April 1905), 190–198 (McD 1905:5). James's annotation in his file of *Mind* (MH Phil.22.4.6*) of "Humanism and Truth" is recorded as WJ/P²⁴. English spellings in *Mind* which have been Americanized in (I) to James's usual practice are not recorded as variants in this collation, nor is the variant English positioning of punctuation in relation to quotation marks or '&c.' *vs.* 'etc.'

37.1   *Mind*] MIND P²⁴
37.2   article] article for July P²⁴
37.19-21   ¹Reprinted . . . made.]
  omit P²⁴
38.3   still] *omit* P²⁴
38.9   'humanism'] 'Humanism' P²⁴
38.11   method.'] ∼ '. ¹ | ¹If further
  egotism be in order, I may say that
  the account of truth given by
  Messrs. Sturt and Schiller and by
  Prof. Dewey and his school (who
  never use the word pragmatism)
  goes beyond any theorising which I
  personally had ever indulged in
  until I read their writings. After
  reading these, I feel almost sure
  that these authors are right in their
  main contentions; but the originality
  is wholly theirs, and I can hardly
  recognise in my own humble
  doctrine that concepts are
  teleological instruments anything
  considerable enough to warrant my
  being called, as I have been, the
  'father' of so important a movement
  forward in philosophy. P²⁴
38.36-37   ²['Practical' . . . physical.]]
  omit P²⁴
[*start* McD 1905:5, pp. 190.17-191.6]
39.2   Humanism] It P²⁴
39.2-3   in fact] *omit* P²⁴
39.4   deep] full P²⁴
39.16-17   some . . . opponents] Mr.
  Joseph P²⁴
39.17   catholic] Catholic P²⁴
39.18   darwinism] Darwinism P²⁴
[*end* McD 1905:5, pp. 190.17-191.6]
[*start* McD 1905:5, p. 191.10-29]
39.31-32   an . . . might] Mr. Joseph
  may probably P²⁴
39.35   term),] ∼)∧ P²⁴
39.35   sincerely to renounce] to
  renounce sincerely P²⁴
40.4   ∧more∧] ' ∼ ' P²⁴

40.9   inductive] *omit* P²⁴
[*end* McD 1905:5, p. 191.10-29]
40.10   pragmatist . . . things] theory
  P²⁴
40.15   'reason'] 'Reason' P²⁴
40.16;41.8   nature] Nature P²⁴
41.12   undulate;] ∼ , P²⁴
41.22   everywhere] anywhere P²⁴
41.24   collaborating with] reacting on
  imperfect P²⁴
41.26   'Collaborating'] 'Reaction' P²⁴
42.8   mass] apperceiving mass P²⁴
42.13   that] which P²⁴
42.25   *denkmittel*] *Denkmittel* P²⁴
42.27   contrary,] ∼ ∧ P²⁴
43.2   rattles] beings P²⁴
43.16   it∧] ∼ , P²⁴
43.29   mental or physical] *omit* P²⁴
44.4;47.11,17,24   absolute] Absolute
  P²⁴
44.5 *et seq. this chap.* Professor]
  Prof. P²⁴
44.6   disciples, . . . physicist] disciples∧
  the physicists Wilbois P²⁴
44.6   thoroughgoing] ∼ - ∼ P²⁴
44.10   school,] ∼ ∧ P²⁴
44.25   determinations,' and] ∼ '?
  And P²⁴
44.34   thing] one P²⁴
44.35   second] second one P²⁴
45.14 (*twice*)   experience] thought P²⁴
45.15   us] us P²⁴
45.20   in some shape] *omit* P²⁴
45.21   be] be there in P²⁴
45.29   in . . . resort] *omit* P²⁴
45.31   'ding∧an∧sich'] ∧Ding-an-Sich∧
  P²⁴
45.32   'absolute'] ∧Absolute∧ P²⁴
46.8-9   exerted . . . own] our own
  mental P²⁴
46.13   deweyite] Deweyite P²⁴
46.25 *et seq. this chap.* tho] though P²⁴
46.31;49.17   truth] Truth P²⁴
47.6   *real*] real P²⁴

47.36 *blaue*] *Blaue* P²⁴
48.4 forever] for ever P²⁴
48.7 *ante-rem*] ∼ ʌ ∼ P²⁴
48.17-18 than . . . ¹humanist] *omit* P²⁴
48.23 ʌheroic devotionʌ] ' ∼ ∼ ' P²⁴
48.30 *inbegriff*] *Inbegriff* P²⁴
49.13 *dramatic temperament*] temperament P²⁴
49.13,14 nature] Nature P²⁴
49.23-40 ⁴[I . . . 248.]] *omit* P²⁴
49.35 bien] *omit* I
50.19 new comer's] newcomer's P²⁴
50.28 *erhöhung . . . daseins*] *Erhöhung . . . Daseins* P²⁴
51.15 mental] correspondence of P²⁴
51.16 the real] *omit* P²⁴
51.18 images . . . sensations] sensations are so often copied by the images P²⁴
52.3 co-ordinates] coordinates P²⁴
52.10 being] *omit* P²⁴
52.11 conceive] conceived P²⁴
52.17 on . . . *mean*] *omit* P²⁴
52.18 intentionally . . . fictitiously] *omit* P²⁴
52.19 real] *omit* P²⁴
52.37 is] *omit* P²⁴
52.38 ⁵Vol. ii, pp. 641 ff.] *omit* P²⁴
53.1 now] is now P²⁴
53.3 perceived to obtain] found P²⁴
53.9 *may*] may P²⁴
53.13 earth's] Earth's P²⁴
53.16 altho] although P²⁴
53.37 ⁶[Mental . . . world.]] *omit* P²⁴
54.6 objects, . . . reality,] ∼ ʌ . . . ∼ ʌ P²⁴
54.8 berkeleyan] Berkeleyan P²⁴
54.13 didn't,] ∼ ʌ P²⁴
54.21 , and . . . believe] *omit* P²⁴
54.27 at that moment] *omit* P²⁴
55.28 experience] Experience P²⁴
55.29 possessed-of] ∼ ʌ ∼ P²⁴
55.30 absolute realities] Absolute Realities P²⁴
55.34 notion] Notion P²⁴
55.34 humanism] Humanism P²⁴
56.2 being] Being P²⁴
56.2 nonentity] Nonentity P²⁴
56.10 'true.'] ʌ ∼ .ʌ P²⁴
56.11 heavens] Heavens P²⁴
56.14 (or long-necked?)] *omit* P²⁴
56.35 your count] it P²⁴
56.35 beforehand] already P²⁴
57.4-5 ³itʌ . . . build] it, build P²⁴
57.18 universe] Universe P²⁴

57.34 motive] object P²⁴; purpose WJ/P²⁴
57.37 published . . . 1904] for this Spring (Montreal, 1904) P²⁴
58.1 copied and] actually P²⁴
58.3-6 The . . . not] *omit* P²⁴
[*start* McD 1905:5, p. 197.2-38]
58.7 ²and . . . pragmatism] he thinks, and pragmatism has to P²⁴
58.7 bankruptcy,] ∼ ʌ P²⁴
58.8 admits] recognises P²⁴
58.8 all?"] ∼ .ʌ P²⁴
58.8 The (*no* ¶)] ¶ There is no room for disagreement about the facts here; but the P²⁴
58.8 such talk] the reasoning P²⁴
58.9 use words] talk P²⁴
58.12 consist.] consist. Mr. Joseph, faithful to the habits of his party, makes no attempt at characterising them, but assumes that their nature is self-evident to all. P²⁴
58.14 absolute reality] Absolute Reality P²⁴
58.16 habits] manners P²⁴
58.16-17 mind's . . . world?] mind? P²⁴
58.19 do] *omit* P²⁴
58.23 as such] *omit* P²⁴
58.31 and] with P²⁴
[*end* McD 1905:5, p. 197.2-38]
[*start* McD 1905:5, p.198.13-37]
58.37 Theoretic truth thus] It P²⁴
59.11 explicitly] *omit* P²⁴
59.21-22 , and . . . attack] *omit* P²⁴
[*end* McD 1905:5, p. 198.13-37]
59.23 I am well] I am leaving many objections for a possible future treatment, and I am P²⁴
59.23 this] my P²⁴
59.23-24 in the extreme] enough P²⁴
59.34 conforming,'] ∼ ʌ' P²⁴
59.35-38 ⁸This . . . account.] *omit* P²⁴
60.1 any] an P²⁴
60.11 advance.] advance. [¶] 6. The two facts, that experiences, conceptual as well as perceptual, claim preservation and yet interfere with one another, is the ground of what is called the 'objectivity' or independence of the reality to which the present experience must conform. P²⁴
60.12 6.] 7. P²⁴
60.12 which] that P²⁴

CHAPTER IV.   The Relation between Knower and Known

The copy-text for Chapter IV is (I), with reference to (P[20]) "A World of Pure Experience," *Journal of Philosophy, Psychology, and Scientific Methods*, 1 (September 29, 1904), 533–543, and 1 (October 13, 1904), 561–570 (McD 1904:10). The chapter is abstracted from pp. 538.3–543.24, and 561.1–562.20, 562.38–564.32. A variant appears in James's marked copy (WJ/I) and also in the plates of the third printing of November 1909 (I[3]).

61.1   Throughout] III. THE COG-
NITIVE RELATION | The first
great pitfall from which such a
radical standing by experience will
save us is an artificial conception
of the *relations between knower and
known*. Throughout P[20]
61.6-7   put . . . intermediary] simply
shoved the subject-object gap a
step farther, getting it now between
the object and the representation P[20]
61.9-10   impossible . . . knowers] im-
passible in the finite realm P[20]
61.10;64.25   absolute] Absolute P[20]
61.11   saltatory] bridging P[20]
61.20-21   [1]Extract . . . 1904.] *omit* P[20]
62.3   ways] types, the ways P[20]
62.5   essay.] essay.[2] | [2]For brevity's
sake I altogether omit mention of the
type constituted by knowledge of
the truth of general propositions.
This type has been thoroughly and,
so far as I can see, satisfactorily,
elucidated in Dewey's 'Studies in
Logical Theory' (Chicago, 1904).
Such propositions are reducible to
the *S-is-P* form; and the 'terminus'
that verifies and fulfills is the *S = P*
as they feel in combination. Of
course percepts may be involved
in the mediating experiences, or in
the 'satisfactoriness' of the *P* in its
new position. P[20]
62.5   treated] just treated P[20]
62.6-7   the *Journal* . . . exist?'] this
JOURNAL for September 1, 1904.
P[20]
62.10   there.] there. Of type 2, the
simplest sort of conceptual knowledge, I have given some account in
two articles, published respectively
in *Mind*, Vol. X., p. 27, 1885, and
in the *Psychological Review*, Vol. II.,
p. 105, 1895.[3] | [3]These articles and
their doctrine, unnoticed aparently

by any one else, have lately gained
favorable comment from Professor
Strong in this JOURNAL, for May 12,
1904. Dr. Dickinson S. Miller has
independently thought out the same
results, which Strong according
dubs the James-Miller theory of
cognition. P[20]
62.12   now] *omit* P[20]
62.13   meanings] experience-value
and meaning P[20]
62.19   an . . . [1]difference] intrinsic
differences P[20]
62.19   makes] make P[20]
62.20   *extrinsic*] extrinsic P[20]
62.24   nothing;] ∼ , P[20]
62.25   Delta;] ∼ , P[20]
62.26   not;] ∼ , P[20]
62.27   *et seq. this chap.* tho] though P[20]
62.33   feel] now feel P[20]
62.34   imperfect] bad P[20]
62.34-35   to have . . . *terminated*] to be
continued P[20]
62.37   other] WJ/I,I[3]; others P[20],I[1-2]
63.2   I] *omit* P[20]
63.5   continues] matches P[20]
63.5   one] *omit* P[20]
63.6   continuing] matching P[20]
63.7-8   *lies . . . signify*] roman P[20]
63.10-11   possiblesʌ . . . cannot,]
∼ , . . . can notʌ P[20]
63.11   pretence] pretense P[20]
63.14   of . . . life] thus lives P[20]
63.19-20   *their . . . known*] roman P[20]
63.19   *starting-point*] ∼ ʌ ∼ P[20]
63.25   *et seq. this chap.* altho] although
P[20]
63.28   gradually] *omit* P[20]
63.30   the object's] *omit* P[20]
63.31   its] *omit* P[20]
63.33   way] thing P[20]
64.3   two . . . oneʌ] union is smitten
into living being, P[20]
64.3   their distinctness] the distinctness of its terms P[20]

64.12 predication] prediction I
64.13 unions] unions realized P[20]
64.17 [1]one] *one* P[20]
64.23 conjunctions . . . experienced]
the conjunctions which we experience P[20]
64.26 stroke. [*space*]] stroke. If, on
the other hand, we had such an
Absolute, not one of our opponents'
theories of knowledge could remain
standing any better than ours could;
for the distinctions as well as the
conjunctions of experience would
impartially fall its prey. The whole
question of how 'one' thing can
know 'another' would cease to be a
real one at all in a world where
otherness itself was an illusion.[4] [*no
space*] | [4]Mr. Bradley, not professing
to know his absolute *aliunde*, nevertheless derealizes Experience by
alleging it to be everywhere infected
with self-contradiction. His arguments seem almost purely verbal,
but this is no place for arguing that
point out. P[20]
64.27 relation∧] ∼ , P[20]
64.31 percept∧ . . . object∧]
∼ , . . . ∼ , P[20]
64.32,33 percept] object P[20]
64.32,36 concept] idea P[20]
64.33 percept's] object's P[20]
64.35 proves . . . be] is P[20]
64.37 for human life] *omit* P[20]
64.37 knowing] knowing for human
life P[20]
65.4-5 [1]sometimes . . . results] yet
leading to the same result P[20]
65.6 ideas] conceptual experiences,
or ideas P[20]
65.7 experiences] experience P[20]
65.12 And this] This P[20]
65.13 substitution. [¶] What] substitution, and some remarks on that
subject seem to be the next thing
in order. | IV. SUSTITUTION | In
Taine's brilliant book on 'Intelligence,' substitution was for the first
time named as a cardinal logical
function, though of course the facts
had always been familiar enough.
What now P[20]
65.14 a system] an absolute system P[20]
65.16 my view] radical empiricism P[20]

65.16 is] wears the form of P[20]
65.24 Others] Others follow them
more livingly, P[20]
65.33 experienced] kind of P[20]
66.2 possible] alternative P[20]
66.10 character] Character P[20]
66.15 -circuits] -circuits which P[20]
66.17 outside] outside of P[20]
66.18 re-enter] reenter P[20]
[*begin* P[20] *part* 2]
66.21 Whosoever] V. WHAT OBJEC-
TIVE REFERENCE IS| Whosoever P[20]
66.21 to be] as P[20]
66.21 substitutional∧] ∼ , P[20]
66.24-41 [3]This . . . made.] *text in* P[20]
66.26 objective] *omit* P[20]
66.26 his] the sense of his P[20]
66.26-27 a . . . [1]percept] an absolutely
continuous perception P[20]
66.27 as a percept] is his perception
P[20]
66.27-28 we . . . it] it may be very
inattentive P[20]
66.28 is the] of a P[20]
66.29 distant parts] rest P[20]
66.29 are] is P[20]
66.30 us . . . objects] each of us, a
conceptual object P[20]
66.30 reality] realities P[20]
66.31-32 their . . . common and] the
nucleus, partly continuous and P[20];
their . . . partly shared and common I
66.32-33 the . . . innumerable] what
we call the physical world of actual
perception, innumerable hosts of P[20]
66.33-34 cogitation,] ∼ ∧ P[20]
66.35-36 all . . . 'reality'] the whole
of the nucleus of relative 'reality,'
as around the Dyak's head of my
late metaphor, there P[20]
66.36 cloud] *nimbus* P[20]
66.39 nuclei] nucleus P[20]
66.41 made.] made. [¶] This notion
of the purely substitutional or conceptual physical world brings us to
the most critical of all the steps in
the development of a philosophy of
pure experience. The paradox of
self-transcendency in knowledge
comes back upon us here, but I
think that our notions of pure experience and of substitution, and our
radically empirical view of conjunctive transitions, are *Denkmittel* that

will carry us safely through the
pass. P[20]
67.2   says . . . and] *omit* P[20]
67.5   difficulty;] ~ , P[20]
67.7   that] *omit* P[20]
67.7-8   is . . . ¹of] to be wholly constituted by P[20]
67.10   fulfils] fulfills P[20]
67.15   lately used] of my former article P[20]
67.20   was] *was* P[20]
67.21   *virtual*] virtual P[20]
67.22   certified] nailed down and
certified P[20]
67.22   knowers,] ~ ∧ P[20]
67.23-25   Just . . . come.] *omit* P[20]
67.33-35   *To . . . sense.*] roman P[20]
67.37   truth or] *omit* P[20]
68.7-8   experiences of tendency]
truncated experiences P[20]
68.9   the] *omit* P[20]
68.9   comes] were P[20]
68.16   appears.] appears. I know full
well that such brief words as these
will leave the hardened transcendentalist unshaken. Conjunctive
experiences *separate* their terms, he
will still say: they are third things
interposed, that have themselves to
be conjoined by new links, and to
invoke them makes our trouble in-
finitely worse. To 'feel' our motion
forward is impossible. Motion implies terminus; and how can terminus
be felt before we have arrived? The
barest start and sally forwards, the
barest tendency to leave the instant,
involves the chasm and the leap.
Conjunctive transitions are the most
superficial of appearances, illusions
of our sensibility which philosophical
reflection pulverizes at a touch.
Conception is our only trustworthy
instrument, conception and the
Absolute working hand in hand.
Conception disintegrates experience
utterly, but its disjunctions are
easily overcome again when the
Absolute takes up the task.

   Such transcendentalists I must
leave, provisionally at least, in full
possession of their creed. I have no
space for polemics in this article, so
I shall simply formulate the em-

piricist doctrine as my hypothesis,
leaving it to work or not work as it
may. P[20]
68.16   Objective (*no* ¶)] ¶ P[20]
68.16   reference] reference, I say then,
P[20]
68.16   an] a mere P[20]
68.17   consists] is P[20]
68.26   but . . . there] there, so that our
knowledge for the most part keeps
only virtual P[20]
68.28   a] a mere P[20]
68.29   , such . . . say,] *omit* P[20]
68.30   and 'true' already,] already,
such a critic might say, P[20]
68.33   fulfilled] carried out P[20]
68.35-36   method. . . . of all] method.
When a dispute arises, that method
consists in auguring what practical
consequences would be different if
one side rather than the other were
true. If no difference can be
thought of, the dispute is a quarrel
over words. [¶] What then would
the *salto mortale*, the immediate self-
transcendency affirmed as something
existing independently of P[20]
68.36-37   *known-as?* What] known∧as,
what P[20]
68.37   for *us*] *omit* P[20]
69.7   and] and such knowledge P[20]
69.8   such knowledge] *omit* P[20]
69.10   *perceptually*] perceptually P[20]
69.14   possess]carry P[20]
69.16   effects] really next effects P[20]
69.20   is] here would be P[20]
69.22-23   fruits— . . . fruits.]
fruits. [¶] Fruits for us, humanistic
fruits, of course. P[20]
69.24-25   The . . . fruits.] *omit* P[20]
plus following excision of P[20] *text*: If an
Absolute were proved to exist for
other reasons, it might well appear
that *his* knowledge is terminated in
innumerable cases where ours is still
incomplete. That, however, would
be a fact indifferent to our knowledge.
The latter would grow neither worse
nor better, whether we acknowledged
such an Absolute or left him out.

   So the notion of a knowledge still
in transitu and on its way joins hands
here with that notion of a 'pure
experience' which I tried to explain

in my recent article entitled 'Does Consciousness Exist?' The instant field of the present is always experience in its 'pure' state, plain unqualified actuality, a simple *that*, as yet undifferentiated into thing and thought, and only virtually classifiable as objective fact or as some one's opinion about fact. This is as true when the field is conceptual as when it is perceptual. 'Memorial Hall' is 'there' in my idea as much as when I stand before it. I proceed to act on its account in either case. Only in the later experience that supersedes the present one is this *naif* immediacy

retrospectively split into two parts, a 'consciousness' and its 'content,' and the content corrected or confirmed. While still pure, or present, any experience—mine, for example, of what I write about in these very lines—passes for 'truth.' The morrow may reduce it to 'opinion.' The transcendentalist in all his particular knowledges is as liable to this reduction as I am: his Absolute does not save him.

69.25 Why] Why, then, P[20]
69.26-28 knowledge ... is] knowing that merely leaves it liable to this inevitable condition? Why insist on its being P[20]

CHAPTER V.   The Essence of Humanism

The copy-text for Chapter V is (I), with reference to (P[20]) "The Essence of Humanism," *Journal of Philosophy, Psychology, and Scientific Methods*, 2 (March 2, 1905), 113–118 (McD 1905:3).

70.1 Humanism] The fact that the January number of *Mind* contains two articles that continue the humanistic (or pragmatistic) controversy, and one that deeply connects with it, makes it more evident than ever that humanism P[20]
70.4 centre] center P[20]
70.14-15 ¹Reprinted ... 1905.] *omit* P[20]
71.10-11 finds ... entertain] has entertained P[20]
71.16-17 guess ... view] construct its meaning P[20]
71.18 this,] ∼ ∧ P[20]
72.3 *et seq. this chap. tho*] though P[20]
72.6-7 Since ... it (*no* ¶)] ¶ Such a formula P[20]
72.14 all-experiencer] All-Experiencer P[20]
72.14 actual] finite P[20]
72.16 defence] defense P[20]
72.22 it] it in philosophical journals P[20]
72.28,31 absolute] Absolute P[20]
72.28 bradleyan] Bradleyan P[20]
72.31 roycean] Roycean P[20]
72.32 knowledge.] knowledge, a treatment of which I have already given a version in two very inade-

quate articles in this JOURNAL for last year.³ | ³'Does Consciousness Exist?' and 'A World of Pure Experience,' Vol. I., 447, 533, 561. P[20]
73.2 thesis,] insight, which I have already P[20]
73.2 above] *omit* P[20]
73.13 in experience] *omit* P[20]
73.13 alternately] both P[20]
73.21 remain] are P[20]
73.26 *identitätsphilosophie*] Identitätsphilosophie P[20]
73.27-28 *does ... itself*] roman P[20]
73.35-36 articles ... 1904.] articles above referred to, especially the first one, 'Does Consciousness Exist?' P[20]
74.9,17,18,19 common∧sense] ∼ - ∼ P[20]
74.10 altho] although P[20]
74.11-12 are ... them,] *omit* P[20]
74.13 dog] dog for him P[20]
74.34-35 no absolute] none but a pragmatic P[20]
75.1 in.] in. They keep to the original common-sense schematism and simply carry it a little farther out. They transcend sense-perception in no other sense than that in which this latter transcends conception. P[20]

75.1   possible] *omit* P[20]
75.2   upon . . . outer] in order upon the hairy P[20]
75.4   conceived] conceived of P[20]
75.9   you and I] we P[20]
75.10   conceive] represent P[20]
75.14   such confluence] *omit* P[20]
75.15   *hand*] hand P[20]
75.19   perfected] perfect P[20]
75.19-20   true . . . muster] sufficiently true P[20]
75.23-24   *that . . . thinking*] roman P[20]
75.25-26   *or . . . ²intervene*] roman P[20]
75.27-28   bears . . . imagination] functions for philosophy just as sensation functions for common-sense P[20]
75.28-29   provisional . . . termini] to be conceived as experiential termini, actual or possible P[20]
75.30-31   , while . . . reality] *omit* P[20]
75.32   philosophical] theoretical P[20]
75.33   'true'] ' ~ ʌ P[20]

76.9-10   , which . . . 'real,'] *omit* P[20]
76.10   *provisionally*] provisionally P[20]
76.11   occupies] includes P[20]
76.12-13   which, . . . experient,] ~ ʌ . . . ~ ʌ P[20]
76.14   *does*] does P[20]
76.17   sensible] perceptual P[20]
76.17   pre-existent] preexistent P[20]
76.21   result.] result. Having written of this point in an article in reply to Mr. Joseph's criticism of my humanism in the January *Mind*, which article I hope may itself appear in *Mind* ere long, I will say no more about truth here, but refer the reader to that review. P[20]
76.21-22   In . . . in a] In any case, it is certain that truth consists in no P[20]
76.23   trans-experiential] transexperiential P[20]
76.26   ¹they . . . *real*,] *omit* P[20]
76.29   'true.'] ʌ ~ .ʌ P[20]

CHAPTER VI.   A Word More about Truth

The copy-text for Chapter VI is (I), with reference to (P[20]) "A Word More about Truth," *Journal of Philosophy, Psychology, and Scientific Methods*, 4 (July 18, 1907), 396–406 (McD 1907:7).

78.1   My] To the Editors of this Journal: | My P[20]
78.1   to my] to the P[20]
78.1   truth] truth which I published in your number for March 14 of this year, P[20]
78.5-6   vary my statements] assail your pages again P[20]
78.7   formulas] statements P[20]
78.10   ʌpragmatists,ʌ] ' ~ , ' P[20]
78.12   as] not as the pragmatist conception, but as P[20]
78.12-13   the first . . . book.] an article in *Mind* bearing the title of 'The Function of Cognition.' P[20]
78.16   knowing . . . together'] Knowing of Things Together' P[20]
78.17   the *Journal* . . . *etc.*,] this Journal P[20]
78.17-79.1   naturalistic . . . reality] Naturalistic Theory of the Reference of Thought to Reality P[20]
78.20   ³The . . . p. 33]] ²*Psychological Review*, Vol. II., p. 105 P[20]

79.11-12   am . . . myself.] beg you for more space in which to express myself. I shall probably not soon offend again in the interests of this particular subject of disputation! P[20]
79.15   Strong] Strong, in the manuscript of a forthcoming work with which he has recently favored me, P[20]
79.21   english] English P[20]
79.26-27   *space*-relations] ~ ʌ ~ P[20]
79.29   other] only other P[20]
79.29   space-relations] ~ ʌ ~ P[20]
79.34   ʌ*Principles of Psychology*,ʌ] 'Principles of Psychology,' P[20]
80.4   readers] readers (Professor Russell,⁵ for example) | ⁵See this Journal, Vol. IV., p. 292 f. P[20]
80.5   may] may easily P[20]
80.12   I . . . know] We know, I say, P[20]
80.13-14   under . . . communicates] with the clue in our hand which the idea gives us P[20]
80.14   in] in common sense, in P[20]

80.15   send] lead P[20]
80.18   'real'] ∧true∧ P[20]
80.19-20   appearances and substitutes] substitutes and representatives P[20]
80.22   towards] to P[20]
80.32   these] these associates P[20]
80.33   an improved] a better P[20]
81.2   Surely not, for] But P[20]
81.6   guide us] guide or point P[20]
81.7   object] *omit* P[20]
81.7   enrich us with] yield us P[20]
81.12   to, or towards,] ∼ ∧ ∼ ∼ ∧ P[20]
81.20   cannot] can not P[20]
81.25   particularities,] ∼ ∧ P[20]
81.33   having become] being now P[20]
81.34   *erkenntnisstheorie*] *Erkenntnisstheorie* P[20]
81.37   what . . . calls] *omit* P[20]
81.37   '*salto mortale*'] ∧ ∼ ∼ ∧ P[20]
82.3   sublime] *omit* P[20]
82.4   explain] overcome P[20]
82.5-6   abstract and saltatory] into a saltatory one P[20]
82.7   the] our P[20]
82.7   concrete] concrete ambulatory P[20]
82.10   defines] explains P[20]
82.10-11   complication∧] ∼ , P[20]
82.11   potentially] *potentially* P[20]
82.19-20   profundity,] ∼ ∧ P[20]
82.23-24   ideational or sensational] ideas or sensations P[20]
83.1   concretely has] actually keeps P[20]
83.4   idea and] idea, P[20]
83.13-14   [2]the . . . of] that faculty *schlechthin*, of its P[20]
83.14   scenes and] scenes, as it were, of its P[20]
83.18-19   *do not*] *don't* P[20]
83.19   *or . . . ignores*] *what it ignores, or positively deny it* P[20]
83.33   armies,] ∼ ∧ P[20]
83.36-37   [6]This . . . 1909.] *omit* P[20]
84.1   of . . . *Pragmatism*,] of my recent little book entitled 'Pragmatism,' P[20]
84.1   used] used for a certain purpose P[20]
84.9   going-round] ∼ ∧ ∼ P[20]
84.13   particular] practical P[20]
84.13   ideas] idea P[20]
84.17 *et seq. this chap.* altho] although P[20]
84.21   any] an P[20]
84.21   nature, which] nature∧ that P[20]
84.22   justly] *omit* P[20]
84.29   quâ] qua P[20]

84.33   pre-existing] preexisting P[20]
84.33-36   There . . . error.] *omit* P[20]
84.37   the man] he P[20]
85.1-2   Or . . . tendencies?] *omit* P[20]
85.6-7   which . . . -through] through which I have to move P[20]
85.9   full] *real* P[20]
85.24   *full*] full P[20]
85.28   full] *omit* P[20]
85.36   experience] cognition P[20]
85.36-37   , with . . . it,] *omit* P[20]
86.10   fulness] fullness P[20]
86.11   abstractional] *omit* P[20]
86.18   man's] *omit* P[20]
86.21   anti-pragmatists] antipragmatists P[20]
86.23   the other] extenuating P[20]
86.26   A still further] Still another P[20]
86.31   sign] sign to us P[20]
86.31   possess] have P[20]
86.33   'truth'] ∧ ∼ ∧ P[20]
86.35   will to believe] Will to Believe P[20]
86.35   [2]will] Will P[20]
87.4   huxleyan] Huxleyan P[20]
87.4   , to . . . truth,] *omit* P[20]
87.8   tho] though P[20]
87.10   then,] *omit* P[20]
87.19   universe] problematic universe P[20]
87.21   them] *them* P[20]
87.23   extreme] maximum P[20]
87.29   sense-perception] ∼ ∧ ∼ P[20]
87.36-37   for . . . purposes] to our speculation P[20]
88.2   than that] *omit* P[20]
88.4   , *as a possibility*,] *omit* P[20]
88.4   *matter*] subject P[20]
88.19-20   result . . . idea] idea would be P[20]
88.26   probably . . . touch] be left, farther from P[20]
88.27   should] should discern a gap, P[20]
88.33   Our] Their P[20]
89.6   ideally perfect] *omit* P[20]
89.7   penetration into] approximation to P[20]
89.12   other] own P[20]
89.13   who] and who P[20]
89.17   *working* or] *omit* P[20]
89.25   is] is P[20]
89.28   logical] *omit* P[20]
89.35   workings and leadings,] leading∧ P[20]
89.36   unskilfully] unskillfully P[20]

CHAPTER VII.   Professor Pratt on Truth

The copy-text for Chapter VII is (I), with reference to (P²⁰) "Professor Pratt on Truth," *Journal of Philosophy, Psychology, and Scientific Methods*, 4 (August 15, 1907), 464–467 (McD 1907:8), which ends at 93.15.

90.2-3   the . . . 1907,] No. 12 of the present volume of this JOURNALΛ P²⁰

90.5 *et seq. this chap.* cannot] can not P²⁰

90.19   anti-pragmatism] antipragmatism P²⁰

90.21   ¹Reprinted . . . 464).] *omit* P²⁰

91.13   an heir] *omit* P²⁰

91.14   one] heir P²⁰

91.14   divided the estate] acted or the estate is divided P²⁰

91.27   itself,] *omit* P²⁰

91.29   verification-processes] ∼ Λ ∼ P²⁰

91.32-33   ²*of . . . idea*] *roman* P²⁰

91.34   exists,] *exists*Λ P²⁰

91.36   possible] *possible* P²⁰

92.4   private] *omit* P²⁰

92.9   altho] although P²⁰

92.23   *substitute*] substitute P²⁰

93.2   truth-relation] ∼ Λ ∼ P²⁰

93.8   'as'-ness] 'as'ness P²⁰

93.9   describable,] ∼ Λ P²⁰

93.16-98.26   *omit* P²⁰

97.14   all] Pratt; all that I

CHAPTER VII.   Material on Deleted Versos of Chapter XIV Manuscript

[*del. fol.* 3ᵛ] '[*pencil*] Pratt seems sometimes to denote by the ['word' *del.*] trueness—of the idea, nothing immediately connected with the idea *itself [*inserted in ink*] but the outward fact that its deliverance, *objectively [*interl. in ink*] obtains or its object really exists. [*ink*] If we think the object exists and the thought is true, then the object does exist.'

[*del. fol.* 6ᵛ] 'Since he himself in turn denies none of the 'workings' for which I have pleaded, *tho he considers them unes- [*above del.* 'as es-|'] |-sential to truth's meaning, it seems as if there were little left to fight about. I admit a reality with which the idea's workings bring it into connexion; I *assume [*above del.* 'allow'] that the idea may be a belief in that very reality's existence; I admit that the idea *has 'trueness' [*above del.* 'may be *called*'] *to use Dr. ['D' *over* 'M'] Pratt's term, [*above del.* 'true'] before it gets itself verified *([*paren over comma*] just as a man has 'mortality' before he dies); I have no objection to saying that by virtue of this trueness the idea may be said to 'transcend' itself, provided you don't mean that it ['transcend' *del.*] goes beyond assignable experience,'

CHAPTER VIII.   The Pragmatist Account of Truth and Its Misunderstanders

The copy-text for Chapter VIII is (I), with reference to P²⁸ "The Pragmatist Account of Truth and Its Misunderstanders," *Philosophical Review*, 17 (January 1908), 1–17 (McD 1908:1). Blue pencil and black ink annotations in James's private offprint at Harvard (Box O, envelope 15, no. 3) are noted as WJ/P²⁸.

99.1   given] given by me in the *Journal of Philosophy* for March 14 of this year (Vol. IV, p. 141) and printed later P²⁸

99.20   ¹Reprint . . . 1).] *omit* P²⁸

100.12   *re-editing*] reëditing P²⁸

100.17   the former doctrines] they P²⁸

100.30   *in case*] in case P²⁸

100.32   ²truthΛ] ∼ , P²⁸

100.35-36   It . . . question.] WJ/P²⁸ ink; *omit* P²⁸, I

101.1-2   particular . . . them] facts altogether P²⁸

101.16   'pragmatism,'] Λ ∼ , Λ P²⁸

101.28   *weltanschauung*] *Weltanschauung* P²⁸

102.6   factors] elements P²⁸

102.20   helpful] hopeful I

102.20-21 October, 1907,] last October, P²⁸; October, 1897, I
102.28 *only* (!)] only∧ P²⁸
102.32 becomes] grows P²⁸,I
103.5-6 *(especially . . . pragmatist)*] , even though the postulator were himself the most hardened pragmatist, P²⁸
103.10-11 conditions . . . grounds] conditions P²⁸
103.12 belief in the headache] supposed belief P²⁸
103.17 it, . . . subject's] it P²⁸
103.35 of . . . in] *omit* P²⁸
103.35-36 belief in] the idea of P²⁸
103.42 indeed] *omit* P²⁸
104.28 profound.] profound.¹ | ¹*Cf.* Russell in the *Journal of Philosophy,* Vol. IV, pp. 292-293, and Pratt, *ibid.,* p. 322. P²⁸
104.36 actually] *omit* P²⁸
105.15 'objective'] ∧ ∼ ∧ P²⁸
105.15-16 beliefs] ideas P²⁸
105.16 'posit'] 'correspond' to P²⁸
105.16-17 'correspond' and] *omit* P²⁸
105.25 pears] WJ/P²⁸ *ink,* I; peas P²⁸
105.27 quart-pot] ∼ ∧ ∼ P²⁸
106.4 *psychological sentiment*] roman P²⁸
106.13 I . . . called] expressly calls P²⁸
106.15 assumed] he assumed P²⁸
106.15 the pragmatist's] his P²⁸
106.20-21 as . . . posited] the pragmatist is forced to posit his P²⁸
106.22 my] his P²⁸
106.22 I remain] he remains P²⁸
106.23 realist.³] realist.∧ P²⁸; P²⁸ *places footnote attached to* possession. (107.14)
106.37 these terms] them P²⁸
107.17 *Fifth*] *Fourth* P²⁸

108.31 *Sixth*] *Fifth* P²⁸
109.5 the . . . my] my manner of P²⁸
109.14-15 ²and∧ . . . pragmatist∧ indeed∧] ∼ , . . . ∼ , ∼ , P²⁸
109.24 *the* truth] the truth P²⁸
110.2 platonic] Platonic P²⁸
110.3 *et seq. this chap.* tho] though P²⁸
110.11-12 backs, . . . feet,] ∼ ∧ . . . ∼ ∧ P²⁸
110.30 backs∧ or feet∧] ∼ , ∼ ∼ , P²⁸
110.31 walls∧] ∼ , P²⁸
111.8 *posse*∧] ∼ , P²⁸
111.8 verification∧] ∼ , P²⁸
111.12 ever] WJ/P²⁸ *blue pencil,* I; even P²⁸
111.12 asserted∧ or] asserted, WJ/P²⁸ *blue pencil; omit* P²⁸
111.15 in posse] *in posse* P²⁸
111.18 *Seventh*] *Sixth* P²⁸
112.8-9 which . . . substitutes] themselves P²⁸
112.9 also] *omit* P²⁸
112.11 and∧] ∼ , P²⁸
112.20 predicaments and perplexities] interests P²⁸
112.36 *et seq. this chap.* altho] although P²⁸
113.9 active or passive] passive or active P²⁸,I
114.2 idiotic] silly P²⁸
114.5 it insists that] *omit* P²⁸
114.7 *Eighth*] *Seventh* P²⁸
115.15 by race-inheritance] *omit* P²⁸
115.18 may be] *omit* P²⁸
115.21 *compatible*] compatible P²⁸
115.22 kantism] Kantism P²⁸
116.13 sollen] WJ/P²⁸ *blue pencil,* I; können P²⁸

CHAPTER IX. The Meaning of the Word Truth

The copy-text for Chapter IX is (I), with reference to (PPr), a privately printed pamphlet (McD 1908:4) and to (P²⁴) "The Meaning of the Word 'Truth'," *Mind,* 17 (July 1908), 455-456 (McD 1908:4). The variants found in (P²⁸) under "The Meaning and Criterion of Truth," *Philosophical Review,* 17 (March 1908), 180-181, are also recorded. English spellings in *Mind* which have been Americanized in (I) to James's usual practice are not recorded as variants in this collation, nor is the difference in English and American typography in the placement of punctuation in respect to quotation marks in *Mind* or in PPr. Bold-face type is used for italic in PPr.

117.0 ∧Truth∧] ' ∼ ' P²⁴

117.2 you∧] ∼ , P²⁴; ∼ : P²⁸

117.3   exists∧"—] ∼ ,"— P²⁸
117.3   true∧] ∼ , P²⁸
117.4   developed] unfolded P²⁸
117.5-6   ask∧ "what] ∼ , "What P²⁸
117.7   ask∧ "does] ∼ , "Does P²⁸
117.8   if∧ moreover∧] ∼ , ∼ , P²⁸
117.8   ²say∧] ∼ , P²⁸
117.8   that] *that* P²⁸
117.11   places;] ∼ ∧ PPr,P²⁴
117.13   ¶ This] no ¶ P²⁸
117.13   either] either one P²⁸
117.15   in order] *omit* P²⁸
117.16   counted ∧true,∧] accounted 'true,' P²⁸
117.16   ∧agree.∧] ' ∼ .' P²⁸
117.16-17   Pragmatism . . . potential.] Pragmatists explain this last term as meaning certain actual or potential 'workings.' P²⁸
117.18   statement∧] ∼, P²⁸
117.18   the] The P²⁸
117.18   ¹desk] thing PPr,P²⁴,²⁸
117.18   exists∧] ∼ , P²⁸
117.18-118.1   a desk . . . you] a determinate reality PPr, P²⁴,²⁸
117.19-20   ¹Remarks . . . 1907.] *omit* P²⁸
118.1   be able to] *omit* P²⁸
118.1   your] *your* P²⁸
118.1-2   ²to . . . words] it must explain itself by terms P²⁸
118.2   that desk] *that* desk P²⁸
118.2-7   mind, . . . agreement,] mind, etc. Only thus does it 'agree' with *that* reality, and give me the satisfaction of your approval. A determinate *reference* and some sort of satisfactory *adaptation* P²⁸
118.4   *that*] that PPr
118.8   of mine] *omit* PPr, P²⁴,²⁸
118.9-10   You . . . workings.] And you can't get at the notion of either 'reference' or 'adaptation' except through the notion of 'workings.' P²⁸
118.10   ∧thing∧] ' ∼ ' P²⁸

118.11   what] *what* P²⁸
118.12-14   'which' . . . object] which means our pointing to a locus P²⁸
118.14   'what'] ∧*what*∧ P²⁸
118.15   conceive it] apperceive the thing P²⁸
118.16   own] *omit* P²⁸
118.16   'that'] ∧*that*∧ P²⁸
118.17-18   for . . . word] these workings are indispensable to constitute the notion of what P²⁸
118.18   'true'] ∧ ∼ ∧ PPr,P²⁴
118.18-22   statement, . . . mediation] statement. Surely anything less is insufficient P²⁸
118.23-26   inessential. . . . -Cinq.'] inessential, and consider that statements are, as it were, *born* true, each of its own object, much as the Count of Chambord was supposed to be born King of France, though he never exercised regal functions,— no need of functioning in either case! P²⁸
118.25   'true'] " ∼ " PPr,P²⁴
118.26   born∧ 'Henri-Cinq.'] ∼ ∧ " ∼ - ∼ ", PPr; ∼ , " ∼ - ∼ , " P²⁴
118.27   and beliefs . . . true] are true thus statically P²⁸
118.28   courtesy:] ∼ ; P²⁸
118.28-29   *cannot* . . . true] can't *define* the particular truth of any one of them P²⁸
118.29   their] its P²⁸
118.30   possibilities] results P²⁸
118.30-119.5   These . . . constitution.] *omit* P²⁸
118.33   withness] witness P²⁴
118.35   ∧*Pragmatism.*∧] 'Pragmatism.' PPr
119.1   empiricism,'] ∼ ,∧ PPr
119.4   reality] Reality PPr,P²⁴

CHAPTER X.   The Existence of Julius Cæsar

The copy-text for Chapter X is (I), with reference to (P²⁰) " 'Truth' versus 'Truthfulness'," *Journal of Philosophy, Psychology, and Scientific Methods*, 5 (March 26, 1908), 179–181 (McD 1908:3) and to (TMs¹) "W. James's Statement," ribbon typescript in the University of Chicago Library, and (TMs²), carbon copy in the Stanford University Library, which James revised by hand together and then independently with variants. In the collation below, the final autograph-revised readings are given for both typescripts distinguished as TMs[1] and TMs[2]; when the typescripts do not differ (whether because of typed readings or identical alterations) the sigil is TMs. For an eclectic text of the typescript and a list of its alterations, see Appendix III. Ampersands in the typescript are not recorded as variants nor is the difference in typography in the placement of punctuation in respect to quotation marks.

120.2;122.5 cannot] can not P[20]

120.2 *word* 'true' *means*] *word* '*true*' *means* TMs; word "true" means P[20]

120.3-4 *concept . . . workings*] roman TMs, P[20]

120.4 ∧*workings*∧.] 'workings'. TMs

120.5 things] facts TMs

120.6 *et seq. this chap.* Cæsar] Caesar TMs

120.7 naively] naively & uncritically TMs[2]

120.7 ∧truth∧] ' ∼ ' TMs

120.9 hold] cognitive hold TMs

120.10 so certainly] necessarily TMs

120.10 Cæsar?—] ∼ ?∧ TMs

120.10-11 so certainly] *omit* TMs

120.11 individual] *omit* TMs

120.12;121.34 (*twice*) 'true'] ∧ ∼ ∧ TMs[2]; " ∼ " P[20]

120.13 and unambiguous] *omit* TMs

120.13-14 'one-to-one-relation']
" ∼ - ∼ - ∼ - ∼ " P[20]

120.14 ultra-simple] ∼ ∧ ∼ P[20]

120.15 the] *omit* TMs[1]

120.15-16 uncertified. . . . The] left indeterminate; the TMs

120.16 truth] | ruth TMs[2]

120.17 incomplete . . . it] incomplete: that universe TMs

120.17 universe of discourse] universe, P[20]

121.3 *shall*] shall TMs

121.4 intention . . . true] statute is enough TMs[1]

121.4 the statement] it TMs[2]

121.7 and∧] ∼ , TMs

121.8 for] for incorporating TMs[1]

121.9 which, . . . *distans*,] ∼ ∧ . . . ∼ ∧ TMs

121.10 unintelligibly] to be unintelligible TMs

121.11 manuscript] real manuscript TMs

121.13 ∧workings∧] " ∼ " P[20]

121.13 determine] determine more fully TMs

121.14 more fully] *omit* TMs

121.16 of him] *omit* TMs

121.17 through] thru TMs

121.18 meant myself] myself meant TMs

121.20-21 [2]of . . . exist] is possible TMs

121.22 But the] The TMs

121.23 ∧truth∧] ' ∼ ' TMs[2]

121.27 2000] 2,000 P[20]

121.29 made] *made* TMs

121.29 effects?] ∼ ∧ | TMs

121.32-33 Well . . . him] Be it so! TMs

121.34 being] *omit* TMs[1]

121.34 established] determined TMs

121.35 as being so] *omit* TMs[1]

121.35 'practically,'] ' ∼ ∧ ' TMs;
" ∼ , " P[20]

121.35 elliptically,] *omit* TMs

121.35-36 in . . . untrue] as being not functionally *untrue* or irrelevant TMs[1]; because not definable as *untrue* or irrelevant TMs[2]

122.4 coming from] in TMs; pertaining to P[20]

122.4 ∧pragmatism∧] ' ∼ ' TMs;
" ∼ " P[20]

122.5 adequately . . . something] *all italic* TMs; *all roman* P[20]

122.5 the something] *that something* TMs

122.6 functional workings] 'workings' wholly TMs

122.7-9 Truth . . . solve.] *omit* TMs

122.10-22 NOTE. . . . 'fact.'] *omit* TMs, P[20]; *for the text for which this substitutes, see below*

Appendix to Chapter X

Both TMs[1-2] *and* P[20] *continue after* 'solve' *at* 224.24 *with the original conclusion*

replaced in (I) *by the* 'Note'. *The copy-text for the reprint below is* P[20], *with* TMs *variants recorded by footnotes.*

People, mixing history with the purely logical inquiry, and falling into[1] inveterate[2] habits of speech, will still say: "The statement is true anyhow, true in advance, born true,[3] true apart from any of its workings, and the workings are themselves determined by that prior truth." This notion of an immanent or[4] inherent truth, meaning a truth with only a part of the constituents of its full definition realized in fact, is, of course,[5] indispensable in practical life. Millions of statements there[6] *pass* for true, for one that lives up to what the full concept implies.

Would it satisfy the repudiators of the fuller definition[7] if we agreed to[8] let them keep the word "true"[9] for what they stickle for so[10] exclusively, namely,[11] the[12] more preliminary and objective conditions of the cognitive relation[13]—so that for any words[14] about Cæsar[15] to be true[16] in that lopped and truncated[17] sense it would[18] suffice that Cæsar should have really existed—while the word "truthful" should be reserved, as having the more concrete sound, for the entire unmutilated notion for which Mr. Schiller and I contend?

Mr. Schiller and I would then appear as fighting the battles of truthfulness against truth.[19] The[20] question would be[21] almost purely academic, for in actual life the true[16] and the truthful[22] would usually denote the same body of actual human statements or beliefs. Even now none of the *facts*[23] which either party emphasizes has ever been denied[24] by the other party, and the quarrel might have the bottom knocked out of it altogether, so far as it related[25] to[26] truth's definition only,[27] by the invention of this or some other pair of new[28] technical terms.

The friends of "truth"[29] would still have to admit, however, that "truthfulness" is the more plenary and fundamental notion, that it includes the whole of "truth" and supplements its deficiencies, and alone defines adequately what correct and perfect knowledge may mean.[30]

1 into] back upon TMs
2 inveterate] inveterate upo TMs[1]
3 born true,] *omit* TMs[2]
4 immanent or] *omit* TMs
5 , of course,] *omit* TMs
6 there] thus TMs
7 definition] concept TMs
8 agreed to] *omit* TMs
9 "true"] ' $\sim$ ' TMs
10 so] *omit* TMs
11 namely,] $\sim$ ∧ TMs
12 the] the fulfilment of the TMs
13 relation∧—] $\sim$?— TMs
14 any words] my statement TMs[2]
15 ∧Cæsar∧] " $\sim$ " TMs[1]
16 ∧true∧] 'true' TMs
17 lopped and truncated] *omit* TMs
18 would] would then TMs
19 that Cæsar ... truth.] for *a [the TMs[2]] real Cæsar to have existed in point of fact? [¶] The more completely determined notion, for which I and Mr. Schiller in our turn stickle, might then be distinguished from

'truth', in that more limited sense, by the name of 'truthfulness', that being a word with a more concrete & *actively-functional [$\sim$ ∧ $\sim$ TMs[2]] sound. TMs
20 The (*no* ¶)] ¶ TMs
21 would be] is TMs
22 ∧truthful∧] ' $\sim$ ' TMs
23 *facts*] facts TMs[2]
24 denied] questioned TMs[1]
25 related] relates TMs[1]
26 to] only to TMs
27 only] *omit* TMs
28 pair of new] new pair of TMs
29 "truth"] ' $\sim$ ' TMs
30 that "truthfulness" ... mean.] that our more concrete notion of 'truthfulness' envelopes *the whole of [*omit* TMs[2]] their own more abstract notion, & defines *in the only adequate fashion [more adequately TMs[2]] what perfect knowledge is. TMs

CHAPTER XI.   The Absolute and the Strenuous Life

The copy-text for Chapter XI is (I), with reference to (P20) "The Absolute and the Strenuous Life," *Journal of Philosophy, Psychology, and Scientific Methods,* 4 (September 26, 1907), 546–548 (McD 1907:9).

123.1   Professor] Mr. P20
123.20   ¹Reprinted . . . 1906.] *omit* P20
124.1   Tho] Though P20
124.11   cannot] can not P20

124.25   the . . . book] my last lecture P20
124.25   admitted] allowed for P20
124.31   great] a great P20

CHAPTER XII.   Professor Hébert on Pragmatism

The copy-text for Chapter XII is (I), with reference to (P20), a review of Marcel Hébert's *Le Pragmatisme; étude de ses diverses formes* in *Journal of Philosophy, Psychology, and Scientific Methods,* 5 (December 3, 1908), 689–694 (McD 1908:8). Not recorded is the use of double quotation marks in the journal which are present invariably whenever (I) (and the present edition) uses single quotes.

126.3   ∧*Le Divin*∧] "Le divin" P20
126.19-21 ¹Reprint . . . 105.)] *omit* P20
126.20   *Le . . . ses*] *Le pragmatisme et ses* I
127.20   admits] even admits P20
127.21   may even] *omit* P20
128.7   reference] *reference* P20
128.21   himself] himself in these pages P20
129.11   fulfils] fulfills P20
130.13   call] *call* P20
130.14   anyhow] *anyhow* P20
130.25   ones∧] ~ , P20
130.27   *absolute*] absolute P20
130.27   *grenzbegriff*] *Grenzbegriff* P20
130.37   escape] can escape P20
130.37   They form] It forms P20
131.1-2 Our . . . them] The belief in it P20
131.2   suggested and satisfied] verified

and validated P20
131.2   our] *omit* P20
131.20-21 the . . . Corot] your propri6-etary interest will be to have it P20
131.23   *them*] them P20
131.25   the rest of] *omit* P20
131.27   of . . . suffice] are all-sufficient P20
131.30   general and] *omit* P20
132.6   altho] although P20
132.20   believe] *believe* P20
132.22-23   ; so . . . situations] *omit* P20
133.2   an objective] a P20
133.10   man.] man. The moth who thinks of a flame as dangerous thinks of it more truly than the moth who only feels its beauty. The workings of such a moth's idea prove more satisfactory in the long run. P20

CHAPTER XIII.   Abstractionism and 'Relativismus'

The copy-text for Chapter XIII is (I), with reference to (P29) "On a Very Prevalent Abuse of Abstraction," *Popular Science Monthly,* 74 (May 1909), 485–493 (McD 1909:4). Variants occurring in James's marked copy of the book are distinguished as WJ/I. Not recorded is the use of double quotation marks in the journal which are present invariably whenever (I) (and the present edition) uses single quotes.

134.5   things,] ~ ∧ P29
134.7   and∧] ~ , P29
135.12   *adding*] adding P29
135.13   unfortunately,] ~ ∧ P29

135.16   *denying*] denying P29
135.20   Some] Certain particular P29
135.20   very] *omit* P29
135.20   own] *omit* P29

135.22　so∧called] ∼ - ∼ P²⁹
135.25　led] often led P²⁹
135.26　often] *omit* P²⁹
135.35　privately] P²⁹,WJ/I,I²; privately I¹
135.35　reducing] we reduce P²⁹
136.8　*class∧names*] ∼ - ∼ P²⁹
136.9　one . . . sins] the original sin P²⁹
136.9　rationalistic] metaphysical P²⁹
136.12　recently] in this magazine not long ago P²⁹
136.21-22　which . . . be] *italics* P²⁹
136.24-25　²seems . . . others] to turn itself towards fact P²⁹
136.34　celarent] Celarent P²⁹
136.35　N. Y.] *omit* P²⁹
136.35　lviii and lix] 58 and 59 P²⁹
137.9　*not before*] not before P²⁹
137.18　no identical passenger,] *omit* P²⁹
137.19-20　shunt . . . chasm] gaping wound which it makes P²⁹
138.8　re-direction] direction P²⁹
138.8　because] because the direction of growth is not unequivocal, and because P²⁹
138.9　of the re-direction] *omit* P²⁹
138.12　connective] continuously connective P²⁹
138.13-14　something] and a life of choices P²⁹
138.14　in] to P²⁹
138.14-15　and . . . choices] *omit* P²⁹
138.19-20　, for . . . Nero] *omit* P²⁹
138.24　defence] defense P²⁹
138.25　beliefs] serious beliefs P²⁹
138.26　situations] concrete situations P²⁹
138.28　no] not the P²⁹
138.29 *et seq. this chap.* tho] though P²⁹
138.29　may] P²⁹,WJ/I,I³; *omit* I¹⁻²
138.30　make the] easily make a prejudiced P²⁹
138.31　will] Will P²⁹
138.34　vol. lviii] Vol. 58 P²⁹
138.35　∧*Some . . . Religion,*∧] "Some . . . Religion," P²⁹
139.3　it∧] ∼ , P²⁹
139.4　branch] brand P²⁹
139.9-10　experience . . . something] experience, something in Being P²⁹
139.15　practically] *omit* P²⁹
139.20　critics,] ∼ ∧ P²⁹
139.32　feel;] ∼ , P²⁹
140.6　concrete] *omit* P²⁹

140.19　abstract and] *omit* P²⁹
140.21-22　the above-cited] his very readable P²⁹
140.22　link] rational link, no link P²⁹
140.22-23　dictionary∧] ∼ , P²⁹
140.24　links] singular links P²⁹
140.24　single] *omit* P²⁹
140.25　perceives . . . there!] perceives. P²⁹
140.25　adds] says P²⁹
140.29　reality] reality of the thing P²⁹, I
140.30　a thing] the thing P²⁹,I
140.33-34　One . . . who] Mr. McTaggart P²⁹
140.37　prevail] permit P²⁹,I
141.8　*insight-giving passion*] roman P²⁹
141.9　*stupid*] stupid P²⁹
141.21　a skeletonized] an P²⁹
141.22　was ever] is P²⁹
141.22+　*no space*] *space* P²⁹
141.25　beliefs] ideas P²⁹
141.27　, I . . . said,] *omit* P²⁹
141.27-28　working∧] ∼ , I have elsewhere said, P²⁹
141.28　beliefs∧] ideas, P²⁹
141.34　book *Pragmatism*] recent book called "Pragmatism"⁵ | ⁵Longmans, Green & Co., 1908. P²⁹
141.34-35　taken . . . energetically] myself taken considerable pains to defend P²⁹
141.35　indeed] *omit* P²⁹
141.35　been] been some of P²⁹
142.5　is . . . have] *omit* P²⁹
142.8-9,11;145.25-26　'relativismus'] "Relativismus" P²⁹
142.17-18　¹*in . . . change*] roman P²⁹
142.17　*sense,*] sense∧ P²⁹
142.28　latter] scheme P²⁹
142.32　individuals] modest individuals P²⁹
142.32　sometimes] *omit* P²⁹
142.34　so] so that P²⁹
142.36-37　⁵Münsterberg's . . . 1909.] *omit* P²⁹
143.11　regulative] WJ/I,I³; constitutive P²⁹, I¹⁻²
143.29　shooting-gallery] ∼ ∧ ∼ P²⁹
143.32　∧*Gegenstand der Erkenntnis,*∧] "Gegenstand der Erkenntniss," P²⁹
143.33　∧*Philosophie der Werte,*∧] "Philosophie der Werte," P²⁹
143.36　all,] ∼ ∧ P²⁹
143.37-38　But . . . critics.] *omit* P²⁹

144.1 to . . . consensus,] *omit* P²⁹
144.7-9 that . . . insists] *omit* P²⁹
144.18 which . . . withal] with which
it coexists P²⁹
144.19 definition] *omit* P²⁹
144.21 think∧] ∼, P²⁹
144.38 grounds] WJ/I; causes P²⁹,I
145.2-3 part ∧ . . . the 'experience']
part. The "experience" P²⁹

145.13-14 one . . . such] the part of P²⁹
145.14 discuss, and] to discuss, and to
P²⁹
145.16 such] the P²⁹
145.21,26 'opinion'] ∧ ∼ ∧ P²⁹
145.26 consist] consists I
145.32 should make] makes P²⁹
145.33 ∧opinion∧ ∧] " ∼, " P²⁹
145.36 *dogmatize*] dogmatize P²⁹

CHAPTER XIV.   Two English Critics

The copy-text for Chapter XIV is (I), with reference to the holograph manuscript (MS) preserved in the Houghton Library. Manuscript ampersands and variant spacing (as sometimes appears in words like *is n't*) are not recorded in this collation.

146.3 it] *omit* MS
146.5 is] means MS
146.6 a] his MS
146.8 that fact] *that* MS
146.8-10 an . . . a fact] which obviously is quite a new proposition, and one MS
146.15 We . . . supposes] What we affirm is nothing so silly MS
146.18 may . . . occasion] may on occasion serve MS
146.19 rather] *omit* MS
146.19 *motive*] motive MS
146.20 *Albany Review*] Albany Review MS
147.2 *causa existendi*] causa existendi MS
147.4 practical] *omit* MS
147.7 ¶ No] *no* ¶ MS
147.11 beliefs] pragmatist beliefs MS
147.13-15 ∧the pragmatist . . . exist.∧] " ∼ ∼ . . . ∼ " (p.410). MS
147.14 exists∧ . . . true,'] ∼, . . . ∼ ∧'
MS (*error of caret placement*)
147.15 *not*] not MS
147.15 slander,] ∼ ∧ MS
147.19 plays∧] ∼, MS
147.23 true∧] ∼ — MS
147.26 own] *own* MS
147.27 the . . . address] their reader himself MS
147.28 not] *not* MS
147.28 for] to MS
147.30 sneers] smiles MS
147.31 true,' tho] ∼ ∧' though MS
147.31-32 , as . . . knows,] *omit* MS

147.32 Mr.] ∼ ∧ MS
147.36 does] *does* MS
147.37 is, of course, . . . exist,]
∼ ∧ ∼ ∼ ∧ . . . ∼ ∧ MS
147.37 *bound*] bound MS
148.1 consequences] the consequences that follow from their nature MS
148.2-3 conceiving . . . 'true'?] having true opinions? MS
148.3,4 an object] objects MS
148.4 shall] *omit* MS
148.4 opinion] opinions MS
148.5 an opinion] opinions MS
148.5-6 by . . . aware] *omit* MS
148.6 else] WJ/I,I³; *omit* MS,I¹⁻²
148.6 of . . . aware] I am aware of I³⁺
148.7 requirement] necessity MS
148.7 have said] say MS
148.7 exists,] ∼ ∧ MS
148.8 *shall*] shall MS
148.12 the] his MS
148.12-13 *secundum artem*] roman MS
148.13 error] untruth MS
148.14-15 procedure] *omit* MS
148.15 it] his procedure MS
148.18 Mr. Russell] him MS
148.18 thinks] even seems to think MS
148.20-21 sin., log.,] *sin∧, log∧,* MS
148.21 of this sort,] *omit* MS
148.21 equated,] ∼ ∧ MS
148.23 , and . . . presently,] (∼ . . . ∼)
MS
148.23 speak] have more to say MS
148.24 seem] seems MS
148.24 also] *omit* MS
148.25 are] are also MS

148.31 Likewise] likewise MS

148.32 *nicht wahr,*] nicht wahr? MS

148.36 'working'] ∧ ∼ ∧ MS

149.1 defined,] ∼ ∧ MS

149.1 interchangeable,] substitutable (*comma uncertain*) MS

149.3-4 by that word] *omit* MS

149.5 ʼdoes] does MS

149.11-15 [Logic . . . mouth.]] ∧ ∼ . . . ∼ , ∧ MS

149.12 Russell] Russell here MS

149.12 both at once] conjointly MS

149.13 'other . . . exist'] " ∼ . . . ∼ " MS

149.13-14 'it . . . *don't,*'] " ∼ . . . ∼ , " MS

149.14 *even . . . don't*] *roman* MS

149.15 mouth.] ∼ , MS

149.18 algebraic] algraic MS

149.19-20 'content'] ∧ ∼ ∧ MS

149.20 or 'deliverance'] *omit* MS

149.24 contents,] contents and MS

149.28 ¹the . . . upon] certain workings on MS

149.28 audience;] ∼ , MS

149.29 'original'] ∧ ∼ ∧ MS

149.29 to mean] as MS

149.30 other] previous MS

149.30 Mr.] *omit* I

149.31,32 about] *about* MS

149.34 *about*] about MS

149.36 discourse,] ∼ ∧ MS

150.4 first;] ∼ , MS

150.5 second;] ∼ , MS

150.8 kind,] ∼ ∧ MS

150.8 men∧'] ∼ , ' MS

150.9 which] which | which MS

150.9 propositions;] ∼ , MS

150.10 insist . . . do] accuse us of doing MS

150.11 + *space*] no *space* MS

150.13 logic,] ∼ ∧ MS

150.15 and . . . argument,] *omit* MS

150.16 the word] the word | the word MS

150.16 allowing] for the sake of the argument he allowing MS

150.21 to say] *omit* MS

150.21 *et seq. this chap.* Cæsar] Caesar MS

150.23 then] *omit* MS

150.25 he says,] *omit* MS

150.28 ²is] is | is MS

150.31 what?—] ∼ ?∧ MS

150.34 believer,] ∼ ∧ MS

150.35 1908.] ∼ ∧ MS

151.1 really exist;] exist, MS

151.2 the] the the MS

151.6 great] *great* MS

151.7 'truth'] ∧ ∼ ∧ MS

151.8 applying] appling MS

151.10 Russell∧] ∼ , MS

151.11-12 invented∧ . . . truth] invented—to foster this confusion— truth they speak of MS

151.14 its] is MS

151.18 make] make a single term MS

151.19 -dead∧' . . . term] -dead,' MS

151.21 *fact*] fact MS

151.22 *belief* that,] belief that∧ MS

151.25-26 ²a . . . belief—] the belief's quality, MS

151.26-27 to . . . possession] left to talk about MS

151.29-30 'Reality . . . belief,'] Reality, idea, and the truth of the idea, MS

151.35 'by definition'] ∧ ∼ ∼ ∧ MS

151.36 'Cæsar exists'] " ∼ ∼ " MS

151.37 'expediency'] " ∼ " MS

151.37 one∧] ∼. MS

151.37 statement] *omit* MS

152.1 'true statements,'] 'truth,' MS

152.1 is like] like MS

152.3 digits] fingers MS

152.5 Messrs.] ∼ ∧ MS

152.12 'truth'] ∧ ∼ ∧ MS

152.12 *Mind*] Mind MS

152.13 vol. xiii] Vol∧ 13 MS

152.19 until] till MS

152.20 the following] this MS

152.21 view:] ∼ — MS

152.26-27 false"— . . . forever !] false", and that all [discussion is thereby terminated. *deleted*] MS

152.28 admiration] great admiration MS

152.30 no] no no MS

152.30-31 and . . . men] (and other men similarly gifted) MS

152.31 having used such] using their great MS

152.32 such] the MS

152.33 as . . . show] which that article exhibits MS

152.34-153.5 P.S. . . . article.] *omit* MS

266

CHAPTER XV. A Dialogue

The copy-text for Chapter XV is (I), with reference to the holograph manuscript (MS) preserved in the Houghton Library. Manuscript ampersands and variant spacing (as sometimes appears in words like *is n't*) are not recorded. The treatment of speech-prefixes is described in the Textual Notes to 154.6, 154.16; details of their variation are not recorded in this collation.

154.0 A DIALOGUE] POST-
SCRIPT. MS
154.3 unconvinced] from being
convinced MS
154.3 try∧ at least∧] ∼ , ∼ ∼ , MS
154.4 dialogue] dialog MS
154.5 begin] reader begin MS
154.7-8 facts∧ for example∧]
∼ , ∼ ∼ , MS
154.12 brother pragmatist] Brother
Pragmatist MS
154.12-13 whether∧ . . . you∧]
∼ , . . . ∼ , MS
154.20 is] *is* MS
154.20 thereby] *omit* MS
155.3 remains∧] ∼ , MS
155.8 so∧] ∼ , MS
155.9 what] *omit* MS
155.9 may be] *omit* MS
155.11 *no*] no MS
155.14 some] some possible MS
155.15 should] may MS
155.15 be] may be MS
155.18 have] must have MS
155.18 innumerable] lots of MS
155.20 yet] and yet MS
155.21 sort of] *omit* MS
155.21 ever] *omit* MS
155.22 thus] then MS
155.22 generically] *omit* MS
155.23 nature;] ∼ , MS
155.24 thus] *omit* MS
155.27 is] *is* MS
155.27 truth∧] ∼ , MS
155.28 shall never] never shall MS
155.29 to] to to MS
155.31 which] that MS
155.31 comprehend.—] ∼ .∧ MS
155.32 a] *omit* MS
155.37 ∧Consists∧?] ' ∼ ' ? MS
155.37 pray] *omit* MS
155.37 'consists'] ∧ ∼ ∧ MS
156.1 or more] and MS
156.1-2 has . . . it obtains] does n't
exist. It obtains MS

156.6 it represents it] represents it
as it is MS
156.8 the . . . it;] *omit* MS
156.8-9 not . . . but] *omit* MS
156.9 *possesses*] possesses MS
156.9 truth. Any] truth, and any MS
156.10 the reality . . . it] it represents
it MS
156.11 thought] tho't MS
156.16 *se*,] ∼ ∧ MS
156.16 actual∧] whether actual, MS
156.18 epistemological,] ∼ ∧ MS
156.19 region] level MS
156.21 *is true*] is true MS
156.21 and-] ∼ ∧ | MS
156.23 '*It*' . . . that∧] '*It*∧ *is true that*'
MS
156.23-24 yield . . . asking] ask MS
156.24 true;] ∼ , MS
156.24-26 I do . . . additional to] does
your phrase mean anything more
than MS
156.26-27 facts themselves.] facts? MS
156.30 value . . . terms.] noetic
value. MS
156.31 them,] ∼ ∧ MS
156.32 may] *omit* MS
156.32 is] *is* MS
156.33 where'—it] where.' It MS
156.34 obtains, absolutely] *omit* MS
157.1 ∧actual∧] 'actual' MS
157.2 knower] knower of the facts MS
157.2 anything] aught MS
157.3 this . . . elusive] the MS
157.3 the facts] them MS
157.5-6 truth . . . truth] truth, it MS
157.8 not . . . ²him] it first, and then
him, not him first, and then it MS
157.10 status] *status* MS
157.12 the] *omit* MS
157.13 numerically . . . it] other than
it, it MS
157.13-14 antecedent . . . thereof]
entirely independent of of a
knower MS

157.14 Is] *Is* MS
157.16 dubious] suspicious MS
157.17 distinguished] distinguisht MS
157.17 an] *omit* MS
157.18 , after all,] *omit* MS
157.18 *would*] roman MS
157.19 *in . . . existed*] roman MS
157.20 conceivableʌ] ∼ , MS
157.20 thereʌ] ∼ , MS
157.21 numerically] *omit* MS
157.22 not only be] be not only MS
157.23 unimaginable,] *omit* MS
157.24 *is*] is MS
157.25 events,] ∼ ʌ MS
157.25 shall ever] ever shall MS
157.28 event,] ∼ ʌ MS
157.29 *if . . . does*] roman MS
157.30 which] that we suppose MS
157.31 of . . . only] is but a name for MS
157.32-33 fact . . . believe] event will have to say MS
157.33 must believe] will have to say MS
157.33 will bring] brings MS
157.34 it] the event MS
157.34 will prove a] proves MS
157.35 it. What] it; and what MS
157.35 something] *omit* MS
157.36;158.5,7 fact] event MS
157.37 ²that] *omit* MS
158.1 pre-exists] preʌexists MS
158.4 *truth*] truth MS
158.4 distinct] different MS
158.7 event] fact MS
158.7-13 Where . . . other.] *omit* MS
158.13 probably] *omit* MS
158.14-16 has . . . things] so often uses the words truth and reality MS
158.16 And has] Does MS
158.17 anything to gain] gain anything MS

158.17 perpetuating and] *omit* MS
158.17-18 ambiguity] confusion MS
158.18 'reality,'] ʌ ∼ ,ʌ MS
158.19 'truth,'] ʌ ∼ ,ʌ MS
158.19-21 ²cognized . . . it,] *omit* MS
158.21 if you] *omit* MS
158.24 you think] *omit* MS
158.29 possibleʌ] ∼ , MS
158.30 truthʌ] thruth. MS
158.31 *actual,*] actualʌ MS
158.32-33 I . . . truth] [¶] Truth MS
158.33-34 *possible . . . virtual . . . conceivable*] roman MS
158.33 exist,] exist, however, MS
158.35 , abstractly taken,] (∼ ∼) MS
159.2 so] *omit* MS
159.2 it does exist,] yesʌ MS
159.7 Never!—so] Never!ʌ MS
159.8 sophistry!] sophistry, with your low particulars. MS
159.8 will] shall MS
159.9 identifying . . . particulars] warping its nature MS
159.11 my dear antagonist] dear anti pragmatist MS
159.11-12 an . . . you;] you, MS
159.13 ineffable conception] inexplicable conception of truth MS
159.13-14 Perhaps . . . will] I must appeal to the rising general. Perhaps they may MS
159.14-15 concrete and] *omit* MS
159.15-16 terms . . . consists] abstract terms which constitutes the pragmatist method MS
159.16 then] *omit* MS
159.17 and natural] *omit* MS
159.17-20 such . . . thought] it so hard to effect an entrance into the heads of other men MS

Alterations in the Manuscripts

All alterations made during the course of writing and of revision are recorded here except for strengthened letters to clarify a reading and a very few mendings over illegible letters. The medium is the black ink of the original inscription unless otherwise specified. It is certain that many of the alterations were made *currente calamo* but others as part of one or more reviews. The two are ordinarily so indistinguishable in the intensity of ink or in the kind of pen, however, as not to yield to systematic recording by categories on the physical evidence. In the description of the alterations when no record of position is given the inference should be that the change was made in the line of the text and during the course of the original writing. *Over* means inscribed over the letters of the original without interlining; *above* always means interlined without a caret unless a caret is specified. When an addition is a simple interlineation the formula is *interl.* or *interl. w. caret*; when a deletion positions the interlineation, the *interl.* is dropped and the formula reads *above del.* 'xyz' or *w. caret above del.* 'xyz'. The word *inserted* ordinarily refers to marginal additions that cannot properly be called interlines but are of the same nature. When reference is made to one or the other of two identical words in the same line of the present edition, either some preceding or following word is added for identification or else the designated word is identified with a superscript [1] or [2] according as it is the first or second occurrence in the line. A vertical stroke | signifies a line ending.

In order to ease the difficulty of reading quoted revised material of some length and complexity, the following convention is adopted. The quoted text will ordinarily be the final version in the manuscript, whereas the processes of revision are described within square brackets. In order to clarify what words in the text are being affected by the description within square brackets, an asterisk is placed before the first word to which the description in brackets applies and thus it is to be taken that all following words before the square brackets are a part of the described material. For example, at 151.19-22 James first wrote 'But the 'that' has the extremely convenient ambiguity for those who wish to demolish pragmatism, that sometimes it means the *fact* that, (Caesar died, for example)—and sometimes the *belief* that he died'. At this point he seems to have stopped and revised the sentence before eventually finishing it with the words 'Caesar is no longer living.' He deleted 'for those' and then 'demolish pragmatism,' and interlined in its place 'give pragmatists trouble,'; he then interlined 'for example' with a caret after 'means', deleted the parentheses about 'Caesar . . . example', deleting 'for example' within the parentheses as well and later included 'Caesar died' to complete the deletion of the parenthesis reading; he interlined 'and' with a caret above the deleted dash, deleted 'he died' and interlined above it 'for example', went back to deleted 'for example' interlined after 'means', and finally deleted the last 'for example' interlined above 'he died'. Later, as part of a major rewriting, the sentence and its context were fully deleted. In formulaic terms this is transcribed as: ['But the 'that' has the extremely convenient ambiguity ['for those' *del.*] who wish to *give pragmatists trouble, [above del.* 'demolish pragmatism,'] that sometimes it means *for example [*interl. w. caret and del.*] the *fact* that, ['(Caesar died, for example)' *del.*] and [*above del. dash*] sometimes the *belief* that ['for example' *del. above del.* 'he died'] Caesar is no longer living.' *del.*]

The lemmata (the readings to the left of the bracket) are ordinarily drawn from the present edition and represent the agreement of book and manuscript. To permit condensed entries, in some cases a single dagger prefixed to the page-line reference warns the user to refer to the Historical Collation for the exact manuscript reading in simple situations when the precise form of the alteration in words or accidentals is (a) not printed in the lemma, or (b) not specified in the descriptive part of the entry. For instance, at 146.5 the edition text reads 'proposition is one the' whereas the MS interlineation is 'proposition means one the'. The daggered entry †146.5 proposition . . . the] *above del.* 'idea is one whose' saves space by referring the user to the Historical Collation, which reads 146.5 is] means MS. On the contrary, the double dagger warns the user that the lemma is not (as in every other circumstance) the reading of the edition text but is instead that of the manuscript. This convention is employed only when the two readings are so similar that a user following the edition text in the Alterations list will be able to identify with certainty the reading that is intended, without recourse to the Historical Collation. A simple example of an accidental difference occurs at 147.37 where the edition text surrounds the phrase 'of course' with commas which are wanting in the MS interlineation. The condensed entry is ††147.37 ∧of course∧] *interl.* A simple substantive example comes at 148.12 in which the edition text reads 'prove the' but the MS alteration is 'prove his'; the alteration in MS is noted as ††148.12 prove his] *above del.* 'clinch the'. The device of the double dagger is not used when the texts are so divergent as to cause trouble in reference; in such cases the lemma is the reading of the present edition and the description of the MS alteration will provide the MS reading.

CHAPTER XIV.   Two English Critics

146.0   Two English Critics] *inscribed over pencil* '1 boat = vehicle = omnibus | book is eloquent ∴ is about eloquence.'
146.2   all] *interl. w. caret*
146.2   clearness] 'c' *over doubtful* 'g' *or* 'y'
146.2   one] 'o' *over* 'w'
146.3   entirely] *follows del.* 'he'
146.3   hit] *above del.* 'place himself at'
146.4   our] *above del.* 'the pragmatist'
146.4   When,] *above del.* 'If we'; *precedes del. interl.* 'we'
146.4   for instance, we] *interl. w. caret*
†146.5   proposition . . . the] *above del.* 'idea is one whose'
146.5   of believing which] *interl. w. caret*
146.6   assumes us] *originally followed*

by 'for instance' *interl. w. caret*; 'for instance' *then moved by guideline to precede* 'assumes' *and finally del.*
146.6   who] *follows del.* 'concrete person' *and precedes del.* 'belief'
146.6   proposition] *above del.* 'idea'
146.8   primarily] *interl. w. caret*
146.8   that fact] MS '*that*' *follows del.* 'the truth of' *interl. w. caret and precedes del.* 'facts *idea proposition, [interl. w. caret]*'
††146.9   obviously] 'obvious' *above del.* 'notorious' *with* 'ly' *undeleted*
146.9-10   a new . . . quite] MS *reads* 'quite a new proposition,'; 'quite' *follows del.* 'something *a [interl.]*'; 'a new proposition,' *precedes del. interl.* 'idea' *above del.* 'different from | from the one *whose truth is in question [above del.* 'originally

believed, in,'] and is'

146.10 and . . . fact] MS *reads*
interl. 'and one' *which precedes del.*
'one' *above del.* 'an idea'

146.11 very] *follows del.* 'hard'

146.11 , it being] *inserted for del.*
'It is'; *comma over period*

146.12 justly] *interl. w. caret*

146.15 We] MS *reads* 'What ['hat'
above del. 'e'] we'

146.15 nothing] *precedes* '['of this
latter' *del.*] so [*inserted*] silly. [*above
del.* 'ridiculous. sort.']'

146.15 Good] *above del.* 'Verification by'

146.16 are] *above del.* 'is'

146.16 proposed] *above del.* 'given'

146.16 merely] *interl. w. caret*

146.16 sure] *w. caret above del.*
'handy mark,'

146.17 by which] *above del.* 'of'

146.17 is . . . tho] *above del.* ', though
it'; 'habitually' *above del.* 'asc'

146.18 may] *follows del.* 'often';
precedes '['often' *del.*] on occasion'
interl. w. caret

†146.19 lurking . . . of] *final* 's' *of*
'motives' *del; above del.* 'essential
['meaning' *del.*] motive of'

146.19 whether] *follows del.* 'on the
part of men, and'

147.1 conscious] *above del.* 'aware'

147.1 such] *inserted for del.* 'this as
his [*above del.* 'the']'

147.2 as the] *precedes del.* '[*fol.* 2] only
['ration' *del.*] reasonable *causal
[*interl. w. caret*] explanation of the
*claim [*comma del.*] *not as its
logical premise; [*interl. w. caret*] and
['the' *del.*] *still less as its objective
content, and [*interl. w. caret*] the
[*inserted*] only clear and definite
*ground ascertainable for [*interl.
w. caret*] [*start earlier deletion*] criterion
which the *critic* may use when he
adjudicates between rival claims.
He ['has ['to' *del.*]' *del.*] uses ['the'
del.] consequences as a criterion. I,
as a pragmatist critic, ['the high
valu' *del.*] | [*fol.* 4ᵛ] am in the posi-
tion *Mr. ['M' *over* 'm'] Russell
imputes to me, when I am talking
about truth at large;'

147.2 our] *follows del.* 'the judgment
of truth'

147.3 cue or] *interl. w. caret*

147.5 beliefs] *final* 's' *doubtfully added*

147.7 No truth-claimer] 'truth-
claimer' *follows del.* 'distinction between truth and falsehood in *the
[*inserted*] meaning which the word
truth comports. No *our belief
comports. No [*above del.* 'one need
be']'; 'No' *then inserted*

147.7 himself] *following comma del.*

147.8 the part] *follows del.* 'the
motive force of'

147.8 in . . . mind] *interl. w. caret*

147.9 himself is] *above del.* 'may be'

147.9-10 may . . . be] *interl. w. caret*;
'at . . . be' *follows del.* 'be' *after* 'may'

147.10 oblivious] *above del.* 'unconscious'

147.10 with respect to] *above del.* 'in
the case of'

147.11 beliefs.] *final* 's.' *over period*

147.12 inform] *follows del.* 'force
upon'

147.13 to] *preceding double quotes del.*

147.13-14 definition . . . that] *above
del.* 'philosophy—a belief can perfectly well it may be perfectly 'true'
to say that A'

†147.14 may be 'true'] *interl. w.
caret; following* 'ev' *del.*; 'A' *del.
above* 'may'

147.14 when] *above del.* 'if'

147.14 does] *follows del.* 'actually'

147.15 exist.] MS 'exist" ' *precedes
del. period and del.* [*foot of fol.* 4]
['(p. 410)' *undel. in margin*] 'at all.
He does nt not mean by this ['that'
del.] just what *our more [*w. caret
above del.* 'the'] vulgar *critics
[*above del.* 'anti-pragmatists' *with
final* 's' *added*] mean [*final* 's' *del.*],
namely [*interl. w. caret*] that
*[*illegible*] since [*above del.* 'it may
be useful to'] falsehoods temporarily
are useful and therefore *we ought
in consistency *to [*inserted*] call them
[*above del.* 'must be counted'] truths.
He is a logician and a mathemati-
cian, accus-| [*fol.* 10]tomed to
think in complicated chains of
identities, and to prove his adversaries absurd, and he applies his
customary method to the pragmatist
belief.'

147.16 They . . . in] *w. caret above del.* 'In'

147.16 concrete] *above del.* 'real'

147.18 I . . . that] 'I may' *above del.* 'if I'; 'hold' *over original* 'say'; 'it true that' *w. caret above del. double quotes*

147.19 the] *above del.* 'those'

†147.19 plays] *following double quotes del.*

147.19 that . . . name,] *inserted for del.* 'and seek to [*above del.* 'and a critic'] may of my words may be both a pragmatist and a 'baconian'. As a pragmatist he will explain my belief'

147.19 express] *inserted for del.* 'seek to impart information to that seek to impart'

147.21 in . . . pragmatist] *interl. w. caret*

147.23 true∧] MS *dash interl.*

147.24 never] *follows del.* 'did nothing of the sort.'

147.26 play] *follows del.* '['or Mr. Hawtrey.' *del.*] This is the usual slander repeated to satiety by our critics. ['But whereas' *del.*] Using the word *'truth' [*above del.* 'true'] absolutely (whereas in any discussion as to *'truth's [*inserted for del.* 'its'] place in human ['human' *del.*] life it can only be used relatively to some particular 'trower') they easily make out that'

147.26 their] *alt. from* 'the'

147.27 ones.] *period replaces del. semicolon*

147.27 If] 'I' *over* 'i'; *follows del.* 'and'

††147.27 reader himself] *interl. w. caret*

147.28 we] *above del.* 'the'

147.28 pragmatists] *final* 's' *added*

147.28 show] *above del.* 'try [*alt. from* 'tries'] to prove'

147.28 those] *w. caret above del.* 'persons [*above del.* 'anyone'] to whom the anyone will believe that it does exist'

147.29 that . . . works] *interl. following interl. w. caret and del.* 'in its existence'; 'it' *inserted for del.* 'A'

147.29 satisfactorily] 'ily' *over* 'y'; *follows del.* 'works perfectly' *and*

precedes del. 'will think that it does [*illegible letters*]'

147.29 always] *interl. w. caret*

147.29 ²it] *w. caret above del.* 'it true that *the [interl. w. caret] belief'

147.29 he] *follows del.* 'they'

147.30 our] *follows del.* 'the'

147.30 is not then] *interl. w. caret*

147.31 in question] *above del.* 'talked of'

147.31 as fact] *interl. w. caret*

147.32 existence?] *question mark before del.* 'in fact.'

147.34 (p. 410).] *interl. w. caret; in* MS *preceding period not del.*

147.34-35 reappears] *follows del.* 'rep'

147.35 adds—] *dash above del. comma*

147.35 belief] *follows del.* 'statem'

147.37-148.9 It . . . currency.] *Separate fol.* 7½*, inserted according to margin instruction* 'Insert next page' *and arrow. Circled instruction at top of fol.* 7½ *reads* 'Insert on previous page.'

††147.37 ∧of course∧] *interl. w. caret*

147.37 sound] *above del.* 'purely'

148.1 consequences.] MS *reads* 'consequences that follow from their *nature. [*above del.* 'assumption.']

148.1 world] 'l' *inserted*

148.1 made] *interl. w. caret*

148.2 for me] *inserted w. caret*

148.2-3 by . . . 'true'?] MS *reads* 'by [*inserted*] *my ['being' *del.*] having [*above* '['if there are' *del.*] true *opinions? [*question mark inserted*] ['in it?' *del.*]']'

148.3 First,] *follows del.* 'First' |

148.3-4 (or . . . found)] *parens over commas*

148.4 such] *above del.* 'those'

148.4 which] *follows del.* 'with' *inserted for del.* 'to'; *precedes* 'agree with' *interl. w. caret*

148.4 opinion.] MS 'opinions.'; *period inserted before del.* '[are]' *interl. w. caret before del.* '['agree' *del.*] shall be in agreement.'

148.6 But in] *above del.* 'In'

††148.8 shall] *above del.* 'does'

148.10 Mr.] *follows del.* 'But' [*continuing original text on fol.* 7]

148.10 himself] *interl. w. caret*

148.11 simply] *follows del.* 'to'

148.11 the] *above del.* 'this'

148.11 Being] *follows del.* 'Trained in mathematical'

††148.12 prove his] *above del.* 'clinch the'

148.17 The . . . logic] WJ *first del. but then inserted* 'stet' *in left margin*

148.19 functions of] *interl. w. caret*

148.19 fact] *follows del.* 'flux of'

148.19 must also mean] *w. caret above del.* 'are dealing with mathematical terms as'; 'mean' *follows del.* 'be'

148.20 as] *interl. w. caret*

148.21 self-sufficient,] *above del.* 'exact and adequate, Only *as [doubtful]'

††148.21 once equated∧] *above del.* 'of the same value'

148.22 without] *follows del.* 'of equations,'

148.25 self-] *follows del.* 'cont'

148.26 context] 'x' *over* 'n'

148.26 varying] 'y' *over start of* 'i'

148.26 be] *follows del.* 'need to be determined'

148.26 further] *inserted w. caret*

148.27 word] *above del.* 'thing'

148.27 The] *follows del.* 'If the definition is true it is'

148.28 claims] *follows del.* 'is exact and'

148.28 it?] *question mark over comma*

148.29 word—] *dash above del.* ', can't it,'

148.29 identical—] *dash for del. question mark*

148.30 two] *inserted*

148.30 can] *above del.* 'must'

148.31 n'est-ce pas?] *above del.* 'nicht wahr?'

††148.31 likewise] *inserted for del.* 'and'

148.32 word,] *precedes del.* 'likewise,'

††148.32 nicht wahr] *precedes question mark over comma and del.* 'etc., etc,'

148.33 self-contradiction] *follows del.* 'absurdity.'

148.34 The] *follows del. non-indented* 'I fo' *and space;* '¶' *in margin*

148.34 rigoristic] 'istic' *above del.* 'ous'

148.35 as working] *w. caret above del.* 'is'

148.36 ¹what] *above del.* 'this. ['I' del.]'

††148.36 ∧working∧] *w. caret above del.* 'it'

148.36 the] *interl.*

148.36 of our ideas] *interl. w. caret*

148.36 means] *underline del.*

148.37 definition] *underline del.*

148.37 meanings . . . things] *final* 's' *added in both*

149.1 equivalent] *final* 's' *del.; follows del.* 'exact'

149.1 interchangeable] MS *reads* 'substitutable' *from which final* 's' *and comma del.*

149.2 and] *inserted*

149.2 its] *above del.* 'the'

149.2-3 be . . . used,] *above del.* 'attach to ['the thing,' *del.*].'; 'a' *inserted for del.* 'any'; 'is used,' *inserted w. caret after* 'term'

149.3 whoso] 'so' *interl. w. caret*

149.4 can] *follows del.* '['cannot imply' *del.*] cannot imply anything about any object, for example; and ['that if' *del.*]'

149.5 nothing but] *w. caret above del.* 'only'

149.5 in particular] *interl. w. caret*

149.5-6 neither . . . anything] *w. caret above del.* 'have no opinion whatever'; 'neither' *inserted before* 'imply' *when* 'nothing' *following* 'imply' *del*; 'n' *added to* 'or'; 'anything' *inserted after del.* 'nothing'

149.7 Mr. Russell] *above del.* 'he says, to'

149.9 merely] 're' *over doubtful* 'a'

149.11 Logic] *In* MS *preceding asterisk and inserted horizontal line above crossing page for footnote del. when following matter ending before next paragraph and including final deletion at* 149.15 *kept as text. Inserted asterisk after* '(p. 400)." ' *del.*

149.11 I . . . passing,] *interl. w. caret*

149.12 to] *follows inserted* 'here'

149.12 them . . . once,] MS 'them conjointly' *above del.* '['both' *del.*] at least *both*, in that case,'

149.14 that] *follows del.* 'that if'

149.14 must be] *above del.* 'are'

†149.15 in . . . mouth.] *interl. w. caret before interl. del. [fol.* 10] 'for the [*above del.* 'in'] pragmatist *mind. [*above del.* 'logician.'] ['Oh' del.]* The

['T' *over* 't'] foolishness of bare
logic, when the terms it uses are
dragged out of their context in
reality ! | [*fol.* 21] and taken in a
vacuum. [¶] He *then [above del.*
'racks the'] puts *the terms, thus
made into [*w. caret above del.* 'the
[*final* 'se' *del.*] bare [*interl. w. caret*]
terms through'] *bare logical entities, through [*inserted*]'

149.16   may not real] 'may' *above del.*
'can' *in* 'cannot'; 'real' *above del.*
'concrete'

149.16   I now ask,] *interl. w. caret*;
'now' *w. caret following* 'I'

149.17   definitions?] *question mark over
comma*

149.17   a] *interl. w. caret before del.
interl.* 'the'

149.17   value] *final* 's' *del.*

149.17   is finally] *above del.* 'are'

149.18   result . . . substituted] *above
del.* 'definitions, abstract'

149.19   all] *interl. w. caret*

149.19   these] 'se' *added*

149.19   accidents] *interl. w. caret*

149.21   workings.] *follows del.*
'['workings.' *del.*] consequences.';
precedes del. 'It is ['both' *del.*] a
content [*comma del.*] and an implication of the truth (or *working
[*final paren del.*] of the belief) that
other men exist, that they *do
[*above del.* 'should'] really exist'

149.22   it] 't' *over* 's'

149.23   Russell's] ''s' *added*

149.24   'by] *follows del.* 'their
existence'

†149.24-25   all . . . associates,] *interl.
w. caret*; 'all . . . as' *inserted*

149.25   would . . . as] *interl. above del.*
inserted 'to'; 'would' *precedes del.*
'seem to'

149.25   translating] 'ing' *over* 'e'

149.26   ¹all] *w. caret above del.* 'the
man's'

149.26   ²belief] *follows del.* 'necessary'
interl. above del. 'sub-'

149.26   itself] *interl. w. caret*

149.27   If] *follows del.* 'If' |

149.27   that] *interl. w. caret*

149.27   explain] *interl.*

149.27-28   as meaning] 'as' *inserted*;
'ing' *over* 's'; *precedes del.* 'effects'

149.28-29   if I say] *interl. w. caret*

149.29-30   to . . . other] MS *reads* 'as
differing from previous' *which is inserted for del.* 'by ['a' *del.*] ['certain'
del.] referring [*alt. from* 'reference']
to what is contained in other'

149.30   if I] *follows del.* 'would,';
precedes 'under-' |

149.30   would] *interl. w. caret*

149.31   doom] *above del.* 'compel'

149.31   agreeing] 'ing' *added*

149.32-33   its truth] 'its' *interl.*; 'th'
over 'e'

149.34   *about* the] MS 'about' *w.
caret above del.* 'in'; 'the' *precedes del.*
'said'

149.35   I] *follows del.* 'the critic who'

149.35   am] *above del.* 'have'

†149.35-36   subject . . . that of] *interl.
above del.* 'universe,' *and del.* 'from'

149.37   thinking] *above del.* 'life'

150.2   expedient] *above del.* 'useful'

150.2   other men] *above del.* 'they'

150.4   believe] 've' *over* 'f'

150.6   object] *above del.* 'cond deliverance'

150.7   one] *above del.* 'the'

150.7-8   power . . . itself.] *above del.*
'genesis.'

150.8   term] *follows del.* 'comm'

150.8   men] *follows del.* 'people'

150.9   contain] *follows del.* 'both';
precedes 'in common,' *interl. w. caret*

150.16   to our fury,] *w. caret above
del.* 'and'; *comma over period before del.*
'H'

150.16   allowing it] 'ing' *over* 's';
follows 'for the sake of the argument
he' *interl. w. caret del. following* 'it'
and moved to precede 'allowing'; 'he'
added

150.18   (as Mr.] 'M' *over* 'D'; *follows
del.* 'to sig' (*or possibly* 'sy')

150.20   therefore,'' he writes,] *interl.
w. caret*

150.21   it] *preceding single quote del.*

150.22   This . . . correctness.''] *follows
del. double quotes; above del.* 'Now
'correctness' *cannot* be identical with
the pragmatist's 'truth,' for if'

150.24   What] *follows del.* 'Cor'

150.24-25   what is] *above del.* 'the'

150.25-26   interchangeable] *above del.*
'substitutable'

150.26 interchange] *above del.*
'substitute'

150.27 " 'Caesar] *single quote over double quotes*

150.30 Mr.] *follows del.* 'Ergo,'; ' ¶' *inserted in margin and vertical line drawn before* 'Ergo' *to indicate paragraph*

150.30 would seem] 'would' *interl. w. caret; final* 's' *of* 'seems' *del.*

150.30 that] *above del.* ', that'

150.31 in] *follows del.* 'is irreconcileable with'

150.31 implies] *follows del.* 'involves old'; *precedes del.* 'that the believer'

150.31 —what?] *dash interl.*

150.32 shall believe] 'shall' *inserted; final* 's' *of* 'believes' *del.*

150.32 his] *follows del.* 'the'

150.32 —or] *dash inserted*

150.33 pragmatist] *follows del.* 'critic' *which is above del.* 'pragmatist [alt. from* 'pragmatically'] *shall believe'*

150.33 about him] *interl. w. caret*

150.34 The] *follows del.* 'Surely the universes are different. When I account for *someone's [first* 's' *over* 'a'] *belief believing Caesar to be dead, I need not share that belief myself.'

150.34 quite] *above del.* 'entirely'

150.34 For] 'F' *over* 'f' *over* 'F'; *follows period over comma over original period*

150.35 The] 'T' *over* 't'

151.1 of course] *interl. w. caret*

151.1 the] *above del.* 'the'

†151.2 the pragmatic deliverance] *follows del.* 'deliverance of'; 'ic deliverance' *above del.* 'ist's opinion'

151.2 as . . . said,] *interl. w. caret*

151.3 altogether] *interl.*

151.3 When] *follows del.* 'We must ['substitute' *del.*] pass from one universe to another in substituting'

151.3 one argues by] *interl. w. caret;* 'one' *inserted for del.* 'we'; 's' *added in ink to pencil* 'argues by'

151.4 substituting] *follows del.* 'we'; 'ing' *over* 'e'

151.4 one needs] 'one' *above del.* 'we ['must' *del.*]'; 's' *added to* 'need'

151.6-7 occurs when we] *interl. preceding del. interl.* 'is the' *above del.* 'comes from'

151.7 carry] *final* 'ing' *del.; above del.* 'making ['m' *over doubtful* 'a']'

151.7 from] *follows del.* 'sometimes carry the subj'

151.8 realm,] *above del.* 'world,'

151.8 applying] MS *reads* 'appling'; 'ng' *over* 'es'

151.8 ¹sometimes] *above del.* 'not only'

151.8 of] *above del.* '['of the' *del.*] our'

151.8 ²sometimes] *above del.* 'but'

151.9 which] *above del.* 'asserted by the in the ob by'

151.9 assert] *follows del.* 'own asser'

151.9 as] *w. caret following del. interl.* '['like' *del.*] *such as [in pencil*]'

151.10 himself,] *interl. w. caret; comma over pencil* '&'

151.10 and others] *in ink above pencil del.* 'and others'

151.10 favor] *above del.* 'use'

††151.11 invented—] *in pencil w. caret above pencil del.* 'meant'; *ink dash over ink comma*

151.12 this] *alt. from* 'the'

151.12 truth] 't' *over* 'T'; *following comma del.; follows dash over period*

151.13 naming] *above del.* 'defining ['ng' *over* 'tion'] a'

151.13 propositions] *final* 's' *added*

151.13 impossible not] *above del.* 'inevitable'

151.14 that] *follows del.* 'is a proposition,'

151.15 propositions.] *precedes del.* 'But the 'that' has the extremely convenient ambiguity ['for those' *del.*] | [*fol.* 17] who wish to *give pragmatists trouble, [*above del.* 'demolish pragmatism,'] that sometimes it means *for example [*interl. w. caret and indep. del.*] the *fact* that, ['(Caesar died, for example)' *del.*] [   ] and [*above del. dash*] sometimes the *belief* that [*del.* 'for example' *above del.* 'he died'] Caesar is no longer living. When I speak of (*begin indep. deletion*) ['the belief's *as [interl.*] satisfactory ['y' *over* 'iness'], I am told "that has nothing to do with the *fact [*above del.* 'proposition']. When I speak of Caesar's existence the fact, truth as meaning its expediency I am told *the [inserted] that truth of *the [*w. caret above del.* 'the'] *of the [*interl. w. caret*] belief *as true, [*interl. w. caret*] I am told that *the [*inserted*] [*pencil interl.* 'a true' *del. in ink*] truth [*above del.* 'the proposition'] *means *the [*w. caret above del.* 'the' *and before del. interl.* 'a'] fact, when I *admit, [*above del.* 'allow'] *claim the [*w. caret above del.* 'speak of'] ['a' *del. above del.* 'the'] fact *also, [*interl. w. caret*] I am told that the ['a' *inserted and del.*] proposition means a belief, and that *truth [*inserted*] in my mouth, *being defined as the ['the' *del.*] belief's workings, [*interl. w. caret*] can only mean *the [*above del.* 'a'] belief and *must exclude the [*above del. inserted* 'and' *and del.* 'not a'] fact,']' (*end indep. deletion*)

151.16 do] *follows del.* 'don't'
151.16 logical] *inserted for del.* 'formal' *above del.* 'logistic'
151.16-17 be . . . treat] *inserted for del.* 'conduce to economy of formulation to ['treat truth as an absolute ['absolute' *del.*] property ['as' *del.*] resident in ['certain' *del.*] propositions *that* etc etc. But the 'that' has the extremely convenient ambiguity for those' *del.*] treat such complexes as 'that-Caesar-is-dead' as 'truths'. But the that has the extremely convenient ambiguity for those ['tru' *del.*]'
151.17-18 as . . . respectively,] *w. caret above del.* 'and false propositions as self-contained logical *entities, [*above del.* 'units,'] and'
151.18 or] *interl. w. caret*
151.18-19 ²of . . . term] MS *reads* 'a single term [*above del.* 'talk'] of *a [*interl. w. caret*] complex [*final* 'es' *del.*] like 'that-Caesar-is-*dead,' [*final* 'd' *over doubtful* 'l' *or* 't']'
151.19 and call it a] *w. caret above del.* 'the *a [*doubtful*]'; 'call' *follows del.* 'treat'
151.21 it] *follows del.* 'it' |
151.24 I am told] *interl. w. caret*
151.25-26 being . . . belief—] MS *reads* 'being a definition only of the belief's quality,' *which is inserted*
151.26-27 truth . . . possession.] MS 'truth left to talk about.' *follows del.* 'leg to stand on.'

151.30 ¹the] *interl. w. caret*
151.30 of the idea] 'of the idea' *above del.* '-relation between them,' *and precedes del. interl.* 'or belief'
151.31 be] *inserted in pencil for pencil del.* 'have kept themselves'
151.31 objection.] *precedes del.* 'In any case the abstract logic-chopping of this class of critic makes one sigh for one breath of concreteness in discussing.'
151.32 terms] 's' *added; follows del.* 'a'
151.32 their] *above del.* 'its settings'
151.33 identifies] *follows del.* 'and handles them'
151.33 treats] *above del.* 'handles'
151.34 ¹risks] *final* 's' *added; follows del.* 'exposes himself to the'; *precedes del.* 'of'
151.34 ²risks] *above del.* 'of committing obvi'
151.35 easily detects] 'easily' *above del.* 'can'; 's' *added to* 'detect'
151.35 prove] *follows del.* 'define "Caesar exists" as a truth, and to define a truth *satisfactory [*above del.* 'as a working'], no more commits me to'
151.36 the statement] *interl. w. caret*
151.36 identical with] *inserted w. caret*
151.36 ²statement] *above del.* 'proposition'
151.37 the one] *double quotes following* 'one.' *del.; above del.* 'is' like proving that because 'truth' *be [*doubtful*] both *statements [*interl. w. caret*] are *true, [*single quotes indep. del.*] is'
†151.37-152.1 ¹is . . . statements,'] *interl.*
152.1 an] *follows del.* 'a boat is'
152.2 vehicles.] *single quotes del.*
152.2 A] *follows del.* 'Who-|ever rides'
152.2 may be] *above del.* 'is'
152.3 Whenever we] *above del.* 'Everyone who'
152.3 see] *final* 's' *del.*
152.4 we see] 'we' *interl. w. caret; final* 's' *del. from* 'sees'
152.4 beast,] *precedes del.* [*fol.* 18] 'but does he see *that he is* such a beast? Messrs. Russell and Hawtrey

would say | [*fol.* 20] it seems to me, that he sees *that he is* such a beast!'

152.4 whenever we] *above del.* 'everyone who'

152.4 believe] *final* 's' *del.*

152.4-5 we believe] 'we' *interl. w. caret; final* 's' *del. from* 'believes'

152.6 here] *interl. w. caret*

152.7 we see] 'we' *above del.* 'he'; *final* 's' *del. from* 'sees'

152.7 a fact] *interl. w. caret*

152.7 notoriously] 'notori' *above del.* 'obvi'

152.10 so much] *above del.* 'the pitfalls of'

152.10 Abstractionism] 'A' *over* 'N'

152.11 trials] *above del.* 'direct constructive attempts'

152.11 positively] *interl. w. caret*

152.13 attempts] *follows del.* 'proceeds to' *interl above del.* 'attempts'

152.13 this] *alt. from* 'the'

152.13 by] *follows del.* 'but'; *precedes del.* 'limit fr'

152.14 its] *alt. from* 'is'

152.16 ¹in] *follows del.* 'with' *inserted for del.* 'in'

152.16 are found] *above del.* 'coexist'

152.19 tortures] *follows del.* 'stretches and'

152.19 rack] *follows del.* 'logical'

152.20 logical] *above del.* 'intellectual'

152.20 gymnastic] *final* 's' *del.*

152.21 portentous] *interl. following del.* 'sophistical' *interl. w. caret*

152.21 believes] *preceding double quotes del.*

152.24 white;] MS 'white,' *precedes del. double quotes*

152.24-26 that . . . false] *inserted*

sideways in margin with arrow and guideline; in MS 'false' *followed by double quotes, comma, del. double quotes and* 'and that ['that closes' *del.*] all ['discussion is thereby terminated.' *del.*]'

152.28 In spite of my] *above del.* 'In spite of'; *follows* ' ¶' *and vertical line; in MS* 'M' *over* 'm' *and not restored to l.c. when* 'In spite of' *restored*

†152.28 admiration] 'great admi' *inserted; follows del.* 'cordial cordial' *above del.* 'cordial admi-'|

152.28 ²of] *above del.* 'for'

152.28 powers,] 's,' *over comma*

152.28-29 I . . . pragmatism,] *above del.* 'would be increased if he I feel as if,'

152.29 even] *inserted*

152.29-30 had it no] *above del.* 'were there'

152.30 function] *over* 'faculties'; *precedes del.* 'it [*interl.*] pragmatism, it'

152.30 and] *above del.* 'or'

†152.31 gifted] *paren over comma*

152.31 used] MS 'using' *above del.* 'using'

152.31 powers] *follows* 'their ['such' *del.*] ['their' *del.*] great' *all w. caret above del.* 'using such'

152.31 in] 'i' *over* 's'

152.31-32 abstraction from reality.] *w. caret above del.* 'unreal material.'

152.33 diseased] *follows caret which follows del.* 'the' *above del.* 'such' |

152.33 abstractionism . . . show.] MS *reads* 'abstractionism [*ink* 'ism' *alters pencil* 'abstractions'] which [*above del.* 'work as'] that article *exhibits. [inserted below del.* 'embodies.']'

Deleted Versos in Chapter XIV Manuscript

[*del. fols.* 19ᵛ, 13ᵛ, *and* 20ᵛ *correspond approximately to text* 148.17–149.6 *and are earlier drafts of this material*] [*fol.* 19ᵛ] 'Such a definition as I give of *the [interl. w. caret*] truth of a ['proposition' *del.*] belief does n't pretend to be an exhaustive account of the whole belief, with *its ['ts' over 's'*] motive [*final* 's' *del.*], causes object, and environment, or *even [interl. w. caret*] of its truth from the point of view of any one but the believer himself. Yet, in the hands of the mathematical logician, it is made to figure as the adequate substitute of the *act [above del.* 'whole fact'] of belief in its full concreteness. The logician considers that a definition *must be an [w. caret above del.* 'give [*final* 's' *del.*] the essence ex full'] exact equivalent of the thing defined, therefore a *full [interl. w. caret*] substitute for the *name of the [*interl. w. caret*] thing, and that two definitions of the same thing, ['have an' *del.*] or two things with the same definition mean identicals and are *therefore ['o' *over* 'u'] mutually | [*fol.* 13ᵛ] substitutable. But when you thus use verbal definitions, *like [*above del.* '['as' *del.*] the a's b's & c's'] so many a-s, b-s, & c's in ['alge-' *del.*] agebraic ['a' *over* 'b'] chains of identity and seek *afterwards ['f' *over* 's'] to restore the real values, you may find subreptions. ['of' *del.*]. Algebraic chains of identity use terms that have no ['other' *del.*] properties outside of what the letters represent; there can be no omission or subreption. But a concrete fact like a belief, or like the truth of a belief has numerous accidents not included in *its [*inserted for del.* 'the'] definition, and substitution is safe only when the accidents are ['rigorously' *del.*] carefully excluded. The belief has its object as well as its truth, and the truth has *its [*inserted*] implications as well as its workings. ['It is an implication of the truth of the | [*fol.* 20ᵛ] belief that Caesar exists, that he does exist,' *del.*] That Caesar does exist, and that one must say that he doesn't, are implications of the truth of the belief that he *does [*following period del.*] exist. But because I define truth only as working, Mesrs. Russell and Hawtrey proceed with their chain of equations as if these implications were excluded '*by definition.*' It depends on what you mean by definition.'

CHAPTER XV. A Dialogue

154.1 correcting] *above del.* 'reading'
154.1 imagine] *follows del.* 'seem to'
154.2 my] *above del.* 'an anti-|prag-matist'
154.2 may] *interl. w. caret*
154.2 keep] *final* 's' *del.*
154.3 may be] *w. caret above del.* 'is'
154.5 the] *above del.* 'the'
154.5 begin:] MS 'begin:—' *follows* 'reader' *interl. w. caret*
154.9 Shall] 'S' *over* 's'
154.9 ²the] *final* 'y' *del.*
154.9 truth about them] *interl. w. caret*
154.10 known?] *question mark added before del.* 'or not?'
154.10-11 (leaving . . . account)] *parens over commas*
††154.12 Brother] 'B' *over* 'b'; *follows del.* 'dear'
154.13 can . . . to be] *w. caret above del.* '*is*'
154.13 any] 'ny' *added*
154.13 at all] *interl. w. caret*
154.14 ²truth,] *comma inserted before del.*', & be it or be it not predestined to be known?'
154.14-15 at any rate] *above del.* 'in any event'; 'any' *of interl. follows del.* 'either'

154.16 PRAGMATIST] *follows del.* 'Why'
154.19 on the] *above del.* 'you'
154.19 one . . . elect] *inserted w. caret*
154.19 to] *inserted*
154.20 that] *interl. w. caret*
154.20-21 whole . . . theory.] *above del.* 'whole case.'
154.21 According . . . theory,] *above del.* 'Your theory of'; 'that' *follows del.* 'you,'
154.21 ideas] *follows del.* 'an'; *final* 's' *added*
154.21 workings] *follows del.* 'its'
155.1 there] *follows del.* 'we have agreed that'
155.1 supposed] *interl. w. caret*
155.2 ideas] *final* 's' *perhaps added*
155.2 exist.] *above del.* 'be found.'
155.3 then] *interl. w. caret*
††155.3 remains,] *final* 's' *and comma doubtfully added*
155.4 Do you wish,] *above del.* 'I am glad to see that you do not,'
155.4 so] *final* 'm' *del. from false start* 'some'
155.4 force me to] *inserted w. caret*
155.5 out] *follows del.* 'of'
155.5 itself?] *inserted following del.* '*per se.*' *interl. above del.* 'itself.'

155.5   I cannot:] *above del.* 'do' *which is above del.* 'Neither do I'

155.5   ³the] 't' *over* 'O'

155.6   or said] *interl. w. caret*

†155.7-8   But . . . say] *above del.* 'But before saying'; 'your' *follows del.* 'that is' *after del.* 'your'

155.8   your] *follows del.* 'the'

155.8-9   ³I . . . to] *interl. w. caret*

155.9   the other] *above del.* 'them both'

155.9   horn] *final* 's' *del.*

155.10   The . . . if] *w. caret above del.* 'If, on the other hand,'

155.13   must] *inserted following del.* ', every determination of reality,'

155.14   truly stateable] *above del.* 'susceptible of *true [inserted]* statement'

155.15   never] *in MS follows* 'may' *interl. w. caret*

155.18   have] *inserted*

155.18   events] *follows del.* 'past'

155.19   of] *interl. w. caret*

155.19   been] *interl. w. caret*

155.19   ²ever] *interl. w. caret*

155.20   abstractly] *above del.* 'that in advance'

155.21   can] *above del.* 'will'

155.21   any such] *above del.* 'these'

155.22   event] *final* 's' *del.*

155.22   event's] *interl. w. caret; alt. from* 'events'

155.23   and] *w. caret above del.* 'of the events, and'; *precedes del. interl.* 'so that'

155.23   accordingly] *above del.* 'therefore'

155.24   virtually] *above del.* 'ideally'

155.29   consistently to] *interl. w. caret*

155.30   do] *interl. w. caret*

155.30   ask me to] *interl. w. caret; final* 's' *del. from* 'asks'

155.31   comprehend.] *interl. following del.* 'represent.' *above del.* 'understand.'

155.32   not,] *comma over del. question mark*

155.35   PRAG:] *follows del.* 'But pra'

155.35   then] *interl. w. caret*

155.35   this] *follows del.* 'does'

155.36   consists.] *final* 's.' *over original period; follows del.* 'exis'

156.1   It . . . nothing] *above del.* 'I

say it *exists [start of underline and following comma del.]* in'

156.1   but] *inserted*

156.1-2   or . . . holds.] MS *reads* 'and properly speaking it does n't *exist*. It obtains, it holds.' *interl. w. caret above del.* 'it doesn't consist in anything *else, [comma over period]*'; *comma following* 'obtains' *doubtfully altered from period; guideline originally preceded* 'It' *and then moved to precede* 'and'

156.3   PRAG:—] *over* 'Anti-pr'; *follows circled* 'rom' *in margin*

156.3   of] *underline del.*

156.4   holds] *above del.* 'obtains'

156.5   ANTI] 'An' *over* 'Pr'

156.5   holds *of* it,] *w. caret above del.* 'obtains concerning it,'; 'holds' *inserted for del.* 'is'

156.6   represents] 'presents' *above del. interl.* 'is aware of' *after inserted* 're' *and is above del.* 'gives'; *preceding comma over period*

156.7   ¹it?] *question mark over comma (or period)*

156.7   represents] *inserted for del.* 'is aware of' *above del.* 'knows'

156.8   The . . . rather] MS *reads* 'The truth does; or rather' *interl. w. caret*

156.9   anyone] 'any' *above del.* 'Any'

††156.9   possesses] *final* 'es' *added; follows del.* 'may'

††156.9   truth, and any] *comma inserted for del. period;* 'and any' *above del.* 'Any'

156.10   idea] *above del.* 'thought'; *precedes inserted* 'of it'

††156.10   represents] *follows del. inserted* 'will'; *final* 's' *above del.* 's'

156.11   we . . . that] *above del.* '['there was supposed' *del.]* there was to be'

156.12   nor any idea] 'nor any' *above del.* 'and no'; *final* 's' *del. from* 'ideas'

156.12   it] *precedes del. comma*

156.14   this] *altered from* 'the'

156.14-15   consists] *precedes del. comma*

156.15   this] *above del.* 'as a'

156.15   facts] *follows del.* 'real state of'

156.16   *per se*] *interl. w. caret*

156.16   one] *follows del.* 'oth'

156.16 all . . . them,] *interl. w. caret
following del.* 'some' *and above del.*
'knower or idea of them,'; 'them'
precedes del. 'it'; 'all' *inserted*

156.16 actual] *in MS follows* 'whether';
alt. from 'either'

156.17 it] *precedes del. question mark*

156.18 built] 't' *over* 'd'

156.19 metaphysical] *follows del.*
'world does it inhabit'; *precedes*
'level' *above del.* 'order'

156.20 ANTI-PRAG:] *follows del.*
'What abs'

156.21 facts are] *follows del.* 'state of';
final 's' *added*; 'are' *over* 'is'

156.21 they] *follows del.* 'it is'

156.23 facts] *final* 's' *added; following
single quote del.; precedes del.* 'u does
that'

156.23 so-and-so] *alt. from* 'such-and-
such'; *precedes del. question mark and
dash but dash restored w. caret*

156.23-25 I . . . phrase] *MS reads*
'I won't ask you *what* is true, but
[*'mean' del.*] does your phrase' *inserted for del.* 'does [*'d' over* 'D'] that'

156.26 really additional] *MS reads*
'more' *inserted w. guideline for del.*
'more' *which is above del.* 'numerically
other than the'

156.26 bare] *follows inserted* 'than
the'; *final* 'ly' *del. from* 'barely'

156.26 of] *follows del.* 'on the part'

156.29 mental . . . for] *above del.*
'noetic aspect of'

156.29 their] *above del.* 'an'

156.30 function,] *inserted for del.*
'their [*interl. w. caret*] mental [*inserted*] equivalent, [*'for them' del.*]'

156.30 value . . . terms.] *MS reads*
'noetic *value*.'; 'noetic' *interl. w.
caret; period inserted before del.* 'for
intelligence.'

156.31 A . . . ghost] *followed by del.*
'of'; *above del.* 'Do you mean *to
call it [*interl. w. caret*] a sort of
second edition'

156.31 apparently!] *w. caret above del.*
'a doubling up of them?'

156.34 ¹obtains] *precedes diagonal
pencil line which cuts through period*

156.36 no] *above del.* 'any'

156.37 assumed.] *follows del.* 'ruled
out.'

157.1 PRAG] 'P' *over* 'A'

††157.1 No 'actual'] 'No' *interl. w.
caret; first* 'a' *over* 'A' *in* "'actual'"

157.1 I agree.] *above del. interl.*
'truly enough.' *interl. above del.* 'yes!
no.'

157.1 you] *precedes del.* 'absolutely'
interl. above del. 'quite'

157.1 that] *precedes del.* [*fol.* 8] '[*begin
indep. del.*] your notion of *the
[*interl.*] truth is out of [*'all' del.*]
relation to whose existence you *so
rightly insist on has no [*above del.*]
'speak of is in no'] degree constituted by ['the' *del.*] relation *to
any [*interl.*] of the facts to *their
[*interl. and del.*] potential *knower
[*final* 's' *and question mark over comma
del.*] who might ideally or in the
nature—of the facts in question?
[¶] ANTI-PRAG:—Of course it has
this relation that if a potential
knower ever became actual [*end
indep. del.*] the notion of a potential
or ideal knower who, if he came to
know the truth at all, *would have
to [*inserted*] know *that* truth, has
['had' *del.*] nothing to do with |
[*fol.* 9ᵛ] *defining [*above del.* 'constituting'] the notion of that truth
in your ['own' *del.*] mind? [¶]
['Nothing' *del.*] ANTI-PRAG:—Of
course if there be a truth, that is the
truth which every possible knower
*will [*above del.* 'would'] have to
know if he *knows [*alt. from* 'knew']
the truth at all. The notion of there
being a'

157.1 no] *inserted for del.* 'the'

157.2 a] *follows del.* 'what'

157.2 knower] *precedes del.* 'would
know'

157.2 has] *follows del.* 'we are considering'; *precedes* 'had aught' *w.
caret above del.* 'nothing'; 'had' *then
del.*

157.6 know] 'k' *over* 'n'

157.8 then it; it] *MS* 'then him, not'
followed by del. 'the other way about.'

157.11 so-|called] *inserted*

157.12 ¹reality] *follows del.* 'the'

157.12 knowledge,] 'ledge' *over* 'er'
and comma inserted; follows del. 'the
*possible [*inserted and del.*]'; *precedes*

del. 'mind, yet having no foothold in either.'

157.12 ²reality] *follows del.* 'the'

157.13 yet] *precedes* 'other than it,' *inserted for del.* 'not identical with'

157.13 at . . . time] *interl. w. caret*

157.14 independent] *in MS precedes* 'of ['a knower of' *del.*] of a knower.'

††157.14 *Is] follows del.* 'It seems to me terribly'

157.14 as] *above del.* 'so'

157.15 knower] *precedes del. question mark*

157.15 suppose] *follows del.* 'vaguely'

157.16 dubious, . . . only] MS 'suspicious, . . . only' *inserted w. guideline following del.* 'like'

157.17 of the reality.] *interl. w. caret; caret over period*

157.17 Isn't] *follows del.* 'It s'

157.18 successful] *interl. w. caret; follows* 'any' *alt. from* 'a'

157.18 have to] *interl. w. caret*

†157.19 *in case] w. caret above del.* 'if'

157.19 where] *follows del. false start* 'wheth'; *precedes del.* 'there were'

157.20 any] *above del.* 'not tru the'

157.20-21 something] *interl. w. caret*

157.21 distinguishable] *originally* 'distinct'; *alt. to* 'distinguisht' *and then to* 'distinguishable'

157.21 find] *follows del.* 'also be non-existent. ['inconceivable?' *del.*]'

157.26 must] *follows del.* 'may'

157.26 also . . . permission] *above del.* 'added the proviso that I should be allowed'

157.27 define the word] *above del.* 'interpret it'

157.27 fashion] *follows del.* 'pragmatist'

157.28 for me] *interl. w. caret*

††157.29 does] *above del.* 'should'

157.31 precedes] *follows* 'we suppose' *interl. w. caret*

157.31 only] MS *reads* 'but a' *interl.; originally* 'an' *interl. w. caret above del.* 'the' *and before* 'abstract'; *then* 'but a' *placed on either side of del.* 'an' *and* 'abstract' *del.*

157.31 what] *above del.* 'the necessary deliverance of'

157.32 knower] *follows del.* 'knowledge of the subject'

157.32 the fact will] MS *interl.* 'the event will' *follows interl. del.* 'the fact' *above del.* 'the subject would'

157.33 He] *precedes* 'will' *above del.* 'would'

157.33 will bring] MS 'brings' *with added* 's'; *follows del.* 'would'

157.34 relations] *follows del.* 'working'

157.34 it] MS *reads* 'the event'; 'event' *follows del.* 'pre-existing reality,' *and precedes* 'that proves' *above del.* 'that would be a possible ['work' *del.*]'

157.35 may] *above del.* 'might'

157.36 ²by] *interl. w. caret*

158.1 anticipated] 'd' *over* 'rs'; *follows del.* 'taken by'

158.3 ANTI-] 'A' *over* 'B'

158.3 know] *precedes del.* 'when it ['comes' *del.*] becomes actual.'

158.4 mustn't] *above del.* 'how can'

†158.4-5 distinct . . . or] *above del.* 'only another name for'; 'either' *inserted*

158.6 what] *interl. w. caret*

158.6 is] *precedes del.* 'the reality,'

158.7 itself, the] *interl. w. caret*

158.7 the reality] *w. caret above del.* 'it'

158.13 common] *inserted*

158.13 which] *precedes del.* 'makes'

158.16 interchangeably?] *precedes del.* 'Truth seems to me a ['collective' *del.*] name for ['facts' *del.*] reality as known or *as [interl. and del.]* knowable, not for reality by itself.'

158.16 And has] MS *reads* 'Does' *altered from* 'do' *after del.* 'And'

158.16-17 philosophy] MS *reads* 'philosophy gain' *above del.* 'we gain'

158.17 consecrating] 'consecrat' *inserted for del.* 'adop' *interl. above del.* 'impor' *which follows del.* 'perpe' |

158.17-18 ambiguity?] MS *reads* 'confusion?'; *question mark inserted before del.* 'into philosophys?'

158.18 ¹call the] *above del.* 'stick to reality as the'

††158.18 ʌreality,ʌ] *interl. w. caret*

158.18 ²call] *follows del.* 'stick to' *above del.* 'call truth'

158.19 ¹cognized] *precedes del.* ', it seems to me'

158.22 this] *follows del.* 'these two'

158.24 that] *follows del.* 'then' *and precedes del.* 'I'

158.26 terms] *follows del.* 'cor'

158.27 as . . . are,] *interl. w. caret*

158.28,29 ¹wherever] 'ver' *added*

158.28 (*twice*) conceivable] *initial* 'in' *inserted and del.*

158.29 ²knowledge] *above del.* 'either'

158.30 truth] MS 'thruth.' *altered from* 'the ['ruth' *over* 'e']'; *precedes del.* 'other'

158.30 Therefore] *follows del.* 'What exists then' *and precedes del.* 'I say,'

158.30 you] *precedes del.* 'asks me whether there be truth of unknown planetary events, *and I reply no, I mean [*w. caret above del.* 'I ['say' *del.*] reply'] no actual truth, *and [*interl.*] *perhaps no possible truth, because [*inserted w. guideline*]* ['possibly' *del.*] no ['possible' *del. with* 'ble' *over* 'tive'] knowledge possible on [*above del.* 'and because no knower with ideas'] *the conditions that obtain. [*inserted for del.* '& their workings.'] But truth conceivable there is, *for knowledge. ['of' *del.*] [*above del.* 'for such a knower'] is conceivable. *of such events, [*w. caret preceding del.* 'So much for the first horn. Nor does the second horn trouble me.'] So when you try to impale me on your second horn, I think of truth as *as abstractly [*interl. w. caret*] conceivable *or virtual. [*w. caret above del.* 'and side'] *I then [*inserted w. caret*] with common sense, and say that even of antediluvian events ['this' *del.*] truth *virtually exists [*above del.* 'is conceivable'] in the shape of ['an account' *del. above del.* 'something that a'] the [*above del.* 'already a'] determinate account which a witness would have to give, were such a witness to ['exist.' *del.*] be brought into existence. [¶] Do not these distinctions release *me [*inserted*] from the dilemma | [*fol.* 15 *head*] word truth, as you use it, and it seems to *me that you [*above del.* 'me'] ['to' *del.*] ought to *abandon your own essentially vague position, & [*interl.*

w. caret] come round to the pragmatist view.'

158.32 by hypothesis] *interl. w. caret*

††158.33 or virtual] *interl. w. caret*

158.33 exist,] MS 'exist, however,' *in which comma following* 'however' *alt. from semicolon*

158.35 in] *follows del.* 'inconceivable'

158.35 nature] *altered from* 'notion'

158.36 that] *follows del.* 'being known like an'

159.1 truth] *follows* 'the' *interl. w. caret; precedes* 'in question' *interl. w. caret*

159.2 possibility] *follows del.* 'conceivability'

159.4 rightly] *interl. w. caret*

159.4-5 embarrassment?] *question mark over comma*

159.5 might] *above del.* 'would'

†159.7-8 avaunt . . . sophistry!] *w. caret above del.* 'never!'; *precedes* 'with your low particulars.' *inserted following del.* 'Let me alone then' *above del.* 'Cease then'

159.8 Truth . . . and] *inserted for del.* 'Truth is truth, *and never will I surrender. [*above del.* 'and exists absolutely.'] You will never get me to subscribe to your *sophistries. ['ries' *over doubtful* 'ication'; *above del.* 'abominable'] fooling [*del. above del.* 'sophistries.'] Even though I cannot articulately tell you what *truth [*w. caret above del.* 'it'] *would [*interl. w. caret*] *consist [*final* 's' *del.*] in,'

††159.8 never shall I] *inserted for del.* '[*begin indep. del.*] had it [*above del.* 'as'] abstraction [*above del.* 'detachment'] *were there [*above del.* 'from any'] [*end indep. del.*] no [*inserted*] conceivable know-| *never [*above del.* ' | er, I'] shall ['never admit its dependence allow that it depends on a knower for its existence ['&' *del.*] conception' *del.*] the *notion [*above del.* 'concept'] of it depends on that of such a knower. *Truth is ['truth,' *del.*] just [*w. caret above del.* 'The concept of it is an'] ['an' *interl. w. caret and del.*] 'inva' *del. above del.* 'absolute'] *truth, and I [*above del.*

'concept. I will'] ['refuse to' *inserted and del. above del.* 'not']'

159.9 by] *precedes* 'warping its nature in the way' *which is above del.* 'giving an account of it in in lower terms of *such [interl. w. caret]* low particulars as'

159.9 way] *interl.*

159.12 so] *follows del.* '['But' *del.*] Nor do I wish to, for I can see no practical advantage in weaning you from your persuasion.'

159.13 conception.] MS 'conception of truth.' *follows* 'own inexplicable' *interl. w. caret and precedes del.* 'as something absolute and absolutely precious. It may'

†159.13-14 Perhaps . . . will] 'must' *above del.* 'shall'

159.13 Perhaps] *precedes del.* 'when

they experience the beneficent workings of the pragmatist method they will'

159.14 will] MS 'may' *above del.* 'will'

159.14 up] *interl. w. caret*

159.16 Perhaps they] *above del.* 'and'; *period added after preceding* 'method' *without deleting original comma*

159.16 wonder] *follows del.* 'some day' *and precedes del. inserted* 'some day'

†159.16-17 so . . . an] *follows del.* 'the'; 'harmless an' *above del.* 'simple a thing as the pragmatist'

159.17 account] *follows del. inserted* 'may'

159.17 as mine] *interl. w. caret*

159.17 have] *follows del.* 'possibly'; *precedes del.* 'met [above del.* 'excited'] with [*inserted*] such opp a violent opposition'

Deleted Versos in Chapter XV Manuscript

[*del. fol.* 5^v *is an earlier draft of text* 154.1-21 *continued on del. fol.* 6^v *for* 154.21-155.3, 155.10-16] '[*fol.* 5^v] Probably the *idea that works as the [*interl. w. caret*] last residual stumbling block in the minds of most anti pragmatists is [*del. false start* 'som' *above del.* 'a thought'] of the following kind. [¶] Assume, hypothetically, they will say, that there is a certain real state of facts *somewhere [*interl. w. caret*] in the universe, concerning which the question may be asked: *Shall ['S' *over* 's'] the truth about it ever be known, or not? *Suppose ['S' *over* 's'; *follows del.* 'And'] *we leave [*above del.* 'the answer to be that (the world being finitely what it is, and'] [*initial paren del.*] the hypothesis of an omniscient absolute ['to be' *interl. w. caret and del. before del.* 'left'] out of the discussion [*final paren del.*] and [*inserted*] that [*inserted below interl.* '['suppose the' *del.*] answer ['to be' *del.*]'] the truth never shall be known to any actual knower that exists or shall exist. [¶] Now, the ['objector' *del.*] anti-pragmatists will probably continue, this *supposition [*interl. w. caret*] puts the pragmatist in a tight place, for he must *then [*precedes del. interl.* 'either' *and above del.* 'either'] say [*precedes inserted del.* 'either'] either [*inserted*] that ['the truth exists' *del.*] there *is* a truth about the state of facts in question, ['which unfortunately' *inserted and del. below del.* 'but that it unfor'] | [*fol.* 6^v] or that there is no truth. If he *says [*final 's' above del.* 's'] there is a truth, *he surrenders his whole case, for [*interl. w. caret; precedes del.* 'thus, since' *which is above del.* 'since'] by the hypothesis there *is no knower of it, and consequently [*w. caret above del.* 'are'; 'and' *follows del.* 'and'] no ideas or workings to constitute *it, [*comma del. then inserted*] *as his theory requires. [*above del.* 'in his mind, the pragmatist surrenders his whole case.'] If on the other hand, he *says [*inserted for inserted del.* 'allows'] that [*above del.* 'say'] *since there are no [*above del.* 'in the absence of'] actual ideas & workings, *there is *no* truth, [*w. caret and moved by guideline; originally followed* 'that'] he flies in the face of common sense. Common sense *believes [*above del.* 'demands'] that every state of facts is *in the nature of things [*interl. w.*

caret] susceptible of statement in some *possible [*interl. w. caret*] kind of a proposition, even tho in point of fact the proposition may never be formulated by
anybody. There must be innumerable *past [*interl. w. caret*] facts ['now' *del.*]
['concerning the' *del.*] in the history of our planet which *neither [*above del.*
'never'] have been ['or' *del.*] nor ever will be formulated, yet the nature of which
already in advance determines ['unequivocally' *del.*]'

[*del. fol.* 1ᵛ: *rejected original continuation of fol.* 5ᵛ, *earlier than fol.* 6ᵛ *revised version,
also rejected*] 'but that neither ideas nor workings constitute it, ['or he mus' *del.*]
—[*interl. w. caret*] which would *amount to ['practically' *del.*] surrendering [*w.
caret above del.* 'be to give up his'] his [*inserted*] whole theory; or he must say that
in the absence of ideas *or [*above del.* 'and'] workings, there ['can b' *del.*] *is *no
[*final* 't' *del.*] truth about these facts, and thus paradoxically fly in the face of
common sense. *For common sense of course [*w. caret above del.* 'What'] demands
that *for every real [*interl. following del.* 'a real' *above del.* 'if there be a ['fact'
del.] real'] state of facts ['exists' *del. above del.* 'at all'] there must ['be some ['possible' *del.*] statement possible' *del.*] in the nature of things be a true account
possible, even though no one should ever be enabled actually to give it.'

[*del. fol.* 13ᵛ: *original of revised fol.* 11 'name . . . know' (157.28-158.3)] '[*begin
indep. del.*] name for the fact that if the event ever should get known, *the [*altered
from* 'there'] *nature of the knowledge is [*above del.* 'is something in its nature
already that'] already ['in advance *is sure helps to, [*interl. w. caret*]' del.*] *to
some degree ['pre' *del.*] determined [*above del.* 'determine [*final* 's' *del.*] which
[*interl. w. caret and del.*] the knowledge shall be.'] *in advance. [*inserted*] The truth
that precedes actual knowledge is the *character ['h' *over* 'a'] ['(so far as the
*sole [*interl. w. caret*] nature of the ['nature of the' *del.*] object already determines
it)' *del.*] of whatever knowledge there may be *in posse*. Its status is the status of
*all [*above del.* 'the'] possibles. [*period inserted*] ['in general, whatever that may be'
del.] For me *possibility [*above del.* 'this' *which was inserted for del.* 'it'] is no third
estate of *present [*w. caret moved from following interl. and del.* 'actual'] being, *it
is only ['whatever' *del.*] *a name for the [*inserted*] present [*above del.* 'but a set of
actual'] conditions ['there may be, are exists' *w. caret and del.*] of future being. The
future being is a knower with his ideas & their workings; the present condition
*of his knowledge [*interl. w. caret*] is the actual *constitution ['s' *over* 'd'] of the
facts to be known. When he comes, his ideas and *the [*final* 'ir' *del.*] latter [*interl.
w. caret*] facts *working [*interl. w. caret*] together ['will determine the truth's
['character' *del.*] nature.' *del.*] [*end indep. del.*] This ['is all' *del.*] conception seems
to cover all that you can possibly mean when you say that truth pre exists to the
knowledge of it. It is that ['con' *del.*] knowledge considered ['under' *del.*] under
the form of possibility merely.'

Word-Division

The following is a list of actual or possible hyphenated compounds divided at the end of the line in the copy-text (I) but which were not confirmed in their forms as printed in the present edition either because the book text did not derive from a journal or manuscript or else because the source (whether journal or manuscript) also broke the compounds at the end of a line and so was not evidential. The latter group are distinguished by prefixed asterisks. In a sense, then, the hyphenation, or the non-hyphenation of possible compounds, in the present list is in the nature of editorial emendation. When the compounds were divided in the copy-text at the ends of lines but their probable form was evidenced in the source, this edition prints the reading of the source (unless emended by record) and no list is provided here.

4.26	turning-point	*127.3	general-utility
95.15	-as-ness	*130.30	sense-objects
95.36	anti-pragmatist	*156.23	-and-so
*110.26	storage-vault		

The following is a list of words divided at the ends of lines in the present edition but which represent authentic hyphenated compounds as found within the lines of the copy-text (I). Except for this list, all other hyphenations at the ends of lines in the present edition are the modern printer's and are not hyphenated forms in the copy-text.

6.15;131.9;147.24	anti-|pragmatists	79.26	*space-*|relations
31.5	matters-|of-	81.33	hocus-|pocus
48.8	self-|stultification	83.34	one-|sidedness
48.25;71.11	anti-|humanists	85.26	experience-|continuum
51.6	copy-|theory	92.36	truth-|relation
61.8	self-|transcending	120.13	-one-|relation
66.15	thought-|paths	132.24	-for-|him
66.36	non-|substitutional	151.18	that-|Cæsar-
69.14,16	self-|transcendency	159.7	hair-|splitting
69.20	self-|transcendent		

The following are actual or possible hyphenated compounds broken at the end of the line in both the copy-text (I) and in the present edition.

71.34	Self-|realization (*i.e.,* Self-realization)	
107.10	truth-|satisfaction (*i.e.,* truth-satisfaction)	

Appendixes

Appendix I

Abstract of "The Knowing of Things Together"

James's abstract in the *Psychological Review*, 2 (March 1895), 152–153, of his presidential address to the American Psychological Association on December 27, 1894, at Princeton University, printed as "The Knowing of Things Together" in the *Psychological Review*, 2 (March 1895), 105–124. Chapter II, "The Tigers in India," in *The Meaning of Truth* is an extract from pages 107–110 of the article. The abstract, subscribed Author's Summary, was reprinted without substantive change in the *Philosophical Review*, 4 (May 1895), 336–337.

Abstracts of Papers.

(1.) *The Knowing of Things Together.*
Address by the President,
Prof. WILLIAM JAMES, Harvard University.

The synthetic unity of consciousness is one of the great dividing questions in the philosophy of mind. We know things singly through as many distinct mental states. But on another occasion we may know the same things together through one state. The problem is as to the relation of the previous many states to the later one state. It will not do to make the mere statement of this problem incidentally involve a particular solution, as we should if we formulated the fact to be explained as *the combination of many states of mind into one*. The fact presents itself, in the first instance, *as the knowing of many things together*, and it is in those terms that the solution must be approached.

In the first place, *what is knowing?* 1. *Conceptual* knowing is an external relation between a state of mind and remote objects. If the state of mind, through a context of associates which the world supplies, leads to the objects smoothly and terminates there, we say it knows them. 2. *Intuitive* knowing is the identity of what, taken in one world-context, we call mental content and in another object. In neither 1 nor 2 is there involved any mysterious self-transcendency or presence in absence. 3. This mystery does, however, seem involved in *the relation between the parts of a mental content itself*. In the minimum real state of consciousness, that of the *passing moment*, past and present are known at once. In desire, memory, etc., earlier and later elements are directly felt to *call for* or *fulfil* each other, and without this sense of mutuality in their parts, such states do not exist. Here is presence in absence; here knowing together; here the original prototype of what we *mean* by knowledge. This ultimate synthetic nature of the smallest real phenomenon of consciousness can neither be explained nor circumvented.

We can only trace the particular conditions by which particular contents come thus to figure with all their parts at once in consciousness. Several attempts were then briefly passed in review. Mere synchronical sense-impression is not a sufficient condition. An additional inner *event* is required. The event has been described: *physiologically* as 1) 'attention;' as 2) ideational processes added to the sensorial processes, the latter giving unity, the former manyness; as 3) motor synergy of processes; *psychologically* as 4) the thinking of relations between the parts of the content-object; as 5) the relating of each part to the self; *spiritually* as 6) an act of the soul; *transcendentally* as 7) the diminution (by unknown causes, possibly physiological) of the obstruction or limitation which the organism imposes on the natural knowing-of-all-things-together by an Absolute Mind. For transcendentalism the problem is, 'How are things known separately at all?'

The speaker dealt with these opinions critically, not espousing either one himself. He concluded by abandoning the attempt made in his Principles of Psychology to formulate mental states as integers, and to refer all plurality to the objects known by them. Practically, the metaphysical view cannot be excluded from psychology-books. 'Contents' have parts, because in intuitive knowledge contents and objects are identical; and Psychology, even as a 'natural science,' will find it easier to solve her problem of tracing the conditions that determine what objects shall be known together, by speaking of 'contents' as complex unities.

[The address is printed in full in the *Psychological Review* for March, 1895.]

Appendix II

Abstract of "The Meaning of the Word Truth"

James's abstract in the *Philosophical Review*, 17 (March 1908), 180–181, of his paper before the American Philosophical Association meeting at Cornell University on December 27–28, 1907, printed as "The Meaning of the Word Truth" in a privately issued pamphlet, then as "The Meaning of the Word 'Truth' " in *Mind*, n.s. 17 (July 1908), 455–456, and finally as Chapter IX in *The Meaning of Truth* in revised form. The *Review* title, "The Meaning and Criterion of Truth," refers not to James's paper but to the series of abstracts of papers on the subject, of which his is the first printed.

Discussion: The Meaning and Criterion of Truth.
WILLIAM JAMES.

My account of truth is realistic, and follows the epistemological dualism of common sense. Suppose I say to you: "The thing exists,"—is that true, or not? How can you tell? Not till my statement has unfolded its meaning farther is it determined as being true, false, or irrelevant to reality altogether. But if now you ask, "What thing?" and I reply "a desk"; if you ask "where?" and I point to a place; if you ask, "Does it exist materially or only in imagination?" and I say "materially"; if, moreover, I say, "I mean *that* desk," and then grasp and shake a desk which you see just as I have described it, you are willing to call my statement true. But you and I are commutable here; we can exchange places; and as you go bail for my desk, so I can go bail for yours. This notion of a reality independent of either one of us, taken from ordinary social experience, lies at the base of the pragmatist definition of truth. With some such reality any statement, to be accounted 'true,' must 'agree.' Pragmatists explain this last term as meaning certain actual or potential 'workings.' Thus, for my statement, "The thing exists," to be true of a determinate reality, it must lead me to shake *your* desk, it must explain itself by terms that suggest *that* desk to your mind, etc. Only thus does it 'agree' with *that* reality, and give me the satisfaction of your approval. A determinate *reference* and some sort of satisfactory *adaptation* are thus constituent elements in the definition of any statement as 'true.'

And you can't get at the notion of either 'reference' or 'adaptation' except through the notion of 'workings.' *That* the 'thing' is, *what* it is, and *which* it is (of all the possible things with that *what*) are points determinable only by the pragmatic method. The *which* means our pointing to a locus; the *what* means choice on our part of an essential aspect to apperceive the thing by (and this is always relative to what Dewey calls our 'situation'); and the *that* means our assumption of the attitude of belief, the reality-recognizing attitude. Surely these workings are indispensable to constitute the notion of what 'true' means as applied to a statement. Surely anything less is insufficient.

Our critics nevertheless call the workings inessential, and consider that statements are, as it were, *born* true, each of its own object, much as the Count of Chambord was supposed to be born King of France, though he never exercised regal functions,—no need of functioning in either case! Pragmatism insists, on the contrary, that statements are true thus statically only by courtesy; they practically pass for true; but you can't *define* the particular truth of any one of them without referring to its functional results.

Appendix III

W. James's Statement

The following early version of Chapter X, "The Existence of Julius Cæsar," offers a transcript of the typescript represented by TMs[1] (University of Chicago Library) ribbon copy, and TMs[2] (Stanford University Library) carbon, in an eclectic text combining the autograph revisions of both documents. In the Alterations list the noted revisions are in ink unless otherwise specified. The x'd-out revisions that represent variant text have been recorded, but simple typed corrections of mechanical error made *currente calamo* have not; nor are the handwritten simple corrections of typing slips noted when alteration of intention was not present. The typewriter had no right-hand margin release, with the result that occasionally several letters were omitted at the ends of lines and had to be supplied by hand; these mechanical corrections are also ignored. When no indication is given of the source of the alteration, both type-scripts agree.

W. James's Statement.

My account of truth is purely logical and relates to its definition only. I contend that you cannot tell what the *word 'true' means*, as applied to a statement, without invoking the concept of the statement's 'workings'.

Assume, to fix our ideas, a universe composed of two facts only: imperial Caesar dead & turned to clay, & me, saying "Caesar really existed". Most persons would naively & uncritically deem 'truth' to be thereby uttered, & say that by a sort of *actio in distans* my statement had taken direct cognitive hold of the other fact.

But have my words necessarily denoted *that* Caesar? or connoted *his* attributes? To fill out the complete measure of what the epithet 'true' may ideally mean, my thought ought to bear a fully determinate 'one-to-one relation' to its own particular object. In the ultra-simple universe imagined, reference is left indeterminate; the conditions of truth thus seem incomplete: that universe must be enlarged.

Transcendentalists enlarge it by invoking an absolute mind which, as it owns all the facts, can sovereignly correlate them. If it intends that my statement *shall* refer to that identical Caesar & that the attributes I have in mind shall mean his attributes, that intention suffices to make it true; I, in turn, enlarge the universe by admitting finite intermediaries between the two original facts. Caesar *had*, & my statement *has*, effects; and, if these effects in any way run together, a concrete medium & bottom is provided for incorporating the determinate cognitive relation, which as a pure *actio in distans* seemed to float too vaguely & to be un-intelligible.

The real Caesar, for example, wrote a real manuscript of which I see a real reprint & say "the Caesar I mean is the author of *that*". The workings of my

~~W. JAMES'S STATEMENT~~
cc

My aƙount of truth is purely logical and relates to its definition
on
ly. I contend that you cannot tell what the word 'tru^eth' means, as applied to a statement, without invoking the concept of the statement's we
'workings'.

imperial
Assume, to fix our ideas, a universe composed of (only) two facts:
ᴧ Caesar dead & turned to clay, & me, saying "Caesar really existed". Most
Say hold
persons would naively deem 'truth' to be thereby uttered, & ~~say~~ that by a
hold
sort of <u>actio in distans</u> my statement had taken direct cognitive ᴧ of the
other fact.

But have my words neceſessarily denoted <u>that</u> Caesar? ⅄ or connoted <u>his</u> attributes? To fill out the complete measure of what the ~~word~~ epithet
c e'
tru<s>th</s> may ideally mean, my thought ought to bear a fully determinate ratza
'one-to-one relation' to its own particular object. In the ultra-simple v
universe imagined, t̶h̶e̶ reference is left indeterminate; the conditions of
at
truth thus seem incomplete; the universe must be enlarged.

Transcendentalists enlarge it by invoking an absolute mind which,
If it
as it owns all the facts, can sovereignly correlate them. ⅄ intends that
my statement <u>shall</u> refer to that identical Caesar & that the attributes
mean statute
I have in mind shall ~~be~~ his attributes, that ~~fact~~ is enough.

Page 1 (reduced) of W. James's Statement (University of Chicago Copy)

thought thus determine more fully both its denotative & its connotative significance. It now defines itself as having been neither irrelevant to the real Caesar
nor false in what it suggests. The absolute mind, seeing me thus working towards
Caesar thru the cosmic intermediaries, might well say: "Such workings only
specify in detail what I myself meant by the statement being true. I decree the
cognitive relation between the two original facts to mean that just that kind of
concrete chain is possible."

The chain involves facts prior to the statement the logical conditions of whose
'truth' we are defining, & facts subsequent to it; and this circumstance, coupled
with the vulgar employment of the terms truth & fact as synonyms, has laid my
account open to misapprehension. "How", it is confusedly asked, "can Caesar's
existence, a truth already 2000 years old, depend for its truth on anything about
to happen now? How can my acknowledgment of it be *made* true by the acknowledgment's own effects? The effects may indeed confirm my belief, but the belief
was made true already by the fact that Caesar really did exist."

Be it so!—but then distinguish between true as being positively & completely
so determined, & true as being so only 'practically' & by courtesy, because not
definable as *un*true or irrelevant. Remember also that Caesar's having existed
in fact may make a present statement false or irrelevant as well as it may make
it true, & that in neither case does it itself have to alter. It being given, whether
truth, untruth, or irrelevancy shall be also given depends on something in the
statement itself. What 'pragmatism' contends for is that you cannot *adequately
define that something* if you leave the notion of the statement's 'workings' wholly
out of your account.

People, mixing history with the purely logical inquiry, & falling back upon
inveterate habits of speech, will still say: "The statement is true anyhow, true in
advance, born true, true apart from any of its workings, & the workings are
themselves determined by that prior truth." This notion of an inherent truth,
meaning a truth with only a part of the constituents of its full definition realized
in fact, is indispensable in practical life. Millions of statements thus *pass* for true,
for one that lives up to what the full concept implies.

Would it satisfy the repudiators of the fuller concept if we let them keep the
word 'true' for what they stickle for exclusively, namely the fulfilment of the
more preliminary & objective conditions of the cognitive relation?—so that for
any words about "Caesar" to be 'true' in that sense it would then suffice for a
real Caesar to have existed in point of fact?

The more completely determined notion, for which I and Mr. Schiller in our
turn stickle, might then be distinguished from 'truth', in that more limited sense,
by the name of 'truthfulness', that being a word with a more concrete & actively
functional sound.

The question is almost purely academic; for in actual life the 'true' & the
'truthful' would usually denote the same body of actual human statements or
beliefs. Even now none of the *facts* which either party emphasizes has ever been
questioned by the other party, & the quarrel might have the bottom knocked

out of it altogether, so far as it relates only to truth's definition, by the invention of this or some other new pair of technical terms.

The friends of 'truth' would still have to admit, however, that our more concrete notion of 'truthfulness' envelopes the whole of their own more abstract notion, & defines in the only adequate fashion what perfect knowledge is.

Alterations in the Typescripts

293.13   W. James's Statement.]
del. TMs[1]

293.15   word 'true' means] *underline
and quotes added;* 'true' *alt. from*
'truth'

293.15   statement,] *comma added*

293.17   only] *moved from before* 'two'

293.17   imperial] *interl. w. caret in
pencil* TMs[1] (*carbon* TMs[2])

293.19   & uncritically] TMs[2] *interl.
in pencil*

293.19   say] *interl. before interl.* 'hold'
above del. 'say'

293.20   hold] *typed interline*

293.22   or] *follows* 'A' *del. in pencil*
TMs[1] (*carbon* TMs[2])

293.23   epithet] *inserted for del.* 'word'
TMs[1] *pencil* (*carbon* TMs[2])

293.23   'true'] *alt. from* 'truth' *in
pencil* TMs[1] (*carbon* TMs[2]); *quotes
added in pencil* TMs[1]

293.24   determinate] *followed by
x'd-out* 'rela'

293.25   imagined,] TMs[1] *comma added
and following* 'the' *del. in pencil*

293.26   that] *alt. from* 'the'; *preceding
colon alt. from semicolon both in
pencil* TMs[1] (*carbon* TMs[2])

293.28   which,] 'ch,' *in pencil* TMs[1]
(*carbon* TMs[2])

293.29   If it] *above del. underlined* 'It'

293.30   mean] *above del.* 'be'

293.31   attributes . . . true;] TMs[1–2]
add 'attributes, that fact is enough.'
TMs[1] *interl.* 'statute' *in pencil
above del.* 'fact'; TMs[2] *del. added*
'fact is enough.' *and interlines*
'intention suffices to make it true;'
*at head of next page typed paragraph
indention not alt. in* TMs[2]

293.31   , in turn,] TMs[1] *w. caret in
pencil* (TMs[2] *ink*)

293.31   the universe] *w. caret above*

del. 'it'

293.32   had] *underlined*

293.33   has,] *underlined and comma added*

293.34   incorporating] TMs[1] *w. caret
in pencil*

293.35   seemed] *alt. from* 'seems'

293.38   reprint∧] *comma del.*

293.38   workings] *above del.*
'consequences'

295.1-2   its denotative . . .
significance.] *alt. from* 'the
denotation & the connotation of
my statement.'

295.2   now] *interl. w. caret in pencil*
TMs[1] (*carbon* TMs[2])

295.2   having been] TMs[1] *interl. w.
caret in pencil*

295.3   false] *follows del.* 'as'

295.4   only] *above del.* 'are'

295.5   meant] 't' *interl. in pencil*
TMs[1] (*ink* TMs[2])

295.6   relation] *follows x'd-out*
'reference'

295.6   original . . . [1]that] *w. caret
above del.* 'terms to consist of'

295.7   is possible."] *added; preceding
period and double quotes del.*

295.8   facts] *typed interline; ink caret*

295.8   statement] 'at' *interl. w. caret
in pencil* TMs[1] (*carbon* TMs[2])

295.8   conditions] *above del.*
'determinants'

295.9   'truth'] TMs[2] *adds quotes*

295.9   it; and] *alt. from* 'it. But'

295.10   employment] *above del.* 'use'

295.10   synonyms,] *alt. from*
'synonymous,'

295.12   its] *precedes del.* 'present'

295.13-14   acknowledgment's]
apostrophe added

295.14   effects?] TMs[1] *adds question
mark; both add* 'ts'

295.14   indeed] *interl. w. caret*

295.14   my] *precedes del.* 'personal'
295.15   made] *interl. w. caret*
295.15   by] *interl. w. caret above del.*
'true *thru [typed above del.* 'true'
and del. in ink] the fact of Caesar
having really existed." thru'
295.16   Be] *preceded by del.* '[¶] Such
a confusion is natural but it ought
to disappear when we note that
the fact of Caesar's existence'
295.16   true] *single quotes del.*
295.16   being] TMs² *interl. w. caret*
295.17   as being so] TMs² *interl.*
w. caret
295.17   courtesy,] *comma added*
295.17   because] TMs² *interl. above*
del. 'as being'
295.18   definable as] TMs² *w. caret*
after del. interl. 'yet' *above del.*
'functionally'
295.18   untrue] 'un' *underlined*; TMs²
added comma del.
295.20   in] *alt. from* 'it'
295.20   have to] *interl. w. caret*
295.21   shall] *interl. w. caret*
295.22   What] *interl. w. caret*; 'p'
of 'pragmatism' *reduced from* 'P'
295.22   for is] *interl. w. caret*
295.22   adequately] *above del.* 'wholly';
following italic words underlined
295.23   statement's] *apostrophe added*
295.26   habits] *follows del.* 'upo'
TMs² *(undel.* TMs¹)
295.27   born true,] TMs¹ *interl. w.*
caret
295.28   themselves] *interl. w. caret*
295.29   the] *follows del.* 'its'
295.30   *pass] underlined*
295.30   true,] *comma added*
295.31   what] *interl. w. caret*
295.31   implies.] *added after del. period*
295.32   fuller concept] *w. caret*

TMs¹ *(no caret* TMs²*) above del.*
'latter'
295.34   preliminary] *precedes del.*
'conditions'
295.34   cognitive] *follows del.* 'full'
295.34   relation?—] *question mark*
and dash w. caret above del. comma
295.35   any words] TMs¹ 'any' *in*
ink above del. 'my', *then* 'words' *in*
pencil above del. 'statement'
295.35   "Caesar"] TMs¹ *quotes added*
295.35   'true'] *quotes added*
295.35   a] TMs¹ *above del.* 'the'
295.36   fact?] *question mark follows*
del. question mark
295.37-38   notion, . . . stickle,]
commas added
295.38   distinguishedʌ] TMs¹ *comma*
added and del.
295.38   'truth',] *quotes and comma*
added
295.38   more limited] *w. caret above*
del. 'specific'
295.39-40   actively functional]
TMs² *hyphen del.*
295.43   *facts]* TMs¹ *underlined*
295.44   questioned] TMs¹ *in pencil*
above del. 'denied'; TMs¹⁻² *type* 'has
ever been' *w. ink caret above ink*
del. 'is'
296.1   relates] TMs¹ *alt. from* 'related'
296.3   ¶The] *continuous text marked*
off by ¶ *sign and vertical stroke*
296.3   still] *interl. above del.* 'then'
296.3   our] *inserted for del.* 'the'
296.4   'truthfulness'] *quotes added*
296.4   the whole of] TMs¹ *interl.*
w. caret
296.5   in . . . fashion] TMs¹ *interl.*
above del. 'more' *and altered*
'adequately'
296.5+   *short rule] added*

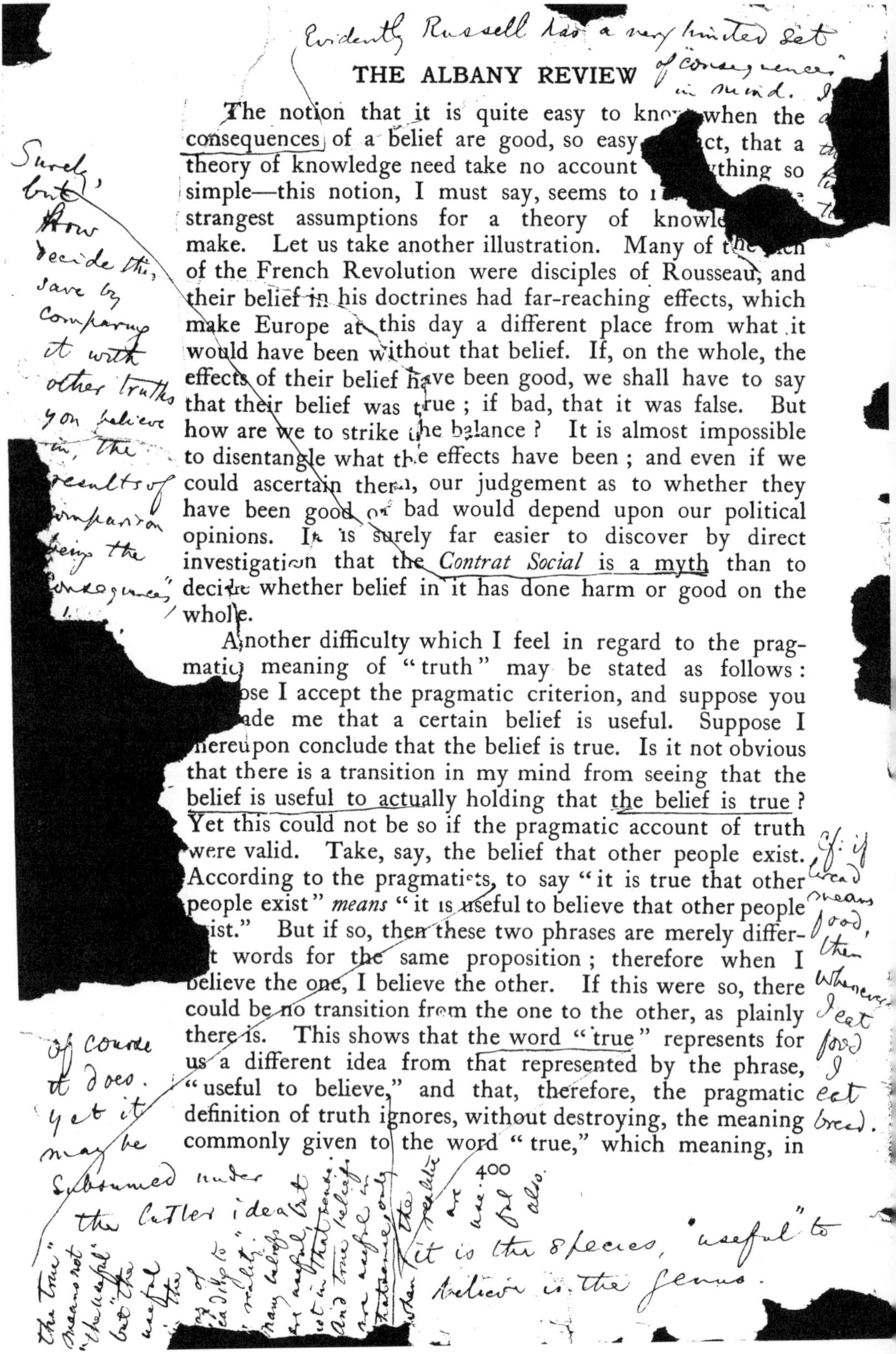

The notion that it is quite easy to know when the consequences of a belief are good, so easy ⟨in fa⟩ct, that a theory of knowledge need take no account ⟨of any⟩thing so simple—this notion, I must say, seems to ⟨me one of the⟩ strangest assumptions for a theory of knowl⟨edge to⟩ make. Let us take another illustration. Many of t⟨he men⟩ of the French Revolution were disciples of Rousseau, and their belief in his doctrines had far-reaching effects, which make Europe at this day a different place from what it would have been without that belief. If, on the whole, the effects of their belief have been good, we shall have to say that their belief was true; if bad, that it was false. But how are we to strike the balance? It is almost impossible to disentangle what the effects have been; and even if we could ascertain them, our judgement as to whether they have been good or bad would depend upon our political opinions. It is surely far easier to discover by direct investigation that the *Contrat Social* is a myth than to decide whether belief in it has done harm or good on the whole.

Another difficulty which I feel in regard to the pragmatic meaning of "truth" may be stated as follows: ⟨Suppo⟩se I accept the pragmatic criterion, and suppose you ⟨persu⟩ade me that a certain belief is useful. Suppose I thereupon conclude that the belief is true. Is it not obvious that there is a transition in my mind from seeing that the belief is useful to actually holding that the belief is true? Yet this could not be so if the pragmatic account of truth were valid. Take, say, the belief that other people exist. According to the pragmatists, to say "it is true that other people exist" *means* "it is useful to believe that other people ⟨ex⟩ist." But if so, then these two phrases are merely differ⟨en⟩t words for the same proposition; therefore when I believe the one, I believe the other. If this were so, there could be no transition from the one to the other, as plainly there is. This shows that the word "true" represents for us a different idea from that represented by the phrase, "useful to believe," and that, therefore, the pragmatic definition of truth ignores, without destroying, the meaning commonly given to the word "true," which meaning, in

400

Handwritten marginalia:

Evidently Russell had a very limited set of consequences in mind. I...

Surely, but how decide this, save by comparing it with other truths you believe in, the results of comparison being the consequences.

Of: if useful mean good, then Whenever I eat food, I eat bread.

Of course it does. Yet it may be subsumed under the "other ideas..." the true" means not "the useful" but the useful ... [it] may always, but ... it in that sense, and true belief ... refer only [to] the reality ... it is the species, "useful" to believe is the genus.

Page 400 (reduced) of "Transatlantic 'Truth'" (McMaster University Copy)

Appendix IV

Annotations in Bertrand Russell's "Transatlantic 'Truth'"

Several letters between James and Bertrand Russell, and two different sets of James's annotations in offprints of Russell's review of *Pragmatism* that appeared as "Transatlantic 'Truth' " in the *Albany Review*, 2 (January, 1908), 393–410, combine with Russell's later "Pragmatism," *Edinburgh Review*, 209 (April 1909), 363–388, to form a background for James's answer and addendum in Chapter XIV, "Two English Critics."

During the summer of 1908, evidently, James wrote an undated letter from Sunbury Lodge, 68 Banbury Road, Oxford, that appears to be a summary of his position addressed to Russell, perhaps at Russell's request. The typed transcript is preserved in the Bertrand Russell Archives (710.051465) at McMaster University.

Sunday P.M.

Dear Russell,

In a nutshell my opinion is this: that instead of being one universal relation sui generis called "truth" between any reality and an idea, there are a host of particular relations varying according to special circumstances and constituted by the manner of "working" or "leading" of the idea through the surrounding experiences of which both the idea and the reality are part.

It is *particularly* of these experiences that I have always had in mind when I have called the workings "Practical", for only with particulars and concretes do we have particular relations. One ought thus *to be able to define empirically* what the truth-relation *consists in* in every instance, and one will probably find it different in most instances.

The ordinary conception makes the same abstract thing in every possible instance. Direct verification by sensible presence is one kind of leading. Where no kind of verification is possible to us it seems to me that the question of our idea being true is irrelevant, except as meaning accord with some enveloping authority who *has* the verification which we are cut off from, and our accord with that observer has itself to be defined pragmatically. I imagine that these views are Schiller's.

Truly yours,
Wm. James

In the autumn, on stationery of the Charing Cross Hotel, London, James wrote again (McMaster 710.151462):

Oct 4 1908

Dear Russell,

I was at Oxford for 3 days last week, & hoped until the last day, when

I found it was going to be quite impossible, to drive out and see you & Mrs. Russell. It was squeezed out by other necessities. I saw Schiller and spent a night at McDougall's most pleasantly. I would fain have spent a night with you, to make up for the rather blunt way in which I declined your invitation last June. I was done-up then, and am comparatively fresh now, but a daughter and a son have come over since then and, as ['is' *del.*] usual, their needs have seemed more urgent than their parent's, so the time has proved too short for many things that I should have liked to accomplish. The son remains at Oxford, in A. L. Smith's family (tutor at Balliol). The rest of us sail on the Saxonia on Tuesday.

One of the first things I am going to do after I get back to my own library is to re-read the Chap. on Truth in your Phil. of M., which I haven't looked at since it *appeared ['ed' *above del.* 'd']. I want to get a better grasp of it than you have of ['th' *del.*] my theory! Your remarks on Dewey (sharp as your formulation is!) in the last Hibbert shows that you haven't yet ['quite caught on!' *del.*] grasped the thing broadly enough. My dying words to you are "Say good-by to mathematical logic if you wish to preserve your relations with concrete realities!" I have just had this morning a 3-hour conversation with Bergson, which possibly may account for this ejaculation! Best regards to you both, in which my wife would join, were she here.

Truly yours, Wm James

To this, Russell responded from Bagley Wood, Oxford (Harvard bMS Am 1092, Russell [813]):

Nov. 6. 1908

Dear Professor James

Your kind letter from London reached me too late to be answered before you sailed, or I should have written at once. I am sorry not to have seen you while you were back in Oxford.

I fear you won't find much about 'Truth' in my Principles of Mathematics. I am sorry I have still failed to understand Pragmatism; it is not for want of serious endeavour, but I suppose we are all born with certain mental blindnesses.

As for the advice to say goodbye to mathematical logic if I wish to preserve my relations with concrete realities, I am not wholly inclined to dispute its wisdom. But I should push it farther, & say that it would be well to give up all philosophy, & abandon the student's life altogether. Ten days of standing for Parliament gave me more relations with concrete realities than a lifetime of thought. But on the whole, I think relations with concrete realities a barrier to understanding the general characteristics which different things have in common, & the general interests me more than the particular. I find the particular chiefly interesting when I can regard it as an "instance".

My wife is away, or she would join me in kind regards to yourself & Mrs. James.

Yours truly
Bertrand Russell.

From the same address Russell wrote in the spring of 1909, and in the course of the note seems to refer to the undated letter James had written from the Banbury Road (Harvard bMS Am 1092, Russell [814]):

April 27. '09

Dear Professor James

Very many thanks for the kind gift of your book on a "Pluralistic Universe", which I found today awaiting me on my return from a holiday (which was also a "moral holiday"). I shall enjoy it all the more from the fact that it will recall the pleasure I had in your visit to Oxford & in hearing your lectures.

I have just published an article on Pragmatism in the "Edinburgh", in which I have tried hard to avoid the misconceptions of which you made me aware last summer. I am permitting myself to send you a copy. If ever you have leisure & inclination to let me know wherein I still misunderstand your position, I shall be most grateful.

Yours very truly
Bertrand Russell.

James replied from 95 Irving Street, Cambridge, Massachusetts (McMaster 710. 051466):

May 14. 09

Dear Russell,

I have both your letter of April 27th. and the Edinburgh Review, which came this A.M. & for which thanks! I have read it *Spannung*, and admired, as always, your unparalleled dialectic dexterity and clearness of statement. But until you give some articulate account of your own of what truth in the *true* sense does mean, you must n't be astonisht if I don't come down. I am "sick and tired" at last of the very name of "truth," being engaged in saying adieu to the subject by putting my collected polemic writings on *it [*above del.* 'the subject'] through the press (including an *unpublisht [*interl.*] retort to your Transatlantic T.), and I am too lazy to try to go into the detail of showing that your *illustrations [*above del.* 'criticisms'] in this article don't work as you mean them to—it would only make complication more complicated still, if I did try, and be useless, for you would think I failed! It is better to keep simple—& the simplest thing is to challenge *you* to give the wonderful true meaning which escapes us. It is simpler also to say that your general social and ethical characterization of pragmatism

301

can be let pass—let us see how *prag, will [*above del.* 'it'] work [*final* 's' *del.*] out! Simplest is it to accuse your mathematical habits of leading you to treat *us* as the sort of abstractionists which your own colleagues are. For instance, your reduction to the absurd on pp. 382–4, etc: Abstractly, truth = what we wish. But no pragmatist ever makes the hegelian optimist conclusion you draw *for him, [*interl.*] because no pragmatist forgets that *concretely* our wish to square ourselves with hard *fact* may be irreconcileable with *our [*interl.*] other wishes. Your abstractionism comes out, it seems to me, very calamitously in the Will to believe criticisms. *My [*above del.* 'That whole'] doctrine deals *explicitly [*interl.*] with our concrete relations with a world where we can only get *probability* in cosmic matters, and where, concretely, belief is a variable of which the ['only' *del.*] willingness to act is the sign without being the measure (I mean that a very little more ['bl' *del.*] belief may let loose all the action possible). You treat me as one ignoring probabilities & treating of hypotheses for which there is *no* evidence! Your own confession of faith in that *Hand*-collection (I have lent *the book [*above del.* 'it'], & forget the *essay's [*interl.*] title) is an exquisite concrete instance of all that I justify in my W. to B. essay, and yet you turn and rend the latter!

It makes one despair of human "understanding" to find men on the whole as similar as you and myself—similar in our ideals *& purposes, [*interl.*] I mean,—so unable to get together in *our [*above del.* 'their'] formulas. No matter! Art is long! I am sending you, along with a recent "offprint," some pp. of a syllabus which I had printed several years ago for use in a course introductory to philosophy, here at Harvard. Possibly *they [*above del.* 'it'] may lead you to soften your animosity to the W. to Believe.

Of course I concede your unlimited dialectic superiority! But don't be satisfied with that alone! *True* truth is the only thing that gives *solid [*above del.* 'a glut of'] satisfaction, and the best thing about it is the definition which you refuse to give! Warm regards to you both, from yours very sincerely

Wm James

This part of the correspondence closes with Russell's reply from Oxford (Harvard bMS Am 1092, Russell [815]):

July 22. 1909

Dear Professor James

I have delayed answering your very kind letter of May 14 until I had had time to read your "Pluralistic Universe" with more attention than one can give in the middle of other work. I have now read it, with great interest & pleasure. Being a pluralist & an opponent of the Absolute, I find myself constantly in agreement with it. As for the points where I imagine myself in disagreement, it may be I over-estimate the difference & I will keep that a "live" hypothesis. With regard to religion, I notice one purely temperamental difference: that the first demand you make of your God is that you should be able to love him, whereas my first demand is that I should be able to worship him. I do not desire familiarity lest it should breed contempt.

"Dialectical dexterity" was not what I was chiefly aiming at in writing about pragmatism. I meant to give a fair statement of it, & a straightforward account of my reasons for not agreeing with it; but I see what you mean about the "prevalent abuse of abstraction", & if I ever write again on pragmatism I will be careful in that direction.

The pragmatic difference that pragmatism makes to me is that it encourages religious belief, & that I consider religious belief pernicious. I dare say this is a prejudice, but it has been fed by reflection on history & current politics. However, my reason for saying this is merely that I do not wish to pretend to be solely influenced by intellectual considerations in the matter.

With much gratitude for your friendliness, I remain

Yours very sincerely
Bertrand Russell.

Annotations in the Harvard Copy of "Transatlantic 'Truth' "

In the James Collection at Harvard University (WJ 500.5) is preserved a lightly annotated offprint of Russell's "Transatlantic 'Truth' " which the evidence suggests was the copy sent to James from Oxford by his graduate student Horace M. Kallen and returned to Kallen on February 12, 1908, 'with some marginal scribbling'. As early as August 6, 1907, when Kallen had received notification that he would be awarded an Oxford fellowship, James had promised to supplement the sum by a hundred dollars, which he paid on February 12, 1908, with the advice, "Spend it for luxuries!" Kallen became acquainted with Russell at Oxford and seemed to enjoy acting the role of intermediary. He must have seen Russell's "Transatlantic 'Truth' " in manuscript or in proof, for he wrote to Russell from London on January 16, 1908: "Prof. James, to whom I wrote some account of your paper on his book and of our subsequent conversations, sends me the enclosed remarks with the suggestion that I pass them on to you. I suspect that it will please him if you write to him about the position he takes in this paper. . . . In the paper I enclose, it does seem to me that James makes some unnecessary terminological concessions. I wonder what you will say to it?" (McMaster U.) In a letter from James to Kallen on February 12, "You don't mention my 'misunderstanding' paper, which I sent you. I hope you think it conducive to clearing up," indicates the strong probability that this was "The Pragmatist Account of Truth and Its Misunderstanders" printed in the *Philosophical Review*, 17 (January 1908), 1–17. This letter of February 12 starts: "I have to thank you for 2 letters, of which the 2nd came this morning along with Russell's article. I have already ordered a copy of the Albany from England, so I return your sheets with some marginal scribbling on them, which Russell may read if you think fit to show them to him. I thank you for sending them. R's article is splendidly written, but R. errs from failure to have grasped my central position. The only way to understand anything is to jump into its centre and work outwards." How this annotated offprint with James's initial reactions to the Russell attack was returned to Harvard is not recorded, but it is reasonable to assume that Kallen deposited it after James's death. No reference appears whether Kallen did in fact show the annotations to Russell. James's diary simply records on February 13, 1908, that he had annotated Russell's article and sent it to Kallen.

In the following transcript the first page-line reference is to "Transatlantic 'Truth'," *Albany Review*, 2 (January 1908), the initial publication; the second reference—in parentheses—is to the reprint of the article entitled "William James's Conception of Truth" in Bertrand Russell's *Philosophical Essays* (New York: Simon & Schuster [1966]). The passage that follows is drawn from "Transatlantic 'Truth'" and ordinarily includes the context of the more specific sentence or sentences on which James commented. A square bracket completes the quotation from Russell and is followed by James's marginal annotation headed by 'JAMES'. For typographical distinction of the two parts, the James annotations are printed in italic, his underlined words being reproduced in roman.

399.7–9 (118.12–13) We may thus sum up the philosophy in the following definition: "A truth is anything which it pays to believe."] JAMES: *The question being in every case whether it really* does *pay.*

399.9–12 (118.13–17) Now, if this definition is to be useful, . . . it must be possible to know that it pays to believe something without knowing anything that pragmatism would call a truth.] JAMES: *Can't it pay to believe in the pragmatist definition?*

399.34–37 (118.37–119.3) It is far easier . . . to settle the plain question of fact: "Have Popes been always infallible?" than to settle the question whether the effects of thinking them infallible are on the whole good.] JAMES: *The "pay" is not a mark, "easy to find" of the truth in a given instance. It is the essence, if the belief is true, and very hard to find in many cases.*

400.1–6 (119.7–11) The notion that it is quite easy to know when the consequences of a belief are good, so easy, in fact, that a theory of knowledge need take no account of anything so simple—this notion, I must say, seems to me one of the strangest assumptions for a theory of knowledge to make.] JAMES: *What other test did any man* ever *employ?*

400.17–20 (119.22–24) It is surely far easier to discover by direct investigation that the *Contrat Social* is a myth than to decide whether belief in it has done harm or good on the whole.] JAMES underlined 'direct investigation' and added a marginal exclamation point.

400.25–27 (119.29–31) Is it not obvious that there is a transition in my mind from seeing that the belief is useful to actually holding that the belief is true?] JAMES underlined 'seeing' and added *NB* in the margin.

400.30–32 (119.33–35) According to the pragmatists, to say "it is true that other people exist" *means* "it is useful to believe that other people exist."] JAMES added an arrowhead pointer in the margin.

400.32–34 (199.35–37) But if so, then these two phrases are merely different words for the same proposition; therefore when I believe the one, I believe the other.] JAMES added an exclamation point in the margin.

403.4–7 (122.14–17) Take the question whether other people exist. It seems perfectly possible to suppose that the hypothesis that they exist will always work, even if they do not in fact exist.] JAMES: *a discovery apparently on the non-existence of others.*

403.16–21 (122.25–31) For what I desire is not that the belief in solipsism should be false in the pragmatic sense, but that other people should in fact exist. And with the pragmatist's meaning of truth, these two do not necessarily go together. The belief in solipsism might be false even if I were the only person or thing in the universe.] JAMES marked the passage with a vertical stroke and *NB* in the margin.

403.36–38 (123.10–12) "Facts," they tell us, are neither true nor false, therefore truth cannot be concerned with them.] JAMES added an exclamation point in the margin.

407.27–34 (128.5–12) Belief, therefore, is a matter of degree. To speak of belief, disbelief, doubt, and suspense of judgement as the only possibilities is as if, from the writing on the thermometer, we were to suppose that blood heat, summer heat, temperate, and freezing were the only temperatures. There is a continuous gradation in belief, and the more firmly we believe anything, the less willing we are to abandon it in case of conflict.] JAMES: Good

Excerpts from two letters from James to Kallen provide some useful background to his opinion of Russell. The first comes in a letter dated January 26, 1908. After commenting on Kallen's description of G. E. Moore at a meeting of the Aristotelian Society, James continues: "I don't know what it is you may have been gaining from Russell, and I have read nothing of his or Moore's of late (except Moore's pretentious fiasco in the last Aristotelian proceedings). But as I remember the Moore-Russell-Meinong epistemology, it seems to me one great merit of my own to cut the ground so easily from under its diseased pedantries and complications. Those propositions or supposals which they make the exclusive vehicles of truth are mongrel curs that have no real place between realities on the one hand and beliefs on the other. The negative, disjunctive and hypothetic truths which they so conveniently express can all be perfectly well (so far as I see) be translated into relations between beliefs and positive realities. 'Propositions' are expressly divised for quibbling between realities & beliefs. They seem to have the objectivity of the one and the subjectivity of the other, and he who uses them can straddle as he likes, owing to the ambiguity of the word *that* which is essential to them. '*That* Caesar existed' is 'true,' sometimes means the *fact that* he existed is real, sometimes the *belief that* he existed is true. You can get no honest discussion out of such terms."

Appendix IV

In the letter of February 12, 1908, in which James included the annotated leaves of Russell's article that Kallen had sent him, he first disposes contemptuously of G. E. Moore and then turns to Russell: "[¶] As for Russell, I find fault with his insisting on the word 'useful' in the narrower sense (for so the reader will take it) to show how absurd I am in saying that the truth is what is 'expedient' or 'what pays.' Much truth *is* useful in the narrower sense, so is much falsehood; but much truth 'pays' without being 'useful' in *that* sense. A developed pragmatism will have to discriminate the various types of truth-making satisfactoriness. Our critics try to head us off from doing this by insisting *in limine* that we *shall* recognize no other kind than the economically or emotionally satisfactory. Then Russell, because I say that truth means 'satisfactory leading towards an object,' first equates 'the true' with 'the satisfactory' at large, then 'the satisfactory' with 'the useful,' and performs his reductio ad absurdum by the mathematical process of substitution, leaving all reference to the 'object' out!! The real way to refute me would be to offer a tenable and intelligible alternative—but this no critic tries to do. [¶] However, we shall certainly win thru, and I personally have no fault to find with the tone in which they handle me. Russell's article tickles me by the splendid style of it, so clear and english." (Kallen correspondence in American-Jewish Archives, Cincinnati, Ohio.)

Annotations in the McMaster Copy of "Transatlantic 'Truth' "

An offprint of "Transatlantic 'Truth' " with more extensive comments is preserved in the Russell Archives in McMaster University, Hamilton, Ontario. In *My Philosophical Development* (New York: Simon & Schuster, 1959), page 181, Russell states, "After James's death I was sent his copy of my article with his comments." According to the Russell archivist, Mr. Kenneth Blackwell, the sender was George Santayana. Whether Santayana acquired this annotated offprint before or after James's death is not to be determined, nor the date when James made this set of annotations, and for whom, except that they must come after the earliest set that James returned to Kallen, now preserved at Harvard. The McMaster offprint is defective on several pages. When a torn-off part of the page includes the annotation, missing text is represented by pointed brackets. Partially preserved letters that may be read with some confidence appear within the brackets.

399.4–12 (118.9–17) "Our account of truth," James tells us, "is an account of processes of leading, realised *in rebus,* and having only this quality in common, that they *pay*" (p. 218). We may thus sum up the philosophy in the following definition: "A truth is anything which it pays to believe." Now, if this definition is to be useful, as pragmatism intends it to be, it must be possible to know that it pays to believe something without knowing anything that pragmatism would call a truth.] JAMES: *Why? This is too deep for my illogical mind.*

399.34–38 (118.37–119.3) It is far easier, it seems to me, to settle the plain question of fact: "Have Popes been always infallible?" than to settle the question whether the effects of thinking them infallible are on the whole good.] JAMES (referring to question of the Pope): *how you can*

306

"settle" that without judging your thinking to have been "good," I fail to imagine. W. J.

400.1–6 (119.7–11) The notion that it is quite easy to know when the consequences of a belief are good, so easy, in fact, that a theory of knowledge need take no account of anything so simple—this notion, I must say, seems to me one of the strangest assumptions for a theory of knowledge to make.] JAMES: *Evidently Russell has a very limited set of "consequences" in mind.* *I <   >*

400.17–20 (119:22–24) It is surely far easier to discover by direct investigation that the *Contrat Social* is a myth than to decide whether belief in it has done harm or good on the whole.] JAMES: *Surely, but how decide this save by comparing it with other truths you believe in, the results of comparison being the "consequences," <however   >*

400.23–32 (119.26–35) Suppose I accept the pragmatic criterion, and suppose you persuade me that a certain belief is useful. Suppose I thereupon conclude that the belief is useful. Suppose I thereupon conclude that the belief is true. Is it not obvious that there is a transition in my mind from seeing that the belief is useful to actually holding that the belief is true? Yet this could not be so if the pragmatic account of truth were valid. Take, say, the belief that other people exist. According to the pragmatists, to say "it is true that other people exist" *means* "it is useful to believe that other people exist."] JAMES: *"the true" means not "the useful" but "the useful in the <w>ay of <l>eading to <a> reality." Many beliefs are useful, but not in that sense. And true beliefs are useful in that sense, only when the realities are useful also.*

400.32–36 (119.35–120.1) But if so, then these two phrases are merely different words for the same proposition; therefore when I believe the one, I believe the other. If this were so, there could be no transition from the one to the other, as plainly there is.] JAMES: *Cf: if bread means food, then whenever I eat food I eat bread.*

400.36–37 (120.2–3) This shows that the word "true" represents for us a different idea] JAMES: *Of course it does. Yet it may be subsumed under the latter idea.*

400.37–38 (120.3) from that represented by the phrase, "useful to believe,"] JAMES: *it is the species, "useful" to believe is the genus.*

401.29–31 (120.34–35) Now if pragmatists only affirmed that utility is a *criterion* of truth, there would be much less to be said against their view.] JAMES: *But it is a miserable criterion for ordinary use, and no pragmatist has so proposed it. It may be the ultimate criterion in doubtful cases. But for me, utility in the sense in which Russell uses it takes a very secondary place in pragmatic epistemology.*

401.36–39 (121.4–6) The arguments of pragmatists are almost wholly directed to proving that utility is a *criterion*; that utility is the *meaning* of truth is then supposed to follow.] JAMES: *who? Surely not W. J.!*

402.25–28 (121.32–35) it should be observed that what constitutes "working" is not the general agreeableness of their results, but the conformity of these results with observed phenomena.] JAMES: *what is that but a most important sort of working?*

403.11–14 (122.21–23) But if I am troubled by solipsism, the discovery that a belief in the existence of others is "true" in the pragmatist's sense is not enough to allay my sense of loneliness:] JAMES (commenting on 'true in the pragmatist's sense'): *i.e. is satisfactory—but I know no pragmatist who considers this discovery as identical to that of the existence of others. We* obey *the satisfactoriness, but it is not the object we believe in. Have I not always emphatically insisted on this point, that any* one *satisfactory way of working makes a belief true only on condition that it is uncontradicted by other ways?* other things equal, *the more satisfactory belief is the truer one.*

403.16–18 (122.25–27) For what I desire is not that the belief in solipsism should be false in the pragmatic sense, but that other people should in fact exist.] JAMES: *And this belief, being satisfactory, keeps Russell from being a solipsist. I don't know what else does, unless he has some logical revelation to that effect.*

403.36–38 (123.10–12) "Facts," they tell us, are neither true nor false, therefore truth cannot be concerned with them.] JAMES*: *It is the* relation to them *of our beliefs, which relation in the book case is that of* picturing *their contents. A catalog does this so far as it is* raisonné, *and then is a substitute for the facts.*

403.38–404.3 (123.12–15) But the truth "A exists," if it is a truth, is concerned with A, who in that case is a fact; and to say that "A exists" may be true even if A does not exist is to give a meaning to "truth" which robs it of all interest.] JAMES: *And flatly denies the pragmatist postulate, at least W. J.'s postulate.*

404.4–5 (123.15–17) Dr. Schiller is fond of attacking the view that truth must correspond with reality;] JAMES: *where?*

404.17–18 (123.28–30) Dr. Schiller, in his essay on "the making of reality," minimises the importance of the basis of "fact,"] JAMES: *Works only from the subjective end of the relation*

404.28–31 (124.3–6) In this paper, therefore, I have considered the difficulties which pragmatism has to face if it admits "facts" rather than those (no less serious) which it has to face if it denies them.] JAMES: *It admits them ab initio; later, in the shape of humanism, it makes a theory about their nature.*

---

*James is here commenting on a lengthy passage in which Russell has used an illustration in which 'facts' are represented by books in a library and 'truths' by the entries in the catalogue.

404.39–405.3 (124.14–17) For their position, if they fully realised it, would, I think, be this: "We cannot know whether, in fact, there is a God or a future life, but we can know that the belief in God and a future life is true."] JAMES: *Silly!*

405.12–15 (124.26–28) these useful consequences flow from the hypothesis that the Absolute is a fact, not from the hypothesis that useful consequences flow from belief in the Absolute.] JAMES (on the first hypothesis): *that is the only hypothesis in the field*

405.15–17 (124.28–31) But we cannot believe the hypothesis that the Absolute is a fact merely because we perceive that useful consequences flow from this hypothesis.] JAMES: *This is all rubbish. The coincidence of the true with the emotionally satisfactory becomes of importance for determining what may count for true, only when there is no other evidence. Surely, other *satisfactions [above del. 'things'] being equal in 2 beliefs, Mr. Russell himself would not adopt the less emotionally satisfactory one, solely for that reason. It seems to me a man would be a fool not to adopt the more satisfactory one.*

405.40–406.4 (125.15–19) "On pragmatistic principles, if the hypothesis of God works satisfactorily in the widest sense of the word, then it works satisfactorily in the widest sense of the word." This would hold even on other than pragmatistic principles;] JAMES: *Will R. kindly explain on his own account what kind of evidence for a non-sensible fact there can ever be except the satisfactory working of the belief—including emotional working, along with other kinds.*

406.12–13 (125.27–28) what religion desires is the conclusion that God exists, which pragmatism never even approaches] JAMES: *In my own treatment of the God problem, I simply illustrated the fact that men do (and always will) use moral satisfactoriness as an ingredient in the truth of a belief.*

406.23–28 (125.37–126.5) so soon as it is admitted that there are things that exist, it is impossible to avoid recognising a distinction, to which we may give what name we please, between believing in the existence of something that exists and believing in the existence of something that does not exist.] JAMES: *What rubbish! when the pragmatists very first assumption is that truth is a relation (which he proceeds to define) between existent realities and our ideas or beliefs.*

407.25–27 (127.3–6) Philosophical beliefs, finally, will, with most people, take a still lower place, since the opposite beliefs of others can hardly fail to induce doubt. Belief, therefore, is a matter of degree.] JAMES (on final sentence): *This fact is the basis of my "Will to believe" doctrine.*

408.39–409.8 (128.19–27) In any science, there is a greater or less degree of obviousness about many of its propositions: those that are obvious are called *data*; other propositions are only accepted because of their connection with the data. This connection itself may be of two kinds, either that the propositions in question can be deduced from the data, or that the data can be deduced from the propositions in question, and we know of no way of deducing the data without assuming the propositions in question.] JAMES: *Methinks that the whole field of* probable *beliefs is left out here. Alongside of the obvious & what can be strictly deduced from the obvious, there is the hypothetical filling in, so that the whole picture may become maximally satisfactory. This is the field of* debatable truth. *In the sensibly and* ['concept' del.] *logically obvious we seem directly to possess reality, our ideas coalesce with it, and the relation becomes one of identity.*

410.4–7 (129.25–28) If, to avoid disputes about words, we agree to accept the pragmatic definition of the word "truth," we find that the belief that A exists may be "true" even when A does not exist.] JAMES: *Silly!*

410.11–12 (129.32) The attempt to get rid of "fact"] JAMES: *by our critics, not by us.*

410.12–13 (129.32–33) turns out to be a failure, and thus the old notion of truth reappears.] JAMES: *will Mr. R. give some definition of this old notion?*

410.13–14 (129.33–34) And if the pragmatist states that utility is to be merely a *criterion* of truth,] JAMES: *definition which may also work some times as a criterion, some times not.*

410.24 (130.6+) B. RUSSELL] JAMES: *does not seem to have discriminated sufficiently between* fact *(or* reality*) and our beliefs about it. The duality of these 2 things is the core of my definition of truth. I seek for a* [interl. 'concrete' del.] *fundamentum relationis, and find it in the concrete world. The reality has a "sphere of influence," and so has the belief. If the two spheres don't touch, I ask* *"what then is* [above del. ' "where does'] *the belief's truth* made *of?" If they do touch, a verification-process becomes possible. I say you can't* define *such a process without recognizing as pertinent to its constitution, in however small a degree, the subjective make up of the believer. A fish that avoids the hook has a "truer" sense of it than one who makes straight at it & swallows it. The mere existence of the hook does n't unambiguously and adequately determine what shall count as true about it.*

Appendix V

Four Letters from William James to James B. Pratt

Three unpublished letters and a postcard from William James to James B. Pratt, all sent from Cambridge, Massachusetts, to Williamstown, where Pratt was Professor of Philosophy, are preserved in the Williams College Archives. These materially supplement the information in "The Text of *The Meaning of Truth*" about the writing and expansion of Chapter VII, "Professor Pratt on Truth." The first two letters and the postcard refer to Pratt's article "Truth and Its Verification," *Journal of Philosophy, Psychology, and Scientific Methods,* 4 (June 6, 1907), 320–324, to which James responded in the same journal in "Professor Pratt on Truth," 4 (Aug. 15, 1907), 464–467, the basis for Chapter VII. The fourth refers to Pratt's book *What is Pragmatism?* which according to his diary James saw on February 21, 1907 (probably the copy he acknowledges in the letter of March 9). This book led to the expansion of Chapter VII in March 1909. The annotated copy of "Truth and Its Verification" which James sent to Pratt on February 28, 1908, has not been found among Pratt's papers in the Williams College Library.

July 1st. [1907]

Dear Pratt — I got your letter in N. H.; and, back to town, I find your article on truth. One of the best written things that have yet appeared— Williams College is playing a fine part—on the false side—in this controversy! I ['have' *del.*] spent yesterday in writing a reply which I have just mailed to the Journal. I have also scribbled some marginal notes on your article, but fearing you may be no longer at Williamstown, I withhold them till I know your address, as printed matter is likely not to be forwarded. Where are you now?

Very truly yours,
WJ.

[p. c.]

Can you possibly send me the J. of Phil IV.12. with your article, in return for my annotated copy?

W. J.

Oct 17 [1907]

Feb. 28. 08

Dear Pratt,

I have your letter and send your article back with some scribbling, which I don't suppose will seem to you to have any point. Nevertheless such industry must go on!

Dewey I don't pretend to fully expound—let him take care of himself.

Yours as ever.
W. J.

Appendix V

Dear Pratt,

Needless to say that I thank you for your book, nor that I read it with mingled feelings, in which the pleasure most decidedly predominated. To begin with, it is *splendidly* written, with a breadth, clearness, good humor, ['and' *del.*] candor, & sincerity that are an honor to American philosophic literature. *Item*, in handling *me*, as a 'modified' pragmatist, you spare me from most of your charges, and you make such cordial concessions to all the elements of healthiness involved in the ['vie' *del.*] concrete view of truth, as significant of 'working,' that your insistance on 'trueness' as the more important conception, appears to me *almost [*interl.*] to vanish in the *total [*interl.*] perspective, & to make you more of an ally than of an enemy.

I believe (against you) that the 'radical' pragmatists are figments of your own imagination, and that Dewey and Schiller mean *exactly* what I do, only ['th' *del.*] we are all talking about universes *of discourse [*interl.*] different in their extent. It is a question of exegesis, and I admit that Dewey is not a clear writer to those who are not already at his point of view, but I am quite sure that the passages you quote are not meant to ['be' *del.*] signify what you get out of them.

I might criticize some of your details. I think the book suffers a little from seeming not to have been composed in a single sweep of plan. But I hate minute polemics, and ['the' *del.*] will make but this one protest against *your ruling [*above del.* 'being ruled'] out of *me* from the "correspondence-theory" of truth, when the very first word of my definition is that it means "agreement with reality."

I am getting ready for the printer all my essays, polemic & dogmatic, on the theory of truth, ['which I' *del.*] and expect to publish them in a volume next September, under the title of "The meaning of truth, a sequel to 'pragmatism'." I shall write a short 'part II,' to the article 'Professor Pratt on truth,' and there make what broad strictures seem to me essential. You will be glad not to be bothered with a detestable *wrangling [*above del.* 'polemic'] correspondence, just after getting that cheerful volume off your hands.

I hope it will sell, and keep the pot of public interest *in the subject [*interl.*] boiling. I hope also, now that you can write so effectively, that you'll keep your pen a-going!

Give my love to Russell whom it is painful never to see in these days, and believe me ever truly yours,

Wm James

[In a letter of March 23, 1909, to John E. Russell, James writes about Pratt:

Pratt's book contains so much good pragmatist stuff, and on the whole lets *me* off so easy, that I can only wonder why he should take so much pains to force a meaning on Dewey and Schiller, which they both repudiate (in spite of the use that can be made of certain of their sentences which the full context ought to explain) and which, if they held it, would make them such donkeys as not to deserve to have ink wasted on them. However, I say no more! But is Pratt getting simply *obstinate,* in his old age?]

Index

This index is a name and subject index for the text of *The Meaning of Truth* and Appendixes II and III. Where these appendixes overlap the text of *The Meaning of Truth*, to facilitate comparison references to them are placed in parentheses immediately after the parallel reference to *The Meaning of Truth*.

It is an index of names only for the "Notes," "A Note on the Editorial Method," "The Text of *The Meaning of Truth*," and Appendixes I, IV, and V. Names of persons, localities, and institutions and titles of books, articles, lectures, and periodicals, where discussed, are indexed. Such items are not indexed if no information about them is provided, if they are only a part of an identification of a discussed item or are used merely to indicate the location of such an item.

References to William James and incidental references to *The Meaning of Truth* are not indexed. Also not indexed is Professor Thayer's Introduction.

Index

Index

Key to the Pagination of Editions

The plates of the Longmans, Green first edition of *The Meaning of Truth* have been reprinted a number of times, but always with the same numbering regardless of the date. Since the original edition has been widely used in scholarly reference, a key is here provided by which the pagination of the original Longmans, Green printing can be readily equated with the text in the present ACLS edition. In the list that follows, the first number refers to the page of the October 1909 original edition and its printings of different date. The number to the right after the colon represents the page(s) of the present edition on which the corresponding text will be found.

v:3	22:23	59:40-41	96:57-58
vi:3-4	23:23	60:41	97:58
vii:4	24:23-24	61:41-42	98:58-59
viii:4-5	25:24	62:42	99:59
ix:5	26:24-25	63:42-43	100:59
x:5-6	27:25	64:43	101:59-60
xi:6	28:25-26	65:43-44	102:61
xii:6-7	29:26	66:44	103:61-62
xiii:7	30:26-27	67:44-45	104:62
xiv:7-8	31:27	68:45	105:62-63
xv:8	32:27-28	69:45-46	106:63
xvi:8-9	33:28	70:46	107:63-64
xvii:9	34:28-29	71:46	108:64
xviii:9	35:29	72:46-47	109:64
xix:9-10	36:29-30	73:47	110:64-65
xx:10	37:30	74:47-48	111:65
1:13	38:30	75:48	112:65-66
2:13-14	39:30-31	76:48-49	113:66
3:14	40:31	77:49	114:66-67
4:14-15	41:31-32	78:49-50	115:67
5:15	42:32	79:50	116:67-68
6:15-16	43:33	80:50-51	117:68
7:16	44:33-34	81:51	118:68-69
8:16	45:34	82:51	119:69
9:17	46:34-35	83:51-52	120:69
10:17	47:35	84:52	121:70
11:17-18	48:35-36	85:52-53	122:70-71
12:18	49:36	86:53	123:71
13:18-19	50:36	87:53-54	124:71-72
14:19	51:37	88:54	125:72
15:19-20	52:37-38	89:54-55	126:72-73
16:20	53:38	90:55	127:73
17:20-21	54:38-39	91:55	128:73-74
18:21	55:39	92:55-56	129:74
19:21-22	56:39-40	93:56	130:74-75
20:22	57:40	94:56-57	131:75
21:22-23	58:40	95:57	132:75